# THE JAZZ SAXOPHONE BOOK

## BY TIM ARMACOST

COVER AND BOOK DESIGN BY MATTHEW HEISTER

©2022 Sher Music Co. • P.O. Box 445, Petaluma, CA 94952 • www.shermusic.com
All Rights Reserved. International Copyright Secured. Made in the U.S.A.
No part of this book, including the video component, may be reproduced in any form
without written permission from the publisher.
ISBN 978-0-9910773-8-0

# ABOUT THE AUTHOR

Grammy nominated saxophonist Tim Armacost is a leading voice on the New York scene. Armacost was born in Los Angeles, but came of age as a musician in Tokyo, New Delhi and Amsterdam, where he burnished his reputation as an upcoming talent, with a big tenor sound and an impeccable rhythmic sense. He began both his touring and teaching careers while living in Europe, heading the saxophone department at the Sweelinck Conservatory, Amsterdam, for five years.

Since he moved to New York in 1993, Armacost has worked with a phenomenal number of jazz greats, including Al Foster, Jimmy Cobb, Kenny Barron, Tom Harrell, Billy Hart, Victor Lewis, Jeff "Tain" Watts, Peter Erskine, Ray Drummond, John Patitucci, Roy Hargrove, Don Friedman and Randy Brecker. He has released 16 critically acclaimed recordings as a leader, performed on more than 60 as a sideman, and has composed and arranged for Wynton Marsalis and the Jazz at Lincoln Center Orchestra, the Brooklyn Big Band, and the New York Standards Quartet. Armacost is a member of Emilio Solla's Grammy nominated nonet, Inestabile de Brooklyn, and played on Solla's big band recording, *Puertos*, which won a Latin Grammy in 2020 for "Best Latin Jazz Album."

Armacost is a widely respected educator, currently teaching at Queens College in New York City and the Jamey Aebersold Summer Jazz Workshops. He has been a guest conductor at the Juilliard School and Temple University, and has taught clinics and master classes at the Stanford Jazz Workshop, IU Bloomington, North Texas State and at universities throughout the U.S., Japan and Europe.

For Charlie Shoemake and Bobby Bradford

# TABLE OF CONTENTS
# PART ONE
## FOUNDATIONAL SKILLS

CHAPTER 1 · WHAT IS IMPROVISATION? – 4

CHAPTER 2 · SOUND – 7

CHAPTER 3 · INTRODUCTION TO CHORDS AND SCALES – 15

CHAPTER 4 · MAJOR CONSIDERATIONS: CHORDS AND SCALES CONTINUED – 28

CHAPTER 5 · THE C MAJOR SCALE CONTAINS THREE MINOR 7TH CHORDS – 35

# PART TWO
## ANATOMY OF A SONG

CHAPTER 6 · THE INTRO – 52

CHAPTER 7 · THE MELODY – 57

CHAPTER 8 · THE SOLO BREAK – 65

CHAPTER 9 · YOUR SOLO - IMPROVISING MELODICALLY – 71

CHAPTER 10 · YOUR SOLO - HARMONIC IMPROVISING – 77

CHAPTER 11 · YOUR SOLO - RHYTHMIC IMPROVISING – 87

CHAPTER 12 · TRADING WITH THE DRUMMER AND A FEW WORDS ABOUT PUTTING TOGETHER A SET – 102

CHAPTER 13 · TURNAROUNDS AND THE HEAD OUT – 110

CHAPTER 14 · PLAYING THE ENDING – 123

# PART THREE
## BUILDING TENSION WITH ADVANCED HARMONY

CHAPTER 15 · THE HARMONIC MINOR SCALE   -   140

CHAPTER 16 · THE DIMINISHED SCALE   -   154

CHAPTER 17 · TRITONE SUBSTITUTIONS   -   171

CHAPTER 18 · HARMONIC IMPROVISING—PASSING TONES   -   189

CHAPTER 19 · PLAYING 'OUT'   -   194

# PART FOUR
## DEEPER MASTERY

CHAPTER 20 · HOW CAN I PRACTICE TO BECOME A CREATIVE IMPROVISER?   -   216

CHAPTER 21 · PHRASING   -   224

CHAPTER 22 · THE BLUES   -   230

CHAPTER 23 · ARMACOST SOLO TRANSCRIPTION ON NYSQ'S "SOUL EYES"   -   249

# SHORT ASIDES

AVOID NOTES - 19

HALF STEP II-V SUBSTITUTION - 39

CYCLE OF FIFTHS - 46

TALKING TO THE AUDIENCE - 106

TURNAROUNDS - 111

TO PLAY LICKS, OR NOT - 147

PATTERNS? - 168

ENHARMONIC SPELLINGS IN JAZZ - 173

RATCHETING UP TENSION - 183

# VIDEO TABLE OF CONTENTS

Videos can be accessed online at www.timarmacost.com, or by searching "Tim Armacost and the Jazz Saxophone Book" on YouTube.

# PART ONE
## CHAPTER 1

- Video 1: Frere Jacques
- Video 2: Frere Jacques Different Keys
- Video 3: Frere Jacques Variations

## CHAPTER 2

- Video 4: Make the Piano Sing
- Video 5: Long Tones Exercise
- Video 6: The Overtone Series
- Video 7: F and G Overtones

## CHAPTER 3

- Video 8: C Major Scale Melodies
- Video 9: Accented C Major Scale
- Video 10: C Major Scale on a D-7 Chord
- Video 11: Blowing Over II-V-I's in All Twelve Keys
- Video 12: Charlie Shoemake Play-Along

## CHAPTER 4

- Video 13: Lydian and Ionian Modes Compared
- Video 14: Major Scale Articulation Exercise

## CHAPTER 5

- Video 15: Simple Piano Exercise

# PART TWO
## CHAPTER 6

- Video 16: Counting Off the Tune
- Video 17: Setting Up the Time for the Band

## CHAPTER 7
- Video 18: Searching for the Melody in Time
- Video 19: Playing in Front and Behind the Time
- Video 20: Playing Just the Melody for Multiple Choruses

## CHAPTER 9
- Video 21: Playing a Known Phrase with Different Notes
- Video 22: Question and Answer Phrases

## CHAPTER 9
- Video 23: Feeling Your Way Through a Song in a Different Key

## CHAPTER 10
- Video 24: Melodic Minor as a IV

## CHAPTER 11
- Video 25: Question and Answer Phrases Over 16 Bars
- Video 26: Rhythmic Melodies and Rhythmic Storytelling

# PART THREE
## CHAPTER 15
- Video 27: The Harmonic Minor Scale on a Dominant 7th Chord

# PART FOUR
## CHAPTER 20
- Video 28: Short Stories
- Video 29: The Inevitable Note
- Video 30: Off the Deep End and Back
- Video 31: Composing in Real Time
- Video 32: Ask Your Fingers to Deliver the Melody in Your Mind

## CHAPTER 22
- Video 33: Three Signposts in the Blues

# ACKNOWLEDGEMENTS

When you write a composition and bring it to a band for the first time, it's always a thrill to hear amazing artists bring your idea to life. I am indebted to the musicians who have engaged with the material in this book in that same way, helping to make it clearer, more interesting, and hopefully, useful.

The book started out as a pithy volume about melody. When Chuck Sher suggested I use that as a chapter in a longer book, I had no idea what I was getting into, but I am grateful for the encouragement to get started two years ago. Chuck has provided insight and advice throughout the process, and was instrumental in organizing the chapters into a coherent whole.

Matthew Heister, in addition to designing a beautiful cover and layout for the book, has read every single word in it (and many that were taken out!). As an editor, Matt has contributed immeasurably more than a watchful eye for errors in the text. In the end, I included very close to 100 percent of his suggestions for ways to clarify and simplify the language. Equally important, Matt is an accomplished guitarist, and has contributed many valuable musical observations, which are embedded throughout the content of the book. Matt's input brought the entire project to a higher plane.

Will Campbell has been a dependable support and an ever-reliable resource. He was willing to read through and help make intelligible the more technical chapters here—an act of true generosity by a deeply committed player and educator.

I also had a small army of additional proofreaders and advice-givers, to whom I am forever grateful. Thanks to:

> David Berkman
> Colin Pohl
> Chris Armacost
> Alex Garnett
> Julian Wakeham
> Lorenzo Toppin
> Rick Wester

Finally, many thanks to Lorenzo Bisogno for the transcription found in Chapter 23.

# PREFACE

Welcome!

This book is addressed to saxophonists, and will have some information that is specific to the saxophone, but it is meant for anyone interested in getting better at improvising. My main teacher, Charlie Shoemake, is a vibes player who teaches the language of jazz. He has taught over 1500 people how to speak this language, and didn't limit himself to vibes players. I have followed that example in my teaching career, working with trumpet players, violinists, vocalists, pianists—anyone who is drawn to the magic of jazz improvisation.

The main goal of each chapter is to give you a tool you can use to practice. I've organized the chapters to identify skills you will need to be a fluent speaker of modern jazz. Feel free to use the book as you see fit—if you like to do things methodically, you can start at the beginning and work your way through in order. If you've been at this a while and want to get better at phrasing, you can jump right in at the phrasing chapter. If you feel the need to develop a disciplined practice routine, you can start at Chapter 20. My goal is for the early chapters to have something worthwhile in them even for someone who's been improvising for 20 years. I want you to have a resource you can turn to for information and inspiration. This is not meant to be the last book you will ever need, but one that can point you toward music and ideas that can help you improve.

In most chapters you will occasionally see a graphic that looks like this:

- Video 30: Off the Deep End and Back

These refer to video demonstrations that you can find on the web. On YouTube you can search for "Tim Armacost and the Jazz Saxophone Book." This will take you to a page where the videos are displayed in lists by chapter. In the chapter lists you can also find links to the musical examples cited in each chapter. You can also find these links at www.timarmacost.com.

## A FEW PRACTICAL MATTERS

Jazz at its best is a highly personal form of expression. In the practice of jazz education that creates a complication—that there isn't an agreed upon set of rules that we can all follow. In fact, a good part of the fun is breaking the rules once you've learned them. If I say 'X' there will always be someone who will say, 'no, Y.' For example, as a player, I like to have a lot of interaction and dialogue with the rhythm section, but there are players who prefer to have the rhythm section lay out a smooth, purely swinging groove. Which one is correct? I say this to point out that I am not here to establish a set of rules for you to follow, but to share the things I've learned through my experience. My hope is that you can use them to grow faster and develop an efficient and inspiring practice routine. If something here doesn't work for you, feel free to toss it out and keep looking…

Transposition:
This book is written assuming that you already have a working knowledge of your instrument and reading music. The most commonly played saxophones are pitched in either Bb or Eb. Rather than giving three versions of every example (Concert, Bb and Eb), I am going to rely on readers to transpose for their respective instruments. For an example in the key of C, let's say a line over a II-V-I progression (D-7, G7, Cmaj7), you can choose to study it in that key and have a piano player transpose it for you, or you can transpose the example yourself.

To clarify that:

An alto player can read the example as is, and ask a piano player to play a II-V-I progression in Eb—F-7, Bb7, Ebmaj7.  Or, she can transpose the line to the key of A and have the piano player play in C.

When I was studying with Charlie Shoemake, he would give me a transcription in Concert, which I would memorize in my key for tenor.  At the beginning I would write out the whole transcription in Bb to make it easier to read.  This had the additional benefit of being a visual representation of what was in my inner ear.  When a line made me think, "Whoa, what is that??" I would write down each note in relation to the chord, to get more detail about the sound that sparked the reaction in me.  Here's how that looks in Bb:

At the beginning I used only the numbers 1 through 7, keeping it simple, and as I learned more about harmony, I got more precise, using 9's 11's and 13's.  As my memorizing and transposing skill increased, I gradually relied more on my ears, and less on the transcriptions to do the work of learning the vocabulary of bebop and straight ahead jazz.

One more thing: The use of gender pronouns is undergoing some evolution in the English language at the moment.  I have adopted the approach of attempting to use 'he,' 'she' and 'their' interchangeably and in roughly equal measure.

Ok, Let's get started.

# INTRODUCTION

## SWING IS A MIRACLE

Swing must be experienced to be known, so it tends to be a slippery thing to describe. But, it is worth saying a few words about it so you know what you're looking for. Swing is what draws most of us into the music in the first place.

I love the way Billy Hart calls it "The Miracle of Swing." The real beauty of swing is that it is something that happens when human beings connect deeply with each other. You're in it, and you can feel yourself in it, but it's bigger than any of the individuals creating it.

I like to describe swing as being similar to love – and I think most people who know swing would also say it comes from love. What I mean by being similar is this:
You can read all the poetry about love there is, listen to love songs all day, watch movies about it—but you only *know* love when you fall into it.

"Oh, *this* is what they're talking about!"

In the same way, you recognize swing. As an audience member you can feel it when the band hits it just right, and there it is. As a player it takes a certain amount of preparation, and a group of simpatico musicians. When you have the experience for the first time, it becomes something you want to experience again and again. It can be something that gives your life pleasure, or it can become a way of life—however much you want it, it's there for you.

It's possible to get a taste of swing on your own, but the real joy and beauty of it is in being together with other musicians and an audience. I look at the work I do in the practice room as preparation for swinging. In order to get a taste, all you need is a few fundamentals in place. To live a swinging life takes more commitment—mastery of melody, harmony and rhythm.

Just as swing is hard to pin down with words, it is also impossible to notate musically. People have tried explaining it as tied triplets, or as dotted 8ths and 16th notes, but it is mysteriously somewhere in between. Generally speaking, it's most effective to write 8th notes, and then the word, "swing." And it's our job to figure out what the word means—or more importantly what it *feels* like.

One more subject before we get started: I want to clarify what I mean when I talk about speaking the language of jazz fluently. The goal of this book is to help you develop the skills you need to go to a jam session, call a tune, and sound good playing it. I believe that learning how to play in time over the changes of traditional standards is a core skill that, once developed, can be beneficial to anything you choose to do with your music afterward. Think of it like learning to draw before doing abstract painting. It's a cliché to look at a late-career Jackson Pollack painting and say, "Anyone could do that." But the fact is—anyone couldn't do that. There is an energy in Pollack's art that comes from the work that he did to arrive at that level of abstraction.

This book is about pointing the way to some skills that will put you in the position to express yourself musically. If I'm successful at helping you learn the skills you need to play "Stella By Starlight," and sound great doing it, then you can take those skills and create whatever type of music that sparks your creativity.

# PART ONE
## FOUNDATIONAL SKILLS

*How can I get started improvising?*

# CHAPTER 1 · WHAT IS IMPROVISATION?

Most simply put, improvising is making it up as you go along.

That's easy to say, but in practice, many people don't know where to start, or are intimidated by the idea of improvising jazz. All of us are already experienced improvisers, though. Every conversation we have, every day, is an improvisation. I may ask someone how she's doing today, and I have no idea what her response will be. I listen to the response, and then proceed with another question, or a statement that follows from what I just heard. Or a person I'm talking with might give an answer and ask another question. The conversation is fluid and open ended, and neither one of us knows where it might go. That open ended-ness is what makes it interesting.

When I started out teaching, I encountered some instructors who would say to their students, "Just go for it. Express yourself!"

While I respect the emphasis on self-expression, I had two problems with this approach. The first is, there was no context for that self-expression—it was as if they were saying, "Let's speak Tibetan, you start!" But the student hadn't studied any Tibetan yet. They may have heard it, but didn't have any understanding of it.

Now, if Tibetan is your native tongue, you didn't start out having long improvised conversations. You also didn't start out learning all of the grammar, before you put your first sentence together. Instead, you started out with a few words like nose, eye, ear, mama, dada. After you learned some words, your mother might have said to you, "Where is Andy's ear?" - while pointing at it. Or "Where is Mommy's nose?" and onward, until you gradually learned a larger vocabulary, and more complex sentences and ideas.

I think of learning jazz in the same way. If we begin with a few simple words—melodies—then we can start by embellishing them and moving them around in the time. After we have a feel for that, we can start learning the grammar of the music—harmony—and begin to add harmonic lines to our improvisation. As we get more fluent, we start figuring out how to balance melody, harmony and rhythm as we learn to speak in paragraphs—and tell a musical story.

To get started, all you need is a melody, your voice, your instrument and a little imagination.

A jazz drummer will play the hi-hat on beats two and four, and emphasize those beats in the ride pattern—I'm going to do the same thing with beats two and four as I play "Frere Jacques," to begin to establish a rhythmic connection with the drums. Two and four are considered 'weak' beats, and 1 and 3 are 'strong' beats—the emphasis gives a little push as the weak beat resolves into the strong beat. Let's call this 'tension and release on a micro level.'

• Video 1: Frere Jacques

A reminder in case you missed it in the Preface: Videos are available online, organized by chapter. You can access them via www.timarmacost.com, or by searching for "Tim Armacost and The Jazz Saxophone Book" on YouTube.

Notice in the video that I'm starting out by improvising with something known. Another of the misconceptions out there is that jazz improvisation is completely new every time. Like it's being born every time someone plays a solo. In fact, it's much closer to a conversation, where 99.9 percent of the words already exist, and it's the discovery of fresh combinations of known elements that makes it fascinating. Some novelists are skillful enough to make up new words that somehow convey the meaning they're aiming for, even though the reader has never seen them before. That is a level of mastery that people like Louis Armstrong, Charlie Parker, Duke Ellington and John Coltrane achieve. They invent 'words' that haven't been heard before, and advance the vocabulary and grammar of the music in the process.

I remember when I first started trying to improvise, the biggest question I had was, "What do I do?"

As I started listening with intention—looking for things to do—I can remember one of the first things I noticed was Phil Woods scooping up into the note A in the first bar of an F blues. I didn't know anything about chords and scales yet, I just thought it sounded cool the way he decorated that note. I remember thinking, "How did he know to do that just then?"

Here's what that would look like on "Frere Jacques," in the second bar:

What I see now is that I was thinking of the music as being something outside of myself. I didn't see how it was possible to decorate something on the fly like that.

Gradually I recognized that the music comes from inside—from my internal singing voice. Now that I know I can *imagine* how the music is going to sound, I can start anticipating what I want to do with that music in advance. We'll get much deeper into this subject as the book progresses.

## SOME THINGS TO PRACTICE

Here are some simple ways to get started working in a manner that will help you become a natural improviser.

First, sing the melody of "Frere Jacques" out loud. It doesn't matter if you have a beautiful singing voice—that's what the saxophone is for.

Now play "Frere Jacques" on the saxophone while you sing it in your mind. Do it enough times until you get to the point where you are certain that what you are singing in your inner ear matches what you hear from the saxophone.

Next, try imagining a variation in your mind, sing it, and then see if you can play that on the saxophone while you sing it.

Here are a few examples of things to try, but remember, these are just suggestions to get you started—it's much more important for you to try to imagine your own variations than to read mine:

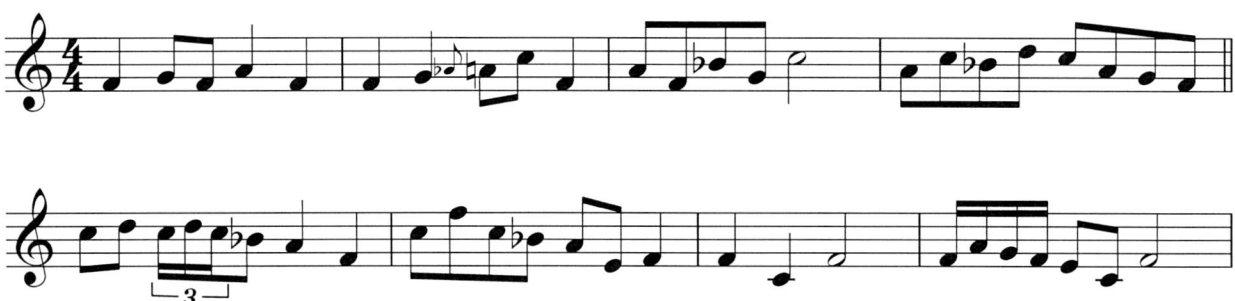

Again, match what's in your mind with what you play on the horn. If you make a mistake, notice how what you have in your mind helps you to *know* whether you're playing correctly or not.

Another interesting way to work on the connection between your ears and your horn is to try picking a random note and see if you can sing the melody of "Frere Jacques" starting from that note. You can just drop your hand on the piano, or sing a random note, then sound your way through it. After you've tried singing it, this next part is extremely important—count off a nice easy tempo, and see if you can find the first note of "Frere Jacques" in the new key. If you miss it, keep it in your head, count four beats, and try again on 'one' of the next bar. Keep going until you find it. After you find the first note, see if you can look for the rest of it, in time. Keep the tempo easy, take your time, and do your searching without leaving the tempo.

- Video 2: Frere Jacques Different Keys

The reason this is important is that what you have just done is the essence of improvisation—imagining a melody, and trying to play it directly through the saxophone, in time. No hesitation, just play what you're hearing in your mind's ear. This is challenging at first, but if you are patient, and practice it every day, you will eventually get extremely skillful at playing what is in your mind.

- Video 3: Frere Jacques Variations

# CHAPTER 2 · SOUND

## TONE

Now that we've established the connection between your inner singing voice and the saxophone, let's talk a little about the quality of the sound that comes from your instrument. At the age of 15, when I switched from clarinet to saxophone, I was lucky to have a teacher who pointed me toward finding my own sound. I started going to Doc Ross at the University of Maryland when I was still in high school. When he felt like I'd progressed to the point where I was ready to commit to a more professional set-up, he sent me down to the local music store with this advice: play all the instruments they have available, and pick the one that feels right to you. For mouthpieces, he gave me a list of five or six brands to try, and told me to pick the one I liked the sound of, but also to pay attention to the way it felt in my mouth. He wanted me to feel physically comfortable with the mouthpiece.

He could have easily told me which saxophonists were playing what sax/mouthpiece/reed combinations—and he already had some information about which players I was interested in, but instead he pointed me toward paying attention to my own aesthetic and physical responses to the instruments. To this day, I am grateful for that advice.

Most of us find our way to the music by hearing someone who sparks our interest, who makes us feel something by the way they play. It's natural to think, "I want to play like that!" It's also natural to ask, "How do they get that sound?" It's normal to investigate which horn they play and which mouthpiece and reed combination they use, and then to try to imitate that. Imitation is an important part of the process of learning how to play. But it's important to note that the end goal is to sound like yourself. The medium-term goal is to gain enough proficiency to sound like one of your heroes. The long-term goal is to listen to your own intuition, and let your responses to the music guide you toward your own style. That can start with putting together a set-up that feels good physically, and gives you pleasure when you hear your sound.

## SOUND IS MORE THAN TONE

In a broader sense, being alert to what grabs your interest will help you build a personal sound, or style, from a wide variety of elements. Studying and analyzing the characteristics of the great players is a good start, and can lead to a high level of craft on your instrument. To take it to the level of becoming an artist, it's necessary to engage your heart throughout the process—to pursue the things that make you *feel* something when you hear them.

Among the additional aspects of playing you'll eventually want to consider as you build your style are:

- Sound—the quality of your tone—big, brash and extroverted like Coleman Hawkins or Sonny Rollins; introspective and poetic like Lee Konitz or Gerry Mulligan; edgy like Jackie McLean or David Sanborn; searching and soaring like John Coltrane and Wayne Shorter.
- Time—where you place yourself in relation to the beat—right in the pocket like Gary Bartz or Zoot Sims; up on top of the beat like Cannonball Adderley or Johnny Griffin; way behind it like Dexter Gordon; or bobbing and weaving with effortless command like Charlie Parker.
- Harmony—how you use harmony to create and release tension—relatively 'in' with an emphasis on melody like Paul Desmond; linear with a high degree of sophistication like Hank Mobley or Stan Getz; relatively 'out,' putting intense harmonic pressure on the music, like John Coltrane and Kenny Garrett; freely allowing the harmony to develop while improvising, like Ornette Coleman and Eric Dolphy; drenched in the blues like Harold Land and Stanley Turrentine.
- Vibrato—the 'waver' on a note which gives it character—fast and tight like Sidney Bechet, broad and slower like Joe Lovano, or almost none at all, like Joe Henderson and Pepper Adams.
- Decoration—scoops and rises like Johnny Hodges, growls and reed slaps like Phil Woods, fully vocal sounding wails and screeches like Pharoah Sanders, Gato Barbieri or Albert Ayler.
- Altissimo register—the octave above the highest fingered note, F, on the horn. Coolly expanding the range of the horn like Warne Marsh; screaming like Coltrane for emotional impact, highly technical use like Michael Brecker, and Bob Berg, through to the effortlessness of the current crop of players like Chris Potter and Mark Turner.
- Subtone—the breathy use of the lower reaches of the horn as exemplified by Ben Webster, Eddie Lockjaw Davis, and Benny Golson.

Pick one of the above elements, and listen with it in mind, to see whose approach matches your aesthetic. You can start with the players named above, and expand from there. Oftentimes younger players adopt the style of the most popular player of their time and miss out on the development of a personal approach to an element. For example, when I first moved to New York in the early '90's many of the younger tenor players were copying Joe Lovano's style of vibrato. There are many ways to use vibrato, and it makes for a richer artistry to improvise with vibrato—playing a long straight note and then adding a touch of vibrato at the very end, for example—rather than simply adopting the style of the times unconsciously.

# GEAR

To get started building your sound, first go to your local music store and take a bunch of horns, mouthpieces and reeds for a test drive, listening for sounds that spark your interest, and feeling your way toward the set-up that fits your body well. This is not something to be decided in one session. Take your time. If you don't have a retail store near you, (internet commerce is making it harder for them to survive) I'd recommend making the trek to a big city so you can have the experience of comparing them, and talking to a knowledgeable salesperson about what's available. It's possible, on the other hand, to take advantage of the internet to order things to try from all over the world, but the process of ordering, trying and returning things you don't like can be expensive and time consuming. Make sure you're clear about the return policy if you go this route, so you don't get stuck with something that doesn't suit you.

If you're at the beginning of the process and want to have something solid to practice on before you take the plunge into a professional set up, I recommend the student models from Yamaha and Yanagisawa. They are well-crafted horns that are consistently in tune. Full disclosure, I endorse D'Addario reeds and Bari mouthpieces, but otherwise have no financial interest in promoting any particular brand of horns.

Here is a list, in alphabetical order so as not to emphasize one brand over another, of companies that offer solid products that are worth trying:

**Saxophones:**
Borgani
Buescher
Buffet Crampon
Conn
H. Couf
Keilwerth
King
Martin
P. Moriat
Selmer
SML
Yamaha
Yanagisawa

**Mouthpieces:**
Bari
Berg Larsen
Brilhart
D'Addario
Dukoff
Francois Louis
Jody Jazz
Meyer
Otto Link
Selmer
SYOS
Vandoren

**Reeds:**
Alexander
Boston Sax Shop
D'Addario
Hemke
Juno
La Voz
Marca
Rigotti
Roberto's Winds
Vandoren

And there are a few companies experimenting with **synthetic reeds,** including:

Bari
Fibracell
Forestone
Hartmann

Legere
Plasticover
Silverstein

In the early stages, the ligatures that come with stock mouthpieces are fine. If you want to branch out a little further, here are some popular brands of **ligatures**:

BG
D'Addario
Brilhart
Francois Louis
Ishimori

Rigotti
Rovner
Silverstein
Vandoren

Regardless of whether you have a student set-up or professional gear, there is one other aspect of sound worth saying a few words about before we get to things to practice.

## PLAYING IN TUNE

My first band teacher, Olivia Gutoff, used to spend what seemed to me a boringly long time tuning the band at the beginning of each class. However, I got used to hearing the band playing in tune—that became our baseline. I didn't stop to think about what it would have been like if we didn't tune up first. She wasn't just teaching us to tune our instruments, but was also training us to play in tune—which is an active, ongoing, and fundamental aspect of playing harmoniously.

The sound wave that is created when you blow a horn cycles a certain number of times per second. If the person sitting next to you is playing with a pitch that is higher (sharper) or lower (flatter) than yours, the waves that are created bounce against each other in conflict, rather than blending into each other and creating a ringing sound. The resulting clash creates a disturbance, called 'beats,' where the ear hears the notes competing against each other. Imagine you painted a wall white, and then came back a year later and just touched up the blemishes on the wall, but with a different shade of white. Despite the fact that both shades are white, your eye would pick up on the discrepancy, and this would generate a feeling of discomfort. I say all this to point out that learning to tune your instrument by looking at a tuner, a machine that tells you if you are in tune, is insufficient. The machine tells you that the pitch you are playing is cycling at the correct rate. Playing an entire solo in tune, though, is different from playing a single note at the correct pitch. There is a need to train your ear to hear the sympathetic vibrations between the instruments in an ongoing way. That's why I recommend tuning to another instrument, rather than a machine. My personal preference is to sit at the piano, depress the sustain pedal, and play a note until the piano 'sings' back to me. If I can make the piano strings vibrate in sympathy with my note, I am learning to play in tune, and am also developing a sound which is rich in overtones. More on overtones shortly.

- Video 4: Make the Piano Sing

## SOME THINGS TO PRACTICE

How can we practice to have a beautiful tone? The conventional wisdom is that the work you do to get a good sound is to play long tones. Long tones are a valuable tool for building stamina and observing the development of your tone, but my goal is, as much as possible, to make practicing fun and inspiring. Playing long tones, at length, and nothing more, is not going to do the job.

There is plenty of work to do to become a solid player, but I also believe that it's important to practice to become the performer you want to be. In other words, without a conscious idea of what you're practicing toward, you lose control over the kind of player you are becoming. If your practice routine is too mechanical, you are practicing to become a mechanical sounding player. If you work extremely hard on technical exercises, but fail to practice improvising, you will sound overly technical. With that in mind, working on tone should be fun and interesting, and engaging to your imagination. This will help you build towards being an interesting and enjoyable improviser, with a beautiful tone.

The first long tones exercise I found that I actually enjoyed doing goes like this:

1. Play a low Bb, the lowest note on the horn, and hold it. I like to do this next to the piano, pressing the sustain pedal.

2. While playing the Bb and trying to make it sound rich and beautiful, imagine the note B natural in your mind, a half step above the note you're playing.

3. Without cutting off the Bb, make a smooth transition to the B a half step away, noticing if it sounds like the B in your mind's ear.

4. Hold the B for a little while, and then release it smoothly before your breath runs out entirely.

5. Take a breath—take your time doing this—and then go back to the Bb. This time imagine the note C natural in your mind's ear while playing the Bb.

6. Same procedure—make a smooth transition to the C while imagining what the interval (a whole step), will sound like.

7. Do it again from Bb to Db, imagining what the interval (a minor third), will sound like.

Proceed as far as you can, up to the top of the horn, imagining the new interval each time before you play it. Tell yourself what the interval is before you play it, like this:

*Now I'm going up to the note D natural, which is a major 3rd above Bb…now I'm playing Bb to Eb, which is a perfect 4th...*and so on. That way you're imagining the sound of the interval, and also memorizing what each interval sounds like.

• Video 5: Long Tones Exercise

One device you can use to help memorize the sound of an interval is to pin it to a familiar melody that contains that interval. Imagine you're about to sing "Here Comes the Bride." What is that first interval?

The first interval in "Here Comes The Bride" is a perfect 4th. You can use that as a way to remember the sound of that interval.

The first interval in the melody of "The Days of Wine and Roses" is a major 6th.

Now you have a way to remember what a major 6th sounds like.

Then, to make it fun, I'll play the interval, and if anything else pops into my mind, I'll try to play that. I turn myself loose to improvise a little based on what the interval fires in my imagination. Then I'll return to Bb and the ever-increasing interval pattern. I'll do this for 15 minutes or so, which helps to warm up my sound, my awareness of what I'm doing, and my imagination. Tomorrow I'll do it again, starting on a different note towards the low end of the horn, so that I hear the intervals in different keys, and don't get bored doing the same thing over and over. I have been doing this exercise for years starting at the bottom of the horn and working my way up, but there's no reason why you couldn't start at the top of the horn and work your way down. Or work from the middle out in both directions. Imagining the intervals and memorizing them in a downward direction would also be beneficial.

In Part Four, Chapter 20, I'll demonstrate another exercise, using melody, that expands on this concept.

One more technical exercise you can use to work on your sound accesses the overtone series. Becoming aware of overtones will help add richness to tone, and will help you learn to fill a room up with ringing waves of ringing sound.

Saxophones use an octave key, so we don't have to 'overblow' to raise a note by an octave, the way a trumpet or flute player does. We can choose, though, to access the overtone series by not using the octave key, and overblowing. If you play a low C natural, for example, you can play the C an octave above it, without using the octave key by increasing the intensity of the air you put through the horn. See if you can do it. If you focus the air a little harder, the next overtone will sound, which is a 5th higher—the note G. This one is a little more squirrelly to get out, but you can play a concert F on the piano, and then try to match that sound. The next note in the series is another C, and the following overtone is the E above that.

1. Fingering the low C without the octave key, try blowing the overtone series from C up to E and back down. You can start on any of the lower notes of the horn for variety.

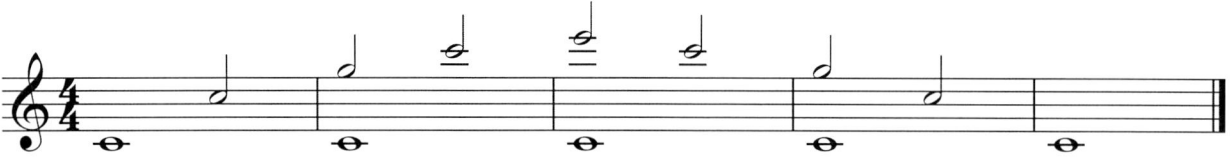

• Video 6: The Overtone Series

2. Now play the note F in the second octave as you usually would, pressing the octave key. Then quickly move to the fingering for low Bb, releasing the octave key, and blow the second overtone—the same F. Notice the difference between the 'overblown' F and the regular F with the octave key. If you are playing in tune, your overblown F should sound rich and full. The idea, then, is to see if you can make the regular F sound as rich as the overtone F. Try going back and forth between the two, noting the difference. You can do this for all of the notes between F and the A natural above it. After the A you get another Bb, so now you have two choices, the second overtone from Eb, and the third overtone, which is two octaves above the fundamental Bb. Meaning, you can 'lip it up' either an octave and a fifth from Eb, or two octaves from Bb.

• Video 7: F and G Overtones

3. Now try blowing a regular F followed by an overtone F, and then move up a half step, and keep going. Each horn will have some quirks. Explore yours and see how it behaves. Here is a chart showing the idea. The first note in each bar is the regular note, and the second is the overtone, with the note to finger shown below it.

The first note in each bar is the regular note, and the second is the overtone, with the note to finger shown below it.

If you want to take a deep dive into this concept, Sigurd M. Rascher wrote an excellent book called *Top-Tones for the Saxophone*. This book will help you develop your mastery of the overtones, giving you a richer sound, and will also help you work on your altissimo register.

And finally, I try to get myself into a beautiful sounding place to practice at least once a week. When I was first starting out, while living in Amsterdam many years ago, my apartment was a couple of small rooms under the eaves of a building, surrounded by neighbors. I couldn't play loudly, but needed to practice, so I would stuff the bell of the horn with socks or a T-shirt and blow into my clothes closet. After I started getting a few gigs and had a little extra money, I would go to a building called the Crea, and rent a dance studio for a couple of hours. It was a large room, with a lot of reflective surfaces, and it was a joy to hear the sound of the horn full out, rebounding around the room. I would try to fill the entire space with sound and would bask in the pleasure of the horn turned loose. Over the years I've found resonant spaces to practice in, including tunnels, concrete stairwells, large concert stages, outdoor amphitheaters, ancient French churches, and the dome of a small palace in India!

If you just want to have some fun playing music by ear, now you have some things to work on that will help you get better at that. There are famous musicians, both living and not, who had such great ears that they were able to develop successful careers without ever learning to read music. James Moody, one of the musicians who I most admire, started out that way. Toward the second half of his life, I had a handful of occasions to spend time with him. By that time he was both deeply knowledgeable and generous with what he'd learned. The first time I met him, he had just finished a concert of two sets of music at the old Bimhuis, in Amsterdam. Full of youthful enthusiasm, I asked him about a specific scale sound he played between the 13th and 16th bars of "Bennie's from Heaven." Not only did he remember what he played, but he took 15 minutes to explain it to me, and sang a number of examples. Then he went on to tell me about a couple of similar things he was working on, and sang those as well.

Moody told me that he'd gotten lucky having some early success in his career, and soon found himself on the bandstand with Dizzy Gillespie. He realized that luck and his ear had gotten him that far, but now he needed to up his game. Gillespie is well known for having urged people to study piano and learn harmony, and he got Moody started. One of the last times I met Moody, 20 years after the first time, he was still finding new things to say on the horn.

The next three chapters are an introduction to the mechanics of harmony. It takes some time to absorb this knowledge, so if you decide to go for it and take it to the next level, be patient, work hard and ask questions. It will be worth your time and effort, and may become a source of inspiration for the rest of your life.

As you embark on your study of harmony, keep this in mind: the point of acquiring knowledge of harmony is not the knowledge itself. Our goal is to use that knowledge to *train our inner ears to hear new things*. As our inner ears become more informed, we can recognize more of what is going on around us. That will make us better communicators with our fellow musicians, and more interesting improvisers.

# CHAPTER 3 · INTRODUCTION TO CHORDS AND SCALES

## WHAT IS A II-V-I PROGRESSION, AND HOW DO I PLAY OVER IT?

We'll go into more detail later, but the goal of this chapter is to introduce you to how chords and scales work together. The word 'harmony' can mean different things, from singing notes other than the melody, to World Peace. What I mean by 'harmony' in this chapter is harmonic theory, the grammar at the core of improvised jazz language. Our specific purpose here is to explain some strategies for creating smooth lines through chord changes. For a deeper dive into harmonic theory, I recommend Mark Levine's *The Jazz Theory Book* and David Berkman's *The Jazz Harmony Book*.

To study the ideas in this chapter, it is ideal if you can sit at a piano, with your horn handy. It's possible to learn harmony without a piano, but we're going for more than just intellectual understanding of harmonic theory. Our objective is to hear a chord and recognize it, not just to memorize the names of the notes in a chord. Further, seeing the shapes of chords on a piano, and seeing the way they move from one to another helps to deepen your understanding of the way chords work.

## THE CLOCKWORK

The following diagram shows the chords that can be built from each scale degree, using only notes in the C major scale.

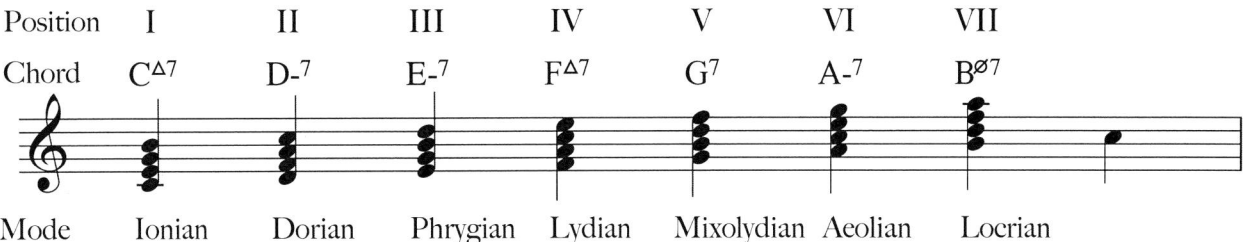

The above illustration is like a blueprint of the gears of a finely crafted watch. Everything is interconnected and working together to create a result that is simultaneously simple and complex. That one diagram contains a template for almost everything you need to understand in order to get a grasp on harmonic theory. If you can master that information, you will be in possession of knowledge that is infinitely fascinating. Whereas simple melodies were the first words you learned to start speaking the language of jazz, harmonic theory is the grammar you can use to make lines—sentences—to help you tell an interesting story.

Since, "A diagram showing the chords that can be built from each scale degree, using only notes in the C major scale" is a bit of a mouthful, I'm going to refer to the above diagram, and variations on it throughout the book, as "The Clockwork."

By the time I had my first lesson with Charlie Shoemake in my freshman year of college, I'd been playing for ten years, and trying to improvise for about four. I'd had some encouragement, having earned first tenor chair in my high school band, and making the all-county band, also on first tenor, and thought I could play a little. I had learned that a Cmaj7 chord had the notes C, E, G, and B in it, but that's about all I knew—beyond that I was playing by ear, and hoping for the best. I studied a few solos, notably Sonny Stitt on "Tune Up," which was fast and difficult, reinforcing my idea that I could play a little…but I also knew that I wasn't really making it.

I was cut down to size when Charlie asked me,
"Ok, Tim, what scale would you play on an E-7b5 chord?"
My answer,
"I don't know. I haven't studied harmony at all yet."
Fortunately Charlie's response was to say, "All right, we know where to start, then."
His second question for me was,
"What do you want to learn to do?"
I said,
"I want to be able to play long, flowing lines."
He said,
"You mean like this?"
and dropped the needle on Sonny Rollins' solo on "Mambo Bounce," from the recording Sonny made with the Modern Jazz Quartet. (For those of you who are digital natives, 'dropping the needle' refers to the way we dinosaurs used to listen to music, on vinyl records. Vinyl is having a bit of a comeback, mainly because it still sounds beautiful. Check it out, if you haven't already.)

I couldn't believe that Charlie seemed to know exactly what I was looking for. I was excited to get started learning how to play like that.

Let's start with a C major scale. No flats, no sharps—it's the easiest one to study since any note that's indicated with a sharp or a flat sign will tell you that it is not in the scale. Note that each note of the scale has a Roman numeral above it. These numbers indicate the position of each note in the scale in relation to the root, or C.

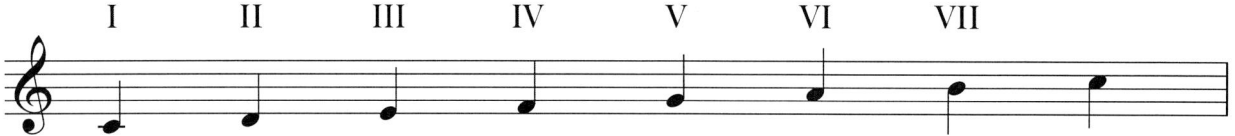

Now, let's make our first chord in the key of C. We create chords by stacking in 3rds. Another way to say that is to take every other note of the scale, and stack them up.

Starting from 1, we'll build 1, 3, 5, and 7, or the notes C, E, G and B, which gives us a Cmaj7 chord. Unfortunately there are a few different ways to notate a major 7th chord, and there isn't an agreed upon standard. In practice you will see: CM7, CMaj7, Cmaj7, C△7 and C△.

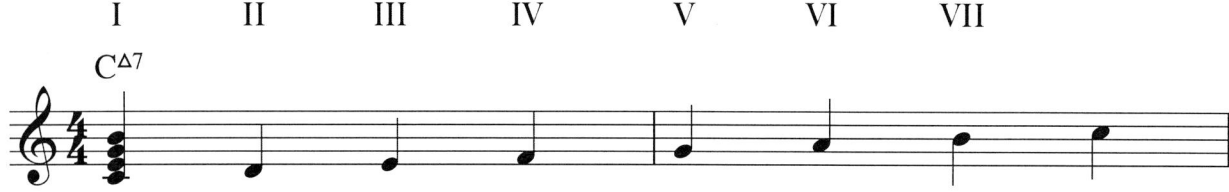

Next, have a seat at the piano, with your horn at the ready, and play a Cmaj7 chord with the sustain pedal on, so you can start playing some melodies and lines against it to see how they sound. First play the basic Cmaj7 voicing by stacking every other note from the scale into a chord. After that you can spread the voicing out for a richer sound by playing 1 and 7 (C and B) in the left hand, and 3 and 5 (E and G) in the right.

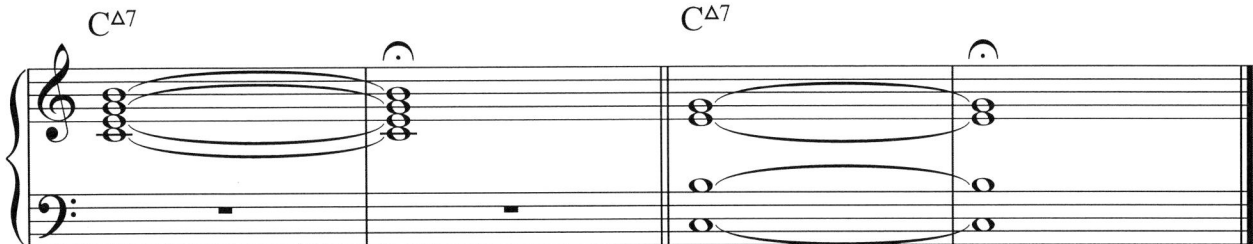

Play the chord, and experiment with the notes of the scale, and see what you find. Can you make some melodies using the C major scale? How does it feel to play the scale as a line that travels through the chord?

• Video 8: C Major Scale Melodies

With the Cmaj7 chord sounding at the piano, play each of the chord tones, one at a time. Can you get a sense of how they feel? Generally, the chord tones C, E, and G should feel relatively 'settled.' They are happy where they are—ringing with the notes that you are sustaining at the piano. The exception is B, which is a half step away from the next C, which has a strong feeling of wanting to be pulled into the C above it, creating tension that wants to resolve.

Now try playing the in-between, or non-chord tones: D, F, and A. They should feel a little less settled, maybe a little more colorful. They feel a bit like they are hanging in the air, wanting to resolve—to release the tension they are creating into a nearby chord tone. Try holding an F, feeling the tension it creates, and then play an E, letting that built up tension release.

Remember how we played accents on the melody of "Frere Jacques" on beats two and four, to connect with the drummer's ride pattern and hi-hat? In so doing, we created a feeling of motion as weak beats moved toward strong beats. As we've just heard, non-chord tones create that same feeling of motion by building tension that can be resolved into chord tones. The horn soloist can line up the non-chord tones of the scale on weak beats, and give them an accent, to push them toward their resolution into the chord tones on the strong beats.

Let's play the C major scale in quarter notes, giving an accent to beats 2 and 4, like the hi-hat does in a traditional setting. Pick a tempo, hear it in your mind's ear, then tap your foot on two and four to that tempo. You can use a metronome to help you decide on a tempo, but for now, let's try to play while feeling the quarter note internally, rather than using an external reference. If you use a metronome to find a tempo, practice hearing it on two and four.

• Video 9: Accented C Major Scale

We can use the scale this way to establish a rhythmic connection to the drummer, in the same way we did with the melody of "Frere Jacques." A swinging rhythm section and soloist are bound together by melody, rhythm and harmony. A skillful soloist can create simultaneous linkage between rhythm and harmony, which will lead to a quicker mastery of swing.

When we play 8th note lines, the same linkage holds, it's simply happening twice as fast.
We can line up the non-chord tones with the up-beats, like so:

Here are some examples of horn soloists playing interesting lines without leaving the C major scale. Try listening and then playing along with them. Here's Harold Land's first phrase on "Take the A Train," from *Study in Brown*:

Don't worry about that D7#11 chord in the third bar for now. Check out how good that line sounds against a Cmaj7 chord. After you can play it along with Harold Land, try playing the piano voicing and playing the line as if it's your own.

Charlie Parker's first phrase on the tune "Half Nelson" sounds both beautiful and interesting. Notice how he starts on a chord tone, lands on a chord tone across the barline, and ends on a chord tone. You can hear this excerpt from take two on the *Miles Davis All Stars* session of 1947 where Parker plays tenor(!).

And here's a characteristically great line from Sonny Rollins from his second solo on "Tune Up," which follows the piano solo, from his album, *Newk's Time* (It's going by pretty fast, but you can find this line at around 5:09 in the track):

## THE SECOND CHORD IN THE CLOCKWORK

Now let's do the same thing from the second note of the C major scale, D. We'll stack every other note on top of each other to make the chord Dmin7. You'll see some different ways to name this chord: Dmin7, Dm7 and D-7 are commonly used.

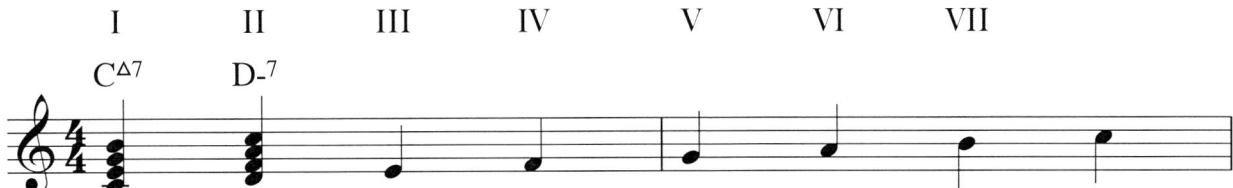

Here is our second chord in the key of C. First play a D-7 at the piano, like we did with the C major chord. You can find it by playing every other note starting from D and holding them, to let the chord ring.

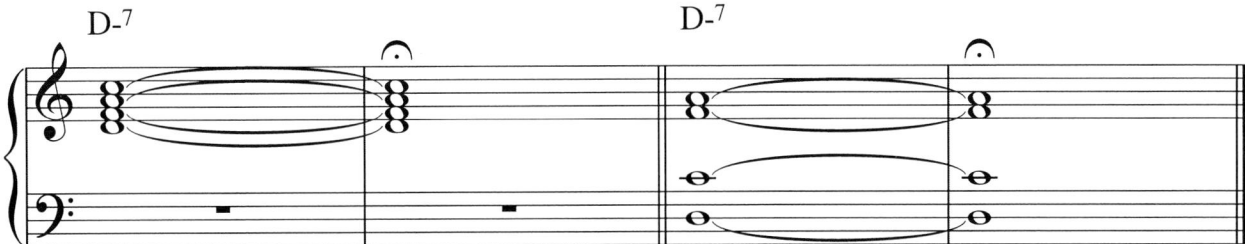

Go through the same procedure as we did with Cmaj7. Play each chord tone—D, F, A, and C, and see how they feel. Next play the in-between tones, E, G and B, and get a feeling for whether they feel settled or not. Pay particular attention to the minor third, the note F. Play the note F on your horn with the D-7 chord sounding at the piano. (Remember to transpose for your instrument.) See how it feels natural? Now play the Cmaj7 chord on the piano, and let that note F sound against it. Hear the difference?

You can try this with the other tones, too. Compare how the note E feels against the Dmin7 chord, and then against the Cmaj7 chord. How about the B?

## A SHORT ASIDE

You might hear someone say that the note F is an "avoid note" on a Cmaj7 chord. Creating a situation in your mind where there is a note to be avoided can easily lead to a bump in the smoothness of your lines and your thinking, or your imagination. Rather than avoiding the 4th tone of a major scale, it makes more sense to think of it as a note that has a strong desire to resolve. That way you can make use of that tension in your playing. Sonny Rollins starts off his solo on "On the Sunny Side of the Street," from Dizzy Gillespie's *Sonny Side Up* with a great melody, using the 4th of the Cmaj7 chord:

And going into his last A section, he references it again, to tie off the story:

We'll get into more of the harmony behind that phrase later, but suffice it to say for now that his great solo couldn't have gotten off the ground if Sonny had been 'avoiding' playing the note F on a C major chord.

## BACK TO D-7

Since we derived the D-7 chord from the C major scale, it makes sense that you would be able to play a C major scale over a D-7 chord, right?

If you start the C major scale on D and play it straight up through the chord, you get a line with exactly one note between each chord tone of Dmin7. The scale travels smoothly through the chord, and also sounds good.

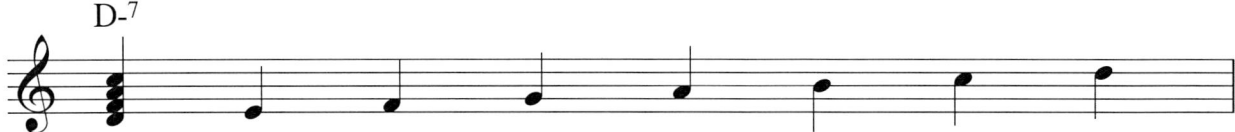

Take a minute to play the C major scale over a D-7 chord, noticing that we're using the same scale as we did on a Cmaj7 chord, but the notes which feel settled and the notes that need to move are different. You can also go back and forth between the two chords, and note the differences.

• Video 10: C Major Scale on a D-7 Chord

Bronislaw Kaper's composition, "Invitation," is a great vehicle for talking about harmony. The form leaves space for experimentation, while simultaneously using functional harmonic movement. The first chord is a concert C-7. With apologies to our Alto and Baritone community, I'm going to show a few transposed examples to stay visually in D minor. Trumpeter Tom Harrell, (not a saxophonist, obviously, but he's one of the most harmonically sophisticated players working today, so we'll have a few occasions to refer to his playing) begins his solo with a beautiful melodic line. This is from his recording, *Total!* (at 1:10 in the track):

Joe Henderson's solo on "Invitation," like Tom Harrell's, is full of harmonic adventure, but here's a great phrase that shows how much you can say with just the C major scale over a D-7 chord. This is from Joe's great recording, *Tetragon*. The excerpt starts in the third bar of the last A section of his first chorus (at 2:39):

## THE II-V-I

The II-V-I chordal movement is one of the most fundamental building blocks of functional harmony in jazz composition. In its most basic form, the sequence of chords is derived from arpeggios starting on the 2nd, 5th and 1st notes of the major scale.

We've looked at the I position in C, which is a CMaj7 chord, and the II position, which is a D-7 chord. In order to complete the II-V-I sequence, we're going to skip ahead of positions III and IV for the moment, and look at the V chord, which in C is a G7, or G dominant 7 chord.

Same procedure as with Cmaj7 and D-7—spend a little time at the piano with the chord ringing, and get a feel for which notes are happy where they are, and which ones want to move.

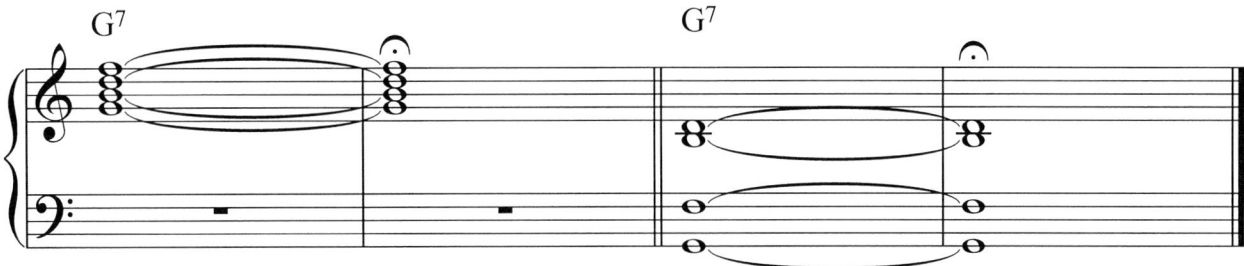

On the first of Cedar Walton's great series of albums under the title *Eastern Rebellion*, George Coleman plays a beautiful solo on "Bolivia." He starts out with some simple phrases, using just the 'home key' of C major (we're back to Concert key here). Here's his first phrase, at 1:08:

If you listen to the whole solo, he takes some harmonic chances later on, and they work especially well because he has established what the home key sounds like in the beginning. This is good storytelling—start simple, raise the tension as the arc develops, and then bring it home at the end.

We've been going to some length to establish how these chords are derived. Now we've seen where the II-V-I chord progression, which is the backbone of the American Songbook, comes from. How can we put that knowledge to practical use?

When I see a chord progression for the first time, my first instinct is to find the simplest possible interpretation of what I see, so I can make my way through the song with relative ease. After I've established the home key or keys, then I'll think about what I can do to be creative with the harmony.

If I see that a song has a II-V-I progression in C in it, I know that I can simply imagine melodies in the key of C for that whole 4 bar space. The C major scale gives me the field of notes from which to make melodies.

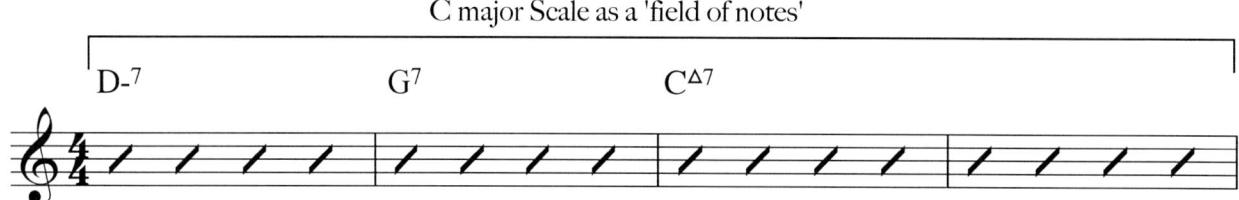

Now that we've found the baseline, or the simplest harmonic choice, we can start paying attention to some of the details. What we know so far is that starting melodies and lines on the chord tones will give them a feeling of clarity and groundedness. Starting on non-chord tones will create the beginnings of a feeling of tension, with a corresponding need to be resolved. Using those ideas we can explore making melodies over the progression, and see what happens.

This might be a good moment to do some playing through some II-V-I's. Grab your favorite play-along recording, and just have some fun. (There are some suggestions for play-alongs in the "Things to Practice" section at the end of this chapter.) Try holding some notes, and seeing how they change as the chords move underneath. See if you can hit some of the chord tones on the downbeat of a bar. Play the scale starting on some different beats, and see what happens. Play a simple melody, and then see if you can play something that sounds like it belongs with what you just played.

Next, we want to start becoming aware of the feeling of moving from one chord to the next. One of the keys to 'making the changes,' or playing sounds that smoothly define the chord progression, is developing the ability to 'play the barlines,' or mark your passage from one bar to the next. Clarity comes from playing chord tones on either side of the barline. If those two notes are a whole step apart it works well, and when they are a half step apart, the transition sounds especially smooth.

In the following illustration, you'll see the chord tones of D-7 to the left of the barline, and of G7 to the right. What we're looking for are places where chord tones on either side of the barline link the chords smoothly together.

Between D-7 and G7 the note C is the 7th of D-7, and the note B is the 3rd of G7. They are a half step apart, and are resolving in a downward direction, all of which contribute to smooth motion.

Here are some lines moving smoothly across the barline:

And here are some examples of great players linking the changes together smoothly. Sonny Stitt's solo on George Gershwin's "S'Wonderful" is a goldmine of good lines. Here's one from 1:01 into the track:

Coleman Hawkins' solo on "Body and Soul," in 1939, is considered the first great example of "vertical improvising." Hawkins wasn't simply making up new melodies on the changes, but was also improvising by outlining the shapes of the chords themselves. This set the stage for the development of harmonic lines by the beboppers in the 1940's.

This line happens as he leaves the bridge in his first chorus. Notice how skillfully he uses the tones of the chords to anchor his lines, and especially how he stays in E for an extra beat before resolving strongly to the Eb major chord.

This is getting a little ahead of the story, but the way John Coltrane plays the first four bars of his solo on his composition, "Giant Steps," is a picture of clarity. The tune is challenging because of the tempo and frequency of changes of key, but have a listen to how Coltrane links the changes together over the barlines at 0:26:

Another popular technique is quoting an existing melody, rather than making up a new one. Here, Charlie Parker quotes his own melody, "Cool Blues," in the first ending of his first chorus (at 0:52) on "Yardbird Suite."

Now we have two approaches to playing over a II-V-I in C:

1. We can simply see it as four bars in the key of C, and we can freely create melodies using the C major scale, and

2. We can take a more scalar approach in order to make lines. In this case we pay more attention to the moment we move from one bar to the next, and link the chords together by playing chord tones on either side of the bar line.

Now let's take a moment and refer back to our clockwork.

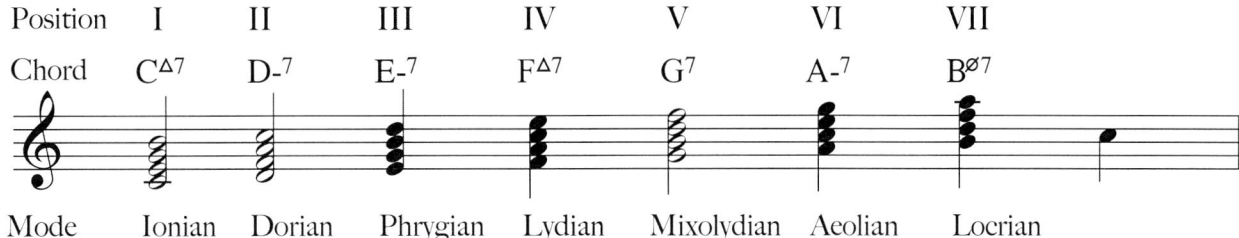

We haven't talked about those words underneath the chords which indicate modes yet. There's a reason for that…at this stage, they can make things unnecessarily complicated. Up to this point, our goal has been to start hearing how the C major scale sounds as we play it over three of the chords that come from the scale—D-7, G7 and Cmaj7.

However, since jazz musicians use the names of the modes to communicate about chords and scales, it is something we need to start becoming familiar with. Especially when we get into the modal style of playing, developed in the late 1950's and into the '60's, it will be helpful if we know how the modes are derived. We are already familiar with them, having looked at the different chords that come from a C major scale. We just haven't named them yet.

Have a look at the word underneath the D-7 chord in the clockwork—Dorian. You can think of the Dorian mode as a version of the C major scale that starts on the note D. Or, the Dorian mode in C is the C major scale, starting on D.

Dorian Mode in C

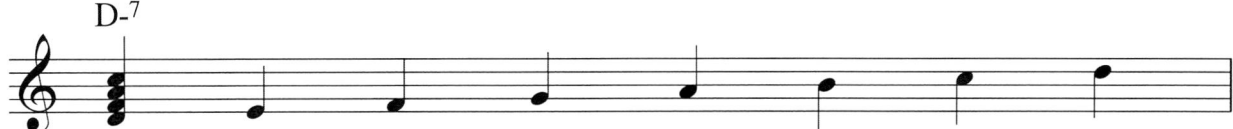

Another way to say the same thing is: the D Dorian scale is the C major scale, starting on the second note of the scale, D.

See the word 'Mixolydian' in the clockwork under the G7 chord? By the same logic, the Mixolydian mode in C, or the G Mixolydian scale, is the version of the C major scale that starts on its fifth note, G:

Mixolydian Mode in C

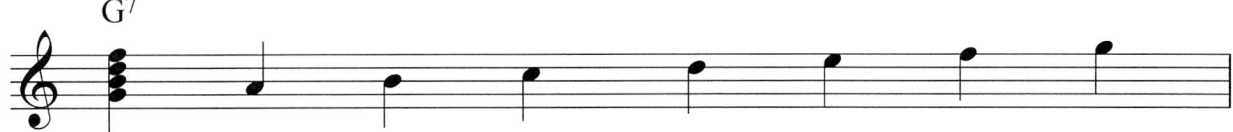

And when C is the home key, we call the C major scale the Ionian mode in C.

If I want to be precise, I could say, in my mind, that over a D-7 chord I'm playing a D Dorian scale, and when I pass into the G7 chord I'm switching over to the G Mixolydian scale, and then, arriving at the C major scale, I use the C Ionian scale.

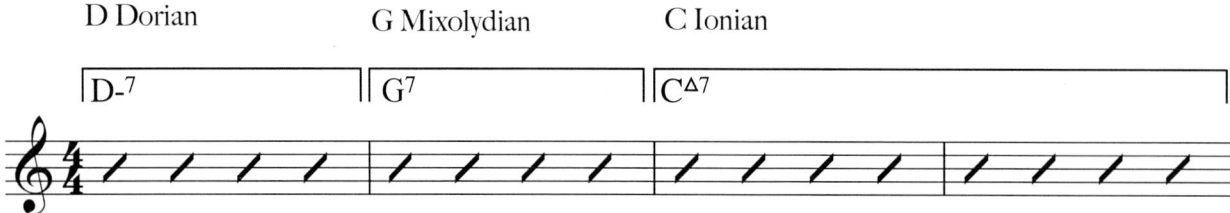

But by the time I've done all that thinking, the chord progression has probably passed me by! Why would I want to think of three different scales, when what I'm playing is only one? I wouldn't, because I want to maximize the hearing, and keep the thinking limited to what I need. So in this case it makes more sense to think of one scale, and concentrate on making good transitions from chord to chord over the barlines.

As we look deeper into chords and scales, we'll find reasons to use the names of the modes. It takes some time to learn these details, but it will gradually become clearer and clearer.

## SOME THINGS TO PRACTICE

1. If you've played the sounds we've explored so far at the piano, great. Keep doing that. If you can do that a little bit every day, D-7 will start to feel like a familiar place. That's what you want.

2. Listen again to Sonny Rollins, Tom Harrell and the other examples. Play the corresponding chords at the piano, and play the phrase again. Now try changing it a little. You can move the phrase around in the bar by starting it on a different beat, or change a note or two, and see if it still sounds good. This is the beginning of the process of making the vocabulary your own.

3. Video 11 shows me playing over a play-along track that Charlie Shoemake made for me 40 years ago… Video 12 is the play-along by itself, so you can practice the II-V-I sounds in all 12 keys.
    - Video 11: Blowing Over II-V-I's in All Twelve Keys
    - Video 12: Charlie Shoemake Play-Along

4. Among the many useful tools Jamey Aebersold has created in the last 50 years, there is a volume dedicated to the II-V-I progression. It's called *Volume 3, The II-V-I Progression*. It has play-along tracks you can use to get more familiar with each major key, and you can try things over the progression. It's important to note that the play-along records are fantastic for giving you some sound references while you try things out, but they are not the same as playing with people. Imagine listening to a recording of a play, or watching a movie where you want to learn the lines. You could recite them along with the movie, as many people love to do, and you could even improvise your own lines or ways of reading the lines—but what you can't do is have a conversation with the people in the movie. When we improvise with other humans, we want to be aware of them, and communicate with them. So remember that the use of play-alongs is a terrific way to master some basic skills, but when you go to play with other musicians, you don't want to make them feel like they are just a play-along record.

5. In that spirit, ask a piano player or a guitarist if they will practice with you, and try working on II-V-I's together. When I was just starting out, I spent a lot of time playing duets with pianists, guitarists, bassists and drummers.

6. Here are some blank staves for you to write down some lines of your own. Try a few in some other keys, and after you write them down, paying attention to what happens as you move over the barlines, try playing your own lines along with one of the play-alongs, and see how they sound.

# CHAPTER 4 · MAJOR CONSIDERATIONS: CHORDS AND SCALES CONTINUED

Here's the clockwork again:

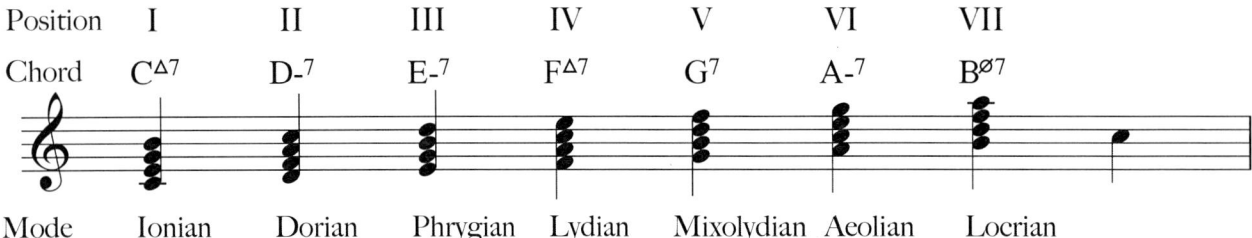

Now it's time to explore the rest of the clockwork diagram and learn a few more details about chord and scale interconnectivity. We're going to skip the III position for a moment and talk about the IV chord, which is an Fmaj7 chord built from the fourth note of the C major scale. As we did before, we will take every other note in the C major scale, starting from F, which gives us F, A, C and E, forming an Fmaj7 chord.

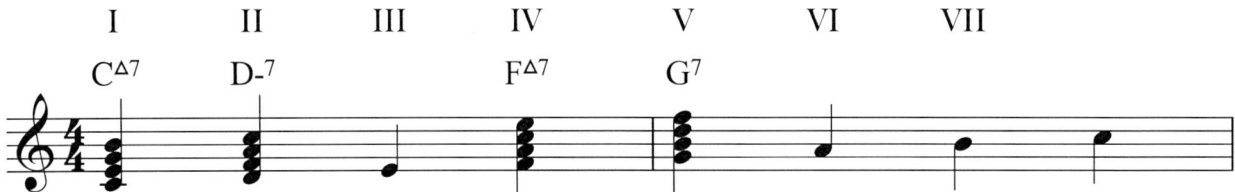

As we have done with each chord in the key, sit down at the piano and play the voicing, and play the notes of the scale, taking some time to get a feeling for which ones ring, and which ones feel like they need to move.

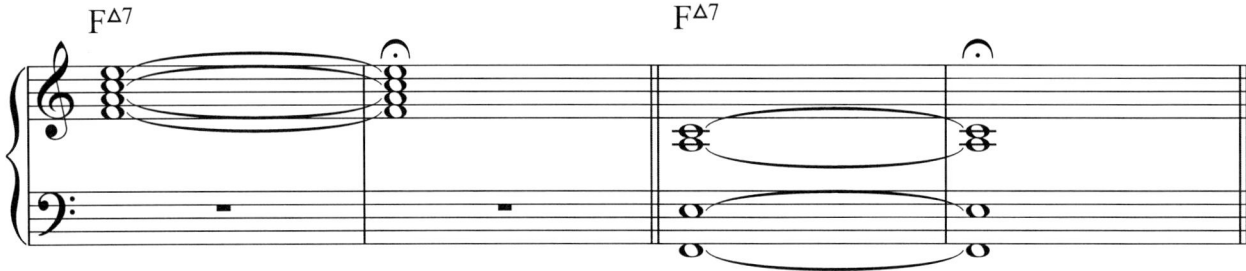

This is the first occasion where the names of the modes come in handy to identify what scale goes with the chord we are playing. Notice that, for the first time, we are looking at a chord type—the Major 7th chord—that appears in two positions in the scale, the first and the fourth.

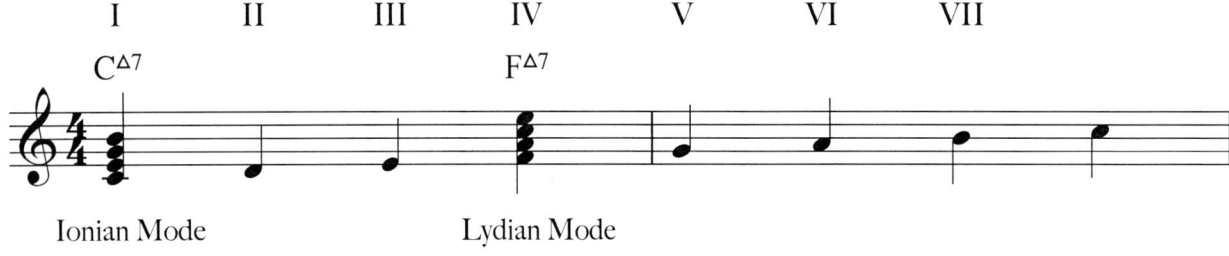

That means that as an improviser, I now have two choices of scales to play over an Fmaj7 chord. I can treat it like a IV chord in the key of C, or I can consider it the I chord in the key of F. If I'm treating it like the IV chord in C, then I am using the Lydian mode of C, or the C major scale starting from F, which we also call the F Lydian scale:

And if I treat it like the I chord in F, I will use the F major scale over it. This is the Ionian mode in F, or the F Ionian scale.

Two things to take notice of:

1. There is only one note different between the two scales.

2. In each case there is still exactly one note between the 3rd note of the chord, A, and the 5th, C. In the F Lydian scale it's a B natural, and in the F Ionian scale it's a B flat.

So both scales get us a smooth line to use to travel through the chord.

• Video 13: Lydian and Ionian Modes Compared

We already looked at some examples of improvisers using the Ionian mode, so now let's study some melodies and lines that use the Lydian mode.

Listen to Joe Henderson's composition "Inner Urge," from the recording of the same name. Here's the melody starting from bar 5:

This first section of the melody is written in the Lydian mode. In this case, an Fmaj7 chord in the key of C.

Notice the chord symbol for the Fmaj7, which includes the flat 5 in parentheses, (b5). This is the first time we've seen that, and it introduces an important concept. There is information given in the name of the chord to tell the pianist which type of Fmaj7 chord he should play. The flat 5 in parentheses (b5), which is the note B natural on an Fmaj7 chord, is called a "tension."

What is a tension? The tension notes are those outside of the four basic notes of the chord. Remember how we played the chord tones one by one and felt how they sounded settled? Remember how the in-between notes sounded less settled? That is tension—the feeling that the note wants to move to a nearby note to release that unsettled feeling.

The chord symbol Fmaj7(b5) is saying to the pianist, "play the Fmaj7 with the note B natural in it."

This is another situation where you will see different spellings for a chord. Fmaj7(b5) can also be written Fmaj7(#4), and these days it is most commonly written as Fmaj7(#11).

That calls for one more bit of explanation, and then we'll get back to listening to some more examples. So far we've talked only about the notes in the first octave of a chord voicing. That gave us the chord tones, 1, 3, 5 and 7, and the non-chord tones, 2, 4, and 6. Now that we're starting to explore the tensions, it is worth taking a minute to see what happens when we extend the scale a little further.

All we've done is to continue the C major scale beyond the first octave.

As we go deeper into harmonic choices, we'll examine the different tensions that are indicated in parentheses in chord symbols. The tensions tell the pianist which type of chord to play. The scale that goes with the chord voicing will give us a field of notes to make melodies with, and a smooth line through that chord.

Let's get back to listening to the sound of the sharp 11 on a major 7th chord, so we can get more familiar with it. The following will be some standard melodies that use the #11 sound.

Ralph Rainger's standard, "If I Should Lose You" has an illustration of the use of the #11 on a major 7th chord. This tune is played in a variety of keys and with some different choices in the chord progression, so for explanation purposes, I'm using simplified changes and we're looking at it in Hank Mobley's key, (Concert F), from his classic recording, *Soul Station*.

Here is the melody, starting from bar 9:

Another beloved standard where we can find this harmony is Dave Brubeck's "In Your Own Sweet Way."

The first A section of the tune has evolved over time. In Brubeck's original version, the melody lands on the note F on a Bb7 chord in the 7th bar of the composition.

Here it is starting from bar 5:

You can hear this on a variety of recordings. The original recording is on the album *Brubeck on Brubeck*.

About a year later, in 1956, Miles Davis recorded the tune with Sonny Rollins on an album entitled *Oleo*. It appears again on his classic 1960 recording, *Workin' with the Miles Davis Quintet*, with John Coltrane. Miles changed the landing note in the 8th bar to an E natural, the flatted 5th of the dominant chord.

By the time Wes Montgomery records the tune in 1960, (*The Incredible Jazz Guitar of Wes Montgomery*) the choice is clear, the last note of the melody is an E natural, and the chord is adjusted to a Bbmaj7.

Here's a line Wes Montgomery uses in his improvisation from that recording, in the first A section of his solo—this happens in the 7th and 8th bars of the tune (2:40):

And here's a line I heard Tom Harrell play at a concert in 1984. I usually carry around a little notebook where I write down lines I hear on live gigs. I loved how Tom set it up for the line to land on the flat 5 of the major chord right on the downbeat of the bar. This is on the first four bars of "On Green Dolphin Street," in Concert Eb. I'll show it in the tenor key of F, since we've been talking a lot about F in the key of C:

You can't find a recording of this one, so try it out on your own at the piano, with a play-along, and with a pianist or guitarist.

Finally, let's talk about choices. *When do I use the Ionian mode and when do I use the Lydian?* Generally speaking, a chord with fewer tensions has more options for interpretation. Put another way, a chord that is played with no tension to start with can support some added tension by the soloist. So, if the pianist is playing a straight Fmaj7 chord, I can treat that as a I in F, or I can add a little spice to it by treating it like a IV in C. But if the piano player is playing an Fmaj7(#11) chord, then it generally sounds better to play the C major scale (or F Lydian), which includes the tension note, B, that appears in the voicing. The F major scale will sound a little clunkier against that voicing. That paragraph is a bit of a mouthful. If you didn't quite get it, go back and read it again, a little more slowly, and see if you can follow everything in it. And better yet, play the different voicings at the piano, and try the scales, and see if you can feel the differences.

We'll see this principle at work in more detail as we ratchet up the tension on Dominant 7th chords in the next section of the book. Put one more way, a high tension chord voicing tends to call for the sound that goes with the tensions being played, whereas a low tension voicing will still work when a soloist adds tension on top of it. So a soloist has more options over a chord voicing with less tension, and has to be more precise as voicings become more complex.

## SOME THINGS TO PRACTICE

Before you go on, take a minute to practice playing some different major 7th chords at the piano, and try playing both of the available major scales against them.

Get used to the idea that you have a choice as an improviser to define the key you are playing in. As you get more fluid with the choices, you'll see that you can play the first chord in "On Green Dolphin Street" in the key of concert Eb one chorus, and in the key of concert Bb the next chorus, and then back again, or not....!

1. If you have a Bbmaj7 chord, your first choice is to treat it like a I in Bb. *What's the second choice?* Answer = F major. *Why?* Bbmaj7 is the fourth chord in the key of F, so I know I can play the F major scale through a Bbmaj7 chord.

2. Try a few others. *What are the two major scales you can play over an Amaj7 chord? What is the sharp 11 of an Amaj7 chord?*

3. To really get a handle on this information, you will eventually have to master it in all 12 keys. If you haven't learned your major scales in all 12 keys yet, now would be a good time to get started on that project. If you can play all 12 major scales, now would be a good time to work on being able to play slowly through all of the chords in each key. People have different ways they go about this. My suggestion is to do a couple of keys per day, so you don't burn yourself out on it. The more keys you learn, the more the sequences of chords will become familiar. Also, make it fun. Improvise!

4. Here's an exercise I use to warm up. Play the major scales in two octaves, in time, imagining the chords you're traveling through as you pass through them. The letter 't' below the staff indicates a tongued note, and the 'h' refers to a note that is not tongued.

- Video 14: Major Scale Articulation Exercise

5. Here are a few lines and melodies you can try out to experiment with the two keys, with a few bars at the end to write a few of your own:

You are now ready to start improvising not just with the melody of the tune, but also with the harmony, in real time.

# CHAPTER 5 · THE C MAJOR SCALE CONTAINS THREE MINOR 7TH CHORDS

One more chapter on harmony and then we'll move on to some other subjects.

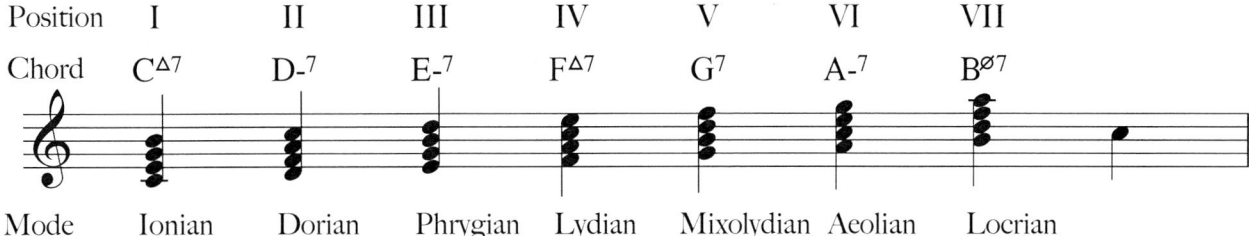

All right—we've seen that there are two major seventh chords in every major scale. This means that each major 7th chord will appear in two different major scales. That allows us to make a choice about which sound we want to emphasize when we improvise on a major 7th chord. It's not a question of making a choice that is correct or not—it's a situation where it's valuable to know what the *options* are. If you can learn to play melodies and lines that indicate clearly which sounds you are choosing in the moment, the musical conversation you generate with the pianist, bassist and other harmonic players can be a source of fun, surprise, negotiation, energy, fascination…

In this chapter we'll look at the minor 7th chords found in the major scales. There are three of them, so we'll have a little more work to do than in Chapter 4. As always, take your time, and get used to the *sounds*, not just the theory, and it will sink in more deeply. Our goals here are twofold:

1. To understand the relationship between the three minor 7th chords and the major scales, and

2. To get used to the idea that a standard chord progression is fluid—we are allowed to improvise with the harmony itself. Our success in that arena is largely determined by how clearly we can play the choices we make in real time.

Now, let's look at our clockwork again, emphasizing the three minor 7th chords.

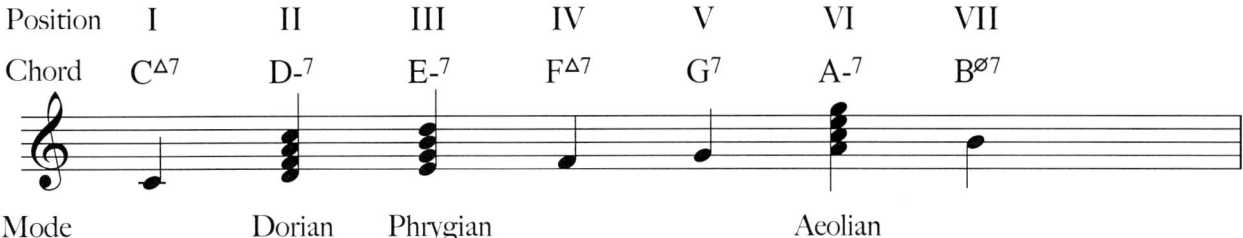

That means two things:

1. We can play the C major scale through all three of the minor 7th chords that appear in the C major scale (D-7, E-7 and A-7), and

2. For each of the minor 7th chords, there will be two other major scales that we can play through them.

Another way to say this is that each minor 7th chord will appear in three different major scales. For example, the D-7 chord will appear in the II position of C major, as we've explored. It will also appear in the Bb major scale in the III position.

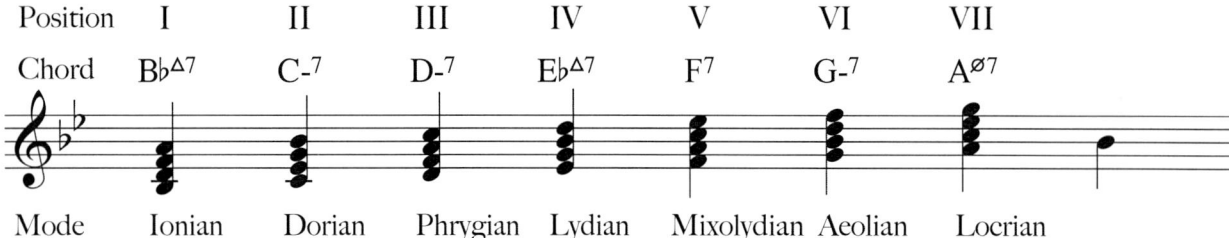

In which scale do you find the D-7 chord in the VI position?

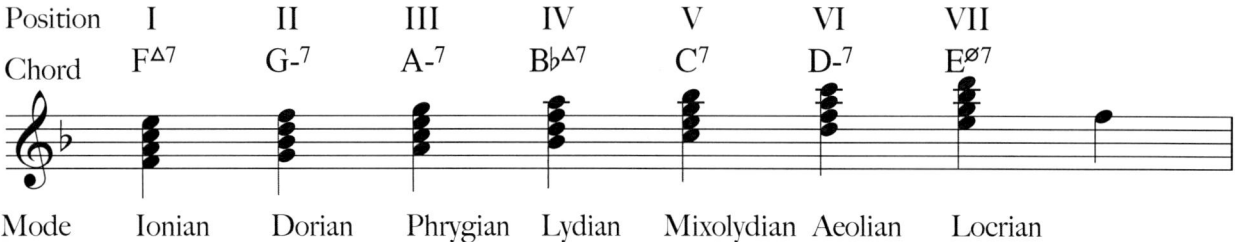

Let's now discuss the quality of the other two minor 7th chords. So far, we've only dealt with minor 7th chords in the II position, which corresponds to the Dorian mode. In the music of the American Songbook, when you encounter a minor 7th chord in the context of a II-V-I progression, the fact that it is meant as a Dorian minor 7th is generally understood. Even in progressions where the II-V doesn't resolve to I, it is most commonly treated as a Dorian minor.

In the case of the Phrygian mode, when a composer intentionally writes a minor 7th chord in another key, he will usually indicate that by writing in the word Phrygian, so you know not to default to the Dorian mode. You might see D-7 (Phrygian), or D Phrygian, or sometimes just D Phryg. Let's get acquainted with the sound of the Phrygian mode.

## MINOR 7TH CHORDS IN THE III POSITION—THE PHRYGIAN MODE

Let's look at the III Position.

In the key of C, we get an Emin7 chord in the third position. Playing the C major scale through an Emin7 chord gives us the E Phrygian mode. One of the ways to remember the sound of the Phrygian mode is that it is closely associated with Flamenco music.

Let's follow our standard procedure and get a taste of what the Phrygian mode sounds and feels like by sounding the chord at the piano and playing through it.

You can start with a straight Emin7 voicing and you could try playing E Phrygian sounds against it (Key of C), and compare that to how it sounds to play E Dorian against it (Key of D). Here are the basic voicings:

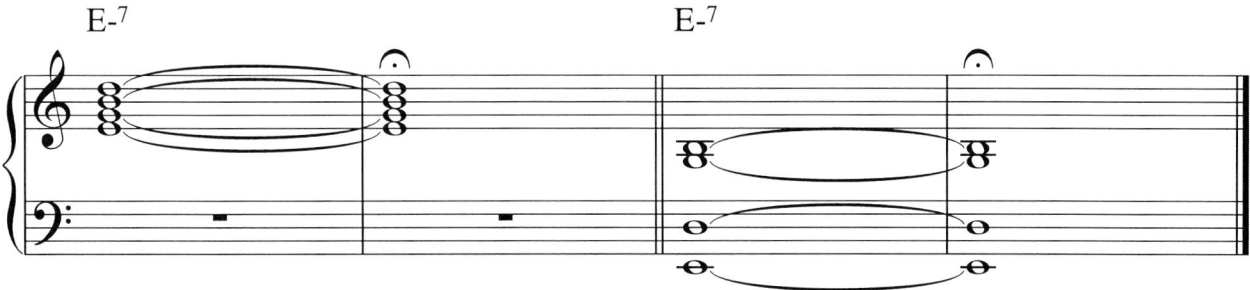

Notice especially how the second note of the scale is a half step away from the root, and has a strong pull to resolve downward. The 6th note of the scale is the other tone that gives the Phrygian mode its color. To me it sounds a bit melancholy. Try experimenting with the Dorian and then the Phrygian modes of E-7. In the Dorian you have a natural 2 and natural 6, and in the Phrygian a b2 and a b6.

Composers will let you know if they want you to choose the Phrygian mode by writing out the name of the mode, but there is one voicing that will indicate the Phrygian mode without spelling it out. It looks like this:

Notice that the voicing contains the Fmaj7(#11) chord, which is the next chord after E-7 in the series of chords in the key of C. Try playing with the scale now against this voicing and get it into your ears.

In the early American Songbook standards, you'll mostly encounter IIIminor7th chords in a key signature, rather than as a mode. In other words, it isn't common to see a minor 7th chord notated as Phrygian in the early standards. You'll see longer spaces of one chord after modal music was developed in the late 1950's and really explored by Miles Davis and John Coltrane, among many others, in the '60's.

Rodgers and Hart's "Have You Met Miss Jones" is a fun and challenging standard that uses the III minor 7th in the traditional way. We'll take a look at that first, and then we'll use Coltrane's composition, "Crescent," as an example of writing that explores the Phrygian mode.

In the 5th bar of the A section of "Have You Met Miss Jones," the melody looks like this:

This is a great example of all three minor 7th chords that appear in F major being used in the progression—A-7, the III; D-7, the VI; and G-7, the II. As our baseline, we can treat the whole four bar section as a walk in the park in the key of F. We can make up new melodies, focus on some of the important chord tones as the changes move, and use the F major scale to develop some lines through the chords. We could also try quoting melodies from other songs, like we saw Charlie Parker do in Chapter 3, on "Yardbird Suite."

For Example, Henry Mancini's classic, "The Days of Wine and Roses," has a similar progression, starting in bar 9:

Try quoting the melody of "Wine and Roses" over the similar progression in "Miss Jones," and vice versa.

(I'd also recommend watching the movie, "The Days of Wine and Roses." Mancini's score is plaintive and beautiful, and the way he adapts the melody and harmony of the title song to match the changing emotions of the story is remarkable.)

Back to Miss Jones—As an improviser, you might want to mix it up after a chorus or two. You could try treating each one of those minor 7th chords as a Dorian minor, for example, and that would put you into some different keys, which would create some new colors. Now you have some more possibilities.

Here's an example of treating each minor 7th chord like a II:

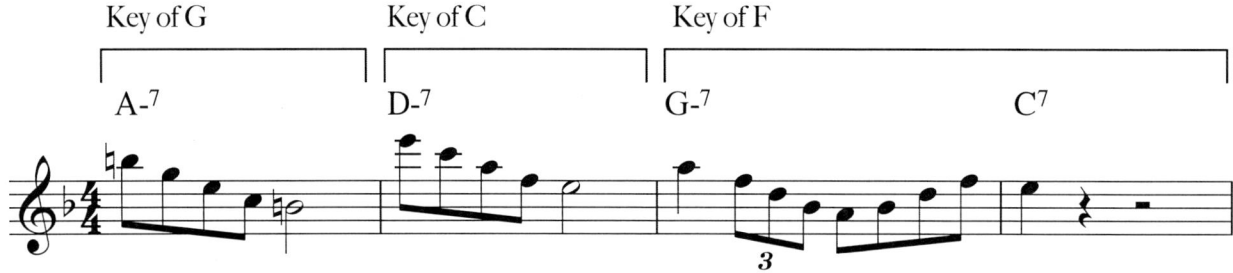

This idea uses repetition to help make the point. It goes: idea, same idea transposed, same idea, but with a variation that carries us forward, so we don't get stuck.

Here's the same idea using rhythmic variety to make it sound more interesting:

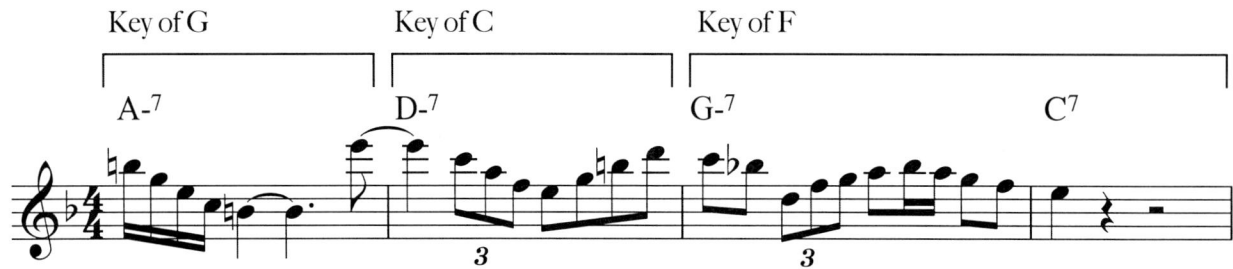

Try playing those ideas with a pianist playing the changes for you, or if you don't have a pianist or guitarist handy, you can always do it slowly, sounding the chords at the piano as you go, or you can use a play along track.

On his debut recording as a leader, *Introducing Kenny Garrett*, here's what Kenny says on his first time through bars 4-7 of "Have You Met Miss Jones," clearly treating it like he's just relaxing in the key of F:

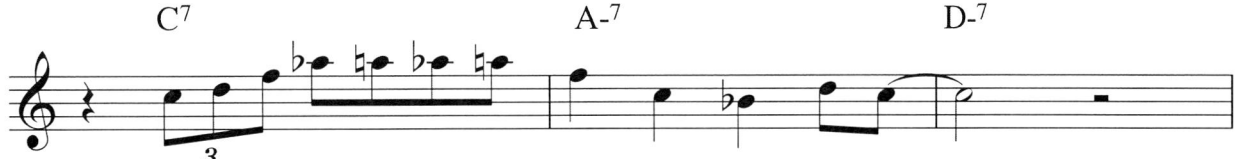

On his trio recording, *Lemuria-Seascape*, Kenny Barron plays the first few choruses treating the A-7 chord as a III in F major, and then he says this in his third chorus (2:15):

Without getting too far into the weeds right here, the presence of the note B natural in his line indicates that Kenny is improvising with the harmony, and treating the A-7 chord in a different key than F major. If he was hearing the key of F major, he would use a Bb, right? So the presence of the B natural means he's probably approaching that A-7 as a II in G major, the Dorian mode.

## ANOTHER SHORT ASIDE...

I've also included this example to draw your attention to the progression Kenny Barron plays in the succeeding bars. Notice after the D-7 chord how, instead of playing G-7 for a bar, and C7 for a bar, he plays Ab-7 Db7 in the first bar, and then G-7 and C7 in the next bar.

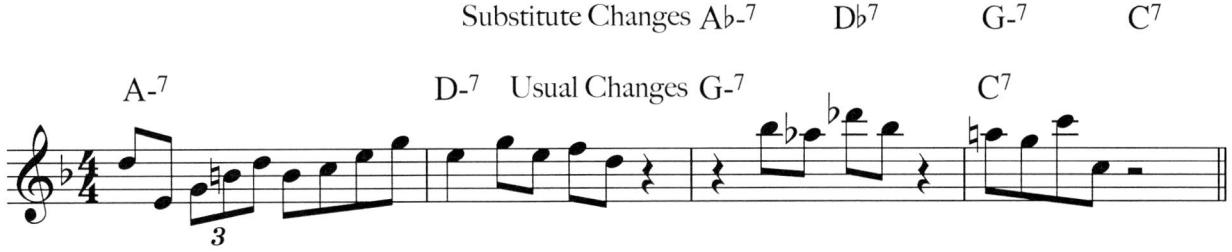

This is a common substitution for a regular II-V over two bars, and most jazz players treat this like the standard changes for the first ending of "Miss Jones," even though you won't see it in most fake books. Try experimenting with this substitution in some other tunes. Two songs where it often shows up are, "It Could Happen to You," and "Like Someone in Love," in both cases in the 15th and 16th bars of the tune.

## BACK TO THE MINOR 7TH CHORD IN THE III POSITION

The examples we've seen so far of a III minor 7th chord show them functioning in progressions that stay rooted to the home key. As musicians started exploring modal music in the early '60's, the III minor 7th chord was pulled out of the context of those traditional chord progressions, and allowed to stand on its own for longer stretches of time. A clear illustration of this is John Coltrane's composition, "Crescent," from the album of the same name.

Here are the first two phrases:

Coltrane has written a melody that is clearly in the key of Eb major, over G in the bass. As we've seen a few times already, there are different ways to name the chord, but they all indicate the Phrygian sound. Two other possible spellings are Abmaj7(#11)/G, and G7sus4(b9).

If we think of it as a G-7 in the key of Eb, note that Coltrane's melody immediately makes use of the two notes that characterize the sound of the Phrygian mode, the b2 and the b6.

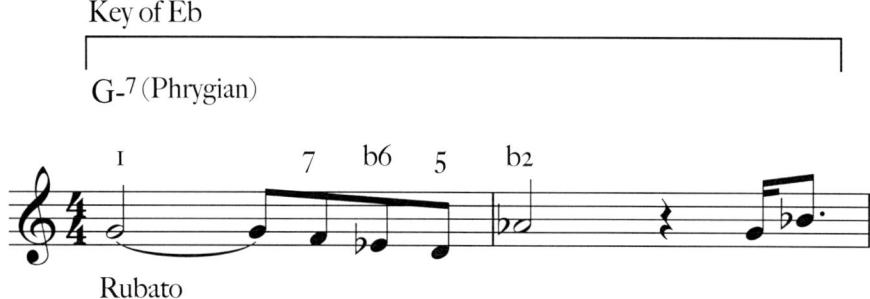

We'll let that example suffice for the moment, and talk about modal music in more detail a little ways down the road.

We're in the homestretch in our discussion of the harmony related to the major scales. Two more chords to look at, and get familiar with. Hopefully, by taking things slowly at this juncture, you will have had time to understand the relationships between the chords and scales well. When we discuss the minor scales, (harmonic minor and melodic minor), we'll use the same process. That should strengthen what we've learned here, and your familiarity with the clockwork model should make it easier to absorb the next set of chord/scale relationships.

## MINOR 7TH CHORDS IN THE VI POSITION—THE AEOLIAN MODE

Now let's look at the last minor 7th chord in the major scales, the VImin7. In C major that will be A-7, in the 6th position. Playing the C major scale through the A-7 chord gives us the Aeolian Mode. Here's the clockwork once again, so you can lock in the visual image, and of course, we will go straight to the piano to explore the sound, and get familiar with it.

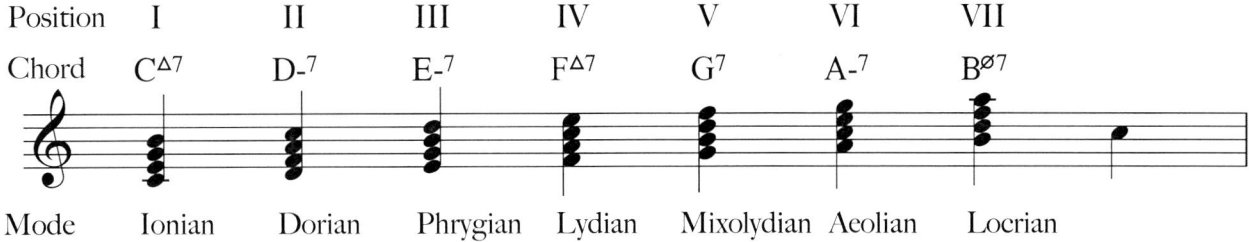

If you've studied classical music, you may know the terms Natural Minor and Relative Minor. These both refer to the sound of the VIminor7 chord.

Here's a picture for your mind of the Aeolian Mode:

And here are the voicings at the piano:

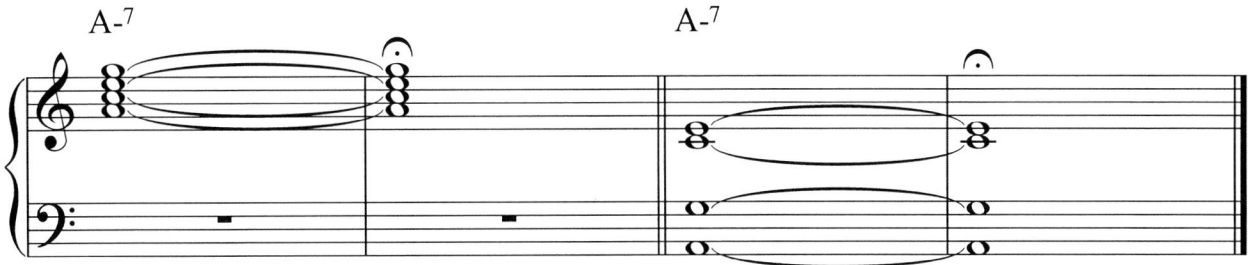

You know what to do to get to know the sound of playing the C major scale through the A minor 7th chord. Take some time to do that, listening for the qualities of the chord tones, and the notes in between the chord tones. Take it slowly, and see if you can get a feeling for how the Natural Minor sounds. It's a little more subtle feeling than the Phrygian sound.

And, we can do the same thing we did with E-7, which is to find the three major scales in which A-7 appears. So you ask yourself, in which major scale does A-7 appear in the II position, as a Dorian minor? Answer is G major. Then, in which position does A-7 appear in the III position—answer is F major. So take a minute to try each of the scales through your simple A-7 voicing, with the chord ringing at the piano.

Here is a voicing you can try at the piano that will suggest the use of the minor 7th chord in the VI position:

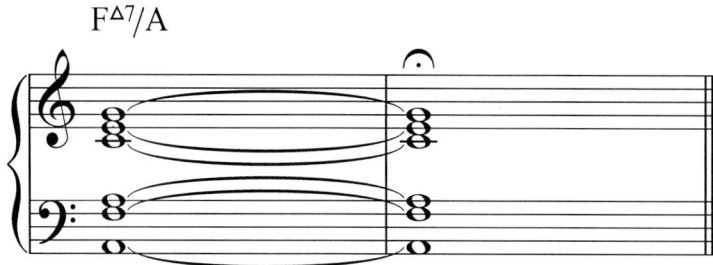

And here's one that is built in 4ths, which gives is a more modal sound:

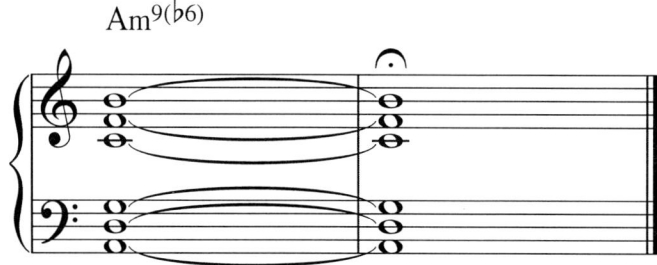

Now that we've checked out the sounds of each of the minor 7th chords, and seen how all three appear in "Have You Met Miss Jones" and "The Days of Wine and Roses," let's take our first dive into a song that will challenge us to put this knowledge to work.

### "ALL THE THINGS YOU ARE" — ALL THREE MINOR 7TH CHORDS, AND MUCH MORE

As of this writing, the second-most recorded standard of all time is "All the Things You Are," by Jerome Kern. You can look it up on Jazzstandards.com, which is one of the best resources for information about songs played and recorded by jazz musicians. "All the Things You Are" has a relatively simple, singable melody, which has just the right amount of unpredictability built in, and the chord progression is brilliant in its balance of functional harmony and surprising twists and turns. It has been a source of inspired blowing for four generations of musicians so far. It's become such a durable vehicle for improvisation because, on the one hand, it can be approached relatively simply, and on the other, there is ample opportunity for a soloist to reinterpret the harmony on the fly without losing the shape of the form.

All three types of minor 7th chords appear in the chord structure of "All the Things You Are." The A and B sections each contain a VI-7 and a II-7. And the D section has all three.

Let's have a look at each one.

The first five bars can all be found in one key on our clockwork diagram. Here's the clockwork in Ab major, the home key of the song, so we can see it clearly.

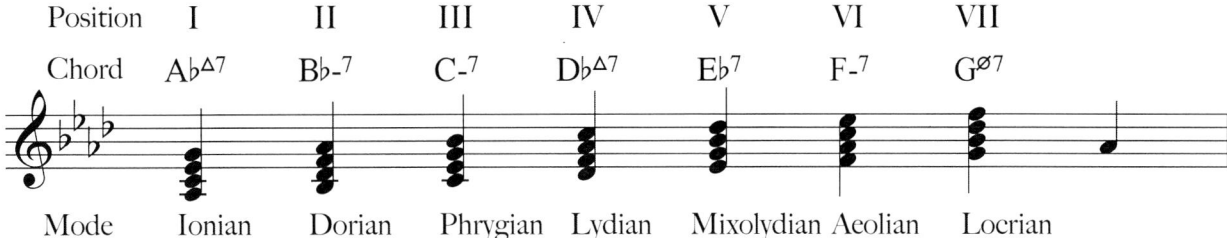

Now, here are the first five bars of "All the Things You Are:"

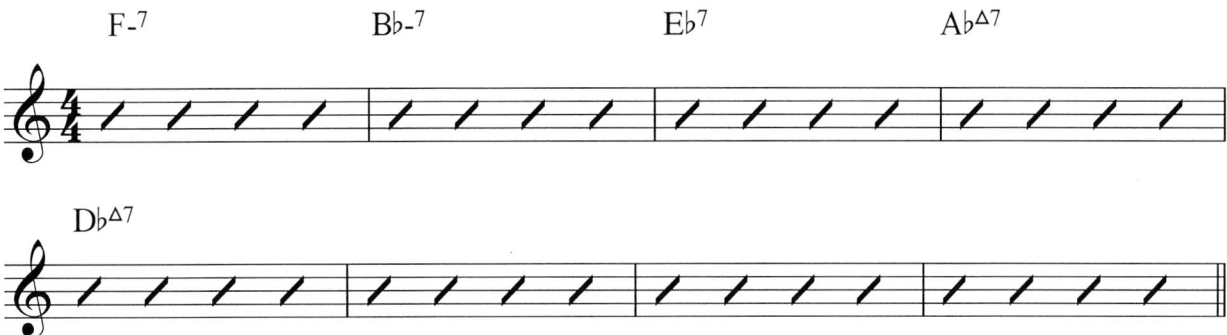

Take a look at that first chord, F-7. Is it functioning as a II, a III, or a VI?

Looking at the clockwork in Ab, we find F-7 in the VI position, right? Grab a pencil and write in a VI above the F-7 chord, and do the same for the rest of the chords in the progression. It should look like this:

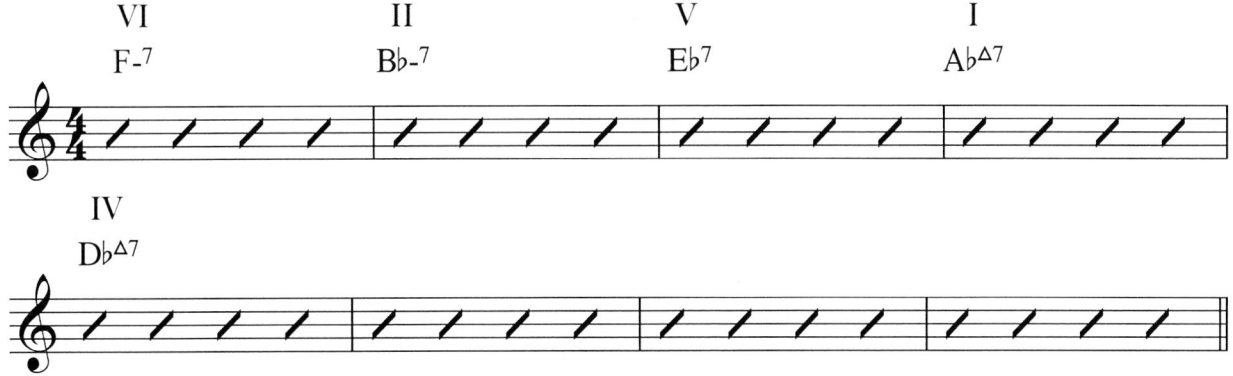

We know that fundamentally we can look for variations of the melody of the tune, and make up new melodies in Ab for those 5 bars without worrying about the key changing.

Our simplest approach to the first 8 bars, then, looks like this:

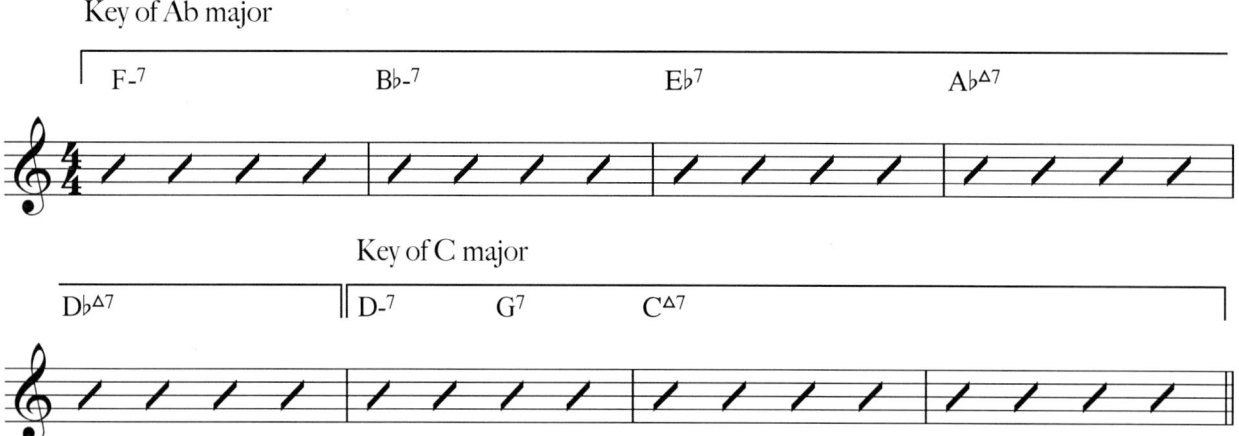

With that in mind, we still have to keep our place in the music. The spot that will show whether we are playing the progression with the band, or just reacting to what we hear after the fact, will be the change of key from bar 5 to bar 6. So as we learn to play "All the Things You Are," one of the first things to do is to find some good lines to make the transition over that bar line.

Here are a few examples:

Try putting on a recording of the tune, or a play-along track, and count through the first four bars. Then play one of these phrases starting in the 5th bar, and see what it feels like to 'make the changes' as you pass from the key of Ab into the key of C.

Then, our next step toward playing the chords more thoughtfully is to emphasize the chord tones, and find melodies that use them.

Here are a few examples from the tradition. Jimmy Heath, from his recording, *On the Trail* (1:15):

That E natural that Jimmy plays in the first bar is not in the key of Ab—we'll get to an explanation of that in the next section of the book. (In Chapter 10, on melodic minor, if you can't wait...) Our goal in these 'setup' chapters is to understand how the chords and scales fit together, and work together. We're adding things one at a time, so you don't get swamped with too many possibilities all at once.

On a record he made with Gigi Gryce, called *Gigi Gryce Quintet/Sextet Vol. 3*, Clifford Brown starts his solo out like this (2:20):

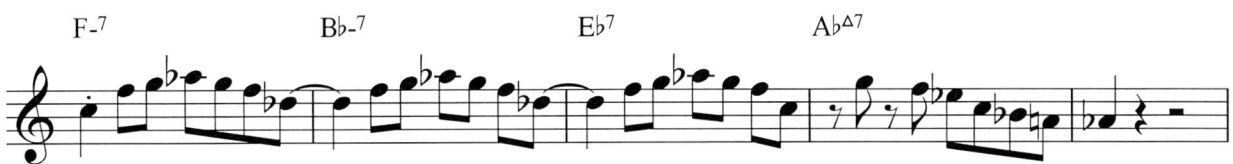

Check out how Clifford adjusts his melody to fit the changes, and how he anticipates the changes by landing on the 'and' of 4 in the first and second bars.

Here's an example where Paul Desmond is clearly treating the F-7 chord as a VI-7. This is from the album *Two of a Mind*, with Gerry Mulligan, and the F-7 chord in question is the first bar after the bridge in Desmond's first chorus (1:09).

And here's another example, from Chris Potter's tour de force solo recording from a master class. This is not a traditionally released recording, but it is widely available on the internet, so I'll trust you to search it up. The phrase happens at the top of his fifth chorus:

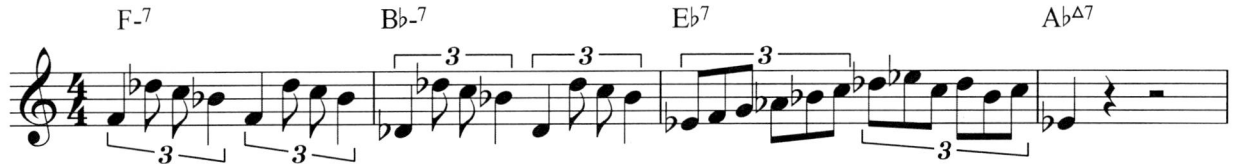

Those examples show the relatively simple approach of staying in the home key over the first five bars of the A section. Now, as we look at the B section let's see how Dexter Gordon takes some liberties with the changes—improvising with the harmony in real time.

The B Section is the same progression as the A section, transposed up a fifth.

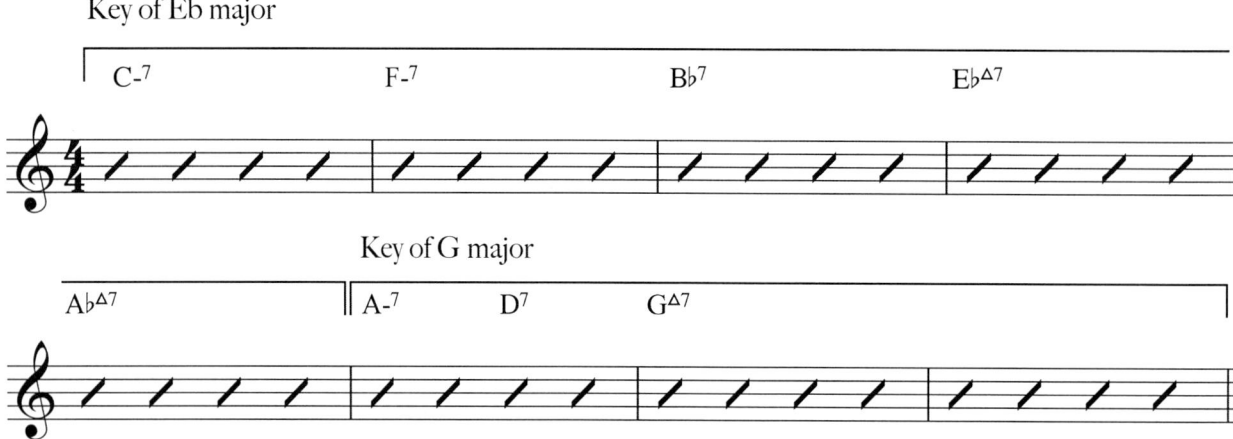

In this example, from a recording on the Steeplechase label, called *After Hours*, Dexter decides to get creative with the changes in his 5th chorus (around 5:28 in the track), and treats the first two bars as a II-V leading to Bb7 in the third bar. Instead of treating the C-7 chord in the first bar as a VI-7 in Eb, he treats it like a II-7 in Bb, and uses Bb major scale instead.

The note A natural in the line tells you that he's not thinking Eb major.

Also, that E natural he uses to get from F to Eb in the middle of the first bar of the example is a passing tone, which is a way of using chromatic notes to smooth out lines. We'll address passing tones in more detail in Chapter 18.

I'm using this example and the next one to point out two things:

1. Dexter is aware of, and is freely choosing the different major scales he can use over a minor 7th chord, and

2. *The harmony is not set in stone.* A common misconception is that the chords have to be played every chorus in the way they appear on a lead sheet. We have the freedom to redefine the sound of the changes in real time, and the trick to doing it successfully is being able to play the sound you want to get across clearly.

# A SLIGHTLY LONGISH ASIDE – THE CYCLE OF FIFTHS

Another thing that makes the chord progression of "All the Things You Are" so compelling is the way the first five chords progress through the cycle of fifths. You can think of the II-V-I progression as a kind of "Ready, Set, Go." The II-7 chord says "Ready" by establishing the key, the V7 chord says "Set" by building up the tension, and the release of that tension into the Imaj7 chord is the "Go."

That release of tension from the V into the I is the engine for much of the feeling of motion in standard songs.  If you move from V to I continuously, it forms a complete circle, which looks like this:

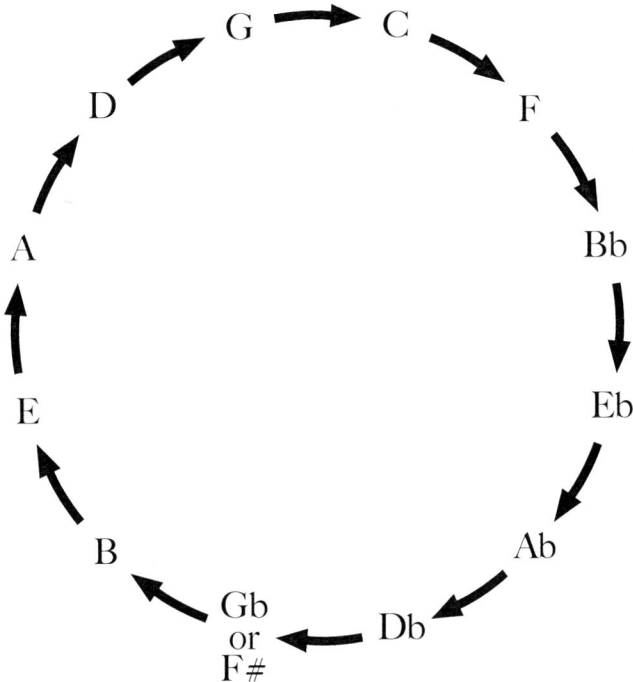

All 12 notes are represented, as are all twelve keys, and the system is perfectly closed.

Looking at the diagram, think back to the first eight bars of "All the Things You Are." Notice how it follows the cycle of 5ths, using the chord qualities associated with the key of Ab major—F-7 to Bb-7 to Eb7 to Abmaj7 to Dbmaj7.  There is a head of steam building up toward the next chord in the cycle of 5ths, which would be a Gb chord.  But Jerome Kern decides to take a left turn at that point, and goes up a half step from Db, to begin a II-V-I that lands us unexpectedly in the key of C.  Genius.  He builds a degree of predictability that the ear unconsciously follows, and then a surprise, with a satisfying release of tension into a new key.

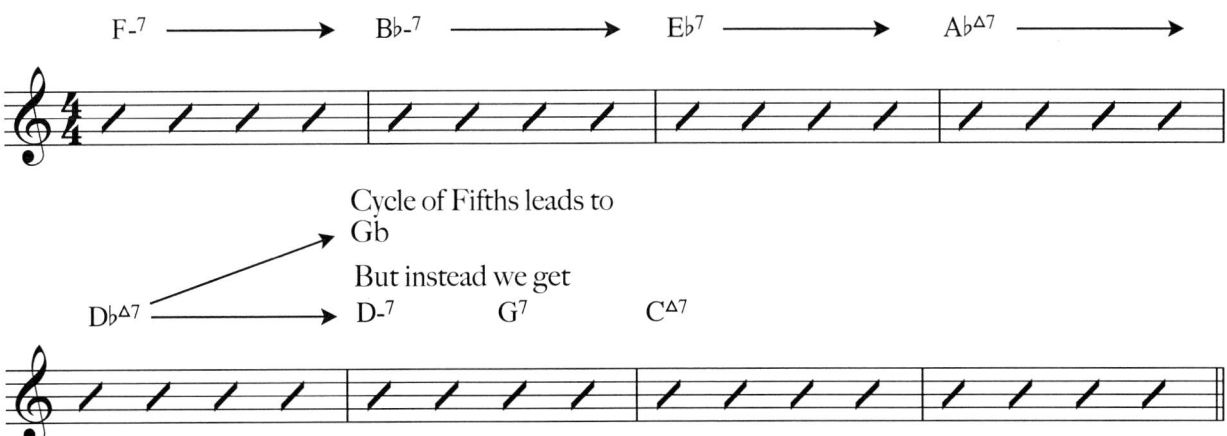

The cycle of fifths will provide us with some other material when we delve into substitute chords, which give us options for improvising with the harmony on the fly.

## THE LAST CHORD IN C MAJOR—THE SEVENTH AND FINAL MODE

At last we come to the 7th chord in the key of C, which will give us the Locrian mode. In C that is a B-7(b5) chord, which is also called a B half-diminished chord. Theoretically, the appearance of the B-7b5 in the 7th position of a C major scale means we can play a C major scale to get lines through the chord. In practice, this is rarely called for. In all my years of playing—40 and counting—I think I've only seen the Locrian mode specifically indicated twice, both times in the writing of one of my favorite contemporary composers, Emilio Solla. So it's worthwhile to note that the Locrian mode is derived from the 7th position of a major scale, but we will see more common scale choices when we discuss half-dimished chords in the harmonic minor and melodic minor scales in upcoming chapters.

## SOME THINGS TO PRACTICE

Here's a summation of the main concepts to get a handle on in these introductory chapters on harmony.

1. Scales provide us with "fields of notes" that we can use to make melodies that will resonate with the chords being played.

2. Chords are derived from the scales by stacking every other note.

3. When a chord type, like a minor 7th chord, appears in multiple positions in a scale, that means that multiple scales can be used to generate lines through the chord.

Specifically, in relation to the material in Chapter 5:

4. Practice playing the different scale choices over the three possibilities on a minor 7th chord. Play a minor 7th chord at the piano, and then ask yourself, "Which three keys does this chord appear in? For G-7 that will be F (as a II), Eb (as a III), and Bb (as a VI). Try playing all three scales and see if you can feel the differences in mood between them—and of course, don't just run the scales, but try improvising in each mode.

5. Return to the examples. Find them in the recordings and listen to them again. Play along with them exactly as the masters played them. Grab a play-along track, and see if you can play the phrases in the same spots in the progression where the masters played them. Then use those phrases as springboards to write and play some of your own.

Let's add a piano exercise to our practice routine. Spend a few minutes each day getting more familiar with the piano, and learning to play it in time. On a tour in Japan a few years ago, David Berkman and I had a day off, and he suggested that we spend some time giving each other a lesson. I showed him some things about how I practice melody, and he gave me this simple piano exercise, which has helped me improve my piano skills a lot.

David showed me a basic piano voicing that delivers all the important information in a chord by playing 1 and 7 in the left hand and 3 in the right. For a G-7 chord that looks like this:

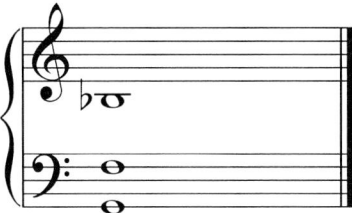

Practice playing that voicing through the cycle of fifths. That will get you comfortable with the voicing itself, and the shape of the cycle of fifths:

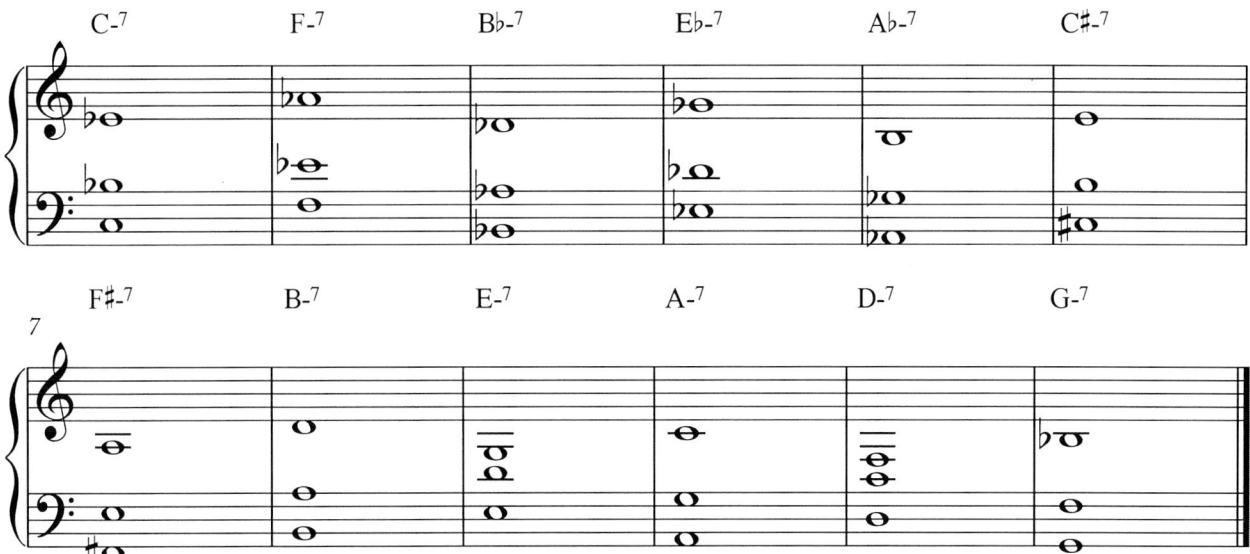

After you've worked your way through it slowly a few times, put on a metronome at a nice slow tempo, and practice playing it in time.

Here's a demonstration of me doing that:

• Video 15: Simple Piano Exercise

Do the same with Dominant 7 chords and Major chords, and then you'll be ready to play through the chord progression of "All the Things You Are," just using these simple three note voicings. Do a little each day until things start to feel more familiar, and then choose another tune and do the same thing.

That's our introduction to harmony. The next section of the book is organized around the skills you should be familiar with in order to perform a standard tune, from the intro through to the last note.

# PART TWO
## ANATOMY OF A SONG

*What Are the Tools I Need to Play a Song from Start to Finish?*

# CHAPTER 6 · THE INTRO

Now that we have some foundational knowledge about how to approach playing a solo on a standard tune, let's prepare to play a song from start to finish. Starting from the intro, through playing the melody and trading with the rhythm section, let's address the skills and knowledge you need to build to navigate successfully through a performance of a standard. What happens first? The intro, or if we're launching straight into the tune, the count-off.

One of the most common mistakes inexperienced players make is getting the tune off to a bad start. How? By counting off the tempo in a way that communicates poorly or not clearly to the band. It sounds obvious, but if you are the person communicating the tempo to other humans, you have to know what the tempo is before you count it off. It's surprising how often you will hear someone count off a tune without establishing the tempo in their own body first. Put another way, if you are feeling the quarter note inside, and you then show that tempo to the band, that will be much stronger than haphazardly searching for the tempo while you count it off. Even if you are using a metronome—say there's a tempo marking at the top of a big band chart, and you know that if you count it off too fast the saxes will fall apart at the soli section—rather than letting the band hear the metronome, you want to listen to the tempo, internalize it, and then count it off for the group. That way they are getting a *feeling* of the tempo. It's coming from a human, not a machine, so you can communicate your feeling about how you want the tune to start in addition to the 'scientific' information of precisely what tempo you want to play.

It's another thing that seems too obvious to say, but this also needs to be done in a way that is audible to the band. If you're turned away from the band, and counting off in a quiet voice, even if your feeling of the tempo is strong, chances are someone won't hear you, and you'll have disunity right off the bat. Then everyone spends the first couple of choruses trying to get the tempo established, which is a great way to lose the attention of the audience. If you sound like amateurs not playing together, the audience will lose interest. But if you come in together, sounding unified, even if you aren't playing on an advanced level, the audience can sense that there is a group of people up there doing something that is bigger than any of the individuals, and they're more likely to tune in.

So, if you want to bring the band in together, clarity of purpose and communication are key.

• Video 16: Counting Off the Tune

## A WORD ABOUT TEMPO

Is there a correct tempo for a tune?
Yes and no.

Or put in the form of a zen joke:
What is the correct tempo for "Softly as in a Morning Sunrise?"
One.

Surprisingly, this simple question touches on some of the most fundamental issues of improvisation. As you've probably heard a bunch already, jazz improvisation is meant to come from this moment, and be an experience that only happens once, in the exact way it happens right now. That is true in the same sense that having a conversation about the same subject with the same people on two successive days is true. If we said the same things in the exact same order as we did yesterday, that conversation would feel dead. It will feel alive and dynamic if we approach it with an open mind—maybe someone has a new thought on it since yesterday, and we can explore that together and see where it leads us. We're not reinventing the English language with every conversation, but it still feels 'of the moment.' Same thing with the language of jazz.

With that in mind, I think the tempo should reflect how I'm feeling when I get the tune started. If I played "Body and Soul" yesterday as a romantic ballad, but have a strong desire to play it today in a medium tempo with lots of interaction with the drummer, if I can communicate that feeling to the band and have them respond to it, I'll be playing the music in a way that is genuinely fresh and coming from how I'm feeling right now. It is necessary for me to develop the skill to communicate that feeling, and it is also incumbent on the rhythm section not to be caught thinking there is a *correct* tempo at which "Body and Soul" *must* be played.

If you are playing a concert that is honoring a composer, a band, or a great soloist, and the goal is to re-create the music of a certain time, in order for the audience to experience the way the music sounds live, then a pretty good argument can be made for playing the same tempo that the music was originally recorded at. Or if there is a practical matter like the big band saxophone section example above, then we might want to aim for a specific tempo, but the point I want to emphasize is that being flexible enough to explore the way the music will sound at different tempos gives you an avenue into creative interpretation of the music, whereas trying to play a song at "the correct tempo" can lock you into playing it more or less the same way every time.

That brings us to the idea of *not* counting the tune off, but starting it with someone playing some music, and having the band respond to that. Generally speaking, this is a more musical way to start the conversation. It's the same thing as feeling the tempo before you count it off, but deeper. By the time the band comes in, there is already a mood and an atmosphere to the music (if you've done it well, of course), and that also avoids the problem created by three of four people trying to figure out exactly what you mean with your count-off.

If I'm playing an intro on saxophone, what should I play?

First of all, look at the word 'introduction.' If you were asked to introduce a person who was about to speak at a conference or an assembly, what would you do? You'd find out some things about that person, and say a few words to give the audience an impression of what they were about to hear. You're setting up the audience to listen to the speaker, and maybe giving them a few hints about what to listen for. If you're going to do the same thing for a song, you can take the same approach.

What makes the song unique? What is it you like most about the song? What would you like the audience to listen for when the band comes in and plays the whole tune? These are all questions that can help you find some things to say in your intro. There is no set of rules to follow, nothing you have to do. It's a space for you to explore on your own. However, if you play the most inspired intro of all time, and then fail to bring the band in effectively, chances are the audience, and the band, will remember the train wreck, and not the intro.

Here are some strategies for getting a tune started without counting it off:

- Play the melody of the last four bars of the tune in time. Say to the band, "I'll play the last four bars by myself, come in at the top."
- Play the last eight bars of the melody in time. Same thing—Say to the band that you're playing the last eight bars, that way there's no confusion when they come in about whether they're coming in at the top, or in the second A section, for example.
- Play the first two A sections (of a 32 bar tune, say) rubato, or freely, out of time. Then bring the band in at the bridge by playing the last two or four bars of the second A section in time. You can keep it simple by playing the melody straight, or take a little more risk by improvising some lines over the changes.
- Take your favorite chunk of the melody, and see if you can make up some variations, on the spot. You could transpose it to some other keys, move it around rhythmically or break it into smaller pieces and try putting them together in different orders.
- Some bandleaders like to play an intro out of time, end it, and then count the tune in.
- One thing I like to do is say to the band, "I'll just start blowing on the changes, and you can fall in

when you feel it." That's a way to enter a tune that moves away from a formulaic approach—playing the head in, some solos, and the head out. Sometimes I'll play the melody at the end of my intro/solo, and sometimes I'll wait and only play the melody at the very end of the tune.

- Improvise on the changes, or play the melody a half step down, and then bring the band in at the usual key. You probably want to mention this to the band before you do it, just in case someone hears the key you're in and thinks that's the key she should come in with.
- If the composition you're playing has a bass ostinato at the beginning, you can also play freely up front, and then bring the group in by playing the bass figure. Or you could improvise for a minute on the ostinato itself, and then play it straight, in time, to bring the band in.

Which brings us to some ways to include the rest of the band…

If you introduced every tune yourself, someone might think you're hogging the stage a bit, so it's good to get everyone involved. You can:

- Ask the piano player to play an intro. If you have an idea about where or how you want to come in, you can communicate that, or you can leave it open and trust the pianist to bring you in. This is a great way to get a ballad started, but it doesn't have to be a ballad.
- Ask the rhythm section to play a chorus or two up front. This is often done on the blues. You might have to count it off to get it going. It's a nice way to get a little mystery into how you're going to play the melody. When you come in, you can adjust the melody to the vibe and energy of the music that's already percolating.
- Ask the drummer to play eight or 16 up front, in time.
- Ask the drummer to play freely out of time, and then to set it up with 8 bars (or 4, or 16) in time. In either of these cases, it's a good idea to be ready in advance to answer the question from the drummer, "What tempo do you want?"
- Ask the bassist to start walking at the top, or over a vamp, and have the rest of the rhythm section come in one by one.
- Especially on a tune with an ostinato pattern or a pedal at the top, ask the bassist to play freely out front, and then set up the pattern in time. Same thing as with the drummer—be ready to show him what tempo you're thinking of.
- Use your imagination and find some other ways to get the proceedings off to an interesting and engaging start.

We can use a variety of intros to keep the music interesting and unpredictable, and we can use clarity to keep it familiar enough that we stay together.

Here's a list of some songs where, if you call them at a jam session, there's a pretty good chance someone in the band will say, "With the intro?" Or someone will just launch into the intro, and you have to know what to do. I've indicated at least one reference recording where you can hear how the intro is usually played.

| | | |
|---|---|---|
| "All Blues" | Miles Davis | *Kind of Blue* |
| "All The Things You Are" | Charlie Parker | *Charlie Parker on Dial* |
| "Autumn Leaves" | Cannonball Adderley | *Somethin' Else* |
| "Bebop" | Charlie Parker | *Charlie Parker on Dial* |
| "Birdlike" | Freddie Hubbard | *Ready for Freddie* |
| "Bouncing with Bud" | Bud Powell | *The Amazing Bud Powell* |
| "Bolivia" | Cedar Walton | *Eastern Rebellion* |
| "Celia" | Bud Powell | *Jazz Giant* |
| "Confirmation" | Dexter Gordon | *Daddy Plays the Horn* |
| "Dance of the Infidels" | Bud Powell | *The Amazing Bud Powell* |
| "Eternal Triangle" | Dizzy Gillespie | *Sonny Side Up* |
| "Footprints" | Wayne Shorter | *Adam's Apple* |
| "I Mean You" | Thelonious Monk | *5 by Monk by 5* |
| "If I Were a Bell" | Miles Davis | *Relaxin'* |
| "I'll Remember April" | Clifford Brown | *Clifford Brown and Max Roach at Basin Street* |
| "Milestones (Old)" | Miles Davis | *Miles Davis All Stars (1947)* |
| "Moment's Notice" | John Coltrane | *Blue Train* |
| "Nica's Dream" | Horace Silver | *Horace-Scope* |
| "A Night in Tunisia" | Dizzy Gillespie | *Birks Works: The Verve Big Band Sessions* |
| "On a Misty Night" | Tadd Dameron | *Mating Call* |
| "On the Trail" | Donald Byrd | *Mustang* |
| "Recorda-Me" | Joe Henderson | *Page One* |
| "Round Midnight" | Thelonious Monk | *Genius of Modern Music Vol. 1* |
| | Miles Davis | *Round About Midnight* |
| "Salt Peanuts" | Charlie Parker | *Jazz at Massey Hall* |
| "Seven Steps to Heaven" | Miles Davis | *Seven Steps to Heaven* |
| "Someday My Prince Will Come" | Miles Davis | *Someday My Prince Will Come* |
| "Star Eyes" | Charlie Parker | *Swedish Schnapps* |
| "Take The A Train" | Duke Ellington | Original Single recorded 1941 |
| "Walkin'" | Miles Davis | *Miles Davis All Stars* |

## SOME THINGS TO PRACTICE

1. Practice counting off a tune in front of a mirror, so you can see what you look like doing it. Are you communicating the time clearly?

2. The first skill to work on if you're going to play the band in instead of counting the tune off, is being able to play a tempo in a way that is clear and demonstrative, so the rhythm section can hear you and come in with confidence. Practice playing a tempo clearly in quarter notes and eighth notes. Then record yourself and see if you can snap your fingers along with it. Can you feel the tempo you're trying to communicate? If you were the drummer, would you know when to come in?

3. After you feel confident that you can bring the band in successfully, start choosing elements of a tune to use as inspiration for your introduction. Practice playing a short introduction, and then moving into time and showing the band where to come in.

4. Try using your horn as a conductor's baton—demonstrating to the band where the quarter note is while you play your cue for the group to come in. Do this in front of a mirror so you can see if you think it's working.

- Video 17: Setting Up the Time for the Band

5. Record yourself playing a handful of intros and listen back—this is another form of looking in the mirror. Make some decisions about what you like and don't like and work on the things you like to make them better. Pluck out the weeds.

# CHAPTER 7 · THE MELODY

There are two goals for this chapter—to discuss some ideas about how to approach playing the melody, and to present some practical suggestions for how to learn a melody.

## APPROACHES TO PLAYING MELODIES

Assuming you are playing an instrumental version of a song, meaning there is no singer and you are playing the melody by yourself, what are your responsibilities? Should you go for accuracy and honoring the composer's written notes?
Yes.

Should you interpret the melody and make it your own, maybe even changing some notes to do that?
Yes.

Are accuracy and creative expression in conflict with each other? It's actually possible to honor the tradition and make it your own simultaneously, if you're willing to put in the work. Let's say you can approach playing the melody on a spectrum that goes from being faithful to the original melody on one side, to being interpretive and giving it a personal spin on the other. Naturally, you can choose to place your approach at a variety of points along the spectrum. You can also choose to improvise with the spectrum itself—playing one tune in a highly interpretive way, and another very specifically and precisely. You could even change your approach from one phrase to another within a song, if you can pull it off effectively.

If you listen to the vocalists Nat King Cole, Frank Sinatra, Ella Fitzgerald and Blossom Dearie, they are each distinct and have personal styles that are identifiable, but they also have in common the fact that they choose to deliver the melody accurately. Each of them infuses the music with their own character, but if you want to learn a melody, listening to any one of these four will put you in the neighborhood of a precise reading of a tune. Honoring the composer's original melody is a good place to start.

Billie Holiday and Abbey Lincoln, and especially Betty Carter, by contrast, choose to present a highly personal interpretation of a melody right from the top. If you want to present a melody with a high degree of artistic personalization, you can learn a lot following their lead. It's important to note, though, that if you start learning a song from Betty Carter, you are studying her interpretation of the melody. If you then interpret that further, and now someone comes along and learns your take on it, and makes more changes, it could become like a game of "telephone," where, by the time a phrase has been whispered to each person in a circle, the original phrase comes out modified so many times that it becomes unrecognizable. These days it's possible to collect a handful of versions quickly. Listening to multiple versions helps us to zero in on what parts of a melody are generally agreed on, and which parts are different artists' interpretations.

If you want to go the other way, and get as close to the original sound of the melody as possible, you can watch the show where the song first appeared. Many of the most popular American Songbook standards appeared first on Broadway or in a movie musical. Watching the original shows can give you a deeper sense of what the lyrics mean, and provide a wider context for the song.

You may ask, are these movies relevant to my life now? It is true that some of these films and shows are already almost 100 years old, and may seem old fashioned. In some ways, they are. However, one fundamental answer to that question is, "Love is always relevant." Most of the songs that have become standards started out as love songs, even if the tradition has delivered them to our doorstep as high-speed burners today.

Another response could be that no one even knows these songs anymore, outside of hardcore jazz fans, so they don't have a living connection to the culture. That is also true—the American Songbook tradition is already multiple generations out of the main stream of popular culture. *But*, the community of hardcore jazz players and fans around the world is substantial. It is now possible to find jazz musicians almost everywhere, and even if you can't speak to each other, someone can start playing "All the Things You Are," and you can immediately stand on common ground. Another important point—these songs became standards for more reasons than just popularity.

Jazz musicians may have originally been attracted to a song because it was a popular hit in its day, but certain standards became long-term vehicles for improvisation because they are so well crafted. The essential core of the tune is strong enough to allow it to be highly flexible and adaptable. So if you're attracted to the complex odd meter music that is popular in the 21st century, listening to "Summertime" while watching a revival of Porgy and Bess on Broadway won't directly address that style of playing; but if you can blow an effective solo on "Summertime" in 4/4, then you can try it in 5/4, 7/4 or 11/8. The song provides some familiarity while you explore something more challenging. If you've done the homework on the standards in the first place, that will give your solos on more contemporary structures some substance, and some deeper reference points. Learning the harmonic language of the American Songbook will also give you tools to use as you seek to reinterpret and improvise on the music that you find in your own contemporary popular culture.

Should I learn the words?
Most definitely. If you're like me and you find it difficult to remember the words to songs, there are still a few good reasons to learn them at the outset.

- As already mentioned, the words signal the emotional meaning of the song. They can inspire your interpretation and guide your emotional approach to the tune.

- The words provide the phrasing for the melody. They let you know when to stop and start your phrases—they provide the motion from one sentence to another.

- Especially if the audience is likely to know the words to the song you are exploring, an accurate rendition of the melody will help the audience 'sing along' with you in their heads, giving them a connection to what you are doing.

- And as a general rule, the more you know about the song you are playing, the deeper your potential for an interesting improvisation gets. If you play the same solo on every song, the audience may lose interest after a couple of tunes.

- If you find yourself in a situation where you are playing behind a singer, called 'obligato,' if you know the words, you have a better chance of creating a complementary line with the singer, rather than stepping on his phrases and getting in his way.

Dexter Gordon is well known for playing melodies in a way that displays a clear connection to the lyrics. It sounds like he is singing the lyrics while he plays them on the horn, which is in fact, what he says he is doing.

Another of the clearest examples available for the more "conservative" approach to playing the melody is Clifford Brown, on one of his masterpieces, *Clifford Brown With Strings*. He delivers the melodies emphasizing beauty of tone, clarity of phrasing, precise time. "Brownie's" readings are so beautiful and complete that he doesn't even need to solo on every track.

At the other end of the spectrum is Miles Davis' approach, especially in a quartet setting. He will play some of the melody, and then, still in the head-in chorus, he'll make up an alternative melody—often so beautiful that it's hard to imagine that it's not the original melody. A great example that I first heard in a master class given by Dave Liebman is Miles' reading of "What's New." You can hear it on a recording called *A Day In Paris*.

Charlie Parker sometimes takes a different tack, playing a chunk of the melody clearly, and then filling the spaces between phrases with brilliant improvisations from his own language. The first sixteen bars of "Autumn in New York," on *Charlie Parker With Strings* is a good example of this.

Lastly, as a general guideline, the more people there are playing a melody, the better it will sound if they play it precisely together. If a saxophone section is playing a melody in unison, the impact lies in their ability to sound like one big voice. If the second tenor player decides he wants to put his own personality into his reading of the melody, instead of improving it he will distract the listener's attention toward himself, weakening the overall unity of the group. If that same tenor player is playing the melody by himself in a quartet setting, there will be much more room for him to play his interpretation—to put his own spin on it. In a classic trumpet and tenor, (or alto) front line, part of the fun is listening to each other and making decisions about when to bend a note together, when to lay back the time, and when to play it straight. The front lines that sound great together are the ones who have found ways to agree on the phrasing of the melody. Here are a few examples of great front lines. I'll leave it to you to search up some recordings where you can find them:

- Charlie Parker and Dizzy Gillespie
- Hank Mobley and Kenny Dorham
- Benny Golson and Lee Morgan
- Wayne Shorter and Freddie Hubbard
- John Coltrane and Miles Davis
- Cannonball and Nat Adderley
- Joe Henderson and Woody Shaw
- Michael and Randy Brecker
- Bob Berg and Tom Harrell
- Branford and Wynton Marsalis
- Donald Harrison and Terence Blanchard

## LEARNING THE MELODY

First and foremost, learn the melody using your ears, not your eyes. If you want to sound like a jazz musician, you have to try to reproduce the sound and feel of the way jazz musicians play melodies. You will not get any information about sound or feel by reading a lead sheet.

Once again, the key is your internal singing voice. I have been amazed to witness, over and over again, with students from everywhere on the planet, the simple fact that almost anyone can sing back directly what they hear, as long as they are focused on the sound. I've done call and response sessions in workshops where I would lay the time way back, or play intentionally complex rhythms, and large groups of people can repeat them back without hesitation. It is this ability you want to tap as you study melodies. The idea is to teach your internal singing voice to sing the melody, and then simply play the melody on your instrument while you sing it in your mind.

How can I practice that?

It takes a bit of discipline, but you can simultaneously:

- Learn a melody
- Train your ears
- Improve your time feel
- Enlarge your improvising vocabulary, and
- Get better and better at playing exactly what is in your mind, directly through your instrument.

We'll discuss the longer-term project of putting together a repertoire of tunes you can play by heart a little later. For now, let's say you've picked a tune to work on, and you have a recording of it that you're using as a reference. Listen to the first phrase of the melody a handful of times. Then choose either the whole phrase or a smaller chunk of it that is short enough to remember, and sing along with the recording. You don't have to have a good singing voice. What you're doing is teaching your internal singing voice a new 'word.'

When you can accurately repeat the first phrase along with the recording, turn it off and sing it, either in your mind or out loud, to confirm that you have internalized it. If you're unsure, check the recording again.

Here comes the most important moment.

There is only one first time for everything, and the first time you play your new 'word' is your opportunity to do some deep training. While singing the melody in your mind, count off a comfortable tempo, and try to play the melody straight into the horn, without thinking about it. Just sing and play. Keep tapping your foot, and search for the melody *in time*. Keep going until you can match what you're hearing in your mind with what you're playing on the horn. If you did the exercise in Chapter 1 of playing "Frere Jacques" in an unfamiliar key, you should recognize this as an extension of that process.

Until you've developed some skill, you won't be able to do it accurately the first time. Avoid the temptation to noodle around on the horn, trying to find the melody with your fingers. Just ask your fingers to deliver what you're hearing with your internal voice.

- Video 18: Searching for the Melody in Time

Why should I do this in time?
If you are able to follow this process, you're not only improving a variety of skills all at once, but most importantly you are practicing to deliver the sounds in your imagination directly through the horn, in real time. Isn't that the ultimate goal of improvisation?

What is a lead sheet for, then?
Lead sheets are for reference and communication. They can help you pinpoint what it is you are hearing as you listen and try to learn with your ears. This is an inexact science, since there are so many ways to go about playing these tunes. There's a learning curve as you grow into trusting what you hear and comparing it to what you see on a lead sheet—you'll discover that you can't always trust the lead sheet.

Lead sheets come in different forms:

- Original sheet music, as written by the composer, which is a great first source
- "Fake books" which tend to present collections of popular songs, often with the simple, "unjazzified" version of the changes
- "Real Books" which are collections of lead sheets transcribed by jazz musicians for their own use, and then copied and shared
- Contemporary collections which take care to present the music with context and maximum accuracy

Among the best of the contemporary collections is the "New Real Book," series presented by Sher Music. (Disclosure, Sher Music is also the publisher of this book.) I mention them not to plug another product from this publisher, but enthusiastically to recommend them because I have been using them for many years—since long before I ever thought about writing a book myself.

A lead sheet can be valuable for reference while you're learning a tune, especially if you're having trouble figuring out exactly what the notes are. I emphasize learning with your ears and not with your eyes so you don't miss out on the opportunity to develop your inner ear as you go. Lead sheets are also helpful to learn about chord sequences. The chord changes on a lead sheet can give you something to listen for as you're learning the tune.

BUT

This is a good moment to remind you that everything is meant to be fluid when you go to improvise on a tune. If you think of the lead sheet as the correct version of the melody and changes, and play them the same way every time, you're missing out on the fun of making decisions on the fly, and negotiating alternate paths with the rhythm section. We'll start looking at those alternate paths in Chapter 10, and get into much more detail in Part Three of the book.

Although digitized versions of both legal and not so legal collections of tunes are temptingly available, I would encourage you, for the benefit of the composers, publishers and your own personal karma, to invest in the legal versions.

The message here is that learning a song is a process. If you grab a piece of sheet music and read the melody without any aural reference, you're missing a lot of vital information about how the song *sounds*.

Since there are often multiple lead sheets for a song with different changes or melody notes, when you go to play the song, unless everyone else learned the song off the same lead sheet, you're likely to fall into disagreement about the melody or the changes. That disagreement can waste time and cause lack of clarity, which leads to people clashing in the music, which can make the music sound bad. So a good lead sheet serves an essential purpose when you go to share a song with your band—good clear communication.

It would be convenient if there were a single authoritative lead sheet for every tune, and we all used the same one. But there is an upside to having to find multiple recordings and multiple lead sheets, and figuring out what the essence of a tune is: it leads us deeper into the culture of jazz. In the process we get turned on to musicians we might not have heard before. And, we learn to distinguish where musicians are interpreting and where they are delivering the melody straight.

How should I figure out which tunes to learn?

One of the quickest ways is to go down to a jam session and listen to what the musicians are playing.

Let's say you're a surfer arriving at a beach you've never been to before. Do you just grab your board and paddle out into 10-foot waves? If you're smart you sit on the beach for a while, watching what the waves are doing and how the locals navigate them.

I recommend to my students to get a little pocket-sized notebook, and every time they hear a tune they don't know, to ask someone the title and write it down. You can also see what other intelligence you can gather—what's a good recording to listen to? Who's version do you like the most?

That's the tune to work on tomorrow, so you'll know it next week if it gets called again.

In my experience, the songs I remember most effortlessly are the ones where I followed this order:

- Listen
- Study
- Perform

*Listen*: Ideally, I like to just listen for a while before I start studying a tune. I use a wake up alarm that I set to play me a song I want to hear a bunch of times, and usually wake up to the same recording for about a week. I can check in on the song later in the day, and try singing it a few times, to see if it's getting lodged in my ear. I want to let the song percolate for a few days, so that by the time I start working on it, I can already pretty much sing it.

*Study*: Gather as much information on the song as you can.

- Composer
- What year it was written
- What show it was in, or what the original recording was
- Original key and most commonly played key
- Best recordings
- If there is more than one lead sheet available, compare them to see if there are places where there is more than one way to play the melody or the changes

This process used to be much more difficult and expensive. All of that information is easily accessible on the internet now, which makes doing the research much quicker. Jazzstandards.com is a great source of information about songs, including a ranked list of the 1000 most recorded songs in history. You can just search up a song on YouTube, or any of a growing variety of music streaming services and instantly find multiple recordings of a song to compare. If you want to be really thorough, you can purchase and download the original sheet music, and check the differences between the original changes and the blowing changes jazz musicians use on their recordings.

The internet is a double edged sword. It is amazing for supplying us with information, but it can have an isolating effect—it's a vast collection of accumulated human knowledge, but gives us the ability to access that knowledge without human contact. The upside of the difficulty of finding information when I was looking for it, was that the human knowledge lived in humans, and we had to talk to each other and share information. That provided a sense of community that is harder to feel in the internet age. Remember that jazz is a living language—you have to speak it with other people to get a sense of how it feels and sounds.

*Perform*: Performing a tune with a band in front of an audience is the best way to test whether you've properly internalized it. If you forget the melody and leave a hole in front of people who are listening, you'll notice! If you're like me, you won't want to feel that feeling again. I'll discuss this in more detail in Chapter 20, but one thing I think many people leave out is practicing to perform. I reserve some time at the end of every practice session to play *as if I'm performing*. That means I kick off a tune and play by myself, without any aids, with the understanding that I am responsible to deliver the melody well, keep my place in the tune, and play clearly over the changes, *without stopping*. On the bandstand, I don't get to ask the band to stop for a second while I make a quick correction to what I just played. I have to continue, and try to make it work.

So you can practice that.

If you can play a tune for 10 minutes by yourself without getting lost, you have a much better chance of staying grounded with the band. And if you have practiced to be responsible for everything—rhythm, melody and harmony—you bring all of that to the table when you go to play with other musicians.

Practicing this way will also help you to improve your time. If you are conscious enough of what you are doing to be sure that you know where you are, you are playing the time. Many musicians depend on the rhythm section to tell them where the time is. If you don't take responsibility for playing the time yourself, the rhythm section will feel the weight of you leaning on them, and that will restrict their freedom to play what they hear.

That gives us a nice segue to playing *against* the time. One of the many (!) fun things you can learn to do is improvise with the placement of your eighth notes in relation to the beat. You can play ahead of the time or "on top" of the beat, directly on the beat, or behind the beat, called "laying back." Here's the kicker—this only works if you're laying back against *your own* sense of the beat. You create tension by feeling a quarter note in your internal clock, and then playing a hair behind it. If you don't feel your own time, and play behind the beat you are hearing from someone else, the result will be to drag the time slower. Same with playing on top of the beat—if you play ahead of the quarter note you are feeling, it will sound tense and lifted, but if you're just playing faster than the rhythm section, you will sound like you're rushing.

For an excellent illustration of the difference, listen to Eddie Harris and Dexter Gordon each play the melody on "Love for Sale." On his recording, *The In Sound*, Harris plays right on the beat, with a tendency to be on top, which gives his solo, especially, an incredible feeling of drive, but he never gets ahead of the band. He always sounds like he's grooving. Dexter Gordon, by contrast, lays it back beautifully on his recording, *Go!*. See if you can play along with Dexter, phrasing the melody exactly as he does. Then see if you can reproduce that feeling playing by yourself.

- Video 19: Playing in Front and Behind the Time

Before we move on, one more thing about sharing the melody with singers. If you find yourself on a gig with a singer, remember that the lyrics make it easier for the audience to relate to a singer, so your job is to complement her delivery. You want to avoid creating any kind of obstruction between the singer, the song, and the audience. As we've seen already, knowing the song well helps a lot to begin with. The next thing is to figure out what kind of accompaniment the singer wants. If I'm meeting a singer for the first time, my first question is usually, "Do you like to have the tenor player involved when you sing the melody, or do you prefer to do it yourself? Or somewhere in between?"

Some singers love to scat and get into it with the saxophonist, and think of themselves as a partner on the front line, like another horn. Others prefer to have the space free to deliver the melody without distraction. As usual, there is no correct way—our job is to figure out how best to work with the singer to make him feel natural and comfortable delivering the lyrics. Remember, the rhythm section is doing this very thing for you *all the time*, so playing with singers is a good opportunity for us to see how it feels to be in a supporting role.

For a couple of examples:

Lester Young is relatively active, but dovetails with the melody beautifully, as sung by Billie Holiday on "Without Your Love." You can find it on *The Complete Billie Holiday on Columbia*.

John Coltrane takes a restrained approach on "They Say It's Wonderful," on the elegant album he recorded with Johnny Hartman, *Johnny Hartman and John Coltrane*.

On Abbey Lincoln's recording, *You Gotta Pay the Band*, Stan Getz gets the balance just right with the vocals, on the tune "I'm in Love," and also plays fills later in the first chorus that contribute to the vibe of the tune.

On Herbie Hancock's tribute album to Joni Mitchell's music, *River: The Joni Letters*, Wayne Shorter takes a slightly different tack on the title track. He gives plenty of space for the lyrics, which in Joni Mitchell's music are often wordier than your average standard, and he also uses long tones to provide color, and finds spots to harmonize with some of Corinne Bailey Rae's held notes, without overshadowing them.

## SOME THINGS TO PRACTICE

1. After you've memorized the melody, try delivering it on your own, at a tempo where you can experience playing it in time, without adding or dropping beats.
2. Try making small changes, starting on a different beat, decorating a note or two.
3. See if you can experience the feeling of laying the melody back, and then snapping it back to the middle of the beat.
4. Practice playing the melody while picturing the chord changes in your mind.
5. Start improvising a little more with the melody. See how many choruses you can play just using the melody as your food for thought.

• Video 20: Playing Just the Melody for Multiple Choruses

In a performance situation, the next thing that happens as we head into the solos is the solo break. It doesn't happen on every tune, but it is a common practice. Chapter 8 will outline some approaches to playing a convincing solo break.

# CHAPTER 8 · THE SOLO BREAK

Now you've delivered the melody beautifully and confidently, with the perfect balance of accuracy and interpretation. What comes next? The solo break. Many standards have a solo break built into the conventional way of playing the tune. At the point where the melody lands at home on the root, commonly the second to last bar of a 32 bar form, the rhythm section hits the downbeat and lays out while the soloist plays a break by himself to get the first solo off and running.

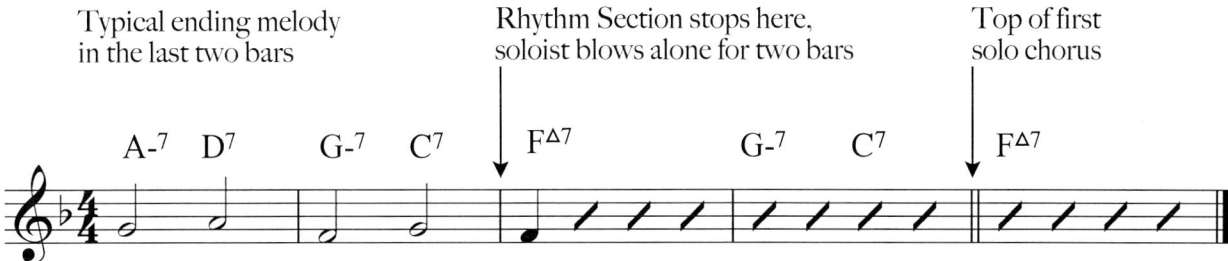

The main objective here is to make it count! Some soloists have an idea in mind ahead of time, others leave it open and sing whatever comes to mind in the spur of the moment. With the release of outtakes from historical recordings, it's possible to hear multiple takes of tunes where a great soloist takes a break. Sometimes the break is pretty similar each time, sometimes you'll hear the soloist going for a different approach on each take. The second option is more risky, and a purer approach to improvisation. Like most things where the risk is elevated, the cost and the payoff are both elevated as well. In this case, the cost is sounding bad during the break, which will send the solo off in a less than optimal direction. The payoff is coming up with something inspired, which inspires the band in turn, and gets the solo going with a jolt of energy.

The argument for having a plan and executing it well is: knowing that it is likely to work. If you play with the same people on the same tunes night after night, though, this approach can lead to a feeling of predictability, and the music can get stale. On the other hand, in a recording situation, if you go in without a plan and miss, there's a chance you have to live with something you don't like, forever…

As always, I advocate for maximum preparation in advance, and then turning yourself loose in the moment.

Here's a short list of some tunes that are commonly played with a solo break in the last two bars:

- "Autumn Leaves"
- "But Not For Me"
- "Bye Bye Blackbird"
- "Cherokee"
- "Days of Wine and Roses"
- "Donna Lee"
- "Four"
- "Have You Met Miss Jones"
- "How High the Moon/Ornithology"
- "I Love You"
- "I'll Remember April"
- "I'm Old Fashioned"
- "It Could Happen to You"
- "It's You or No One"
- "Joy Spring"
- "Lover"
- "Moment's Notice"
- "On Green Dolphin Street"
- "Secret Love"
- "Speak Low"
- "The Song is You"
- "Star Eyes"
- "Take the 'A' Train"
- "There is No Greater Love"
- "There Will Never Be Another You"
- "What is This Thing Called Love"
- "You Stepped Out of a Dream"

Here are a few that have built-in interludes leading to a solo break:

- "A Night in Tunisia"
- "Bouncing With Bud"
- "Celia"
- "Daahoud"
- "Groovin' High"
- "If I Were a Bell"
- "Moment's Notice"
- "Nica's Dream"

## TUNES OFTEN PLAYED WITH A SOLO BREAK

The following are examples of solo breaks taken from recordings of standards where the melody lands on the root in the second to last bar, setting up a natural two bar break. Notice how many different ways there are to go about it.

Here's Oscar Peterson's break on "Autumn Leaves," from *Live in Belgrade*:

Kenny Garrett takes a relaxed approach, and substitutes GbMaj7(#11) for the root chord, releasing into FMaj7 in the first bar of the new chorus on "Have You Met Miss Jones," from his record, *Introducing Kenny Garrett*:

Sonny Stitt likes to jump in a couple of bars before the break—he'll ignore the last phrase of the melody and blaze into his improvisation early. On "All God's Children Got Rhythm," (usually written "All God's Chillun") from his recording of the same name, Stitt is already blowing 5 bars before the end of the melody chorus:

On the classic recording *Study in Brown*, Harold Land goes the opposite way and starts a phrase at the break that carries through the first two bars of his first chorus on "Take The A Train:"

Jackie McLean takes a minimalist approach on "It's You Or No One," playing a familiar rhythmic figure, using only one pitch. This is on his debut recording as a leader, *Presenting...Jackie McLean*:

Miles Davis, after cutting his teeth alongside Charlie Parker, developed an understated style, epitomized by this beautiful laid back break on "Surrey with the Fringe on Top," from *Steamin'*:

Notice how Miles leaves a nice big space after landing his break phrase, and lets another whole bar go by after his second phrase. This is the definition of taking the time to let your story unfold.

On his recording, *Rollins Plays for Bird*, Sonny Rollins takes the tune "I Remember You" at a relaxed tempo, and then contrasts that with a double time break, including a typical Rollins-esque humorous quote:

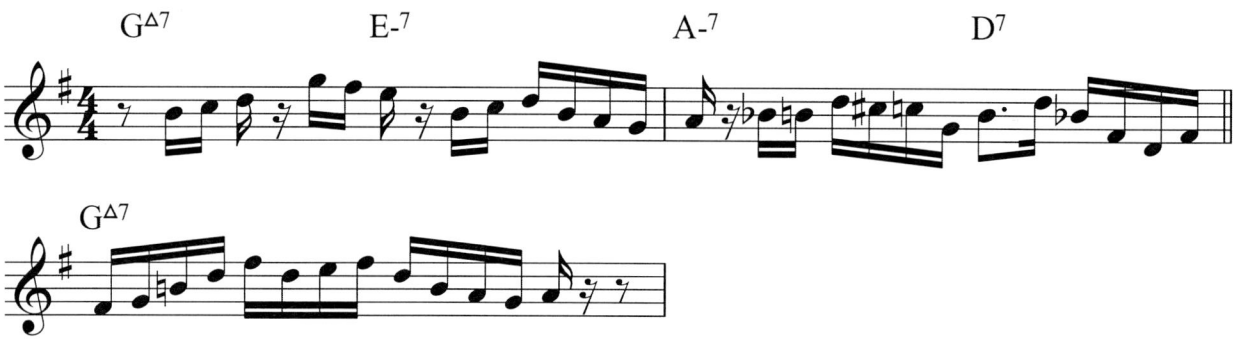

This is a great example of getting the solo off with a jolt of energy. Drummer Max Roach responds by diving in after the break with a double time feel, settling back into the original groove in the 5th bar.

## TUNES WITH AN INTERLUDE AND SOLO BREAK BUILT IN:

The most famous break of all time is Charlie Parker's four-bar break on "A Night in Tunisia," from the 1946 Dial sessions. For context, bebop was ascendant at the time, but there were still very few musicians alive who could think up, much less execute, such a stunning break.

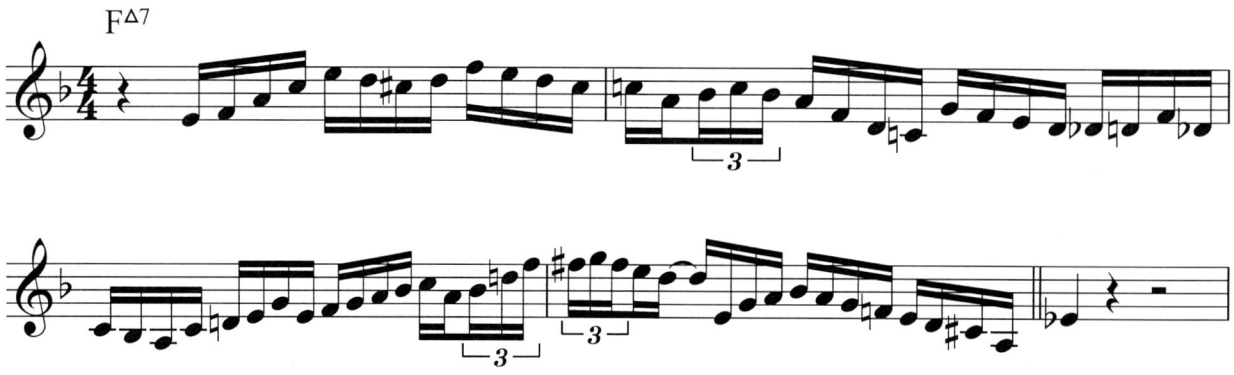

Bud Powell packs a lot of information into a two-bar break on his tune "Celia," from his recording, *Jazz Giant*.

Hank Mobley consistently combines laid back elegance with harmonic sophistication. Those qualities are on display throughout his solo on "Nica's Dream." He gets it started after the iconic interlude on the first Jazz Messengers album from 1956:

Finally, John Coltrane built a two-bar break into every chorus of "Moment's Notice."

Here's the first one, as a send off to the solo, at 0:58 in the track:

Second break, at 1:35:

And the third break, at 2:12:

## SOME THINGS TO PRACTICE

1. Your success in playing a solo break is mostly dependent on how well you play the time through the space where no one else is playing. If you play a great break and the band comes ripping in behind you, your solo will be off and running, and the audience might spontaneously applaud their satisfaction at the surprise. If your time is unclear, though, and the band is confused about where to come in, even if the content of your break was great, that content will be diluted by the confusion, and now you're playing catch-up. So the focus in your practice should be on feeling the time and delivering that feeling to the band.

    If you haven't done it already, you can start by playing some of the breaks we've been listening to in the chapter. First play them straight, and when you can deliver the time clearly, then start changing notes and using the breaks as templates for your own ideas. Try playing the last eight bars of a tune, and then a solo break, feeling the continuity of the time. Take a handful of approaches to the break, and see if you can pull them all off. If you're not feeling it, slow down to a tempo where you can be sure of where you are at all times.

2. When you start to feel pretty solid working with known materials, practice taking breaks without deciding beforehand what you're going to play. Keep at it until you have a few experiences that feel successful. Then push a little further until you get used to the feeling of successfully executed solo breaks.

3. Record yourself and try snapping your fingers or clapping along with it, and see if the time feels good. Pretend you're the drummer, and see if it's clear where you would come in based on what you're hearing on the recording.

4. Cannonball Adderley is one of the all-time great players of solo breaks. Rather than transcribe them for you, I decided to leave a few for you to do yourself. Here is a list of a handful of amazing solo breaks Cannonball played. Check out how the feeling of passion is conveyed in all of them, even though the approaches are quite different:

    - "You Got It" on *The Cannonball Adderley Quintet in San Francisco*
    - "Azule Serape" on *The Cannonball Adderley Quintet at the Lighthouse*
    - "Limehouse Blues," "Wabash" and "Grand Central," all on *Cannonball and Coltrane*

5. Get together with some other humans and practice playing breaks in a real situation.

# CHAPTER 9 · YOUR SOLO – IMPROVISING MELODICALLY

Now you've played the melody with the perfect balance of representing the tradition and personal expression, and you've delivered a killer solo break. How should you approach your solo? Think about a juggler keeping three balls in the air for a minute. She has to keep all three balls in motion, which takes a certain amount of practice before she can do it in a way that looks effortless. She can emphasize one ball for a little while by throwing it higher than the others, but still keeps everything in motion.

The three balls we are juggling are melody, harmony and rhythm, so the following chapters will address:

> Melodic Improvisation
> Harmonic Improvisation
> Rhythmic Improvisation

## IMPROVISING WITH THE MELODY

When I moved to New York for good in 1993, I decided to expand my knowledge by learning more about the nuts and bolts of jazz drumming. (I know this sounds like a rhythm story right after I said 'Improvising with the Melody,' but trust me, it's a melody story...) Specifically, I was interested in polyrhythm, and wanted to experience how drummers set up layers of rhythm on top of each other. Michael Carvin was giving lessons at Michiko Studios in Midtown, where I was renting a practice space regularly, so I approached him one day and asked for a lesson. After experiencing me as a novice on drums for a while, Michael asked me bring my horn to a lesson, and to play him some recordings so he could get a sense of where I was on my first instrument. Listening to a live recording from a gig I played in Japan, he gave me a push that is still affecting my playing 25 years later. He asked me, "You set up a vibe in your playing of the melody. Why does it sound like you step into a different room as soon as you start your solo?"

He was pointing out a fundamental flaw in my approach to improvising—that I was thinking of the changes as a vehicle for me to play "my shit" on, (pardon my language). Think about that. If the melody is just something to get out of the way, so that I can deliver all the stuff I've been practicing over the changes, aren't my solos all going to sound pretty much the same?

Not only that, but I was also introducing a discontinuity in the flow of the song. If I'm really improvising, what I just said should be influencing what I'm saying now, which in turn influences where I go next. A really fine improviser is able to be in the past, present and future, all at once! He can reference where he came from, play what he's playing now, and suggest some possibilities of where he might go.

That might seem like a lofty goal, but it's actually quite normal—a conversation works the same way. We flow from one idea to another. It's not always directly linear, but a good dialogue has a natural flow. Now, to get a sense of a conversation that is *not* organic, imagine if the first few sentences of a dialogue went like this:

"Hello."

"Hi. How are you?"

"I'm great, how are you?"

"I'm good, too. What are you up to? Four score and seven years ago our fathers brought forth on this continent, a new nation, conceived in Liberty, and dedicated to the proposition that all men are created equal."

That last bit is an interesting subject, but the speaker hasn't introduced it in a way that makes sense. The flow is broken. And the response from the first speaker might be:

"Uhh…"

Imagine that the speaker just went on and recited Lincoln's entire Gettysburg Address, without letting you get a word in edgewise. You might not seek out conversations with that guy very often after that…

The idea Michael Carvin got me thinking about was how to take the first few steps into my solo in a way that flows naturally from the melody, rather than just launching into a bunch of stuff that I'd been working on in the practice room.

The other important thing he was pointing out was that my solo should have a relationship with the song I'm playing. Seems obvious when you say it on paper, but you'd be surprised how often people adopt the approach of just playing the same stuff over every tune, regardless of the context.

The goal is for solos over "Cheryl" and "Relaxin' at Camarillo" to be distinct, even though they are both Charlie Parker tunes written over the blues in C.

When the music was still young, jazz musicians started out by improvising on the melody, and that's one of the fundamentals that will never go out of style. To be a contemporary jazz player, there is a lot more material to master and assimilate, but if you can hear melodies in your imagination and play them on your instrument in real time, you're well on your way to being an improviser.

Here are some suggestions for practicing to improvise with the melody of the song you are playing.

- As we talked about back in Chapter 1, you can start with simple decorations of the existing melody.
- Try playing the melody a little more freely, like a singer does. Listen to Frank Sinatra sing a melody, and see if you can steal a few of the techniques he uses to make the melody sound like a living thing, as opposed to something that is stuck on the page and must be played a certain way. Get some clues from some other singers as well. Remember to maintain your awareness of where you are in the time and the form as you practice, so you're not dependent on the rhythm section to do that work for you.
- See if you can count off a tune, and improvise a few choruses just by playing variations of the melody.
- Take a phrase from the melody and keep the rhythm the same, but change the notes. This is a good step toward feeling the energy of playing something that is partially familiar, but unfamiliar at the same time. You can do this with any phrase, but one that has a distinct rhythmic character will have more impact and be easier to recognize as familiar.

- Video 21: Playing a Known Phrase with Different Notes

    - Play a phrase from the melody, thinking of it as a melodic question, and then find some answers to that question that are different from the answer the composer wrote.

• Video 22: Question and Answer Phrases

   • Try picking a phrase and finding as many variations of that phrase as you can.

   • Learn from yourself. Put on a pair of headphones and listen to something that you love, and sing along to it, imagining that you are in the band on the recording session. Set up a recording device to hear just your singing, not the song you are using as inspiration, and sing away. Listen back to the recording and see if you sang anything that sounds great to you. Learn that on your instrument, and try playing it in the same place in the tune where you sang it. If you sang something that sounds almost good, see if you can hear what would make it better, and learn that on your instrument.

Now we've gotten deeper into the existing melody, and we're moving in the direction of making up new melodies over the changes. The natural progression in the evolution of the music was for musicians to start out by embellishing the existing melody, then to make up new melodies in real time. To do that, they had to gather more information about chord structures and scales. Once jazz players got some knowledge about the chords, they started finding ways to play lines through the progressions, and also started tinkering with the changes themselves. That led to improvising with the chord progressions as well—substituting chords and making up new progressions in real time.

Each time you master an element of the music new ways to improvise emerge.

So—if we're going to start making up new melodies on the changes, what makes a melody? What's the difference between improvising lines and melodies?

Whereas harmony is relatively scientific and can be discussed with a certain level of assurance that we agree on what it is, melody is a little more mysterious. Remember back at the beginning when we talked about love as something that you 'recognize?' You can write down a description of it, but a person has to experience it to know it. Melody can be described, but when it comes down to it, how do you know a good melody when you hear one??? You don't know it like you know that 2 + 2 = 4. You know it because it makes you *feel* something. The faculty, or sense, that we use to recognize melody is different than the one we use to study mathematics or chemistry—or harmony. As humans we have, among many other mysteries, an analytical side and an intuitive side to our brains. One of the things that makes jazz music so beautiful and powerful and universally attractive is that it engages both sides of the brain.

"That's all very interesting and philosophical," you might say, "but I've just played my solo break, and I need to play my solo. Can you get to the point, please?"

Right, I hear you—stop talking about it and show me how to do it. I'm getting there.

The point is that learning to create new melodies over the changes is something you're going to have to do by trial and error, and the way that you judge your success at it is to use your own intuition about how you're doing.

Yikes.

Self-reliance is rarely a bad thing, so let's think of this as a challenge and embrace it.

- First of all, pay attention to when the melody of a song makes you feel something. It's essential to become more deeply aware of what your own mind is telling you about what is beautiful, powerful, interesting, infuriating, motivational, inspiring. Some songs really speak to you, others don't. In the case of a song you have to play that doesn't particularly spark your interest, see if you can find a detail about it that is worth expanding on.
- As we've said, we can describe melodies, so let's get at some of the things that will put us in the neighborhood we're trying to explore. A melody is:
    - Tuneful, singable. There are more complex forms of melody, but what we're focusing on at the moment is the type of melody you'll find in a typical jazz standard, in the tradition of Tin Pan Alley and Broadway.
    - Relatively Simple, and therefore,
    - Memorable

When I started out trying to improvise, a key moment for me came when I stopped noodling, and took a moment to try to listen for something to play. I imagined a melody—heard it in my inner ear, and went to try to play it. I succeeded in playing what I was hearing for the first time, and the hair stood up on my neck. "That was it!" If you're not hearing anything, you can always listen to the music around you and grab something someone else plays and try to work with that. Rather than trying to fill the space so you don't get lost, take your time and listen.

One of the best examples of this I know was recommended to me by the great tenor player, Bennie Wallace. It is Sonny Rollins' solo on a blues called "Sumphin," from Dizzy Gillespie's recording, *Duets*. Sonny's solo starts around three and a half minutes into the track. Listen to how he leaves big spaces between phrases, and how simple his first few phrases are. Sonny developed into one of the greatest melodic improvisers of all time, and "Sumphin" is a perfect place to get a sense of that. See if you can adopt the same approach, and play a few choruses that hang together melodically.

- Notice how Sonny's simple melody is based around the 3rd and the root of the first chord of the blues. (the notes A and F on an F7 chord) Try playing some simple melodies starting from the other chord tones of an F7.
- Leonard Bernstein, in a beautiful lecture he gave in the Young People Concert Series called "What is a Melody," says:
    - Melody is the singing side of music and rhythm is the dancing side of music
    - He goes on to make some distinctions:
        - A Theme is a melody that leaves something to be said
        - A Tune is fully fledged, a song that has been completed

What we're talking about here is working with pieces of melody—what Bernstein calls themes—that leave something to be said. And we're exploring making up melodies like this in real time, and listening for what comes next, and trying to play that.

Bernstein goes on to explain to the young people something to watch for in classical music, which is what he calls the "1-2-3 method," which is:

1. A short phrase, followed by
2. The same phrase, with a variation, followed by
3. The tune soaring off in an inspired direction from there.

See if you can practice that. You may have put together that the 1-2-3 method is very close to a description of the blues. The classic blues form is just like that:

1. My man don't love me, He treats me oh so mean
2. My man, he don't love me, he treats me awful mean
3. He's the lowest man, that I've ever seen

That's the first chorus of "Fine and Mellow," as sung by Billie Holiday on a CBS broadcast from 1957. There's a difference from Bernstein's description. He talks about the third phrase soaring off into inspiration—his point of reference is the beginning of a long piece of composed music. The blues form is more like:

1. Statement
2. Same statement with variation
3. Conclusion

Then the second chorus will be a variation on the first, developing the idea in groups of three phrases. See if you can "write" a melody for a blues by making it up in real time. If you keep it simple enough to remember, it'll be easier to find variations.

Incidentally, Lester Young's chorus on "Fine and Mellow" (which starts about a minute and a half into the track) is another amazing example of an improviser taking his time, and playing from one beautiful melody to the next.

Remember playing "Frere Jacques" in an unfamiliar key back in Chapter 1? I learned that idea from James Moody. Here's the way he used it, which contributes to improving your ear, deepening your relationship with a melody, and checking to see if you are confident that you have all the details of the melody in place. Play the melody of a standard in the key you usually play it in, to get it going in your mind. Then pick any note at random, and try starting the melody from there. Don't think about anything. Just see if you can hear your way through the entire melody, and let your fingers find it in response to your inner singing voice. It's more challenging, and thus more valuable, to do this in time. No need to rush through it. Pick a tempo that is slow enough that you can enjoy the process. There is a significant difference in long-term results if you do this slowly and in time, rather than fumbling through it out of time.

- Video 23: Feeling Your Way Through a Song in a Different Key

## SOME THINGS TO PRACTICE

1. Some players to listen to who are known for great melodic development:
   - Sonny Rollins
   - Paul Desmond
   - Miles Davis
   - Lee Konitz
   - Wayne Shorter
   - Dexter Gordon
   - Stan Getz

It's important to listen with your focus tuned to how they are moving from one melody to the next. If you listen to Wayne Shorter hoping to hear him play like Charlie Parker, but on tenor, you'll be disappointed. But if you listen to hear how Shorter 'writes' new melodies with each new improvised chorus, you'll hear something deeply inspiring.

2. In addition to the practice suggestions given along the way in this chapter, there is a detailed description of a method to practice melody, and ways to incorporate that into your daily routine, in Chapter 20.

# CHAPTER 10 · YOUR SOLO – HARMONIC IMPROVISING

## USING SCALES TO CREATE HARMONIC LINES

While soloists in the early years of jazz were developing their ability to improvise on the melodies of popular songs, swing era composers like Duke Ellington, Billy Strayhorn and Mary Lou Williams were mastering harmony and writing increasingly sophisticated arrangements. The players found themselves surrounded by beautiful harmonies, and it makes sense that some of them would start to wonder if they could take their improvisation to a higher level.

Coleman Hawkins' 1939 recording of "Body and Soul" is generally thought to be the solo that pointed in the direction of improvising 'vertically,' or using the shapes of the chords for material to improvise on, in addition to using the melody for inspiration. You could say that Hawkins decided to "look under the hood" of the song, to see what was going on in the chord progression, and try tinkering with that. A similar development had been going on for decades in the art world, where painters were moving away from depicting the world realistically on canvas, to experimenting with the elements that made up a picture. They were improvising with color itself, rather than simply using it to show what they saw. Hawkins' decision to improvise with the harmony itself is a similar move.

The beboppers embraced that approach and ran with it. After mastering the shapes of chords, players like Dizzy Gillespie, Charlie Parker and Bud Powell started discovering how to make harmonic lines—lines that used scales to create a smooth path from one chord to another. If melodies are horizontal, and chords are vertical, the beboppers were able to synthesize the two into music that combined horizontal and vertical approaches simultaneously. It's like moving from two-dimensional chess to three dimensions. Sounds like genius, right? It was, but that doesn't mean we mere mortals can't learn how to do it, now that they've shown us the way.

By way of illustration, let's look at the melodies of Cole Porter's "What Is This Thing Called Love," and Tadd Dameron's "Hot House." We can compare Porter's traditional melody with Dameron's, which is a bebop style melodic line over the same set of chord changes. A new melody on a familiar or established set of changes is called a contrafact.

The melody in the first four bars of "What Is This Thing Called Love" is simple and easy to sing.

"Hot House," by contrast, is more of a harmonic line than what has been considered a melody to this point.

Notice the addition of the G half diminished chord in the first bar. The beboppers were acquiring a more sophisticated grasp of harmony, and were using it to create more interesting progressions, and a new kind of melody to go with them. This was unfamiliar to the ears of the general public, and met with some resistance at the time, but it was coming from a place of curiosity and innovation, so it was only a matter of time before listeners started to hear and accept what the boppers were exploring.

Remember the idea of tensions we discussed back in chapter four? This chapter is going to begin the process of examining that at length, especially in relation to dominant 7th chords.

The II-V-I became a staple of song forms because of the way it builds and then releases tension in a manner that our ears can follow. As we said earlier, it sounds like, "Ready, Set, Go!" with the "Go!" happening as the dominant chord releases its built up tension into the tonic chord. There are three additional scales we can use, which create an increasing amount of tension against dominant chords, and we're going to look at them one at a time, in the order of how much tension they create on a dominant 7. We'll use our clockwork framework, which will reveal additional chord/scale relationships to discuss. The three scales are melodic minor, harmonic minor, and the diminished scale.

## THE MELODIC MINOR SCALE

The first of our new scales will be the melodic minor. We will work on some uses of the melodic minor in this chapter as a way to get a taste of what it is like to improvise with the harmony itself—to redefine the qualities of the chords from one chorus to the next, making the chord sequence into a fluid, living thing. We'll address this concept in more detail in Part Three—Building Tension with Advanced Harmony.

Here's the melodic minor scale in C.

If you've encountered this scale in a classical context, you'll think of it as being a scale with different notes ascending and descending. In a jazz context the ascending half is used. The scale is the same ascending and descending.

Here is our "Clockwork" illustration of the melodic minor scale:

A couple of things to point your attention toward:

- Notice that there are two dominant chords, in the IV and V positions.
- Notice that there are no modes indicated. There are some names used to describe the modes of the melodic minor, but, for the sake of consistency and speed, we're going to focus on the clockwork model here. The aim is to learn to put these ideas to work in your playing as soon as possible, and not get too bogged down in naming things.

Ok, time to go to the piano and listen to the sound of a melodic minor scale. Here is the basic voicing for a C-△7 chord, and a more ringing voicing. Try playing the scale against each chord with the sustain pedal down so you can hear your lines interact with the sound of the chord. See if you can make some melodies.

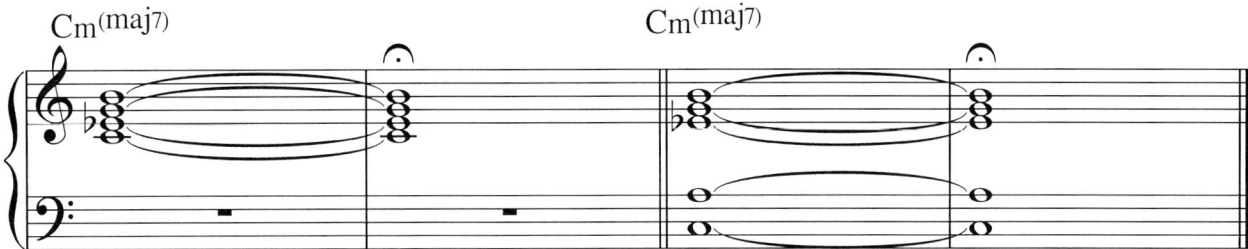

Here are a few lines you can try out that you'll hear players use once you start listening for them:

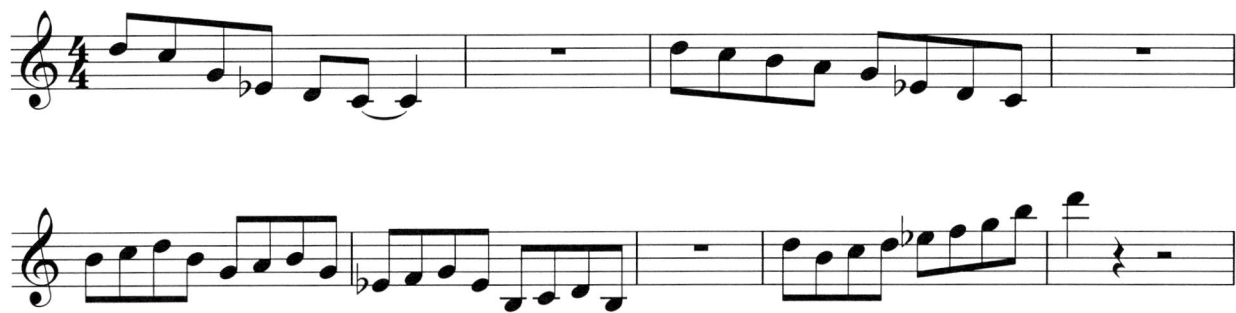

The first one is a quote of the melody of "Cry Me a River," and is probably the most commonly used quote in all of straight ahead jazz. I think it was Jerry Coker who joked that it isn't a jazz solo if it doesn't have a "Cry Me a River" quote.

Now that you have some familiarity with the sound, let's talk about the situations where this scale comes in handy. If you think back to our major scale clockwork, there are seven chords, built from each tone in the scale. We can use the scale to make melodies and lines through each one of those seven chords, but we found that in practice, we generally only use six of them, some more often than others.

The same is true of the chords you can build from the melodic minor scale—theoretically you can use the scale in all seven situations, but in practice there are only four that come up frequently. You could be the person who finds a way to use the three less well-traveled paths...

The I, IV and VI positions are the ones encountered most often. The III comes up occasionally, and although the V is technically correct, there are other choices that are more colorful, which makes this one a bit bland by comparison, so it's not used very often. We will explore the I and IV positions in this chapter, and the VI towards the end of Chapter 17.

## MELODIC MINOR AS A 'I' CHORD

Billy Strayhorn's "Chelsea Bridge" and Horace Silver's "Nica's Dream" both have a
Bb-△7 chord in the first bar. We can address that as a I in melodic minor, meaning we'll play melodies and lines using the Bb melodic minor scale for the first two bars of each tune.

At around the two and a half minute mark of "Nica's Dream," from Horace Silver's recording, *Horace-Scope*, Blue Mitchell plays this line starting from the fifth bar of his solo:

And here's Joe Henderson at the outset of his solo on "Chelsea Bridge" from his *Big Band* recording from 1996:

Notice in both examples how the soloists shift from Bb melodic minor to Ab melodic minor as the chords change.

So far we've been looking at the changes to find our baseline key, with the idea of finding chunks of bars where we can just freely play in a key without thinking too much, like on a II-V-I in a major key. In this chapter we're going to find more ways to improvise with the harmony itself, which will take us in the direction of making decisions about each bar in a progression.

When we wanted to play with a little more detail, we focused on precisely what to play over the barline, as one chord moved to another. That will be even more important as we begin to try playing in different keys from one bar to the next. We can still choose the simpler path, but now we're going to have more options.

To tie off a loose end—we were talking about the first bar of "All the Things You Are" back in Chapter 5. Now we have our explanation for the use of the note E natural on an F-7 chord. As a soloist, you can choose to *improvise with the quality* of that F-7 chord. Or another way to think of it is to substitute an F-△7 chord for the F-7 chord. Either way, the result is that you can choose to approach the first bar as a I in F melodic minor.

Here's an example from the recording, *Monday Nights at Birdland*. Lee Morgan, coming out of the bridge of his first chorus (at around 5:20 in the track) plays the following:

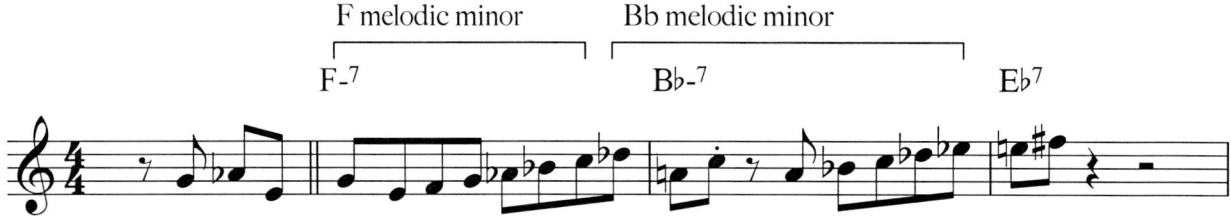

Notice how he treats both the F-7 and the Bb-7 as I's in melodic minor. If landing on the note E natural on the Eb7 chord seems mysterious, we'll get to an explanation of that shortly. What we are emphasizing at the moment is the idea that the harmony is not stuck on a lead sheet, but is fluid in the moment, and improvisers can make choices of how to define the harmony on the fly. The trick is to play something clear enough that the choice can be heard, and Lee Morgan does that beautifully in the example above. This is something that is commonly used, and now that your ears are tuned in to it, you'll start hearing it a lot.

Does the piano player have to respond by playing an F-△7 chord?

Good question!

If the piano player hears what you are playing she has the option to adjust and play an F-△7 chord, but she can also stay with the straight F-7 chord, which will result in a little extra tension as the two sounds "rub" against each other.

## MELODIC MINOR AS A IV

Have a look at that clockwork again.

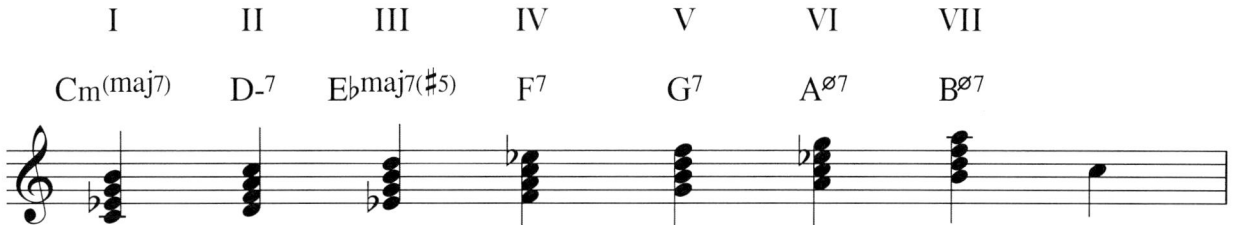

See how there are two dominant 7 chords right next to each other? The one in the IV position is the really interesting one. So far, the dominant 7th chords we've dealt with have been functioning as chords that build tension and then release it into a Imaj7 chord. Now we will look at a new situation, a dominant 7 that is *not* moving to I. Instead of moving strongly toward resolution, dominants that are not going home have a static, or hanging feeling.

The blues is the first place to look for this situation.

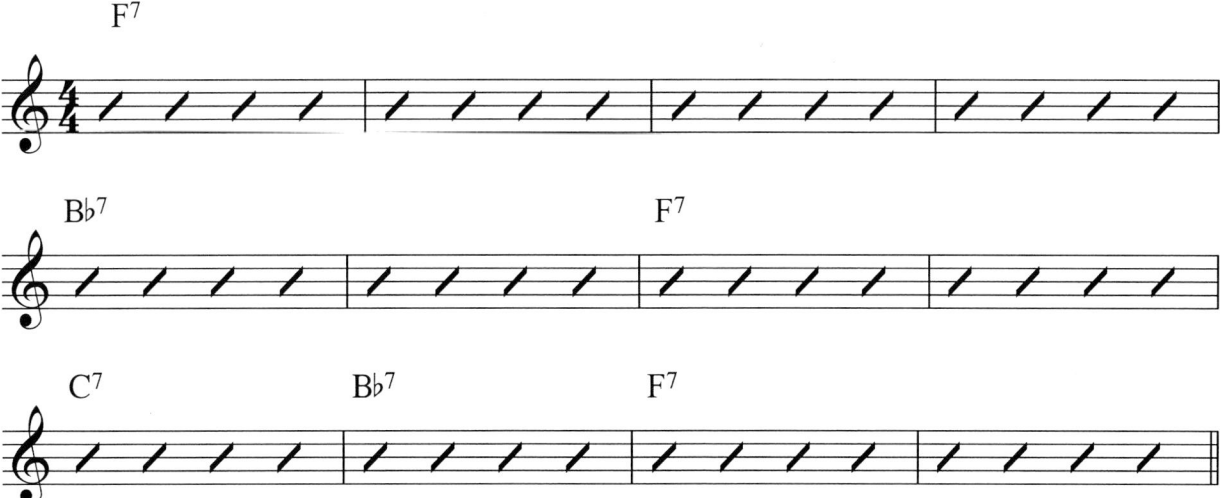

See the Bb7 chord in the 5th bar? Where is it going? If it were resolving to I, where would it go? Bb7 usually resolves to Eb, but in this case the next chord, in bar 7, is an F7, so we have a dominant 7th chord that is not going to I.

All right, so the question is, in which melodic minor scale will we find at Bb7 chord in the IV position?

Here's the clockwork diagram in the key of F melodic minor.

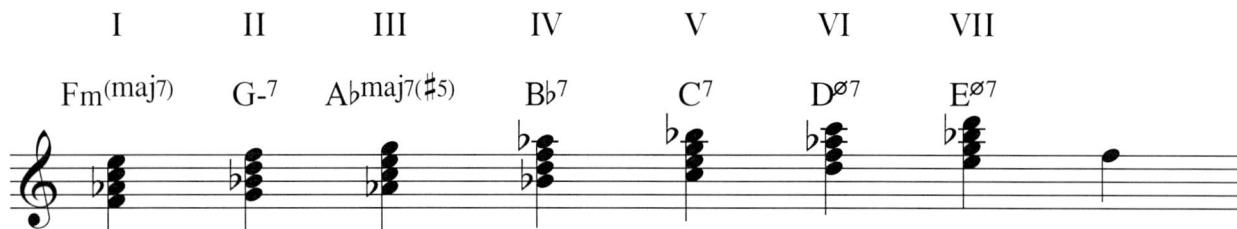

Notice that the F melodic minor scale gives you the note E natural, which is the #11 of a Bb7 chord.

Ok, time to sit at the piano and hear how this sounds. First play a straight Bb7 chord on the piano, and try playing the F melodic minor scale, and some of the lines we experimented with at the beginning of the chapter. Here are some basic voicings:

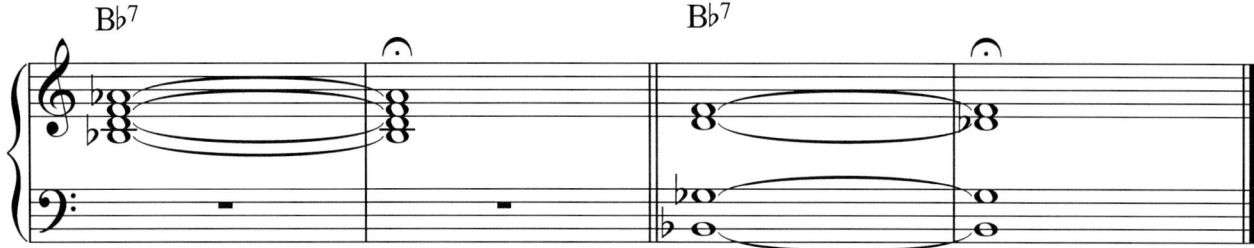

And here are the lines we played around with earlier, transposed to F melodic minor:

We can also play a more colorful voicing for the Bb7 chord, which includes the #11:

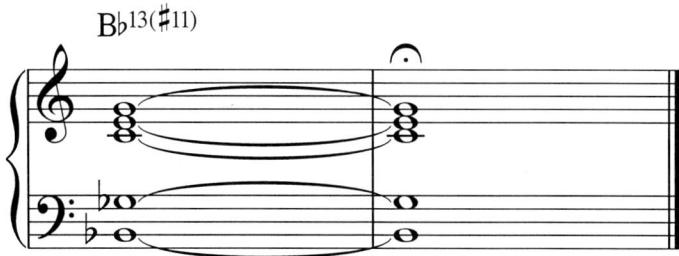

- Video 24: Melodic Minor as a IV

Now that you hear what the sound is like, let's check out a few of the masters using it in their solos.

This is Sonny Rollins on "Mambo Bounce." He plays this line at the 5th bar of his second chorus, about a minute into the track:

Hank Mobley's solos are a mother lode of harmonic information, performed with understated elegance. We will have more than one occasion to refer to his solo on "The Best Things in Life are Free," which is a masterpiece of hard bop blowing on his album, *Workout*.

Here are the changes Mobley uses on the bridge of "The Best Things in Life Are Free:"

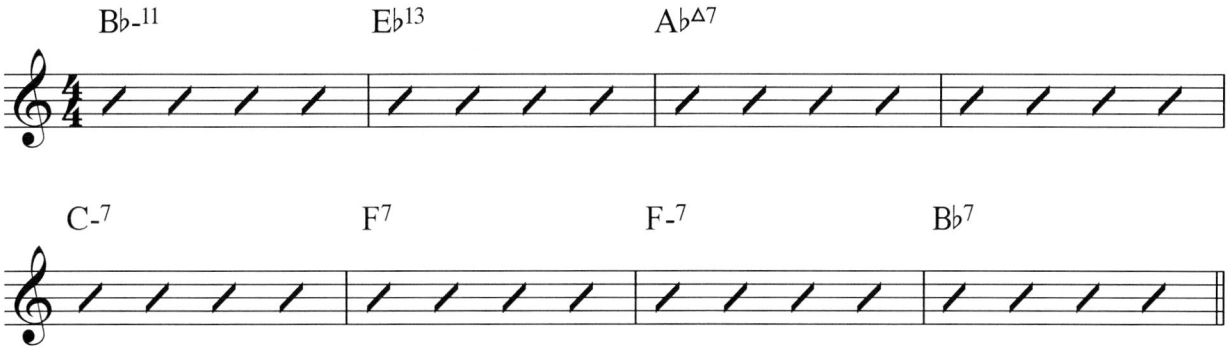

Can you see the spot where there is a dominant 7th chord not moving to I?

The F7 chord is not resolving to I, right? In that situation, we have a new choice—we can treat C-7 and F7 like a I and a IV in C melodic minor, which is what Hank Mobley does on his second chorus. This happens at about 1:50 in the track:

Note that using the melodic minor is a choice here, not a necessity.  We can still go with the basic choice of treating C-7 and F7 as a II-V in Bb major.  This means we can approach that pair of bars in at least two different ways from chorus to chorus.  And we'll get a few more harmonic choices together before we're done.  Here's an illustration of some different ways you could choose to approach those two bars:

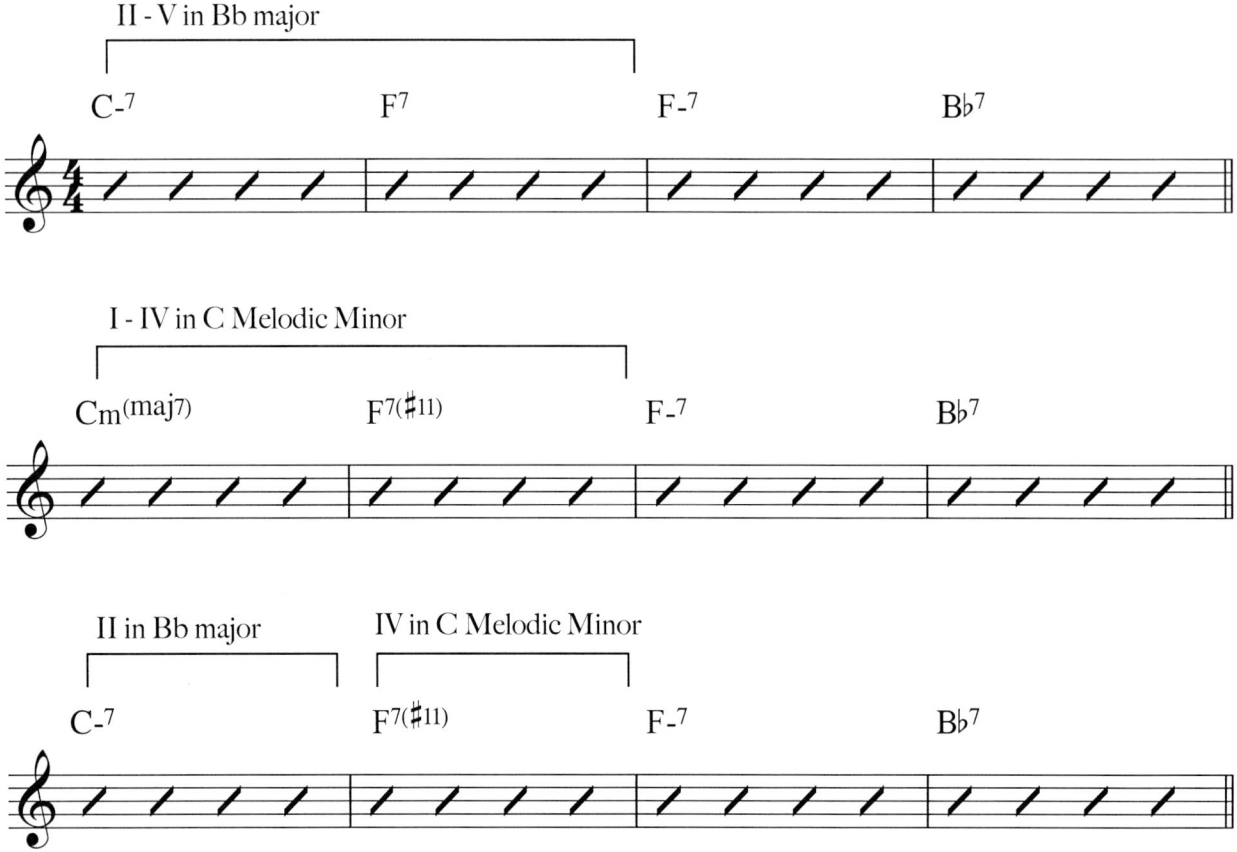

There's only one note different between the Bb major scale, and the C melodic minor scale.  Bb major has a Bb in it, and C melodic minor has a B natural.  But that one note gives the C melodic minor a colorful sound.

"There Will Never Be Another You" is another song that gets called a lot at jam sessions, and has a similar progression, in the same key, as the second half of the bridge of "The Best Things in Life Are Free."  Here are the second eight bars of "There Will Never Be Another You".  See if you can spot two places where there is a dominant 7th not moving to I.

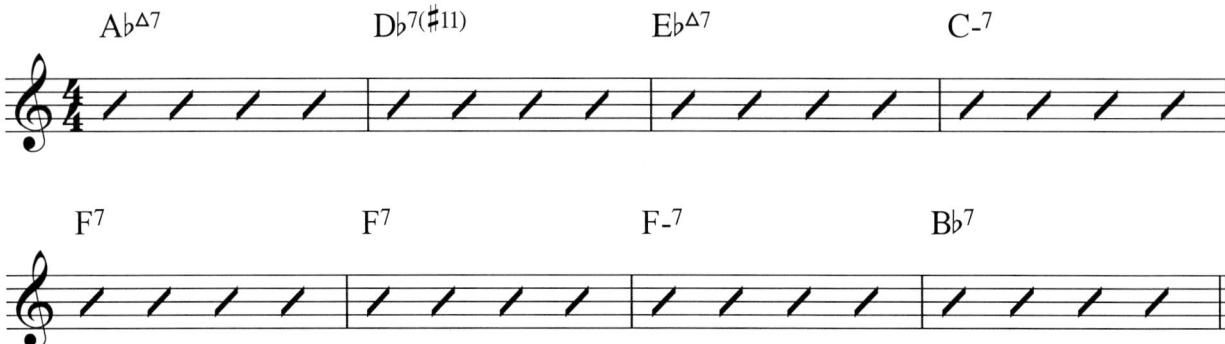

That Db7(#11) is a candidate, yes? The question to ask yourself is, "In which melodic minor scale does Db7 sit in the IV position?" Think about it for a second, before you read this next sentence.......Db7 is the fourth chord in the Ab melodic minor scale, which means the Ab melodic minor scale will give you a smooth line through a Db7 chord, when it is not moving toward a I chord.

On Woody Shaw's deep-swinging record *Solid*, Woody, Kenny Garrett and Kenny Barron all use the melodic minor scale through the F7(#11) chord, each in his own way. Barron plays particularly clearly through both situations in his first chorus, at around 3:18 in the track. This is a superb example of harmonic knowledge, modern swinging 8th notes, and great phrasing on "There Will Never Be Another You:"

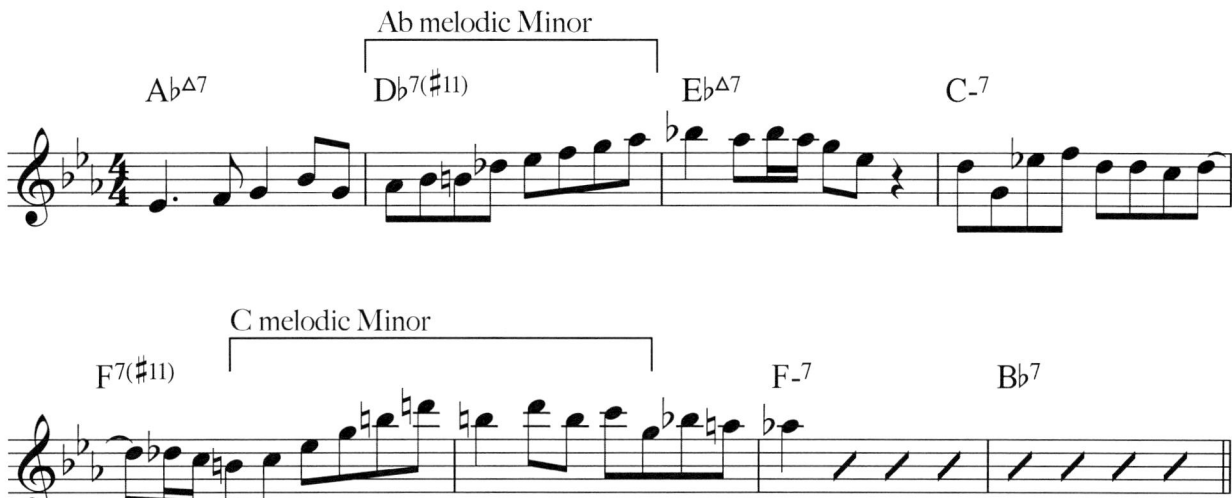

One of the characteristics of Duke Ellington and Billy Strayhorn's writing is dominant 7th chords that hang in the air, not resolving to I. Here's a short list of seven of their compositions where you'll find a dominant 7th chord you can treat as a IV in melodic minor. Work out which melodic minor scale belongs with the "hanging dominant" chords, and give it a test run in the right spot during the progression.

- "Come Sunday"
- "In a Sentimental Mood"
- "Isfahan"
- "Prelude to a Kiss"
- "Sophisticated Lady"
- "Take the 'A' Train"
- "Warm Valley"

We will get to two more common uses of the melodic minor scale after the chapter on the diminished scale. In the meantime, let's take some steps toward mastering the melodic minor as a I and as a IV.

## SOME THINGS TO PRACTICE

1. Now you've encountered quite a few examples of masters of jazz using the melodic minor scale on the fly in their solos. Try putting on a play-along track of, say, "There Will Never Be Another You," and play Kenny Barron's line using the Ab melodic minor scale in the right place in the progression. You can improvise your way through the 9 bars of the form that precede it, or just count them out and wait for the Db7(#11) bar to come around. Do it many times, until you feel sure that you know where you are in the form, and keep playing it until it *feels good to play it*.

2. After you feel confident about playing that line, or one like it from the other examples, see if you can find four 8th notes to play on beats 3 and 4 of the previous bar that will lead you to the start of Kenny Barron's line. Like this:

3. Then you can look for four more 8th notes so you have built a full bar's worth of good sounding notes leading you to the Kenny Barron line:

4. You can do the same thing in the bar after Kenny Barron's line. Find four good notes to play to keep the line moving after you enter the bar of Ebmaj7.

5. Try playing a tune like "Invitation," which has some longer sections of minor 7th chords, and see if you can play over them using the melodic minor scale—so C melodic minor over a C-7 chord—and see how it sounds.

# CHAPTER 11 · YOUR SOLO – RHYTHMIC IMPROVISING

Here's the main thing about rhythm:

You need to practice it until it feels good. In your body.

There is a fundamental difference between being able to play something right, and being able to deliver something that feels good. Mulgrew Miller talks about this in a video you can look up by searching "Mulgrew Miller Comping." You might not think a comping video applies to you, but Mulgrew makes so many points in this short video that are applicable to everyone, that I show it to all of my students regardless of their instrument. Mulgrew recommends practicing to comp on your own, until it feels good, saying:

"In order to be *assured* that you can do it, you have to be able to do it so that it feels good to *you*."

He goes on to say that the bassist has to walk lines until it feels good to him. The drummer has to play time until it feels good to him. And I would add, the saxophonists and trumpet players *and* all single note players have to play lines and melodies until they feel good to them.

Mulgrew:

"Then when you come into a group, and everybody feels good, you're feeling good together…and nobody is leaning on somebody else."

The ideas in this chapter will help you strengthen your time, but will help you more if you have already done some homework to establish a foundation of good time. How can you do that? Here are some reminders of things we've touched on before.

1. Start small. Learn a short phrase from someone who played something that you think is beautiful or attractive or cool or swinging…and do it in this order:
    a) Listen multiple times and first learn to sing it.
    b) Only after you can sing it, try playing it on your instrument, matching what you're singing in your mind's ear with what you are playing.
    c) Keep working on it until you can play it exactly as the artist you love played it originally. Play it many times, slow it down if it helps, and keep after it until you can play it precisely along with the original—until it feels good.
    d) Then see if you can play it by yourself, unaccompanied, and do it until it feels good.
2. Play along with recordings, imagining that you are in the band at the recording session. Choose recordings that feel good, and play along with them until it feels good!
3. See if you can continue playing the song, but without the recording. Now you are responsible for everything—time, harmony and melody. Keep it simple and keep it grooving.
4. If you've been working on something and want to try adding it into your playing, slow the tempo down until you can play it without disturbing the groove. If you practice something too fast, say 10 times, and you only pull it off once, 90% of your practice time was just devoted to playing inaccurately. Slow it down until you can make it feel good, and practice *that*.

Most often when someone is playing with shaky time, it's because they are trying to 'think' the music, rather than sing it. If a student is trying to learn a line by Freddie Hubbard, for example, and they can't deliver it in time, I'll suggest we listen to Freddie play it a couple of times, and then I'll ask them to sing it. It is almost universal that students can sing something accurately if they listen carefully, and then repeat what they hear, without thinking about it. If they can sing it accurately, then it becomes a matter of conscious repetition—playing the phrase while matching it to the singing in their inner ear—until they can play it well and make it feel good.

There is a more detailed discussion of this in Chapter 20—on developing a daily practice routine.

As we discussed in Chapter 7, there is a balance to be struck between playing the melody clearly—honoring the melody as originally composed—and interpreting it, or giving it a personal character. Now that you're in your solo, you are encouraged to explore more, and one of the ways you can do that is by moving the melody around in the time. If you've practiced the tune already by improvising multiple choruses playing only iterations of the melody, you've already gotten the process started. Here we'll look at a few examples to get some inspiration for rhythmic exploration of the melody.

Thelonious Monk is one of the all-time great rhythmic improvisers, which is logical since he is also one of the greatest rhythmic composers of all time. For Monk, it was standard practice to move the melody around in the beat for at least the first chorus of his improvisation, and he would often continue that exploration for an entire solo.

Check out "Well You Needn't," from Monk's recording, *Monk's Music*. Monk takes the first solo, stretching and squashing the melody in a variety of ways. Here are the first two phrases as they are played in the melody chorus:

Here are the variations Monk plays in his first chorus:

By the way, notice the difference between the way Monk plays the original melody and the commonly played Miles Davis version. Miles also uses a different bridge. If you call "Well You Needn't" on a gig or at a jam session, you should be prepared to answer the question,

"Monk's bridge or Miles'?"

(And of course, you should know both, so you can go either way.)

The *Thelonious Monk Fake Book* is a great resource. No jazz book collection should be without it. Once again, though, the story doesn't end once someone writes it down—Monk played his compositions different ways with different bands, so there are often multiple versions of a tune. It can be hard to pin down exactly what the original version of a Monk tune is, so if you want to be thorough, it's best to check out multiple versions and make some decisions about which details you prefer.

Another way you can work on rhythmic iterations of a melody is to start it on a different beat and see how it behaves. You can use accents to make it sound like it belongs on the new beat. Here are some new possibilities for ways to play the first two bars of "Well You Needn't:"

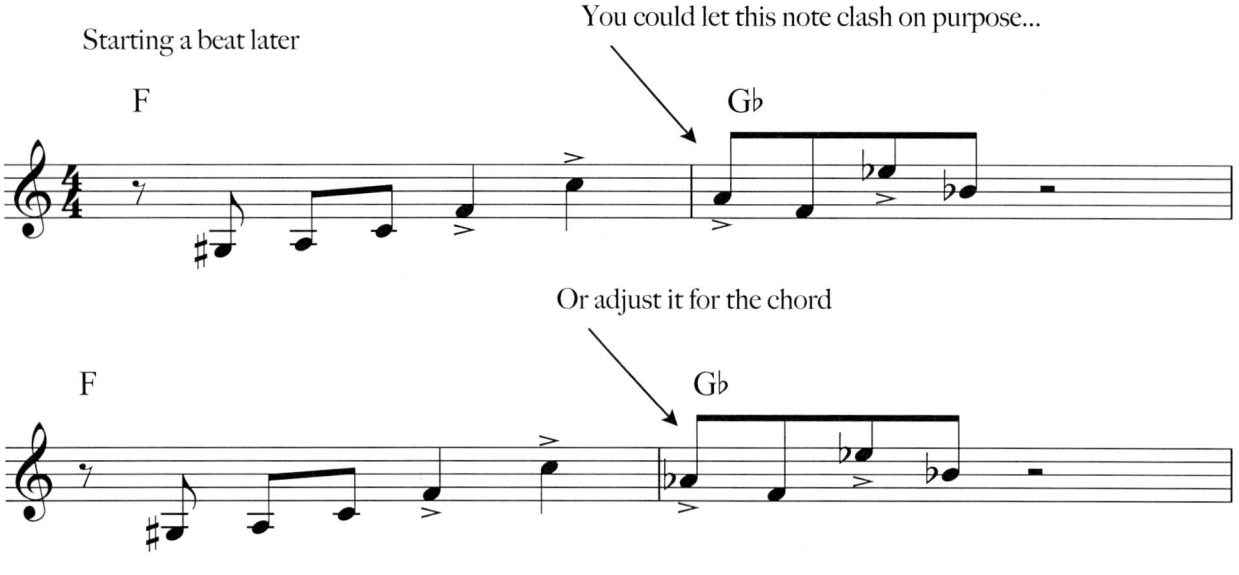

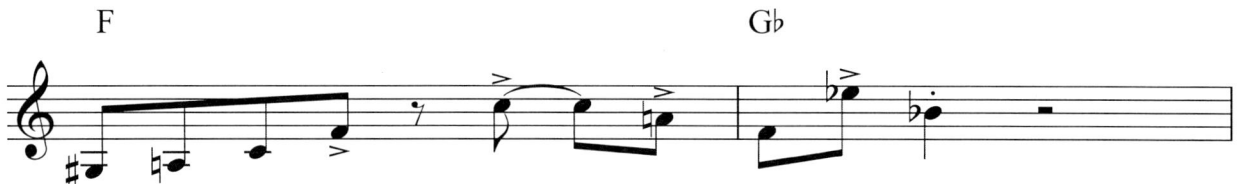

Thelonious Monk also had a particular genius for writing *rhythmic melodies*—where the rhythmic component is essential to the character of the melody. These great rhythmic melodies serve as hooks, making the melody memorable, and they can also function as anchors in the form while improvising. This can help the improviser keep his place in the music, and can help keep the audience (and the band) engaged as well. A skillful listener will recognize the recurring element in a solo, and start to wonder,

"Is she going to do that again this chorus?"

or

"I haven't heard that little hook in a while……..ah there it is again!"

The rhythmic elements of the song are there for you to use in your improvisation, and can be a readily available source of connection within the band.

In particular, Monk's concluding phrases at the ends of A sections often contain a rhythmic quirk that sounds attractive. Here are a few examples.

The last phrase of the A section of "In Walked Bud" goes:

"Bye-Ya" has a propulsive one:

The first A and the second A are different in "Eronel," which creates a kind of a question and answer from one A to the next:

First A Ending

Second A Ending

Here's a next level challenge:

See if you can improvise through an A section of "Eronel" and pose a musical question in the 7th or 8th bar. Then blow through the second A, and see if you can find an answer to your question phrase to make the whole 16 bars hang together as one paragraph.

• Video 25: Question and Answer Phrases Over 16 Bars

In "Pannonica," the first two A sections end with the same phrase, but the last A has a twist:

Here's one more, from "Hackensack:"

Each of those melodies has a strong rhythmic character. They will stand up to being moved around and experimented with. Try starting them in some different places in the beat and see if you can play them convincingly. You can also try coming up with some different combinations of notes to match the rhythms. Have at it.

When Keith Jarrett's first standards album with Gary Peacock and Jack DeJohnette came out in 1983 (*Standards Vol. 1*), he chose to play familiar melodies, but to start interpreting them right from the first chorus of the tune. The freedom of Jarrett's rhythmic interpretation of the melody of "All the Things You Are" influenced a whole generation of improvisers. Here was a trio that could play the melody chorus as if they were already deep into an improvised solo. There is a vast archive of the trio's recordings and performances available now. Listen to Keith's interpretations of melodies and compare them to the early versions and to the original sheet music for a master class in rhythmic interpretation of well-known melodies.

## EXPAND YOUR VOCABULARY BY STUDYING THE LANGUAGE OF DRUMMING

If you quote the first two bars of Monk's tune "Nutty" on another tune with similar changes (almost any Rhythm Changes composition), most experienced drummers will answer you with beats three and four from the third bar:

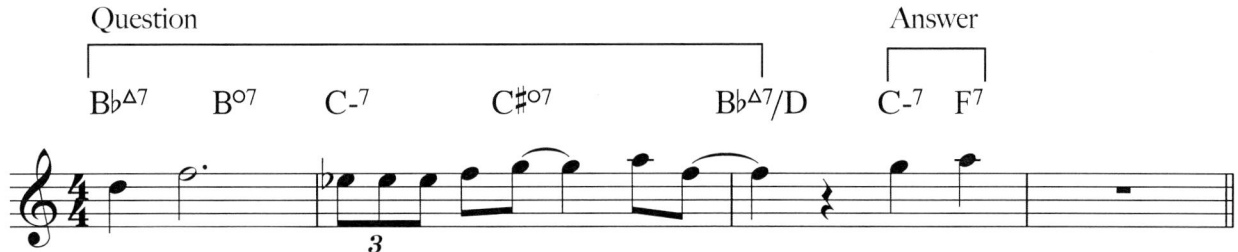

They know to do that because they've done their homework, and learned the melody of "Nutty," *and* maybe they've hung out in clubs and heard other drummers pick up on that quote. We can return the favor by getting familiar with some of the language drummers use regularly. And while we're at it, we can assign notes to some rhythmic language, and generate some rhythmic melodies of our own.

We don't have space here to describe the history of how modern drumming developed, but Kenny Clarke is the drummer generally credited with codifying the style to which most modern drummers are indebted. In the 1940's, as Charlie Parker, Dizzy Gillespie, Thelonious Monk and Bud Powell were developing a new harmonic and melodic language, Kenny Clarke innovated the style in which:

- The main time keeping function rests in the right hand, on the ride cymbal.
- The left foot on the hi-hat complements the right hand, keeping steady time on beats two and four.
- The left hand on the snare and toms, and the right foot on the bass drum are free to "comment" on what the drummer hears going on around him. This freedom to propel the music not just with strict time keeping, but with rhythmic commentary opened the door to the highly interactive drumming style that is prevalent today.
- Instead of playing the bass drum on every beat, (four on the floor), the drummer can play strong, often unexpected accents with the bass drum and crash cymbal, which is what people mean when they talk about Kenny Clarke "dropping bombs."

What a drummer does with his left hand is often described with the word, "patter," which is somewhat unfortunate since that word carries a little bit of a connotation of mindlessness. A good drummer is doing anything but mindless chatter with his left hand. He can support the soloist with punctuation, generate repeated patterns to build tension with the bassist and pianist, accentuate important points in the form, and tell rhythmic stories of his own within the structure of the tune. We are interested in all of these activities—if we know what the drummer is up to, we can participate and create some dialogue with him.

Let's steal some drum language, and set it to melody. Kenny Clarke and Dexter Gordon play interactively on "Scrapple from the Apple," from Dexter's recording, *Our Man in Paris*.

Here's the phrase Kenny Clarke plays to set Dexter's solo in motion after the head in. This starts on beat three of the last bar of the form, at around 0:42 into the track. The top line is the snare drum and the bottom line is the bass drum:

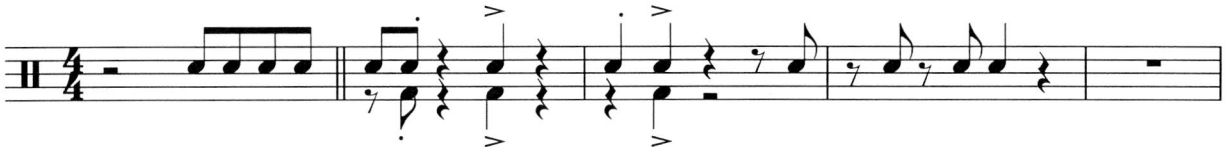

We can create some phrases using that rhythm as a template.  Here are a few lines for the first four bars of "Scrapple" to get you started:

Using some rhythmic language that will be familiar to the drummer is an invitation to interact, and that interaction will provide your solo with some energy you wouldn't be able to generate by yourself.

Listen to how rhythmically Dexter Gordon plays throughout his first chorus.  There is a lot of material to mine here, but here's one more favorite of mine. (from around 4:38 in the track.)  It's the last four bars of the second A section of a chorus, and Kenny Clarke plays:

Notice that Clarke plays the same idea three times and then concludes the thought with the last two quarter notes.  Try using that shape as inspiration to find some phrases of your own.  Here's an example:

And if you wanted to expand on that, you could say:

And now you're off developing some language of your own.

By way of making sure you're aware of one of the swingingest rhythm sections on record, here's a similar example Billy Higgins plays during Freddie Hubbard's solo on "The Maze," from Herbie Hancock's first record as a leader, *Takin' Off*. You can find this at around 1:46 in the track. It's a similar shape, a simple phrase repeated three times with a conclusion at the end. This one happens across the barlines, though:

Try adding notes to that sometime, and see if the rhythm section picks up on what you're doing. Here's one example:

This is a simple eight bar blowing form, but notice how Billy Higgins is playing the form. His phrase builds tension over the first 4 bar section which has only one chord, and releases it on the 'and' of four into the next section, where the changes move from bar to bar. While you are studying 'drummer language,' pay attention the ways in which drummers mark the form. A good drummer knows the length of the form and the phrases that make it up. A really good drummer also knows the changes, and matches her 'commentary' to the tensions and releases happening in the harmony. Listen for the ways drummers do this, and see if you can meet them on the 'and' of four at the end of an eight bar section, or beat one of the new one.

On "Ah-Leu-Cha" from Miles Davis' *Round About Midnight*, Philly Joe Jones is a great source for rhythmic phrases to steal. Here's one landing on the 'and' of four, (at about 1:17 in the track):

And here's one where he uses upbeats to set up a satisfying hit on one (at 2:20 in the same track):

Here is a short list of drummers to look out for whose language you can study to expand your vocabulary, and increase your odds of developing a rapport with the drummer in your band.

- Kenny Clarke
- Max Roach
- Art Blakey
- Roy Haynes
- Philly Joe Jones
- Billy Higgins

For more contemporary language, and a highly interactive approach to supporting the soloist, check out:

- Elvin Jones
- Tony Williams
- Billy Hart
- Jack DeJohnette
- Al Foster
- Jeff "Tain" Watts

There are many others, of course, but for the immediate subject at hand, that list will point you toward some excellent sources. Follow the same procedure as you would when transcribing a melody. Listen intently, focusing on the drummer's left hand. When he plays something you like, learn to sing it. See if you can repeat it back, making it feel good. Get it to the point where you can sing along with the original, precisely. Set it to notes and see what you come up with.

## WORKING CREATIVELY WITH THE LANGUAGE OF THE DRUMS

In the same way that we create questions and answers with melody, we can use rhythmic phrases to ask questions and answer them.

Here are a few common phrases you're likely to hear played by drummers who have absorbed some tradition:

Let's take that first one and see if we can pair it with another to make a "couplet." Here are three iterations of questions and answers using that first phrase as a jump off point:

After you have learned to make rhythmic couplets, you can try making longer paragraphs with rhythmic ideas, and eventually become a rhythmic storyteller as well.

Check the video for a demonstration of making up rhythmic melodies in real time, and then setting them to notes.

- Video 26: Rhythmic Melodies and Rhythmic Storytelling

The point of this chapter is to help you balance your approach to improvising. You can come at your solo from the point of view of melody, like Lee Konitz and Wayne Shorter do exceptionally well; or with harmony at the forefront, as great line players like Hank Mobley and Freddie Hubbard do; and you can also use rhythm as the front edge of your ideas. Sonny Rollins, John Coltrane and James Moody are examples of players who are able to juggle all three balls so well that you never know what they're going to do next.

Another way you can lead with rhythm is to use short bursts of notes with bits of space between them. I'm not sure if it was musicians or writers who came up with the term, but this is often referred to as "pecking." The word is a good description of how it sounds. For a classic example of pecking, listen to John Coltrane on "Chasin' the Trane," from *Live at the Village Vanguard*. Check out how he mixes lines in with bursts of pecking, and at times goes for long stretches playing two or three note phrases. See if you can imitate that.

A few more examples of pecking from the tradition:

On Freddie Hubbard's composition, "Happy Times," from his recording, *The Artistry of Freddie Hubbard*, the melody of the tune itself sounds like it was inspired by pecking. For most of his solo Freddie approaches the tune from his wheelhouse—long, flowing harmonic lines—but he does do a bit of pecking in his last chorus. In another composition on the same recording, "Bob's Place," you can hear Freddie peck at a minor blues, starting at around 1:15 in the track. You can find another example on Sonny Rollins' solo on "I Want To Be Happy," on the recording he made with Monk in 1954 (*Thelonious Monk and Sonny Rollins)*. There's a nice bit of playing between 3:03 and 3:10 on the track where Sonny plays short bursts of notes that hang together as a longer thought, even though the phrases are broken up by space.

Another technique you can try is something I think of as "leaving breadcrumbs," although, come to think of it, in this case the 'crumbs' are more an indication of where you're going than where you've been …It was inspired by something I heard Charlie Parker play on a recording, where he plays a long, beautiful four bar phrase, ending it abruptly with two 8th notes on the third beat of the fourth bar of the phrase. Then he does it again in the next four bar phrase, playing the two hanging 8th notes in the fourth bar again. By the third time, the drummer knows it's coming and hits it with him. Here's an example of what that might look like on a blues:

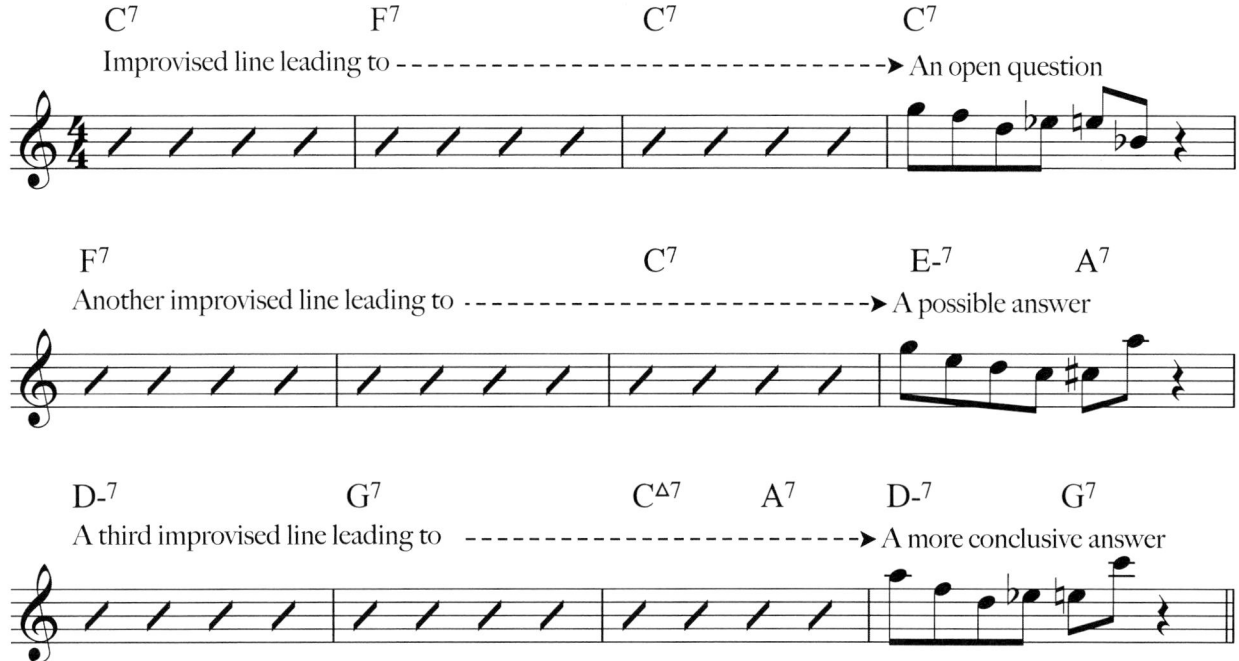

If you're having fun with it, there's no reason you can't play an inconclusive phrase on the third time, and keep going. Or play the conclusive phrase and keep going anyway…!
It's a matter of taste when you decide to move on to something else.

James Moody used to love to play the blues in Db, and he would do a similar thing with a phrase that used groupings of six 8th notes, like this:

And then he would play the phrase over the barlines all the way through the chorus, adjusting for a more complex set of changes, like so:

The repetition establishes predictability, the changing harmonic content creates surprise, and the entire idea is an invitation to the rhythm section to engage with what he is doing.

I once heard him do this while circular breathing, changing the harmonic content each chorus, for five or six choruses, maybe more. The whole band jumped on the train, playing over the barlines while staying rooted in the form, and the final release of that built-up tension was intensely satisfying...

## SOME THINGS TO PRACTICE

1. Take some rhythmic hooks from Monk's music and set them to your own notes.

2. Try playing the one you just invented in real time.

3. Now try keeping the rhythm, but making up the notes in real time.

4. Do the same thing with some drum language, looking further afield than the examples here in the book. In the process, see which drummers make you feel really good when you're playing along with their recordings. Some people are naturally drawn to Elvin Jones, some to Tony Williams, some to both. Knowing what makes you feel good will help you choose drummers that are right for what you want to do.

5. Work on knowing exactly where you are in the form, and aim to land lines on the 'and' of four to anticipate moving into a new four or eight bar phrase.

6. Find ways to invite the rhythm section to participate in what you are playing.

7. Get inspiration in real time by listening to what the drummer is playing and using it to start a fresh idea.

8. See Chapter 19 for some more ideas on rhythmic approaches to improvising.

# CHAPTER 12 • TRADING WITH THE DRUMMER AND A FEW WORDS ABOUT PUTTING TOGETHER A SET

Now we've come to the point in the performance of a tune where there have been a few solos, and the end of the song is starting to become visible on the horizon. If you're the leader, the next moment calls for a decision. Do we go straight to the head out, (the melody of the tune), or have one more solo?

A bunch of factors come into play in this decision, like the length of the tune, the energy of the performance, the length of the set, and making sure the solos are distributed in a way that features everyone satisfactorily. If everyone in the band solos on every tune, the set can get bogged down in predictability, and the tunes can get too long. Doing some strategic planning can help keep the set moving.

Drummers and bassists are often the ones who wind up sacrificing some of their time in the spotlight, so, especially when I'm leading a group, I try to make it a point to involve them in the decisions I make about the shape of the tune. This can be done before the set, checking with everyone to see if they have strong feelings about particular tunes they want to solo on, and including that in your planning. If you're like me, and you prefer to leave it a little more open to allow for things to happen that you *didn't* plan, then the communication has to happen while the tune is ongoing. I usually make it a point to try to catch the bassist's eye sometime during the tune, and give him a question in the form of a hand signal. I'll usually play a little 'air bass' with a question-mark facial expression, and the bassist can nod yes or no. Done.

If I'm not able to communicate with the bassist, and I decide to go straight to a drum solo, I'll say that out loud, or point to the drummer at the next transition. If the bassist was looking forward to his solo, this can create a moment of disappointment, so if I've made that executive decision, I'll try to acknowledge the bassist on the mic between tunes and feature him more prominently on the next tune, just to make it clear to the audience that I value his role in the music.

The same goes for the drummer. If I haven't already written a certain type of drum solo into the arrangement, (a little more detail about that shortly) I'll try to catch her eye and give her a signal, maybe my right hand imitating a ride cymbal, and I might mouth the word, "Solo?" Or, I might want to do some trading, so I'll make a 'you-and-me' motion with my hand, and say "Trading?" If the drummer nods to the trading signal, we're on, and if she says to me, "I got it," then I turn it over to her and forgo the trading. Sometimes I'll just make a decision and start trading, or make the decision to hand it straight to the drummer. I don't always make the right call, but I do try to pay close attention to whether people are getting enough soloing space, and when I make a decision about someone's else's solo, I'll check back with them later if I feel like I could have done it better or should have done it differently.

I've used the word 'trading' a couple of times already, so if you're unclear about what that is, check out the tune, "Four," on Miles Davis' classic album, *Workin'*. The trading starts after the piano solo, at around the 5:50 mark in the track. Miles solos over the first four bars of a chorus with the whole rhythm section, and then Philly Joe takes the next four bars by himself, then Miles again, and so on through a complete chorus.

Note that, even though you don't hear the chords during the drummer's sections of the trading, the harmonic motion continues. In other words, the chorus is always ongoing. If the soloist plays the first four, after the drummer takes four bars, the rhythm section and soloist enter again at bar 9.

Trading fours is probably the most common way to do it, and could even be considered the default option, but that leads to an important point. In the same way that letting everyone solo on every tune can lead to predictability, and allows for the danger of band members going on autopilot, if trading is done the same way every time, it can get formulaic and stale.  Since fours is the default position, I make it a point almost never to start trading with fours—not to be a contrarian, but to keep things fresh and unpredictable. Naturally, if I wind up starting out with eights every time, I'll run the risk of that getting stale. With that in mind, I try to mix it up as much as I can.

Like every other element of the music, trading allows for lots of room to improvise.  The two most common choices are:

- Trading fours for a couple of choruses and head out
- Trading eights for a chorus or two, fours for a chorus or two, and out

It's not uncommon, especially in a 'tenor battle' type of situation to go:

- Eights for a chorus or two, then fours, then twos, sometimes even ones, and then a chorus or two of soloing together, leading to a big climax point before returning to the head

Sonny Rollins is well-known for trading fours for so many choruses that you can't believe he still has more to say.  He takes the predictability out of it by pushing it further and further, and creates an amazing head of steam, coming up with a seemingly endless series of ideas.  Another way to create some tension is to choose longer lengths to trade over.  On a thirty-two bar tune, starting out trading full choruses or half choruses is a fun way to go.  Especially if the drummer likes to take risks, this can create a game of focusing hard and staying with the form—and the payoff of all coming in together at the next entrance of the band can be really satisfying.  Likewise, if everyone *doesn't* come in together, working it out in real time and solving the problem can be fun, too.  Train wrecks, of course, are less fun.

Although there are some conventions around trading, there are no rules. Good decision making and clear communication can make any number of approaches work.  Trading on a 12 bar blues offers some interesting options, like the expected:

- Trading twelves
- Trading fours

But you can also try:

- Trading eights, so that it takes two choruses to come around to the top again
- Horn soloist takes eight, drums takes four
- Other way around, horn takes four, drums eight
- Trading sixes, which divides the chorus in half, but the handoff point is in an unexpected place in the harmony

Then you can also try trading groups of 3, 5, or 7 bars.  This can work, especially if you have the chance to rehearse it enough for it to become natural sounding, BUT, if it's not natural sounding and winds up making everyone think too much, it can easily drive a stake through the heart of an otherwise great performance…

Trading on a tune with an odd number of bars, or an odd number of phrases can create some other challenges.  Once again, sometimes a bit of discussion is called for beforehand, and other times good decision making can do the trick.  "All the Things You Are" is structured 8, 8, 8, 12—so if you start with eights, the simplest solution is to let the drummer have 12 at the bottom of the chorus, which creates a little extra tension.  If you're trading fours or eights and you keep it strict, the spaces will flip flop in the second chorus, and you'll have to play through two choruses for the back and forth to reset at the top.

When I'm playing a tune with a form other than 12 or 32 bars, if the band hasn't discussed the trading beforehand, and I feel like trying it, I'll watch the form go by a few times during the piano solo, and make a plan for how I want to trade, and then will give big signals to the drummer when I mean to play and where I intend to hand it to him.

Another thing I like to do occasionally with groups that know each other well, is to trade organically. I just play whatever number of bars I feel like playing, and then leave the drummer for as long as I feel like it. This can have a dovetail effect and its unpredictability makes it a nice change from the usual pattern. I'll say something beforehand if I intend to try this, so that everyone stays in the form the whole time and is always ready to jump in and out. This works great in a saxophone trio setting.

Having pointed out an unconventional way to go about trading, it's also worth mentioning a few of the conventions:

- Generally speaking, the person who took the first solo takes the first entrance in the trading
- If there are multiple horn soloists, the trading generally follows the solo order, so if the tenor player played the first solo, followed by piano and then trumpet, then the trading goes: tenor, drums, piano, drums, trumpet, drums, and so on. And the odd number of soloists means that everyone has to pay attention to where they are in the chorus, because they won't be trading over the same section each time around.
- Usually the drummer will be the person to play last. It sounds good to have the head out follow the drummer playing alone.

In the example we listened to at the beginning of the chapter, Miles Davis was the only soloist trading with Philly Joe Jones, even though Red Garland and John Coltrane each took solos during the tune. That's another way to do it. If there are multiple horns playing on a tune, sometimes I'll choose not to play a solo, and just trade with the drummer as my contribution.

Trading isn't the only way for a drummer to solo on a tune, of course, so saying a few words on drum solos in general is in order. Most drummers don't expect to play on every tune, but they also expect not to be taken for granted…so it's worth considering where to place the drum solos in a set, and there are different ways to do it.

Among some of the options available for a drum solo are:

- A completely free space, like a cadenza, where the drummer can define the solo however she wants, in or out of time
- A solo over the form, where the drummer plays choruses like everyone else, with or without accompaniment
- A "Shout" chorus, where the band plays a repeated climactic melodic figure, followed by responses from the drummer
- A through-composed drum solo, where the band plays accompanying figures
- Trading for a few choruses, followed by a chorus or more of solo drums playing on the form
- Drummer playing over an open vamp, either before or after the head out. And of course this could happen elsewhere to keep it interesting

# AND FINALLY, A FEW WORDS ABOUT BUILDING SETS

This is an area where there is a lot of room for personal preference. I have my preferences, so I'll explain a few of mine, and you can take them or leave them, as you see fit.

If you think of an improvised solo on a tune as a story that has a beginning, middle and end, you can think of the tunes of a set as being chapters in a larger, longer story. My two main goals in creating sets are:

- Making sure the arc of that larger story is interesting for the audience, and
- Putting myself in contrasting environments, so I feel like each tune is fresh and inspiring to play on.

If I play a medium tempo version of "Have You Met Miss Jones" in F, followed by a medium tempo version of "The Days of Wine and Roses," in F, there's a pretty good chance that I'll start finding myself leaning toward saying some of the same things on the second tune that I said on the first. Even if I try to dedicate myself to really playing the tunes as they are, and not just treating them as vehicles for blowing in F, I'll still likely hear some of the same ideas in my mind's ear. I can avoid that by taking care to provide myself with a different atmosphere to play on with each tune in the set. With that in mind, thinking about the harmonic content of each tune can help me to choose a set order that won't sound repetitive.

Here are a few of the guidelines I use to create contrast in harmonic atmosphere:

- A half step away gives the greatest contrast in key. If you play a blues in C, you can follow it with one of the many beautiful standards in Db, like "Isfahan." If you play one of the many fine tunes written in G, like "Willow Weep for Me," you can follow it with something in Ab, like "Time Was" or "Like Someone in Love," which makes for good contrast.
- A whole step also works. Playing a tune in F after one in Eb tends to have a feeling of the atmosphere brightening. Conversely, moving down a whole step removes a sharp from the key signature, or adds a flat if you're in the flat keys, which gives a 'darkening' type of contrast.
- A major third away makes for excellent contrast. The tune "Gone with the Wind" moves from Eb to G within the first eight bars. This works great from tune to tune as well. A tune like "Strollin," in Db could be followed by "If I Were a Bell", in F.
- A predominantly major sounding tune, like "Bye Bye Blackbird," of course, will contrast well with a mostly minor song, like "Softly, as in a Morning Sunrise."
- You can also take harmonic rhythm, which refers to the density of chords in a progression, and the motion from chord to chord in a song, into account. A tune like "Stablemates," which has a lot of chords, moving quickly, would pose a contrast to "Impressions," which has long spaces of only one chord.

I'll also try to pick tunes that have distinct rhythmic atmospheres, to sharpen the contrast from tune to tune in a set. I might start with an up-tempo burner in 4/4 if I feel like some excitement. After that, a medium-up tempo would make for a little contrast, but a ballad would widen the difference. Tempo is one area to find difference, but I could also choose to go from a standard in straight ahead 4/4 to an original tune in an odd meter. From straight ahead to straight eighths. From hard, loud expressive blowing, to quiet and introspective poetry.

The idea is for each tune to be distinct from the last, and to present a different set of challenges for the band, so that everyone is engaged all the way through the set. If I can keep myself inspired, I'm likely to infect the band with that inspiration, and if the band is inspired, the audience will feel it.

One last thing I've noticed about sets—first and last impressions matter. With that in mind, I tend to lean toward using tunes with clear and detailed arrangements at the beginnings and ends of sets. I like to show the audience how well the band works together. If the first tune has a well-designed ending, it creates an invitation for the audience to interact with the band—with a burst of enthusiastic applause, which gets your set moving in the right direction.

Then, without it becoming formulaic, I also like to look for a space where I can let each band member play by himself, for a moment of pure spotlight. That of course, gets more difficult as the numbers of band members increase. Everything within reason. And finally, I like to try to plan for a number of different types of drum solos, in order to keep it fresh for the drummer and the audience, and to help shape the overall arc of the set in a way that is unpredictable as it unfolds.

## A SHORT ASIDE ON TALKING TO THE AUDIENCE

The way I see it, if you are the one introducing the band you have three things to accomplish:

- Giving the audience the names of the players
- Allowing the audience to acknowledge the musicianship of each player
- Telling the audience something about the music and the players they are hearing

If, like me, you have a tendency to forget peoples' names in the heat of the moment, it's a great idea to write them down. I'm lucky not to be too troubled by stage fright, and really enjoy performing and talking to the audience, but the one thing that can freak me out is if I forget someone's name. I might be sounding like a crusty old curmudgeon here, but don't use a smart phone to prompt you on the names of the members of the band. It looks unprofessional. Use a pen and paper, or print it out, and try to keep it discretely out of sight. You only want to use it if you need the prompt. It is best if you can do it from memory. If you're in a situation where you're playing with a musician for the first time, take a second to make sure you know how to pronounce their name correctly. That's just a basic sign of respect.

And—

Slow　　　　　　　　down.

Relax. Make sure the audience can hear you, and take care to say each person's name clearly. It seems obvious, but so many people rush through their introductions, and the audience doesn't get to hear each musician's name properly.

That goes for the individual names, and also for moving from one musician to the next. I think of this moment as one where I have an opportunity to set each musician up to get some individual love from the audience. If I rush from one name to the next, I lose the chance to create that moment for each member of the band.

David Berkman has a fun game he plays, where he tries to come up with a different superlative for each player as he goes along:

"On saxophone, we have the brilliance of Dick Oatts. Give it up for Dick Oatts."
"And on bass we have the insouciant stylings of Ugonna Okegwo. Ugonna Okegwo on bass."

And then, just for fun, instead of coming up with a third one, he might say,

"Our drummer is exactly as brilliant and insouciant as Dick and Ugonna. No difference at all. Exactly equal in brilliance. And insouciance. Gene Jackson on drums everyone."

It's clever and entertaining, but it's also highly functional. He creates a little space of expectation before saying each person's name, then gives the name. It's another kind of tension and release. He's also shown each musician respect, even though it's humorous—and the audience sees that and responds to it.

A little more serious way I'll do it sometimes is to say something like,

"Our pianist, and the man who played that spectacular solo introduction to the ballad a couple of tunes ago, is Bruce Barth."

That's another way to draw the audience's attention to the reason they're clapping for someone.

And the third element is delivering information about the music to the audience. When I'm in the audience, I like it when the person introducing the band tells me some key pieces of information about the music. Fundamentally, I like to know the title of the tune, and who wrote it. If it's an original composition, I'm interested to know some of the backstory—what the composer was aiming for, or if there's an interesting story about the title. If these things are delivered in a way that is brief and engaging, I enjoy hearing them. Some announcers like to give the background on standards, like the name of the Broadway show or movie in which they premiered. That often gives me something to watch later that will provide more context on the tune, especially if I'm thinking about playing it.

Two things that I don't want from the introduction:

1. A long, drawn out biography of each musician. Some basic information is great, but I don't want too much of my time listening to music to be taken up with biographical information I can look up on the web later if I want to, and
2. To be told what to experience from the music. I get annoyed if a leader tells me the next tune is meant to make me feel like I'm sitting on a beach, relaxing to the sound of breakers pounding the shore….. One of the exquisite beauties of musical language is that it is non-verbal, making it possible for people to respond to it in individual ways.

## A SHORT ASIDE WITHIN A SHORT ASIDE

To illustrate the last point, a quick story. I was on tour in Europe with a quartet in the early days of my career. We played a fairly high-profile gig in Holland for a live radio broadcast, with a good sized audience in the studio. We played one long set, and the first tune was Benny Golson's "Stablemates." I don't remember anymore how I felt about my own performance on "Stablemates" at the time, but what happened after the set was remarkable. As we left the bandstand, we were greeted by a line of people who wanted to say hi and engage with us about the music. The first person I talked to said to me,

"Wow, what a great set of music. I really enjoyed the band. I thought you guys got off to a bit of a rocky start with "Stablemates," but the set just picked up steam all the way through after that."

The second person said to me,

"Wow, you guys' version of "Stablemates" was the best version of that song I've ever heard live! The rest of the set didn't do so much for me, but thanks for "Stablemates."

What I learned from those encounters was that I don't control how the audience responds to the music. Each person is bringing her own life experience to the music that day. For that reason, I take care to be neutral about my own performance—I carefully avoid scowling or projecting to the audience my unhappiness if I do something I don't like. Instead I'll just try to stay in the moment and work it out. I've had band members who know me really well say that the note I thought sounded terrible was the most interesting moment of the solo.

So those are some of my personal preferences around talking to the audience. This is yet another thing where you can develop a personal approach. If you're nervous talking to the audience, just think about the function of what you have to do, and deliver the information. You're inviting the audience inside your music. You can keep it short and sweet and get the job done. If you're more outgoing, or have a talent for comedy, getting the audience to laugh a bit is a great skill. Have fun, but keep the focus on the music.

And, at the risk of being repetitious, this is yet another area where improvisation plays a role. If you talk to the audience after every tune, that can become predictable, like anything else that falls into a pattern. It's good to let a few tunes go by in a set without verbal interruption. Sometimes I'll announce directly that we're going to play two or three tunes in a row, which I like to do in order to help the audience follow the proceedings. When I don't do it that way, I'll take a minute and catch them up afterward.

One last thing along the same lines: James Moody, in addition to being delightful and hilarious on the mic, was also great at letting the audience know what to expect. Toward the end of the set, he would say something like,

"Next we're going to play a ballad, and we'll follow that with the last tune of the set, "Giant Steps."

I was often grateful for that little bit of guidance when I was in the audience. It let me know that I had two more tunes to concentrate my attention on, and then I could look forward to ordering a drink and chilling with my 'table-mates' on the break.

## SOME THINGS TO PRACTICE

1. Trading, by nature, is something you do with others, so the best way to practice it is to do it.

2. Like most everything else, though, you can go to the recordings and work with them as well. One suggestion: Play along with Miles' recording of "Four," and see if you can grab an idea from Philly Joe Jones to work with. At the end of the second exchange, Philly Joe plays this figure (at about 6:06 on the track):

You could take that figure and start your line on the next four bars with a melody using it:

3. Try using some of the suggestions here to put some interesting sets together. Take note of what works, and what doesn't. If you find yourself feeling like you played two tunes that were too similar, look for more contrast.

4. For introducing the band, try doing it while looking in the mirror. Hold a mic and practice, like you would if you were learning the lines to a play. You can make a video as well, and get a feeling for how you look doing it. If you want to do it with more confidence, imagine how you think that should look, practice it, and record it. Use the video to gauge whether you're projecting the image you want to see.

# CHAPTER 13 · TURNAROUNDS AND THE HEAD OUT

Coming out of the trading or the last solo, a cue to the band for the head out is often in order. The universal symbol for "head out" is pointing to your head. Pretty straightforward, as long as everyone knows that the melody choruses are called "head in" and "head out." It's a good idea if you're trading, to keep an eye on the drummer, and try to respond to where he feels ready to return to the head. This can be a smooth transition, and it can also be a moment for a bit of drama, if you're so inclined. If you're going for the smooth transition, and the energy is high from some trading, it makes sense to interpret the melody to fit the energy of the moment. Taking some chances can be fun here, as long as you don't mislead the band into thinking that you're still trading. Or, you can just take the simplest route and play the head straight, go to the ending, and you're home.

If you want to do more with it, though, there are lots of options available. Let's do a little Q and A:

*"Does the head in have to match the head out?"*

Do they have to be played the same way? No. They can be, but the heads certainly don't have to be the same. There's a strong argument to be made for playing the head in clearly and as accurately as possible, to set a solid baseline from which to improvise. On the other hand, Miles Davis started interpreting right away, sometimes coming up with new melodies that sound like they *should* have been the original melody! As in many things, you can find someone to argue either direction with passion, so it's ultimately up to you to decide.

*"If you played the head in with a two feel, do you have to go back to a two feel for the head out?"*

No. Just like there's no rule about how many solo choruses you play in a two-feel, there's no rule that says you have to go back to a two-feel on the head out. Especially if the energy is high during the trading, it can sound like someone jammed on the brakes if you go back to a two-feel right at the top of the head out, especially if everyone isn't on the same page about what's happening. On the other hand, if everyone in the band knows you're going to go back to a two-feel, and everyone does it together, it can create a satisfying moment of surprise for the audience. You can decide this beforehand, as a part of the arrangement, or make it happen with a clear cue as you leave the trading. Another way to go is to carry the energy from the blowing into the head out, and then halfway through, or at the last eight, downshift to a two-feel to ease the tune into a soft landing.

*"If I played the head in twice, do I have to play it out twice?"*

Nope. You can, but you don't have to. Twice in, once out is a common choice. It depends on the length of the head and the energy of the performance. If you're feeling like it'll get repetitive, go with your gut and take it out after one time through. Some tunes with a short form, like Sam Rivers' "Beatrice," can go either way. Playing it twice at the end is no problem, but if you do it once, and then play a clear ending, it'll work great. The main thing is to communicate clearly what you want to do, so the band can end together. As legendary trumpeter and arranger Michael Mossman might say, your performance can be like a beautiful Armani suit, but if you make a mess of the ending, it'll be like a big mustard spot on your tie. What people will remember is the spot, not the suit!

*"Do I have to play the entire head out?"*

Probably more often than not, the whole head out gets played, but again, it's not a rule. There are lots of ways to go about it, and in recording situations, arrangers often make choices that will shorten the song. This happens on the bandstand as well. One example is on a ballad. It's common to choose to take the head out from the bridge. You might play a melody chorus, say, a chorus each of a tenor solo and piano solo, and then at the end of the piano chorus, you cut off the first half of the tune, and go straight to the bridge. Or you can play a melody chorus, a half chorus each for alto, piano and bass, and then you take it out from the bridge, only playing the second half of the melody of the tune. If you want to feature the bassist, you could give her a chorus and a half, and take the bridge out. Or two choruses, and then go straight to the bridge.

An option often used on medium-tempo tunes is to play a shout chorus for the first half of the head out, and then catch the melody for the second half.

Thinking more like an arranger, it's nice to have the head out be arranged somewhat differently from the head in, to bring the story to a conclusion, but with a twist. One fairly common arranger's move is to take the head out up a half step. Frank Sinatra's version of "New York, New York" is probably the most famous version of this technique.

The story of a tune can continue to unfold from the first note to the last vibrations of the crash cymbal punctuating the ending—organizing things so that the story is interesting all the way through is one of the challenges worth meeting.

You've decided to rise to that challenge. You created a solid frame for the tune with an intro and interesting transitions between solos; you told a great story in your own solo; you made excellent decisions about trading and guided the band through a strong performance. Now you need a great ending. If you're an arranger, now's your opportunity to bind together the elements of your work, and bring things to a satisfying conclusion. If you're a bandleader, a great ending is one of the moments where your band has a chance to execute something together. It's a highlight for the group as a whole, beyond what individual improvisers bring to the table. And if you're at a jam session, or playing with people you don't know, chances are the group will be looking at you, the horn player, to lead the group through to the end of the song. Learning some different ways to bring the proceedings to a smooth close is yet another skill worth spending some time developing. As we've done throughout the book, we'll discuss here some of the conventions, and you can use them as a springboard to invent some endings of your own.

After playing the melody out, on standards like "If I Were a Bell," where the harmony resolves to the root chord in the second to last bar, there is one more door you can step through before ending the song. You can create a loop out of the last four bars and stay there for some more blowing before cuing the ending. Miles Davis' groups in the '50's and early '60's used this type of "Tag Ending" a lot, and John Coltrane liked to use it for an extended second solo on "Bye Bye Blackbird."

## A REALLY LONG ASIDE ON TURNAROUNDS

First, what is a turnaround? Before we get to its use in a "Tag Ending," let's explore in detail what a turnaround looks like where you most often encounter it in a song. We'll use this 'Aside' to do that, and return to the ending loop afterward.

A basic turnaround is a quick-moving cadence that gets you from the root back to the root. It most commonly appears as a two bar phrase, with two chords per bar.

## TWO BAR TURNAROUNDS

Let's build one from scratch so you can see how it functions. Here is the simplest version of the last four bars of "Bye Bye Blackbird," with the melody and no turnaround:

The last two bars of the tune are Fmaj7, and where that is headed at the top of the next chorus is four more bars of Fmaj7. Nothing inherently wrong with that, but it makes for a pretty long space of no harmonic motion. Especially if you're playing multiple choruses of a solo, you might want to generate a little energy from the end of one chorus to the beginning of the next one. That's where a turnaround comes in handy.

A lead sheet on a tune like this will often show the last four bars like this:

The parentheses around the G-7 and C7 are there to tell you that those chords might not be in the original composer's changes, but in practice most jazz musicians choose to play them to set up the Fmaj7 at the top of the next chorus. Some lead sheets will just add the II-V without the parentheses, acknowledging that playing that progression is accepted practice.

Now we have a solid resolution to the root, Fmaj7, in the second to last bar of the form, and some harmonic pull toward the top of the next chorus. If we want to add a little more motion without leaving the key signature, we can insert a D-7 in front of the G-7, the D-7 being the VI in the key of F. That'll look like this:

We've built a I-VI-II-V progression, which is one of two types of turnarounds you'll see frequently.

Being jazz musicians, we wouldn't want the fun to stop there, though, so now we'll start improvising with the qualities of those chords. That opens the door to a variety of scale sounds and different levels of tension, which as we know, create more and more pull toward resolution.

The first move we'll make is to turn the D-7 into a D7 chord. The third of D7 is the note F#, so now we've left the key of F major. Here's what that looks like: (the next few examples will be just the two bar turnaround, we'll get back to the last four bars of "Bye Bye Blackbird" in a little while.)

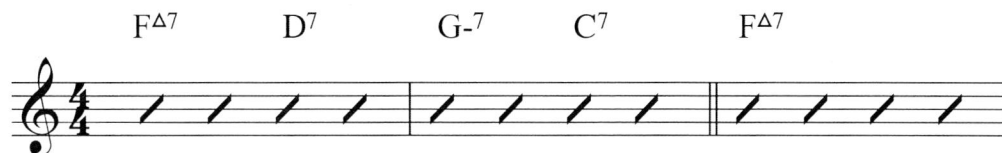

Here are a couple of straightforward passes through the turnaround:

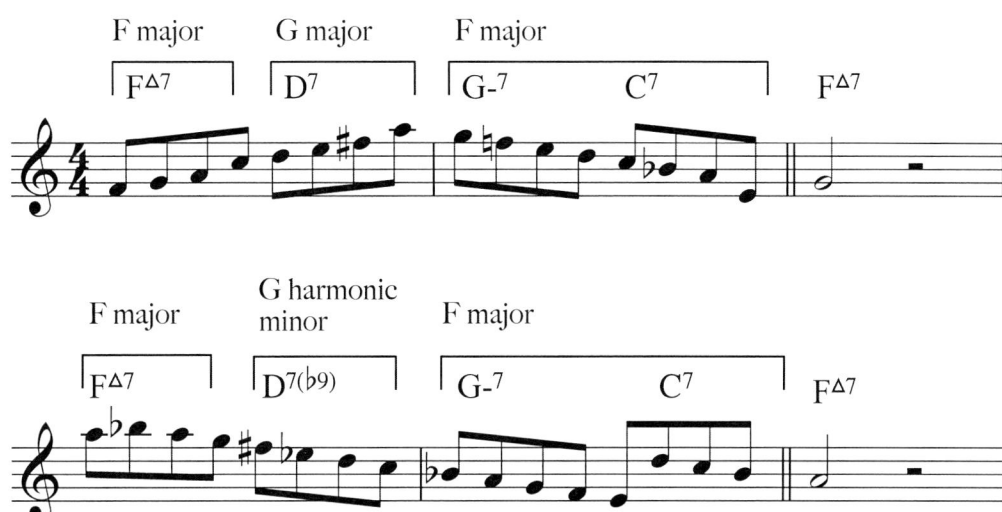

Here's Hank Mobley's solo break on "The Best Things in Life Are Free:"

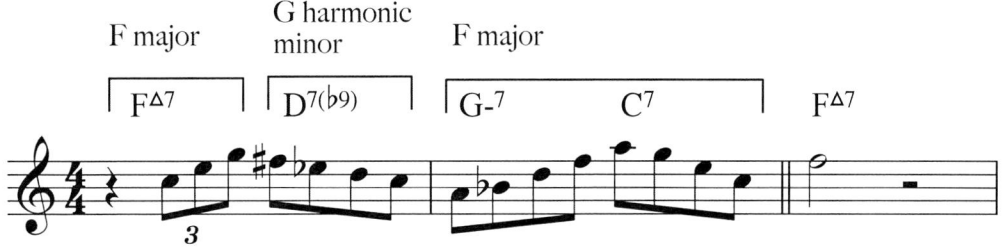

And here are a handful of lines that gradually increase the amount of tension being played through the progression. Notice how we started from no tension—treating all four chords like they're in the key of F, to maximum tension—treating each chord like it's in a different key. Any combination is possible. The following examples will give you a taste of some of the more advanced harmonic options available. These are explained in detail in Chapters 15-17.

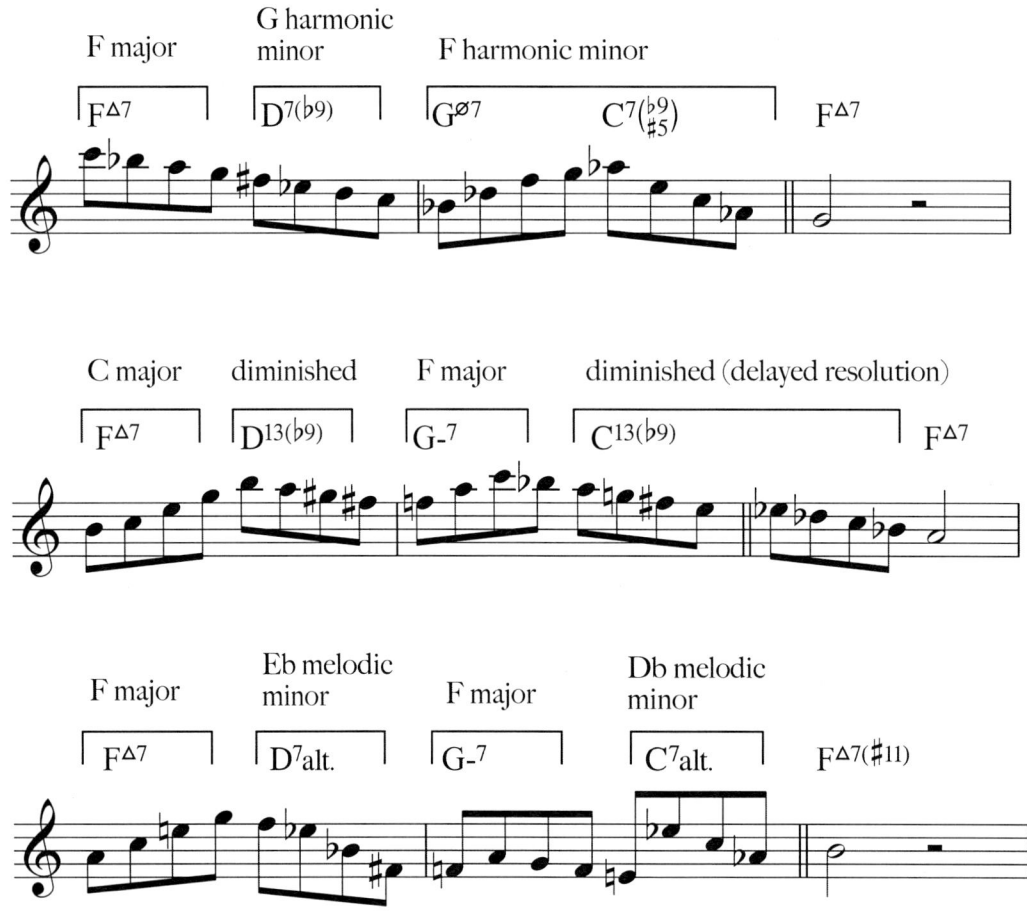

See if you can find some more lines that you like the sound of, using the above examples as templates.

We found a bunch of different ways to play through the progression based on altering the qualities of the chords. We can take another harmonic approach, and change the chords themselves by using substitutions.

For example, look what happens if we substitute an A-7 chord for the Fmaj7 in the simplest version of the progression:

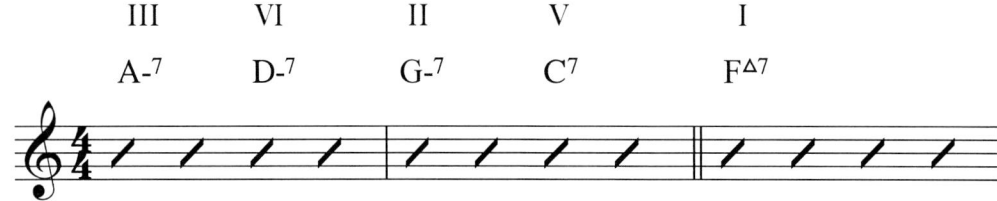

A-7 is the III in F major, and if you think about it, an A-7 chord is also the same as an Fmaj9, without the F, so A-7 makes sense as a replacement for Fmaj7. This gives us the other most common form of a turnaround—the III-VI-II-V.

Turnarounds aren't only found in the last two bars of the form.  You'll often encounter the III-VI-II-V version of the turnaround in the first ending of an AABA type standard.
Check the first endings of these tunes for some examples:

- "Ceora"
- "Cherokee"
- "Darn That Dream"
- "Easy Living"
- "Ghost of a Chance"
- "Jitterbug Waltz"
- "Misty"
- "The Nearness of You"
- "The Song is You"

Here are a few ABAC type forms, where you get a turnaround at the end of the B section, heading back to the second A:

- "Here's That Rainy Day"
- "Love Walked In"
- "Moon River"
- "Soon"

Notice what happens when we make the D-7 into a D7 chord—the A-7 becomes the II of a II-V in G.

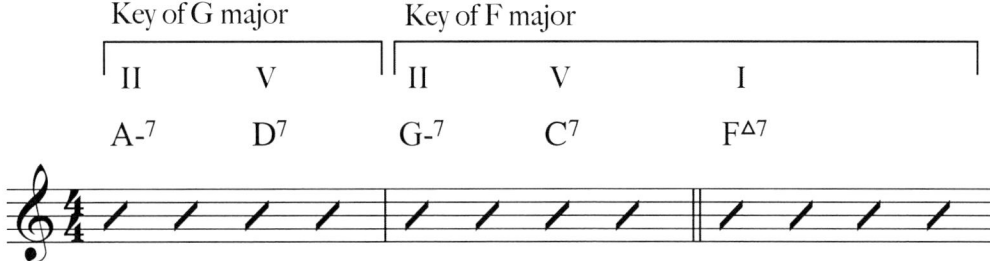

Now that we're using substitutions, let's try the tri-tones of the dominants.  Here's what that looks like, with a line to illustrate it:

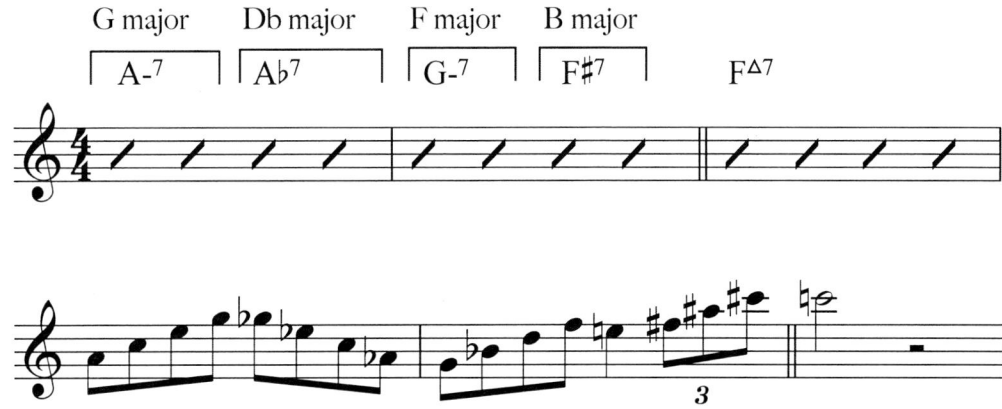

Then we could play the II's for those tri-tones:

And here's one more iteration, with a line to match:

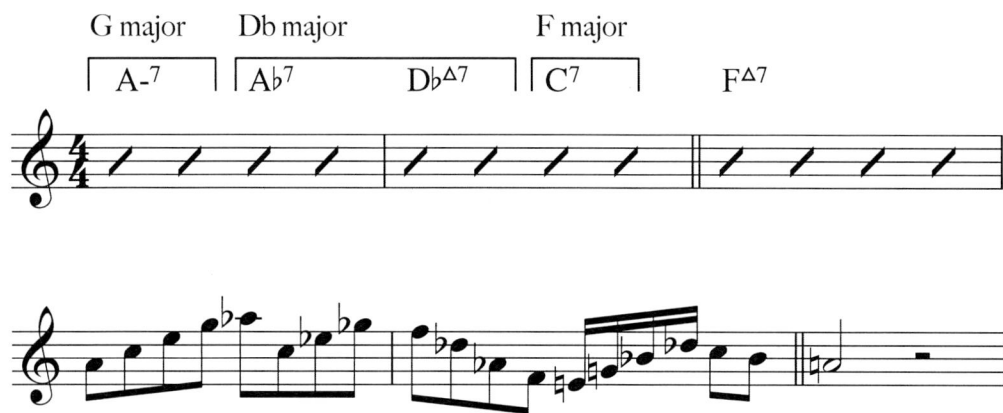

The turnaround at the end of Tadd Dameron's "Lady Bird," is an iconic one, where he took the tritone motion to another level by changing them to all Maj7 chords. Here it is in F, so you can see it in relation to the rest of the examples:

Try that in a few more keys and try substituting it into some different songs. That'll give you something to work on for a few weeks…or a lifetime.

This is not meant to be an exhaustive list of all the possibilities—exhaustive lists can get pretty exhausting. The point here is to see how using harmonic logic allows you to play a different set of changes every chorus if you want to keep things fresh. Thelonious Monk found this mother lode of information, and used it as the basis for many of his compositions.

Here's one last version:

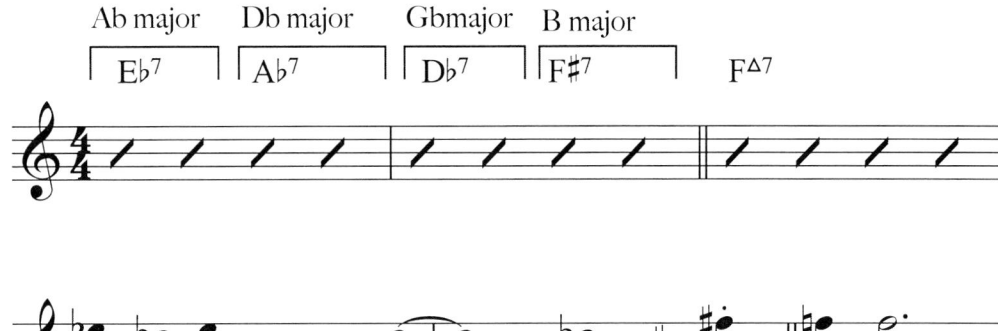

You'll find one like that starting in the fourth bar of Monk's "Trinkle Tinkle." Have a look at "Off Minor," "Think of One," "Bemsha Swing" and "Shuffle Boil" to see how Monk used the subtle differences between turnarounds to generate sounds for a whole host of compositions.

---

## USING A TURNAROUND TO CREATE AN ENDING

Leaving our longest "Aside," let's get back to stepping through that last remaining door before playing the ending in our outstanding performance of a song.

In the 1930's and '40's, when composers like Duke Ellington, Cole Porter and Hoagy Carmichael were developing the 32 bar song form, one of the conventions of the era was to bring the chord sequence home to the root in the second-to-last, or 31st bar of the form. Here are the last four bars of the tunes we're about to discuss, in their simple forms:

"Bye Bye Blackbird"

"I Could Write a Book"

"If I Were a Bell"

As we've seen, jazz musicians in the bebop era modified show tunes to make them smoother vehicles for improvising. Adding a turnaround to the last two bars of a chorus generated energy toward the top of the next chorus, making it easier and more fun to play multiple choruses in a solo.

Small groups in the 1950's and early '60's started getting more ambitious about arranging their music. They developed more complex intros, interludes and endings, and as a result were able to present their music in a more polished and artistic way. Groups led by great bandleaders like Horace Silver, Max Roach, Clifford Brown, Art Blakey and Miles Davis blazed this trail, and their music was labeled "Hard Bop." They found new ways to use turnarounds and substitutions to create original endings.

Miles Davis recorded "Bye Bye Blackbird" on his 1957 album, *'Round About Midnight*. When they get to the 31st bar of the head out, where the harmony would ordinarily resolve to the root, they use a substitution and double back.

Here are the regular changes for the last four bars again:

And here are the last four bars, as played by Miles' group in the head out. You can hear this at around 7:35 in the track:

See how that A-7(b5), D7 progression loops you back to G-7?

Listen again, noticing how the group then repeats the last four bars, and brings the tune to a close with an arranged ending. That little loop-back sets up the ending, and keeps the audience briefly in suspense before setting them back down happily with a rhythmically interesting cadence. A last little taste of tension and release.

Notice also how Miles hits the note Eb as the A-7(b5) chord arrives. That note, the flatted 5th of the chord, is the note that most clearly sounds the difference between the expected chord, Fmaj7, and the substitution, A-7(b5). Remember that situation, it will be useful as a cue when you try to do this yourself.

Let's look at the other two tunes cited above, "I Could Write a Book," and "If I Were a Bell." Both appear on Miles' recording *Relaxin'*, released in 1958.

Miles plays "I Could Write a Book" in Eb. Let's look at the ending. In this case, there is a two bar turnaround—I-VI-II-V—starting from bar 29 which lands us at the root in bar 31. Here are the last four bars in Eb in their simple form:

And here are the last four bars as played by Miles's group on the head out. You can find it at about 4:47 in the track:

This time, instead of just looping back once, they stay in the loop a few times before ending the song. See if you can count how many times the loop goes around.

After the loop, Miles quotes the melody, and they go with a short ending. They stay pretty close to the basic set of changes during the loop, but take note that, just like we did with the two bar version of the turnaround, we can redefine the qualities of the chords, and also use substitutes once we're in the loop. This can be another space to 'negotiate' the changes each time through with the pianist and bassist.

Miles' version of "If I Were a Bell," from the same recording, in addition to being the source of the famous quote, "I'll play it and tell you what it is later," has another great example of an arranged ending using the turnaround loop.

Here's the simple version of the last four bars of the melody again:

This time, at around 7:38 in the track, instead of substituting A-7(b5) for the final Fmaj7 chord, they use a more dramatic substitution, and go up a minor third, to Bb-7.

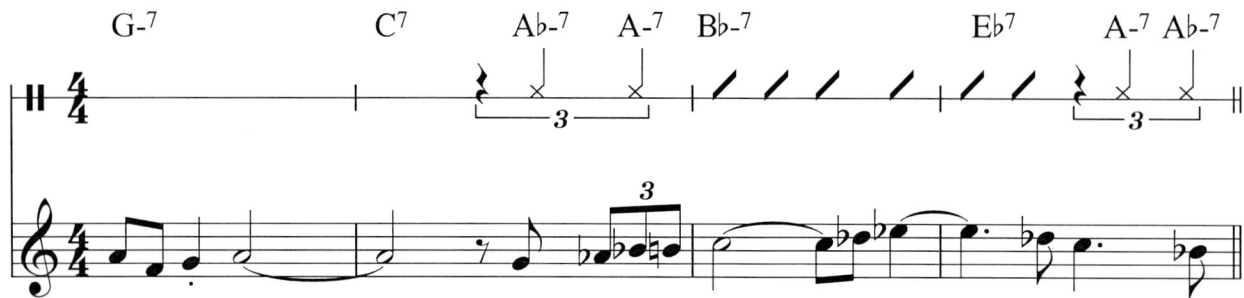

Going back down the minor third, they drop into a turnaround loop that looks like this:

After a few times around, Miles plays the melody as a cue at 8:01, which takes them to the ending.

## USING TURNAROUND LOOPS TO EXTEND SOLOS AND ENDINGS

Now that you're familiar with the way the loop works, go back and listen to "If I Were a Bell" from the beginning. You may notice that each soloist cues into the loop at the end of his solo (not just at the very end of the tune). This has become one of the conventions for playing "If I Were a Bell." You don't have to, but you have the option of cuing into and then playing over the loop during your solo. This gives you some options for approaches to your solo as well. You could:

- Play one chorus, then cue in and spend the bulk of your solo in the loop
- Divide it up evenly; a few choruses followed by a few minutes in the loop
- A chorus or two, a few times in through the loop, and back to a regular chorus
- No solo during the main body of the tune, and then a solo only after the head out, on the loop

By the mid 1960's Coltrane was running with this idea. He played magnificent solos stretching out on the turnaround loop, especially on "Bye Bye Blackbird."

There are a number of examples of this, but look for the version from 1962, in Stockholm, with his great quartet featuring McCoy Tyner, Jimmy Garrison and Elvin Jones. Check out the whole song, of course, not just Trane in the turnaround loop. McCoy's solo is a great source of traditional vocabulary intermixed with modern ideas.

After Garrison's solo, Coltrane chooses to come in halfway through the chorus and take the head out from the bridge. (This happens at about 12:08 in the track, which is 17:55 long). The last four bars start at the 12:25 mark, and two bars later, the band enters the loop.

As you can hear from Coltrane's example, once the loop is established, the sky's the limit for creating tension and releasing it. With a pianist or guitarist with big ears, you can have an ongoing dialogue about what substitutions to use, and the game can get fierce, in a good way, to see if you can stay together while constantly making choices about the changes. You can use all of the harmonic choices we've discussed over G-7 and C7, and you can do the same over the A-7 and D7. You can stay with a sound for a while, or switch it up with each pass. Coming up in Part Three we'll discuss some more advanced harmonic concepts which will also apply here.

## SOME THINGS TO PRACTICE

1. Use the lines and examples given in the chapter as templates to find some lines of your own.
2. See how many different ways you can find to define the root motion of a turnaround, and see if you can find lines and melodies that define them clearly.
3. Remember to put your knowledge to work. It isn't enough just to write some things down—make sure you take the next couple of steps to incorporate your ideas into your soloing.
    a) If you find a path through a turnaround you like, get it under your fingers and then play it over a play-along or a recording *a bunch of times* so you can hear it and feel it in context.
    b) Play a highly complex turnaround against a play-along that is using a simpler version of the changes, so you can hear and experience the tension created by your substitutions.
    c) Get with a pianist or guitarist and see what happens when you try out your ideas in real time, with a human!
4. Learn "Bye Bye Blackbird" and some other songs like it, with a major 7th chord at the top and a II-V-I over the last 4 bars, and practice to cueing the rhythm section into a loop. Here are a few suggestions in some different keys:
    - "East of the Sun" (G)
    - "My Secret Love" (Eb)
    - "My Shining Hour" (C)
    - "There Is No Greater Love" (Bb)

5. And here's one more loop idea to try.  I heard George Coleman do this at Bradley's in NYC back in the good old days, but I haven't been able to find a recorded version of it.  Remember the cue from "If I Were a Bell" where they went up a minor third and back down?  You can use that as a loop as well:

After playing a few times through that loop, George Coleman takes it to the next level, and continues going up in minor thirds until it brings him back to G-7, and then drops back into the regular turnaround:

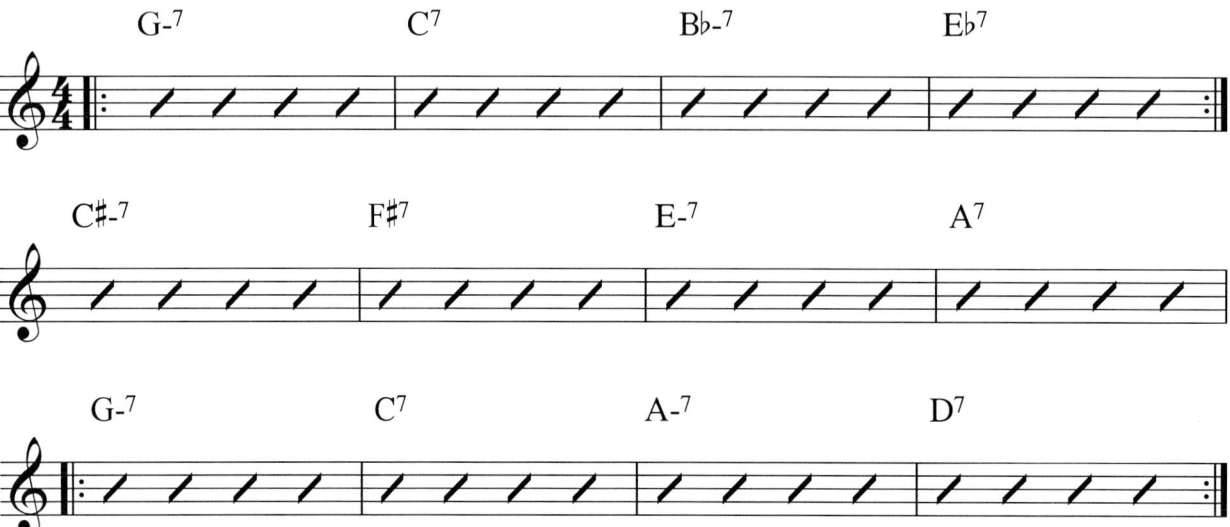

That last one sounds particularly good with minor 9 chords instead of minor 7ths.

Have fun…!

# CHAPTER 14 · PLAYING THE ENDING

Especially if you're the leader, and *especially* if you're a vocalist, the band will be looking to you to lead them through the ending, so it's in your interest to train yourself to do it well. In a jam session environment or one where there's no obvious leader, the rhythm section will generally be looking to the players of the melody to cue the ending.

If you've browsed your way here without reading through in order, when we get to the part about loops, you'll find more information about them in the previous chapter. If you've come straight from the last chapter to this one, keep that loop going in your mind a little longer, and we'll discuss how to get out of it and play the ending about midway through this chapter.

Our purpose here is to get to know some of the common types of endings. Knowing what you are doing will help you navigate the group through to a successful ending, and having an idea ahead of time of what type of ending you want to execute is also helpful. If you can set the tune down with the band all together the audience will respond.

Everyone can relate to a well-crafted conclusion, and it is especially attractive to people who are less familiar with jazz. You'll find that rhythm section players also appreciate playing with a horn player who knows how to end a tune well.

## THE SHORT ENDING

The simplest way to end a song is to play the head out and stop after the last note. Seems easy enough, but unless you're playing a tune where that is the generally accepted way to end the song, chances are the rhythm section will be expecting more. If you've thought about it, and what you want is a short ending, then it's best to communicate that to the band before you start the head out if you're already performing it. If you have time for a rehearsal, you can practice it, of course. On the fly, you can turn to the band and say, "short ending," and then when you get there, use your horn to drive the point home by making a clear downward motion on the last beat. Especially if you've given some warning, this will usually work.

Charlie Parker's "Donna Lee" is a clear example of a tune that is usually ended on the last note. Check his 1947 recording with Miles Davis to see how it sounds. You'll find most people end the tune this way.

The next simplest way to end a tune is to play the head out down to the last note, leave a short space, and then add a final chord, often with a dominant 7 sharp nine sound. Here's how Miles Davis plays the last phrase of "Four," from the recording *Workin'*. You can use the last two notes Miles plays to signal to the band that you want that sharp nine sound. They'll hear it.

A slightly more standardized way to say that is like this:

And Dexter Gordon's take on the last phrase goes:

That's on Dexter's recording *Bouncin' With Dex*. Check out how he adds a little turnaround between the last note of the melody and his final ending. Dexter gets that from a Miles Davis recording, *Blue Haze*. Here's how Miles plays it:

Most people don't play that turnaround when they end the tune "Four," so you'll want to make sure everyone knows what it is if you want to try it. It's a great device to know about, and the melodic line flows beautifully through the two extra bars.

## REPEATING THE LAST PHRASE OF THE MELODY

Probably the most frequently used convention is to play the last phrase of the melody three times to set up the ending.

Kenny Garrett uses this method on the version of "Have You Met Miss Jones" referred to in Chapter 5. He plays it straight, with a nice little touch of vibrato on the second iteration, and a slight rhythmic variation on the third. Here's what it looks like:

Note how Kenny lands on the root, but the rhythm section treats that note like the major 7th of F#maj7(#11), and then resolves to the expected Fmaj7 a bar later. This is a very common choice used to add one last surprise to a tune.

You can take it a step further, and add another chord before the F#maj7. What would be the chord that comes before F# in the cycle of 5ths? C#, right? Go to the piano, and see what this sounds like:

That should get you started looking for interesting ways to redefine the root when you get there. Try some minor 7th chords and some dominants as well, and see what you can find. Bill Evans (the pianist) is a master at creating interesting final chord sequences, as is Cedar Walton. They're both great sources, if you run out of ideas.

For a slightly different approach to playing the last phrase three times, listen to Dexter Gordon's ending on "There Will Never Be Another You," from *The Montmartre Collection*. He repeats the last four-bar phrase. To be precise, they play the last four bars of the form, and then repeat it twice, for a total of three times. Check out the rhythm Kenny Drew plays on the final chord.

And just for fun, have a listen to Elvin Jones' group playing "It Don't Mean a Thing…" from the album of the same name, for a drum-centric version of the last phrase repeated style of ending.

## ADDING A "CAPPING PHRASE" AFTER THE LAST NOTE OF THE MELODY

As far as I know, there isn't a term for adding a phrase after arriving at the last note of the melody to set up the ending, so I'm using "capping phrase." The ending of Duke Ellington's "Take the 'A' Train" is the most famous version of this type of ending. For the sake of historical accuracy, here's the way the last phrase is played on the original recording from 1941:

Three things to note about this example:

1. The ending is in the key of Eb, which is a part of the big band arrangement. In small group contexts the tune is usually played in C, the key in which the big band arrangement begins.
2. The first note with an arrow above it, the E natural, is sometimes played as an F. You should know that the original melody is the E natural.
3. The second note with an arrow over it is the anticipation the Ellington band plays. The most common way to play it now is without the anticipation.

Here's what it looks like in the key of C, and as it's usually played:

And here's a Dexter Gordon version, from his album *Take the A Train*, where he combines the traditional ending with the Miles Davis style final sharp 9 chord we heard on "Four:"

It has become standard practice to use that "capping phrase" on "Take the 'A' Train" and also "C Jam Blues," but if you use it in other contexts it can sound a bit too predictable, so you want to learn some other good capping phrases. After you've collected a bunch of them, you'll get better at making them up in real time, if you work on it a bit.

Sonny Stitt was a master at ending tunes on the fly. He spent a good deal of his career traveling as a soloist playing with pickup rhythm sections, and as a result, developed ways to send clear musical messages to people he might not have had a chance to get to know much before the gig. (He was also notorious for just starting tunes without announcing them, in whatever key he felt like playing. So if you wanted to accompany him you had to have done your homework. Or you got really good at learning tunes after one chorus—assuming the bassist was competent and friendly enough to teach you the form in a hurry…)

Here are a few examples of Stitt's capping phrases. These come from the early recordings he made for the Prestige label, available now as *Sonny Stitt Complete 1949/1950 Prestige Masters*. You might also find them under the title *Sonny Stitt/Bud Powell/J.J. Johnson*.

Here is Stitt's capping phrase on "All God's Chillun Got Rhythm:"

And here he is on "Bud's Blues:"

On "I Want to Be Happy" Stitt chooses to improvise the last phrase instead of playing the final melody, and then plays a nice capping phrase to show the rhythm section where he's aiming to finish:

On "Fine and Dandy," instead of playing a capping phrase beyond the last note of the melody, Stitt replaces the last phrase of the melody with a quote of Charlie Parker's "Little Willie Leaps," leading to a short ending:

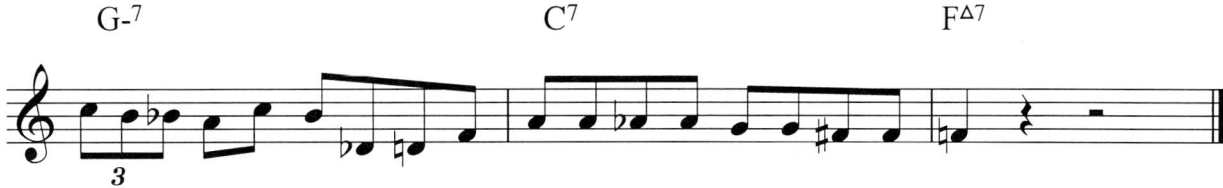

You could also use that phrase as a capping phrase…

Hopefully you're hearing how this works, and are ready to start trying them on your own. You can also start paying closer attention to how horn players end songs when you're listening to music. For good measure, here's one last one, this one on "Avalon." Stitt again uses the strategy of improvising the last phrase and then using a capping phrase:

## BRINGING THE BAND HOME AFTER PLAYING A LOOP

Ok, now that we've acquired a few more skills for ending songs, we can finally address cuing the band out of the loop.

To recap from Chapter 13, you've successfully cued the band into a turnaround loop after playing the head out. You've had some fun with the rhythm section playing with the harmony of the loop, and you sense that the tune is ready to come to its final conclusion. What do you do? You could simply play the last phrase of the melody as a cue, but this can be a little abrupt, and the rhythm section might miss the cue, and you wind up feeling stuck in the loop. You could solve this problem by turning to the rhythm section before you play the last phrase and saying, "Here we go," and then playing the last phrase of the melody. That'll work pretty well in most cases, and a hand sign like a raised fist can also work, if you get the timing right and if everyone in the band knows the meaning of your hand signals. It's also worth learning some musical vocabulary, so you can give the cue with your music, rather than with words or signs.

A good cue out of a loop is a three step process, and when it's done well, sets up the rhythm section to hit beat one of the second to last bar, giving you a chance to play a final capping phrase, and bring the song to a satisfying conclusion, giving the audience the signal to erupt into rapturous applause. There's your incentive to learn how to do this, right there.

Here are the three steps to cuing the band out of the loop, assuming you're in a four bar, II-V-III-VI loop:

1. Play a phrase in the first two bars (II-V) that sounds like a question.
2. Play another two bar phrase that answers it in the next two bars (III-VI).
3. Play a final two bar phrase that leads everyone's ears toward the root (II-V leading to I).

Our man of the chapter, Sonny Stitt, recorded "Bye Bye Blackbird" with the Hank Jones Trio on his record, *The Good Life*, and his cue to the ending is about as clear as you can get. The band enters a loop at around 4:08 in the track, and Sonny's cue for the ending starts at 4:20. Have a listen. Here's what the question and answer look like:

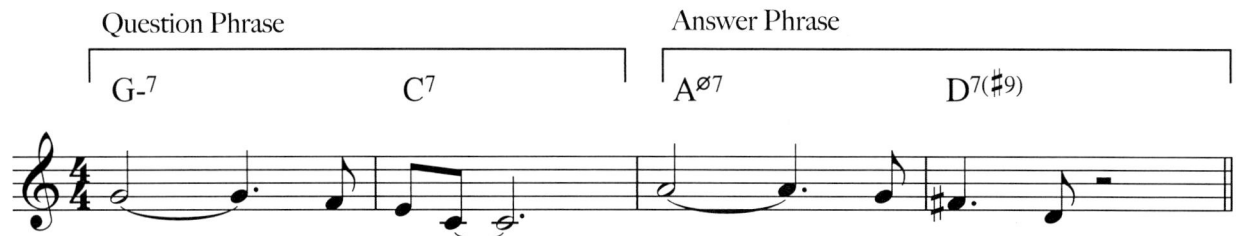

And here it is with the final phrase—notice how inevitably it aims for and lands on the root:

If you listen carefully, you can hear the rhythm section searching a bit for the changes after Stitt lands on the root, but they're solid on beat four right after that, which is typical of this type of ending.

If you want to make that even clearer, you can use the rhythmic phrase that sets up that beat four, like this:

That last rhythm is used commonly by experienced rhythm sections, so if you quote it they'll know right away what you mean.

Here are a few variations on Stitt's question and answer pair.

Now that you get the overall shape of things, you can start mixing and matching these phrases to make an ending of your own.

Here's one example:

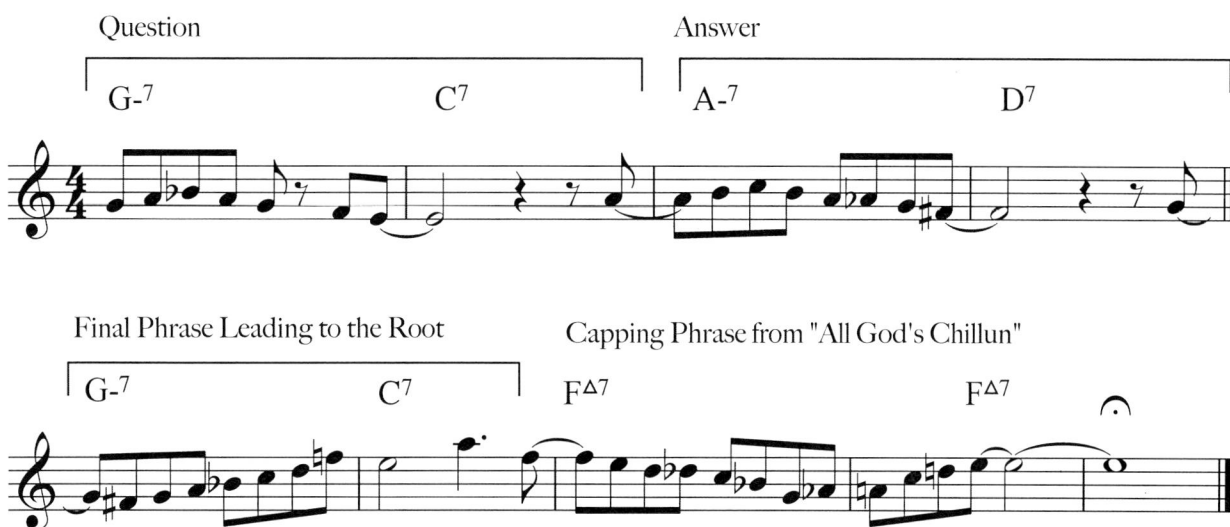

And here's one more with a capping phrase that Stitt uses a lot:

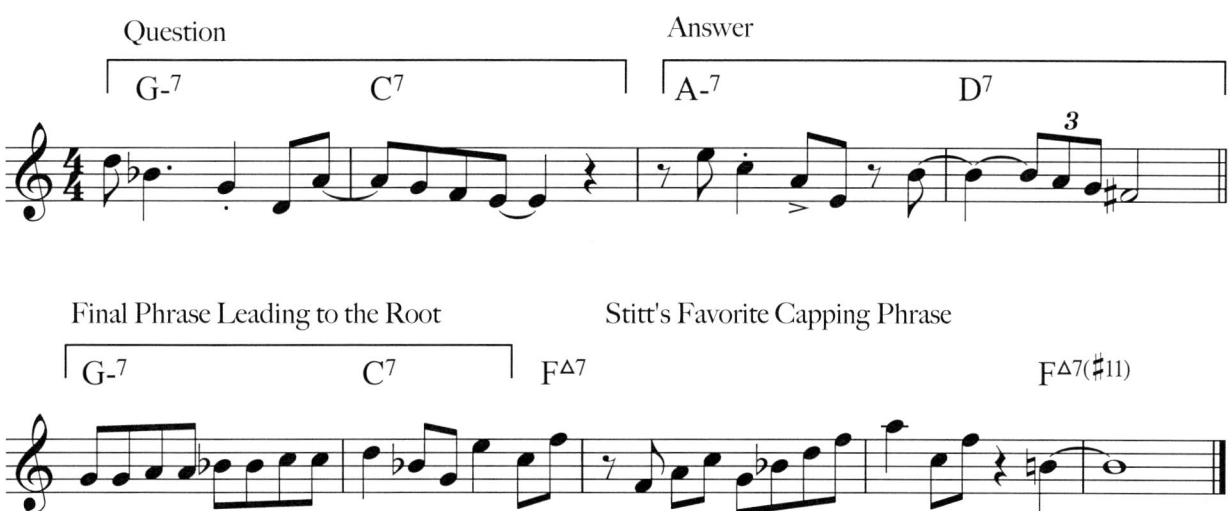

Make up a few more of your own, and also practice to see if you can make up some question and answer melodies in real time that will communicate where you want to go. Gather a rhythm section and try giving them the cue, and see if you can successfully lead them through to a solid ending.

Here's a short list of standards that lend themselves to the loop style ending:

- "All of You"
- "But Not For Me"
- "Bye Bye Blackbird"
- "Gone With the Wind"
- "How Deep Is the Ocean"
- "I Love You"
- "If I Were a Bell"
- "My Secret Love"
- "My Shining Hour"
- "Old Folks"
- "Stella by Starlight"
- "There Is No Greater Love"
- "You Stepped Out of a Dream"

## SOME OTHER TYPES OF ENDINGS

There are some variations on the "last phrase played three times" type of ending. It seems like there are as many ways to play the ending of "It Could Happen to You" as there are jazz musicians. It has a II-V-I in the last four bars, so it lends itself both to looping and to the two repeats and a capping phrase style of ending. It is also common around New York to hear players take the first repeat of the last phrase up a half step.

Frank Wess used this ending on one of his last recordings, *Magic 201*, when he was 91 years old…..I hope I'll be recording at 91…

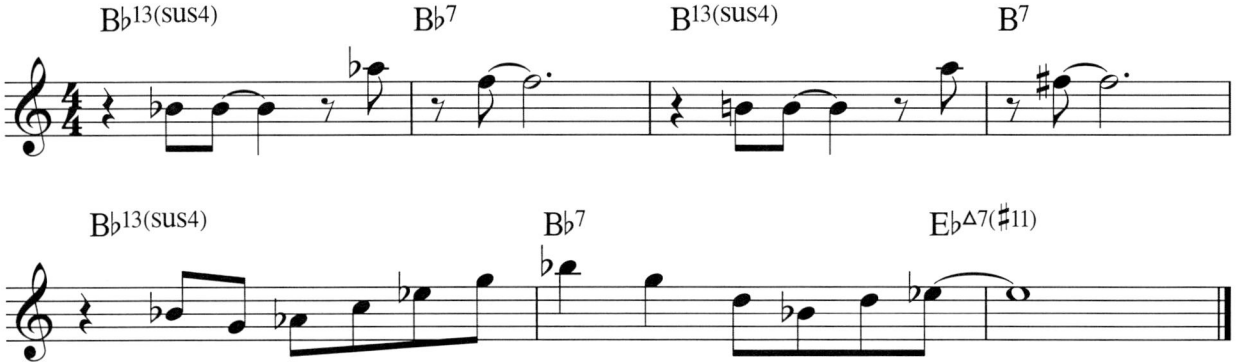

On his debut recording, *Presenting…Jackie McLean,* Jackie used the half step up technique on "It's You or No One:"

On "I Remember You" the second iteration is often played a minor third up. You can hear Cannonball Adderley do this on his recording, *Cannonball Takes Charge*:

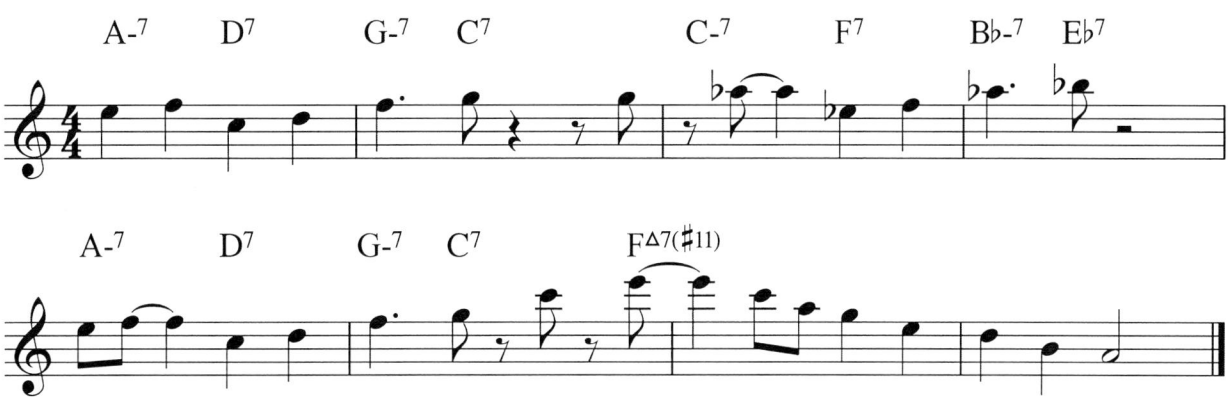

There are lots of other ways to end a tune, but these are some skills that will help you function well when you get a chance to work with a rhythm section that has been around the tradition. When you go to repeat the last phrase three times, if you keep it in the same key there's no need to say anything, although you might want to pay close attention in case the pianist goes up a half step just to see if you're listening. If you go up the half step on a tune like "It Could Happen to You," or "It's You or No One" where it is commonly done, you can probably get away without saying anything, although it never hurts to communicate your intention. And in the case of a minor third, it helps to mention it ahead of time, since it's less common. And of course, you can use the minor third option on other tunes—but a quick rehearsal or verbal run-through is appropriate if you want to do that on a tune where it isn't standard practice. Hopefully you're getting the message—mix it up and have fun. It's important to hang out and learn the ropes, so you know what the usual practices are, and after you know them, be free and find your own way.

A few more tunes that have particular endings that are useful to know about:

- Cherokee is often ended in the way Clifford Brown and Max Roach played it on *Study in Brown*. In place of the last two bars of the melody, they play a riff, and then repeat it one more time, landing on the flatted fifth of Bbmaj7. Listen to how they do it on the recording. It looks like this:

You have to listen closely, but you can also hear Sonny Rollins use this ending on "B. Quick," an extremely fast take on the changes of "Cherokee," also with Max Roach.

- "All the Things You Are" is often ended by returning to the intro instead of landing on the root, like this:

You can hear that played by Lee Morgan and Hank Mobley on *Monday Nights at Birdland*, which we also referenced in Chapter 10.

You can, and many people do, make the Intro section into a loop, and then cue then ending from there, which looks like this:

There are some variations on the way to play the final chord—have a listen to some different recordings for ideas about how to get there.

It's important here to be mindful of how long the tune has been going on, and how many people have soloed on it. If you cue back into the intro vamp, it can go long, and then you might exhaust your rhythm section and/or the audience. If it feels right, there's nothing wrong with letting the vamp build up some momentum and creating one last wave, but only if the energy is there in the room to support it.

If that last wave is not needed, for a short, clean ending you can enter the loop for a couple of repeats, play a *ritardando* and get out fast.

For another alternative, listen to the way Keith Jarrett uses a short ending on "All the Things You Are" on his classic album *Standards Volume 1*.

- "Round Midnight" is another tune where most people play the arranged ending, so it's good to know how it goes. You can get the shape of it from Dizzy Gillespie's 1946 recording, and they play the intro that has also become standard on this recording.

- Also worth learning is the Miles Davis interlude, introduced on his album *'Round About Midnight* and made deeply dramatic in the ensuing years after Tony Williams joined the band. (After you've listened a few times and tried to figure it out with your ears, you can check your work by comparing it to the chart in Sher Music's *The Standards Real Book*.) Miles plays the traditional ending on this recording as well, so you can get a second take on it.

That should get you started being more aware of the possibilities for ending tunes. Mix and match, be creative, and learn to be clear. When you get the chance to play with a group in a regular kind of way and you can build trust, then leaving things open and making up the ending together can also be highly rewarding. Chaos endings can be lots of fun, but can get old fast if every song ends in a disorganized way.

A final word, and then we will be finished with the second section of the book. In the case of a ballad, the horn player often gets a space to herself to play a cadenza. The most common way this happens is the horn player leads the band up to the second to last chord, often with a *ritard* to make it clear what is happening. If you're on top of it, you can dive right into a cadenza before the band plays the last chord, and they'll know what you're up to. The cadenza is your space to showcase whatever you want. You can:

- Play your instrument. Now is a good time to show off your love of your instrument and what you can do on it, but don't stop there.
- As with other things—play the song, otherwise every cadenza will sound the same.
- You can play freely over the changes, in time or rubato—over just one A section or the bridge, or over the whole form. The challenge is to keep it interesting and tell a good story.
- Play the melody, or a fragment of the melody and find some variations.
- Find a rhythmic device to develop.
- You can make your cadenza short or long, depending on how much you have to say, and how long the song went on before you got to this moment.

For a short example, Sonny Stitt plays just a few phrases at the end of "Ghost of a Chance," on his recording, *Constellation*.

A beautiful arrangement of "Skylark" gives Freddie Hubbard a little space to blow on the Jazz Messengers' great recording *Caravan*.

John Coltrane took cadenzas to a whole new level with his great quartet of the early to mid-1960's. The one not to miss is "I Want to Talk About You." There are a number of different cadenzas on this tune. Seek them out. They may change your life…

And just for fun, Michael Brecker made a splash in the mid-1980's when he brought an EWI with him on tour. His runs through five octaves on his cadenzas on "In a Sentimental Mood" would routinely bring the house down.

You can play the most beautiful cadenza of all time, and still drop the ball if you don't bring the band in for the last chord or chords elegantly. So it's worth practicing to get the band home as well. Some suggestions:

- Learn to lead the band to the last chord. Remember those capping phrases, and the phrases just before them, that lead inevitably toward the root? If you can play some of those you have an idea of how to play a melody that will tell the band when you want them to come back in.

- You play a solid last phrase, inviting the band back in at the root—this is a good opportunity to give the piano player a nudge to reharmonize the ending a bit. If you play the root, that can be an invitation to the pianist to improvise a final sequence. But if you don't play the root, the tendency is for the band to play a sound to match your note. Put another way, if the horn player plays the root, the pianist or guitarist has lots of freedom to find some interesting sounds. If you play a different note, their tendency will be to play a final chord and Bob's your uncle.

- Some good notes to end on besides the root:
    - The flat 5—this generally suggests a Major 7(#11) chord
    - The 9—suggests Maj 7th, but can be some different qualities, so gives the pianist some leeway
    - The major 7th —similar to the 9th
    - End on the root and immediately signal half step up—if you're in C, playing a clear phrase leading you to the note C, then when you land on it, play a C# major 7 arpeggio, starting from the note C. That'll let the pianist know that you want a little harmonic surprise there, and maybe a few more chords, if you hear it…

## SOME THINGS TO PRACTICE

Hopefully it has become clear throughout this chapter that there are skills that take some practice, that don't have to do just with your own personal solo. Just like the rhythm section players also have to learn to become good accompanists, we horn players are responsible for becoming skillful at leading the band through to the end of the song. A solid ending, played well, as we said earlier in the chapter, can be a real source of pleasure for the audience, and they will reward you for a good ending with enthusiastic applause. You can help deliver that applause to your deserving bandmates by:

1. Learning a variety of endings that you can use on the fly
2. Developing a vocabulary of question and answer phrases, phrases that lead to the root, and capping phrases
3. Learning to cue into and out of loops
4. Learning the conventional endings (and intros) for commonly played standards
5. Learning to play an interesting cadenza, and being able to bring the band home to the last chord with clarity and elegance
6. Learning to feel the appropriate length of loops and vamps at the end of tunes, so you don't overstay your welcome with the rhythm section

After doing some of the homework, gather a simpatico rhythm section and ask them to help you work on these skills. Their feedback will let you know if you are communicating clearly.

# PART THREE
## BUILDING TENSION WITH ADVANCED HARMONY

*How Can I Make My Storytelling More Colorful?*

# CHAPTER 15 · THE HARMONIC MINOR SCALE

When Charlie Parker started playing lines using the sound of the harmonic minor scale, he was connecting jazz with both its past and its future. The sound of harmonic minor is present in ancient traditions like Hindustani Classical music in India, Persian music, and North African music. You'll hear it in the folk traditions of places like Bulgaria, Greece and Turkey. It is a defining element of the sound of the Klezmer tradition. J.S. Bach used the harmonic minor extensively in his work, establishing it as an important element in European classical music in the early 1700's. Jazz has become a true world music precisely because elements from around the world were knitted into the fabric of the music by innovators like Charlie Parker.

Let's take a look and a listen to the harmonic minor scale. If you've been following from the beginning of the book, you know the drill by now: grab your horn and get to a piano, and we'll explore the sound of the scale, and the relationships between the scale and the chords generated from each of its notes.

Here's the scale, in the key of C harmonic minor:

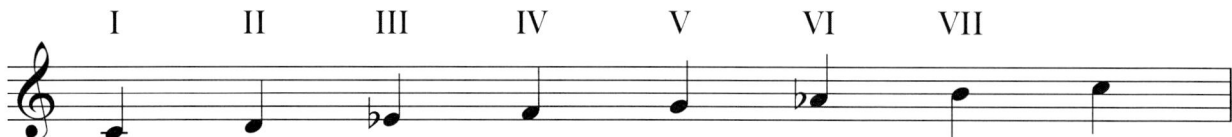

Two things to notice right off the bat:

1. There are two notes that are different from the C major scale, the b3 and the b6.

2. All of the other scales we've looked at so far are composed of whole steps and half steps. The interval between the b6 and the major 7 of a harmonic minor scale is a minor 3rd. In C that is the leap from Ab to B natural. This relatively large leap gives the scale its characteristic sound.

3. Notice that we are proceeding in order of the number of notes that are different from the major scale. The C melodic minor has one note different, the b3. The C harmonic minor has two notes that are different, the b3 and b6.

Here's the clockwork for harmonic minor in C.

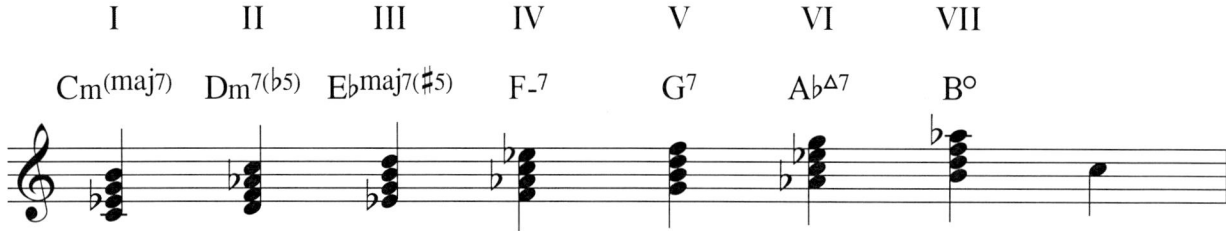

The first chord in harmonic minor in the key of C is C-△7, which is the same as melodic minor, so we can use the same voicings:

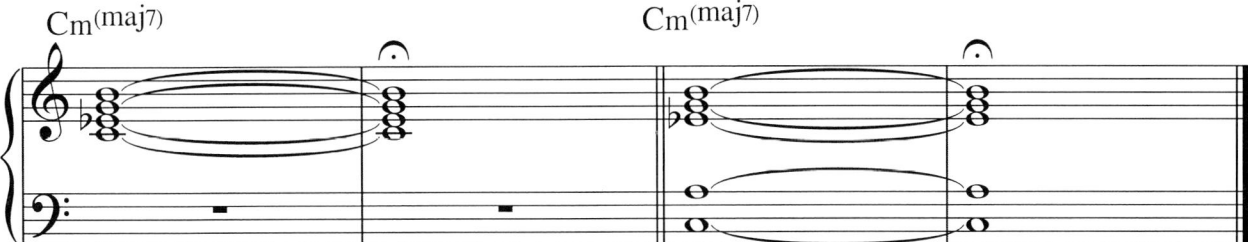

Familiarize yourself with the sound of the scale, while you sustain the chord at the piano. Take some time to feel the chord tones (C, Eb, G and B) and non-chord tones (D, F, Ab). Hold the note Ab, for example, and see if you can hear where it wants to move. Experiment with it. Tinker. Try playing the scale in 3rds and 4ths. Try playing the arpeggios one after another, then one up and the next one down, then the other way around. Try playing an arpeggio up, and the scale down four notes. See how many different ways you can come up with to explore the sound of the scale.

## THE I CHORD IN HARMONIC MINOR—I MIN MAJ7

Let's check out how some of the masters used the harmonic minor in real time. Remember "Nica's Dream" from the recording *Horace-Scope*? We saw how Blue Mitchell treated the first two chords as I's in melodic minor. Let's look at how Junior Cook uses harmonic minor in his pass through the same changes.

Here's his first phrase at the top of his first chorus:

See if you can imagine some lines that use Junior Cook's idea as a starting point. Here are a couple of examples. Try playing these lines against a play-along, or along with the Horace Silver recording. Then see if you can find a few more of your own.

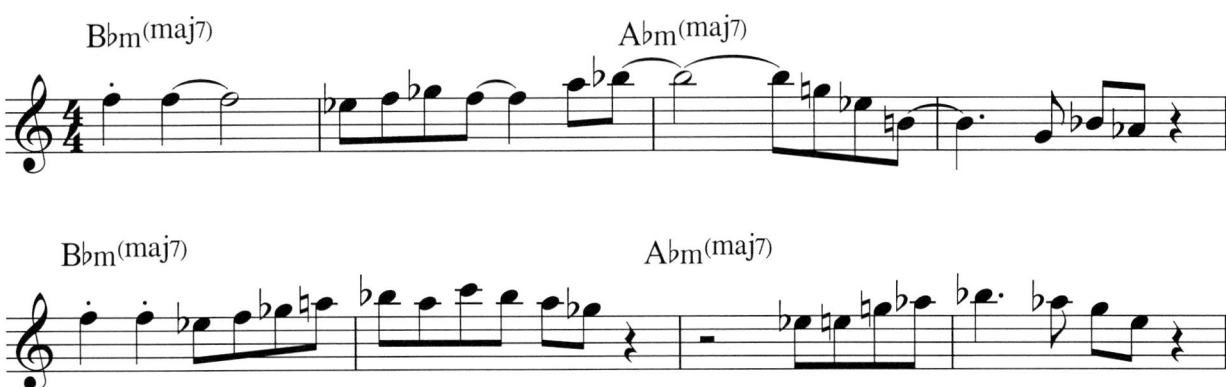

On the way out of the bridge, at the top of his last A section, Junior says this:

Here are a few iterations of those lines. Notice how I'm trying to use the scale and also play two phrases that fit together. You can think of the first phrase as a "question" and the second as an "answer:"

The tune, "Invitation" gives you a four bar section of C-7 to play with. Try looking for some melodies using the harmonic minor scale on that section. Starting in bar 9 you get another four bar section, this one in Eb. You could take a C harmonic minor melody that you like from the first 8, and transpose it to Eb harmonic minor. Now you're engaging more deeply with the variety of sounds available to you as an improviser, and you're also developing a theme through a chorus…enjoy…

## THE V CHORD IN HARMONIC MINOR—V7(+5♭9)

If you look at the clockwork again, you'll see G7 in the 5th position. Notice that by just stacking every other note in the harmonic minor scale starting from G, you get G, B, D and F, which make a straight G7, the same G7 you get in C major.

Try sounding the G7 chord at the piano with the sustain pedal, and playing the C harmonic minor scale through it. Use the straight voicing, without tensions.

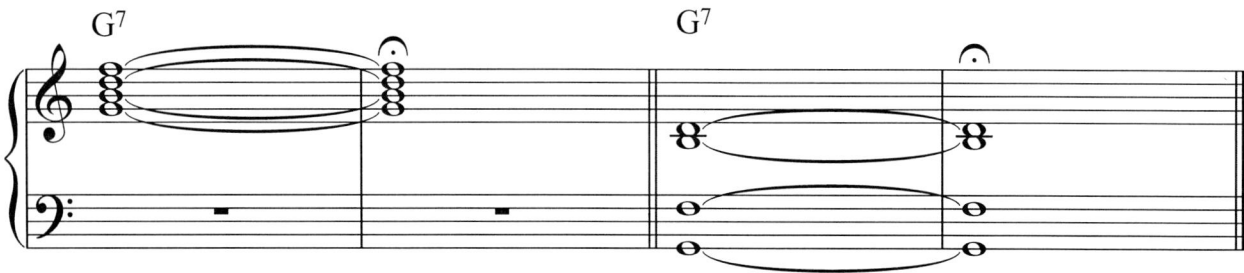

Does it work?

Try contrasting that with the C major scale against the G7 chord. Notice that the simple chord voicing will support both the major and minor scales. When you play the tension notes created by the harmonic minor scale, they will pull harder toward nearby chord tones, but they don't sound wrong, especially if you move them to the note they are pulling toward, and release the tension.

Some people get confused at this point and start wondering why we're playing a C harmonic minor scale through a G7 chord. The reason is that G7 is the fifth arpeggio in C harmonic minor. Look at the clockwork again and find it. The G7 chord is embedded in the C harmonic minor scale.

That means that when a pianist or other chord instrument is sounding a straight G7 chord, you can freely use the C harmonic minor scale against it. This gives you a new way to create tension while playing through the G7 chord. You can play the C harmonic minor scale and all of the arpeggios associated with it against the G7. Try it out and see how it feels.

The trick is to use the sound of the scale clearly enough so that what you're doing can be heard by your rhythm section partners. The examples in the chapter will get you started doing just that.

• Video 27: The Harmonic Minor Scale on a Dominant 7th Chord

Next let's sound a G7 at the piano that includes the two tension notes that are generated by the harmonic minor scale. Here are a couple of voicings you can try:

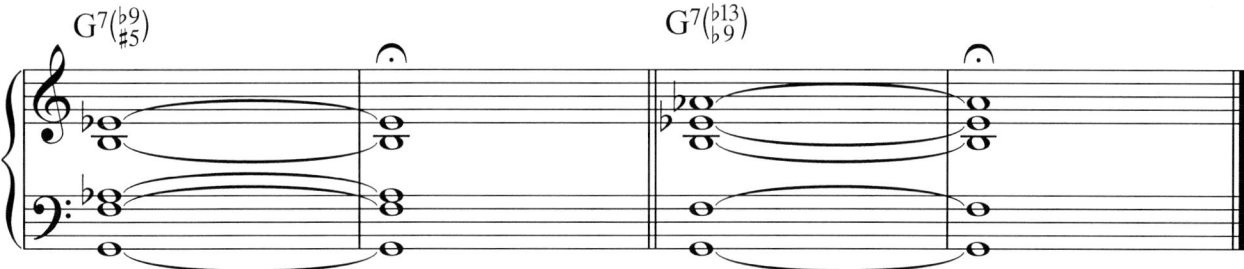

Notice how, now that the b9, the note Ab, is present in the voicing, that note doesn't create as much tension when you play it on your horn. It still wants to move, but the chord voicing supports it. The harmonic minor scale 'belongs' with this voicing. Play around with the sound and get used to it.

Then, try playing the *C major* scale against the G7(+5b9) chord. See how it clashes? The idea, again, is this: if the pianist is using a voicing with no tension, the soloist has more room to make choices about how much tension to play—how much pressure to put—on the chord. But if a pianist or guitarist uses a chord voicing with tension in it, then the soloist is better off if she knows which sound belongs with that voicing. That's the reason I'm stressing that you sit at a piano while you learn these sounds. It makes a big difference if you get to know the sounds while also learning how to produce them at the piano.

Let's go to the tradition again, and hear how the greats make lines using harmonic minor. The most common situation where you'll hear it used is when a dominant 7 chord is moving in a V-I progression, where the I is a minor 7 chord, for example C7(+5b9) to F-7.

I chose to use C7 as an example because it is in Hank Mobley's key for "The Best Things in Life Are Free." At the start of the B section of the tune, (the second eight bars of the form) the harmony cycles back and forth between C7 and F-7. Here's how Mobley navigates it in his first chorus, starting from around 0:53 in the track:

And here's the slightly different take on it at the same spot in his second chorus (at around 1:37):

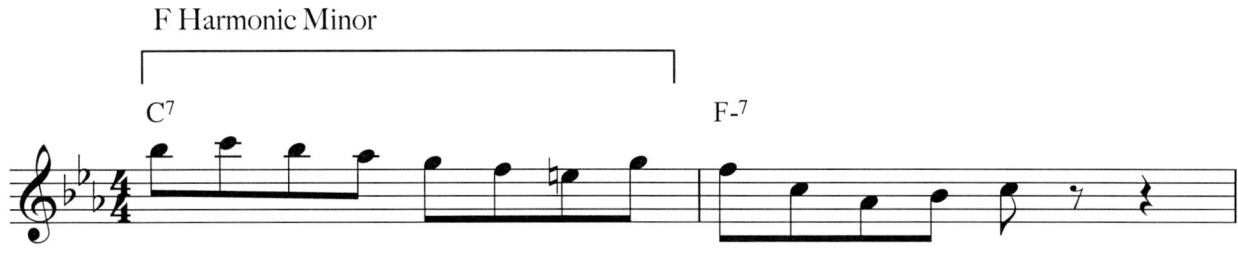

If we use Hank's line as a starting point and play around with it a little, we can find some more lines that sound great through the C7, and stick the landing across the barline into F-7.

Try these:

Next, play along with the recording and see if you can land some of these lines in the spots where they belong in the form. Imagine that you are the soloist in the band, and see if you can feel your lines swinging with the rhythm section.

Now see if you can find some more lines of your own. Try them out.

We will progressively add more tension as we study the scales in this section of the book. The lines derived from these scales have a tendency to increase the feeling of complexity in the music. Remember, though, that each of these scales gives you a field of notes from which you can also create simple melodies!

A simple melody within a complex sound—that's an interesting zone to live in for a while…

Here's another harmonic minor example from Charlie Parker's tune, "Confirmation." This is the first phrase of his solo from his 1953 studio recording of the song:

That Ab at the end of the second bar is not in the D harmonic minor scale. Parker is using it as a way to smooth out the line and carry him to the note A across the barline, so he lands clearly on a chord tone of the D-7 chord in the next bar. People have some different names for this type of situation, but I think it's simplest to think of it as a "passing tone." There is a detailed discussion of passing tones in Chapter 18.

Notice also, that the II in the II-V is an E half diminished chord, and that the second chord in the harmonic minor clockwork is also half-diminished. Here's the harmonic minor clockwork in D minor, so you can see it:

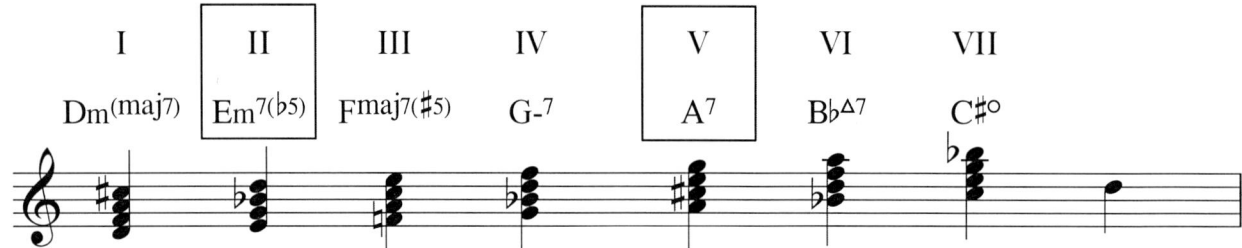

All that is to point out—when you see a IImin7(b5)-V-Imin7, those chords are telling you that harmonic minor is a solid scale sound to use to flow through those chords smoothly.

If you are able to learn Charlie Parker's line and play it precisely along with him, you will experience how it feels to play swinging eighth notes like a master. Then, if you can pull that line out of Charlie Parker's solo and use it in your own solo by plugging it into the spot in the form where it belongs, you'll have the experience of playing something great that fits with the harmony. You'll also build your awareness of where you are in the changes.

All of that is great.

As you've seen earlier in the chapter, I think it's important not to stop there. The next step is to understand where his idea comes from—to get at the grammar, which, in this case is the use of the harmonic minor scale—and use that to generate some lines of your own.

Here are a few iterations of Parker's idea:

## A LONGISH, PHILOSOPHICAL ASIDE ON WHETHER OR NOT TO PLAY LICKS

Two of the questions I get asked most frequently by students are:

1. Should I play licks?
And,
2. Should I learn licks in all keys?

For the purpose of this 'aside' we'll define a lick as a short, familiar piece of melody that is commonly used by jazz musicians. The definition can be expanded to include a phrase that you like the sound of in someone else's playing, and think about adding to your solo vocabulary. For an example and a laugh, do a quick search on "the lick jazz" and you'll hear a famous one being played by a wide variety of musicians from John Coltrane to Kenny G. But don't get stuck in the online information vortex, come back here and continue reading…

My answer to both questions is, "No if you do it by rote like a robot, and yes, if you can do it creatively."

What I mean by that is: if I just learn the notes of a lick, and then plug it in exactly the same way chorus after chorus, I will sound like I'm reading a script off a teleprompter, rather than conversing freely in a language.

Let's use the phrase we learned from Charlie Parker as an example. Here it is again, with the changes that follow it written in:

See how the changes after the second bar are following a pattern? It's II-V's going down in whole steps. The D-7 and C-7 chords are not half-diminished, but that's ok. We're improvising, so we can make some decisions about that on the fly.

If I take Parker's lick and transpose it for the next two bars, adjusting it for the natural 5th on the D-7 and C-7, it looks like this:

Try it. It sounds good, and the first time you play it, it will sound pretty smooth, like you have command of the changes. But if you play it again the same way on the second A section, it'll sound like something you've worked out over the changes, not like something you're imagining and pulling off in real time. You could be creative with the harmony, and make the minor 7ths into half-diminished chords, like this:

Now you're working with the idea and making it your own, which is good, but if you leave it there, you'll be stuck with playing variations on a group of notes. That's where understanding the underlying harmony comes in handy. If you know that the lick is embedded in the harmonic minor scale, you can use that to widen your possibilities.

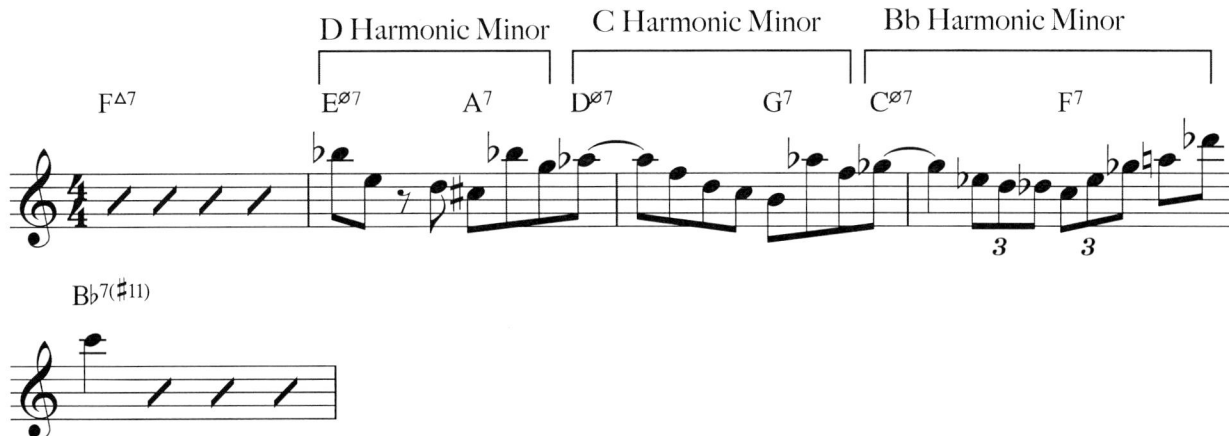

And here's one more iteration using Parker's idea as a starting point and making up my own set of lines.

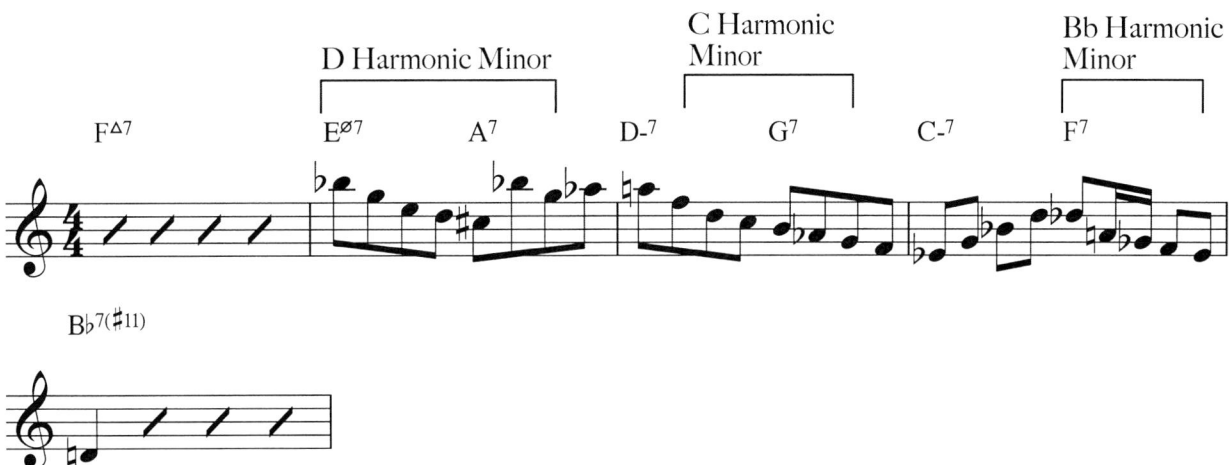

Get the idea? If I can be clear, and find lines that sound good, I can improvise with more than just notes—I can create numerous variations on a simple idea. To return to the language analogy, I know that I need words (licks) to make sentences (lines), and I know that certain words are frequently used. Just because they're used a lot doesn't mean I should avoid them. What I want to do is use the words I know to make interesting sentences. In conversation we speak naturally about our thoughts and feelings in the moment. We don't make up sentences in advance and then repeat them verbatim. Same thing with the language of jazz.

Back to the harmonic minor scale—we'll discuss one more situation where harmonic minor comes up in functional harmony. You know how the "Clockwork" system works now, so you should be able to explore (on your own) the remaining chords we haven't dealt with directly in the book.

Here's your clockwork one last time.

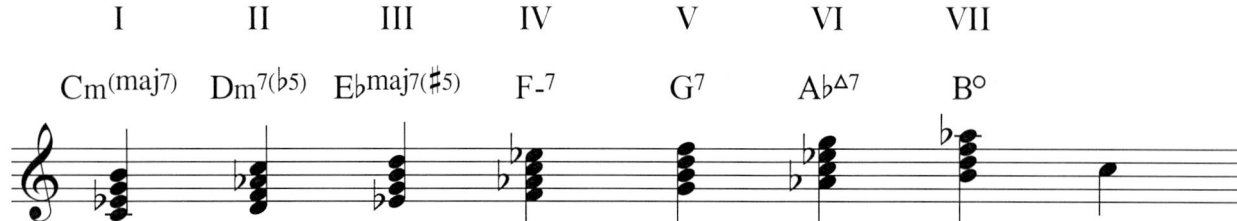

The B diminished chord in the VII position will be our last subject in this chapter, and we will explore the diminished chords and scales in more detail in Chapter 16. Here are some voicings for B diminished to play at the piano. Try sustaining them and playing some C harmonic minor lines and melodies with them.

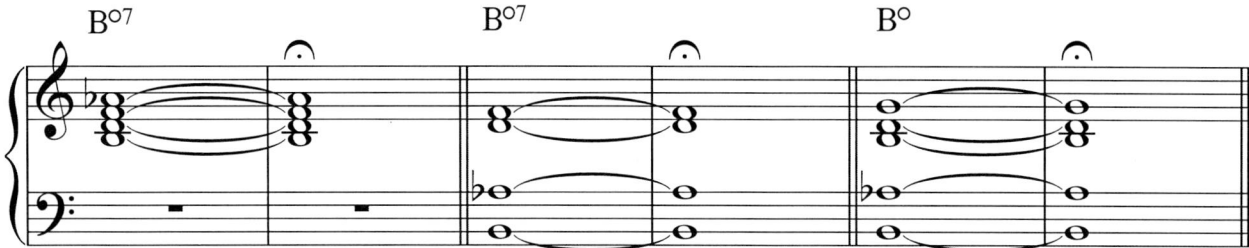

A VII-I progression, in this case Bdim7 to C-7, is a little bit unusual, but occurs often enough that it is worth knowing about. The Bdim7 acts like a V chord resolving to I, but allows for a different bass motion.

Here are a few ways to play the progression, so you hear how the diminished chord releases into the minor 7th chord. Notice that, technically, to be in the harmonic minor scale it should release to a C-maj7 chord, but in practice you will most often see the diminished chord resolving up a half step to a regular minor 7th:

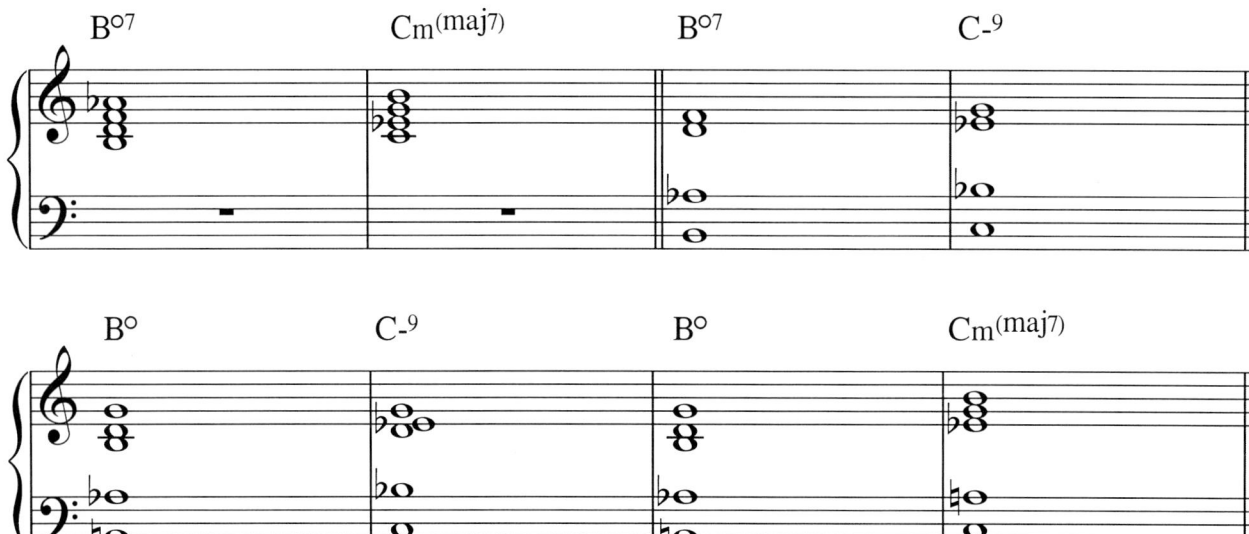

Charlie Shoemake introduced me to this concept by having me learn Sonny Rollins' solo on "Slow Boat to China." Sonny uses the harmonic minor sound in a number of ways during this solo. See if you can spot them. Here's one right at the beginning of the solo:

"It Could Happen to You" has a similar progression. "Donna Lee" has a Bdim7 moving to C-7 in the fifth bar before the end of the form. "Like Someone in Love" has the same progression heading into the last four bars of the form—Bdim7 to C-7 when it's played in Ab major. (Many people like to play it in Eb.) Those are some situations where you can try out the C harmonic minor scale on the B diminished chord.

There is one more thing to note before we move on. If you take a Bdim7 chord and put a G in the bass, what do you get?

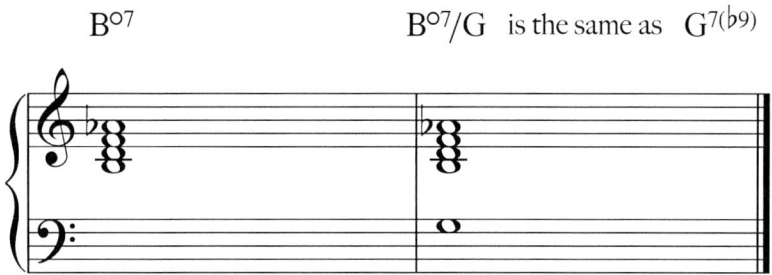

Since the B diminished chord and the G7(b9) chord both live in the C harmonic minor scale, you will often find musicians simply replacing the diminished chord with the dominant. The dominant chord gives a little more flexibility for blowing, so it is often preferred. But the diminished shouldn't just be shunted aside in favor of a dominant all the time. Diminished chords are quirky little animals, and we'll see some different ways to use them and approach playing on them in the next chapter.

Grab a piano player or maybe a vibes player just for fun, and have him play the above progressions for you. Play some harmonic minor lines over the diminished chord. See if it feels different if you have the pianist play a G7 instead. See if you can get your lines to resolve smoothly into Cmin7. Then ask the pianist what choices he would make in this situation. Ask the pianist about ideas for additional approaches to the diminished chord, and have her teach you some different voicings to try.

## SOME THINGS TO PRACTICE

1. Now that you're familiar with the sound of the harmonic minor, try putting it to use. Use the scale as a field of notes to imagine some melodies. Try making up a harmonic minor based melody, and then see if you can play some variations on it as you travel through the form.

2. Find a tune that has a similar progression to "The Best Things in Life Are Free." Take some of the lines you learned from Hank Mobley's solo and transpose them into some different songs. "Secret Love" and "Bye Bye Blackbird" are compositions that have similar B sections.

3. Play the line precisely a few times, and then see if you can modify it in real time to make it come alive. Try to surprise yourself. After you're confident that you can land the idea across a barline, experiment with the feeling of not knowing exactly what you're going to play.

4. Try playing a little "harmonic misdirection." Take a line like this:

The line is setting up your ear for the resolution into G-7. Now play it like this, and see what it feels like to land it, surprisingly, in G major.

5. Now might be a good time, if you haven't already, to try memorizing a transcribed solo. Like most things in jazz, people disagree about whether this is a good way to learn to play the music. If done well, I think it's one of the best tools for getting to know the language. When I was first starting out, Charlie complimented me on how well I played Sonny Rollins' solo on "Mambo Bounce." Eager to get some more of that praise, I set out to play my next solo perfectly a week later. I spent all of my practice time on the transcription. After performing the transcribed solo (I think it was Rollins again, on "Almost Like Being in Love"), it was immediately apparent that I didn't really know the tune when I tried to take a solo myself. Charlie was quick to point out that it sounded like I had prepared a "piece" for him, rather than improving my improvisation that week. No praise, but a critique that got right at the heart of the matter.

So, the advantages to memorizing solos from the masters are:

- Learning to play things that sound good (!)
- Adding to your soloing vocabulary
- Experiencing what swinging eighth notes *feel* like
- Having the experience of playing a solo that works from start to finish
- Accessing lines and melodies that inspire variations of your own, which results in the development of your personal sound
- The only downside is getting stuck in someone else's style of playing, or repeating things too robotically, but you're not going to do that.

6. The best place to start is a solo from a master that gets your attention and makes you say, "I want to play like *that*." Sometimes, though, it really helps to be pointed toward something for a specific reason. You can always ask your teacher or another musician for a suggestion. There is an outstanding resource online that was created by Mike Tracy, of the University of Louisville's great jazz program. Mike canvassed the faculty of Jamey Aebersold's Summer Jazz Workshop a few years ago, and collected a large set of recommendations of solos that are worth learning. He posted the results on his blog, along with some suggestions for studying solos. The solos are also helpfully sorted into two groups—ones to get started with, and "next level" solos, which are a little more challenging. Here's a link to the web location:

http://www.michaeltracy.com/blog/wp-content/uploads/Transcription-complete-2-5-20.pdf

7. Chapter 20 has more detail on the mechanics of working with transcriptions.

# CHAPTER 16 · THE DIMINISHED SCALE

The Diminished scale is a different sort of animal than the three we've discussed so far. First of all, it's an eight-note scale, instead of seven. For this reason it is also called the "Octotonic Scale." Secondly, it has a kind of symmetry built in. Whereas all of the previous scales had more whole steps than half steps in them, the diminished scale is exactly even. A whole step is always followed by a half step, and a half step is always followed by a whole step. Here's what one looks like:

The symmetry of whole steps and half steps gives this scale a distinct sound, and a particular feeling as it moves in time. It also makes for some interesting and unusual harmonic outcomes. Instead of a straightforward clockwork that works the same way in all twelve keys, we get a different set of combinations.

Practically speaking, there are two main playing situations where the diminished scale is a logical choice. We will look at those two first: using the diminished scale on diminished chords, and using the diminished scale on dominant 7th chords. After you've mastered those two, there are a number of creative ways to apply the scale, which we'll explore last.

## PLAYING DIMINISHED SCALES THROUGH DIMINISHED CHORDS

Let's get the sound of the scale into our ears in relation to a diminished chord.

Here are two voicings for a C diminished chord. As usual, we make the C diminished chord by stacking every other note in the scale, which gives us C, Eb, Gb, A. Try playing the C diminished scale with the chord sustaining at the piano.

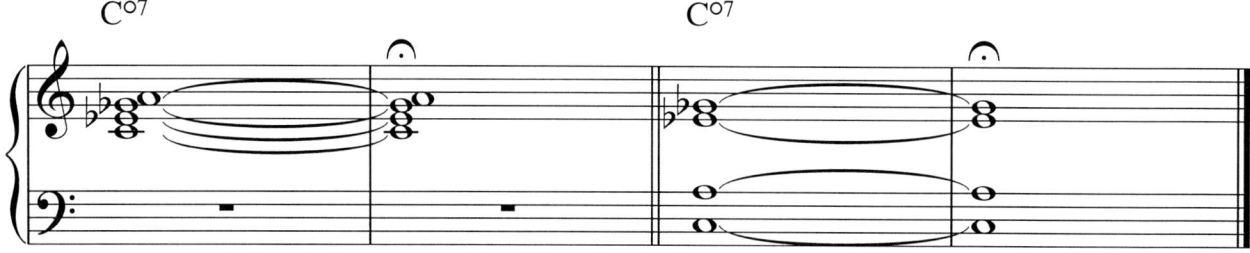

Notice that the C diminished scale starts with a whole step—C to D. This is sometimes referred to as a "Whole Step Half Step" diminished scale. You'll also hear "Half Step Whole Step" diminished scale, and we'll check that out next, when we discuss dominant 7th chords.

We saw in Chapter 15 how a diminished chord has a function within the harmonic minor scale, and is found resolving in a VII-I motion. Here we'll look at situations where the diminished chord is *not* resolving in that type of motion.

Antonio Carlos Jobim uses diminished chords liberally in his compositions. Let's listen to a few players play lines through "Wave," one of Jobim's most popular tunes.

Our old stalwart Dexter Gordon can always be counted to be making the changes. Listen how on "Wave" he anticipates the sound of the Ab diminished chord by starting it two beats before the chord arrives. This is from Volume 2 of the *Swiss Nights* series of live recordings he made for Steeplechase. (This happens leaving the bridge of his first chorus, at around 2:25 on the recording.)

Two things to note about this recording—First, Dexter is not playing it in the original key. "Wave" is usually played in Jobim's key, a whole step higher, in D. So if you study Dexter's solo here to get some information, it's worth transposing what you learn into the usual key. If you call "Wave" at a jam session or gig, the assumption will be that you'll be in D.

And secondly, notice where Dexter lines up the whole steps and half steps.

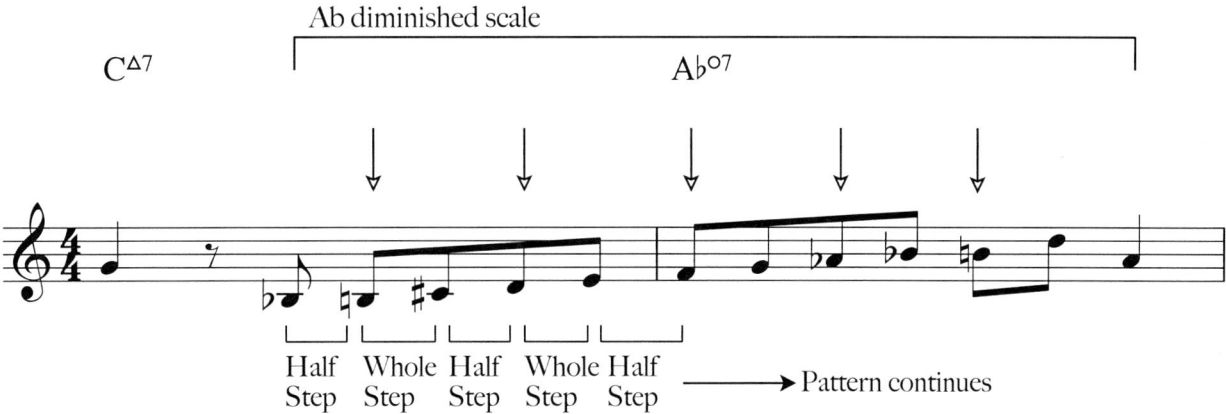

See how the Dexter starts the scale on an upbeat (the 'and' of two), with a half step to get to beat three? Since the scale is symmetrical, all the succeeding upbeats will resolve to a downbeat with a half step. When you go to use the diminished scale on a diminished chord, you want to line up the scale so that the half steps resolve to the downbeats.

Try putting on a play-along of "Wave" and playing the diminished scale through the second chord, lining the scale up in the beat like Dexter does. Here are a couple of examples in the original key:

It should feel smooth as it travels through the chord and the beat. Notice that the melody of "Wave" also follows this pattern.

Now try playing it "wrong," with a half step from the downbeat to the upbeat.

See how it feels a little blocky and unnatural? It just doesn't lay very well if you play it that way. Of course, that doesn't mean you *aren't allowed* to play it that way—you just need to be ready for that feeling of 'not-smoothness' and be able to resolve it into the next chord in a way that makes sense, if you choose to do that. I think you'll find that 'whole step half step' feels better and will be your default usage of the scale on diminished chords.

One of the many quirks of the diminished scale is that the way the scale lays in the beat is the same going up as it is going down. Meaning, if you start a line on the beat you want to start with a whole step, so that the upbeats line up with the half steps, whether you're going up or down.

To illustrate—if you start an ascending line from the root on a Cdim7 chord it'll look like this:

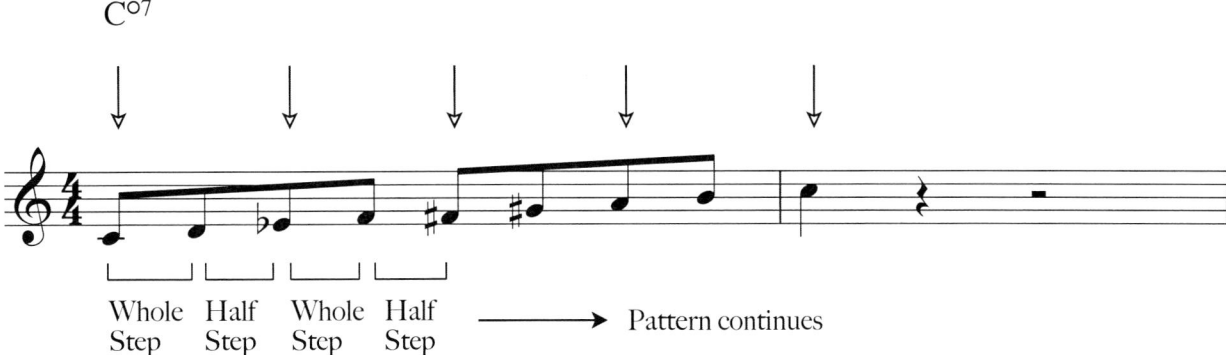

But if you start from the note C going downward, it will sound smoother if you play the note C on an upbeat, in order to make the half steps line up with the upbeats, like so:

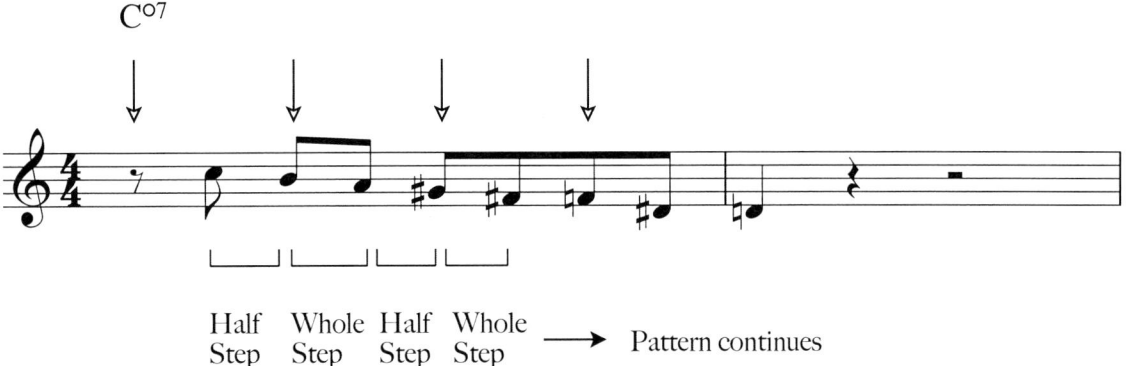

This is something that has to do with feel, so don't take my word for it, or just read through the information on this page. Go ahead and play along with something that has some diminished chords in it, and try using the scale going up and down, and confirm for yourself how it feels.

Now that you have a sense of the way the scale feels, try playing it through some more interesting voicings for a C diminished 7th chord. Here are two of them:

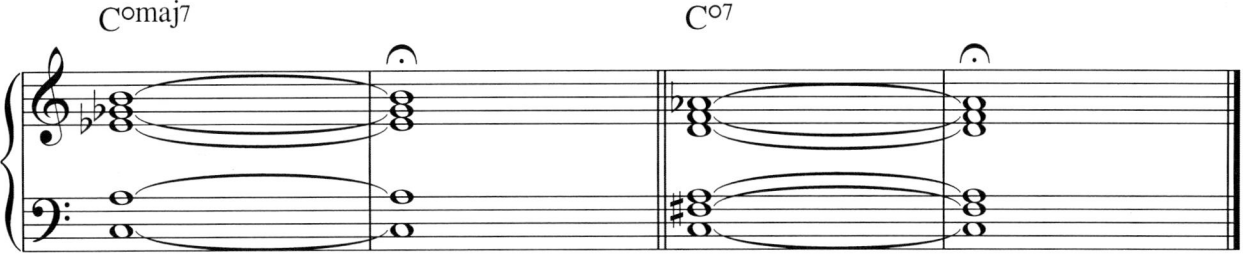

James Moody used to love to play "Wave," and surprisingly, the track I found that had a good example of him using the diminished scale in the second bar is also in the key of C. This one is a little off the beaten track, but if you search for Moody playing "Wave" with the RIAS Big Band, you should be able to locate it. (You can also find it in the "JazzSaxBook Ch.16" playlist on my YouTube channel.) This example happens as he enters the second A section of his solo, at around 1:54 in the track:

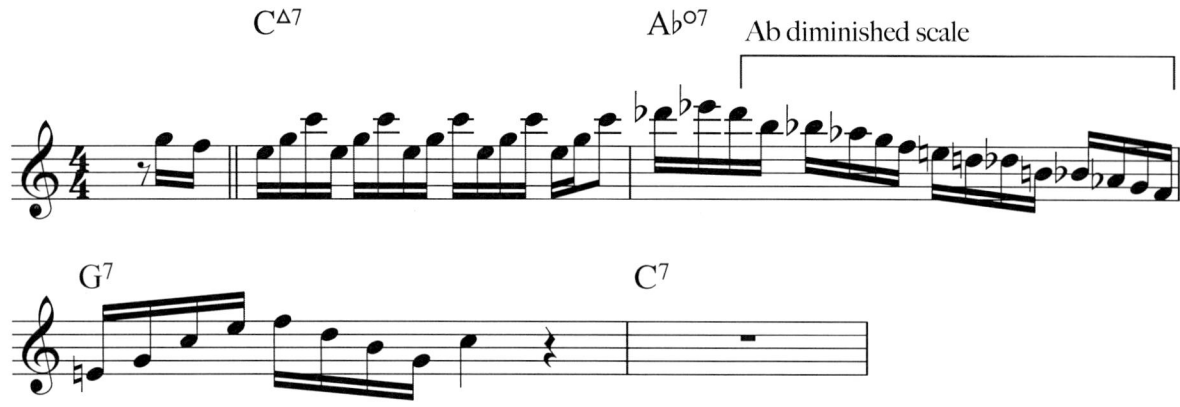

Here's another way to work on putting together good lines on a diminished chord. Stan Getz is a great line player, but is even more known for being an outstanding melodist. He was instrumental in popularizing Jobim's music around the world. We can take a melody Getz played, and use that to inspire a diminished line.

On the iconic *Getz/Gilberto*, Stan starts his solo on "Corcovado" by quoting the melody, but giving the second phrase a different shape, like so:

We could use the diminished scale to fill in the space in the third bar, aiming for a good landing note on the Gmin7 chord that's coming up in bar 5. Here are a couple of examples:

There's another interesting thing to point out about "Corcovado" before we move on. If you listen carefully to the seventh and eighth bars of the first statement of the melody, when Astrud Gilberto is singing, Jobim doesn't land on Fmaj7 in the 7th bar. He substitutes Fdim7 for a bar, and then resolves it to an Fmaj7 in the eighth bar. Joao Gilberto, comping on guitar for Getz's solo plays Fmaj7 for both bars. These days many people treat the Fdim7 to Fmaj7 progression as the standard one for that spot in the tune, and it's another good place to make use of the diminished scale.

Billy Strayhorn used a similar progression in the seventh bar of "UMMG," and you can also find this substitution as an important sound in the changes of "If I Should Lose You."

Any time you see a II-V heading to Imaj7, you can try using this substitution if there is enough space to let it sound. Herbie Hancock uses this device in his improvisation all the time, creating a surprise at a place where your ear is expecting a resolution.

## WHAT HAPPENS IF WE BUILD A "CLOCKWORK" DIAGRAM WITH THE DIMINISHED SCALE?

If you've worked hard to this point to understand how the clockwork diagrams illustrate the functions of the chords in the major, melodic minor and harmonic minor scales, congratulations! You've laid a sound foundation by equipping yourself with the knowledge that will help you to become an intelligent improviser. Now we're going to dive a little deeper into the odd nature of the diminished scale, and we'll find that in some ways it is simpler to understand, and in other ways its symmetry creates new possibilities that you may be working on for decades…

Let's build a chord from each of the tones of a C diminished scale and see what happens.

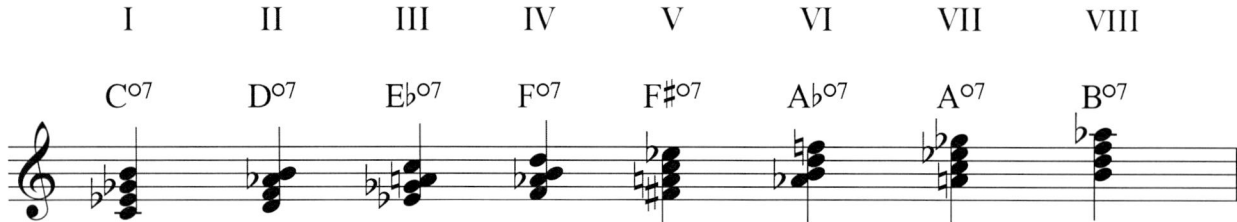

Okay, that's different.

## THING ONE

The first thing that stands out is that all of the chords are diminished 7ths. So now we're in a different zone than the functional harmony of the other three scales we've studied.

## THING TWO

Look at positions I, III, V and VII. The second thing that stands out is that the diminished chords that start on C, Eb, Gb and A each use the same four notes. The only difference is which note is the root.

That means that you'll play the same diminished scale on all four of those chords, Cdim7, Ebdim7, Gbdim7 and Adim7. As a way of confirming that for yourself, start on the note Eb, and proceed by playing a whole step, and then a half step, and so on. See how that gives you the same scale as the one that started on C? You get the idea, but do it again starting from Gb and A, and see what happens.

Remember how we had to learn the major and minor scales in all 12 keys? The diminished gives us a break. There are only three diminished scales to learn.

Here are all three diminished scales. Take a minute to get them under your fingers.

You can also grab a pencil and write in all the different diminished chords above each tone of the scales, so you have a good mental picture of them.

## THING THREE

Notice how those four chords, C, Eb, Gb and A are all a minor third apart. A minor third above C is what? Eb. The minor third of an Eb chord is Gb. And a minor third above Gb (or F#) is an A natural. If you're classically trained that will be a Bbb, or B double flat, but in jazz there's a tendency to simplify things because of the need for quick recognition while making things up on the fly, so you'll almost never see a double flat notated. Now, notice that the minor third of an A chord is C again—so it's a closed loop. That will come back to give us some ideas later on.

## THING FOUR

Here's a fourth thing to point out about the diminished scale: go back to the diminished clockwork and see how the first two chords are Cdim7 and Ddim7. Those two chords give you all eight notes of the scale. Every other chord in the diagram is an inversion of one of those two diminished chords.

Getting back to practical applications, here's an example, and an illustration of the thought process in finding something to play on a diminished chord. In the third bar of "Corcovado" there's an Abdim7 chord. Of the three diminished scales, the way to find the one that'll work best is to start on the root and play whole step half step. That'll give us this scale:

In the diminished clockwork we know that the first two positions in the scale are both diminished chords, so we could use that to generate a line.

Try playing this in the third and fourth bars of "Corcovado" and see how it sounds:

When the beboppers started exploring more complex harmony in the 1940's, they worked out a lot of their new ideas on the blues. If you've ever played Charlie Parker's blues head, "Now's the Time," you may remember the diminished chord in the 6th bar. Starting from the fifth bar of the form, instead of playing two bars of Bb7, Parker plays Bb7 in the fifth bar, and Bdim7 in the 6th bar. That has become a common move, and you can use your diminished scale there. Parker himself tends to end phrases in the 5th bar, often leaving the 6th bar empty, so there isn't a treasure trove to tap of him playing the diminished scale in this situation.

Some years later, though, Herbie Hancock gives us a beautiful example on Sonny Rollins' recording of "Now's the Time," from Rollins' record of the same name. I don't know why it's become a thing in this chapter, but once again, we're encountering a recording in a different key than the original. Rollins chose to record "Now's the Time" in Eb. That means the 5th bar will be an Ab7, with Adim7 coming in the 6th bar. Here's what Herbie plays in his second chorus. (At around 2:04 in the track)

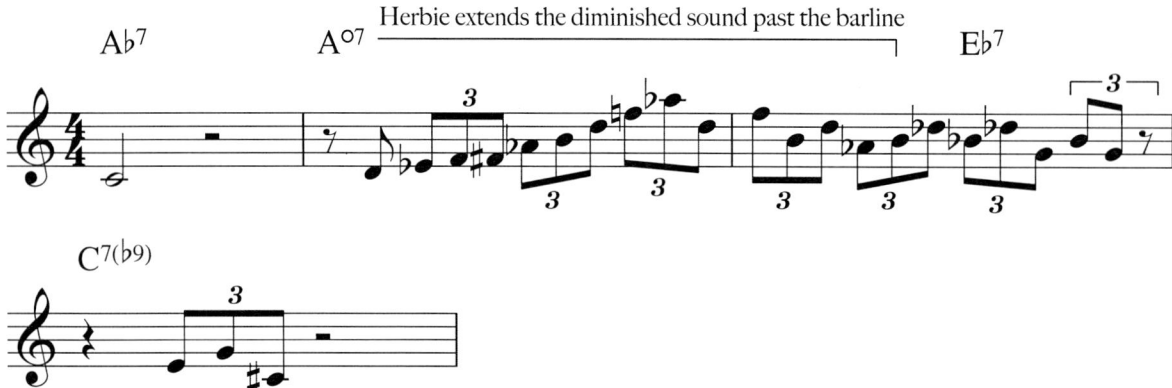

Herbie's delivery of the diminished scale in triplets is particularly attractive.

Sonny Stitt mastered the diminished sound, using it in a variety of places. Before we get into the use of the diminished scale on dominant 7th chords, let's listen to one more example on a diminished chord. Stitt uses the 6th bar substitution in his first chorus of "Au Privave," on the recording he made with Oscar Peterson, *Sonny Stitt Sits in with the Oscar Peterson Trio*:

Like Dexter Gordon did on "Wave," Stitt starts the diminished sound before he enters the bar of Bdim7. This creates some tension on the Bb7, while telegraphing to the pianist that he is planning to use the Bdim7 substitution in the 6th bar. It's a solid bit of musical communication.

We could use Stitt's line for inspiration, extending it all the way through the Bdim7 in the sixth bar of the form, like so:

Try using that line as a template to inspire some more lines of your own.

## PLAYING THE DIMINISHED SCALE ON DOMINANT 7TH CHORDS

Now it's time to get a little creative with our analysis of the diminished scale. Up to now, we've used the clockwork to show us how chords appear in a scale by building the chords from every other note in the scale. Because of its symmetry, the diminished scale behaves a little differently, as we've seen. So we're going to be a little cavalier and explore some things that don't look strictly logical, but work, nevertheless.

Here's the C diminished scale again, with some different notes emphasized:

If we stack up those emphasized notes, what do we get?

That means we can use the diminished scale on a D7 chord. Notice that the next note in the scale after D is Eb, which is a half step from the root of the D7. So the shortcut to remember which diminished scale works on a dominant 7th is: from the root proceed half step, whole step.

Here's the scale written out in the context of a D7 chord, with the tensions indicated above.

Notice how there are now three tensions: b9, #9 and #11.

Let's get some voicings ringing on the piano, so we can hear what the diminished scale sounds like as it travels through a dominant 7th chord. The clearest indication that the diminished scale will work best on a dominant is when it is spelled with a natural 13 and a b9, like this: D13(b9).

Here is a basic voicing and a more complex voicing for dominants that are appropriate for the use of the diminished scale:

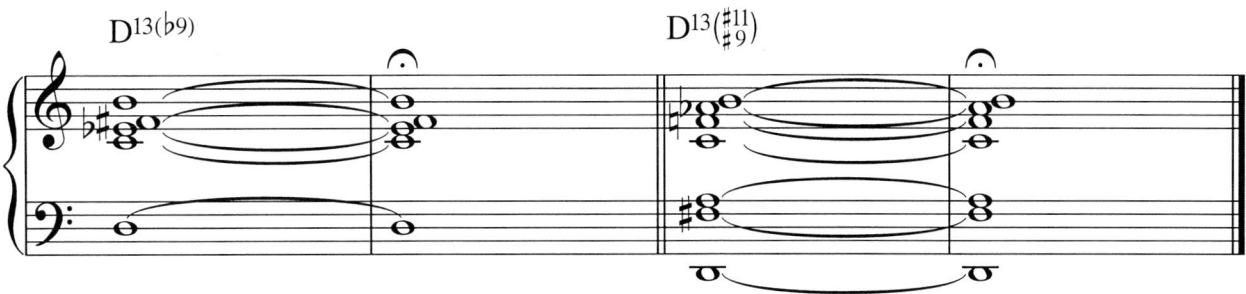

Try playing the scale through the chord, with it ringing at the piano, and get used to the sound of it for a while. Try also playing a simpler D13 chord, without the b9. See if the scale still travels smoothly through it. It should. Then go the opposite direction and try playing a G major scale against the D13(#9#11) voicing. You'll probably find that that one sounds more "clashy." This is to reiterate the point—if the piano voicing has very little tension, there is more room for adding tension with your choice of scale sound. The more tension the pianist uses in the voicing, the more it works better to choose the scale that incorporates all of the tension notes included in the voicing. In this case, the only scale that contains the #9, #11 and the natural 13 is the diminished scale.

Another characteristic unique to the diminished scale is that, because it is an eight-note symmetrical scale, it will land on the same note you started on, an octave away, if you play the scale straight through a bar.

Here it is starting on the root of a D13(b9) chord, and landing on the same note, D, an octave lower, which is the 5th of a Gmaj7 chord:

And here it is starting on the 13, the note B, and landing on the same note, B, which is the 3rd of Gmaj7:

In the same way we did over a diminished chord, we are lining up the whole steps with the downbeats and the half steps with the upbeats.

If we start a line on the 3rd of the D13(b9) chord, the note F#, then it works better to play a quarter note first, so that we can get everything flowing smoothly after that, like so:

WS = Whole Step
HS = Half Step

But notice that if we keep going we'll land on the note Ab on the first beat of the Gmaj7 chord, which will sound like a clunker if we don't resolve it well.  One solution would be to skip a couple of notes and land on the note F#, which will provide a bit of a surprise, and a resolution at the same time.  This is something that Tom Harrell does masterfully, which makes for satisfying phrase endings.

And another way we can address the situation is to use the sound of the scale to extend our line past the barline, and resolve it two beats later.  Get a pianist or guitarist to work on this with you, and have them play the Gmaj7 on the first beat, while you extend the tension for two beats.  Check out how it feels to resolve the tension two beats late.

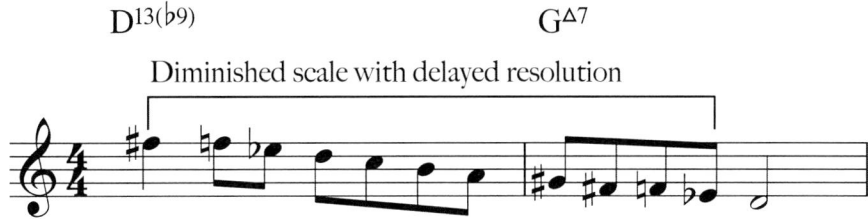

Try finding some other diminished lines that land you on a note that is wrong for Gmaj7, but resolve later.

The symmetry of the half steps and whole steps in the diminished scale helps the ear to follow what's happening when you extend the tension by playing past a barline, or when you anticipate a barline by starting the sound early.  Take your time working on this.  If you can develop your ability to see yourself playing past a barline without losing your place in the form or turning the beat around, it will deepen your awareness of form generally.

This is a next-level skill—earlier in the book we learned how to play precisely over the barline as one chord moves to another.  If you mastered that skill, now you can take that precise resolution and move it around.  Say, for example, you have a II-V-I in G over four bars.  You could anticipate the arrival of the D7 chord with the diminished scale and play it past the next barline into the Gmaj7 chord, creating the illusion that the bar with the dominant chord has been expanded like the folds of an accordion.

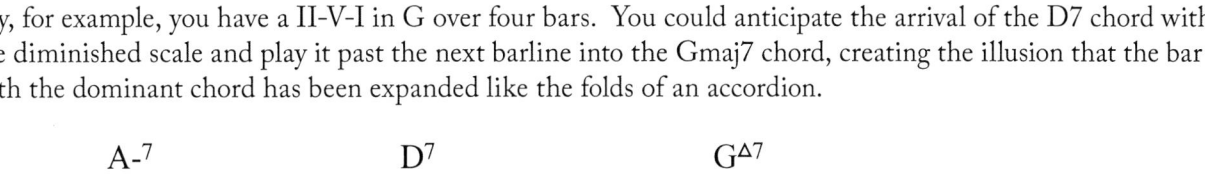

Now you're improvising with the barlines a la Keith Jarrett on "All the Things You Are."

One more thing before we observe this animal in it's natural habitat—remember how we could play the same diminished scale on four different diminished chords because they were a minor third apart? The same is true for dominants. So we should be able to play the same diminished scale on a D13(b9) chord as we do for the dominant chord that is a minor third above it, right? A minor third up from D is F. Try starting a diminished scale on the note F, proceeding half step whole step. Do you get the same diminished scale that you played on the D13(b9) chord?

You'll be able to play the same diminished scale on each of the four dominant 7th chords you can build from the scale:

Ok, let's listen to some players using the diminished scale in context. As always, don't stop at reading through these examples, and don't stop at listening to them while you read them. Listen a couple of times and then play along with the pros, transposing for your instrument. That way you can get to know how they feel, and begin to imprint the sound in your internal voice's memory banks.

Let's listen first to Tom Harrell using the scale in a way that sounds melodic. This is from the opening track, "Barbara," from one of Horace Silver's all-time great recordings, *Silver 'n Brass*. Here's Tom's opening statement on a Bb13(b9) chord, at around 1:25 in the track:

And at 2:04 in the same track, Harrell plays this over the Ab13(b9) chord:

Sonny Stitt uses the diminished scale in a beautiful idea on a ballad, "Ghost of a Chance," from a record he made with Barry Harris called *Constellation*. Here's the improvised line he played in the first ending of his statement of the melody, at around 0:30 in the track. He's actually triple-timing:

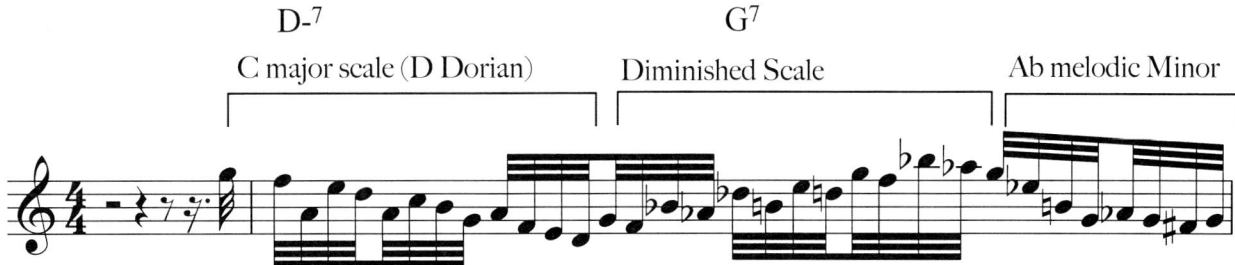

That may look a little intimidating, but by now nothing scares you, so let's unpack that a bit. I've put the G7 at the halfway point in the bar to illustrate how Stitt anticipates the arrival of that chord by starting the diminished line early. Also, we haven't talked about why Stitt is using an Ab melodic minor scale for the last beat of the bar. We'll get to that in the next chapter.

Let's take that line and play it as a double time line on "Take the 'A' Train."

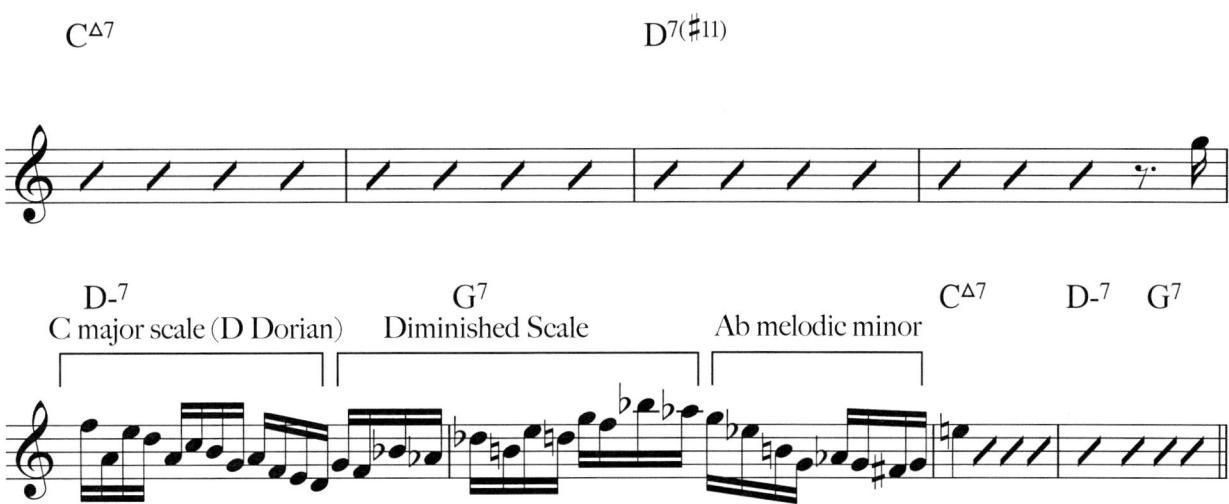

To pull that off, you'll want to play "Take the 'A' Train" at a slower tempo than the original. Try it at around 110 bpm and see if you can manage it. Then see if you can play it not like a quote, but as if it's your own idea, and keep going into the next bar of C major. Then you can start changing some notes and making it more your own…

Let's expand that one more time, and make it into an eighth note line. We'll need a tune with a four bar long space of C major. The A section of "My Shining Hour" should work nicely. Let's use that to experiment a bit. Since Sonny Stitt's idea begins on tones that line up with D-7, let's make up a line that matches Cmaj7 in front of it, and then start our Stitt phrase in the second bar. Play it a handful of times. You can pull up John Coltrane's version of "My Shining Hour" (from *Coltrane Jazz*), which feels great at a bouncing medium tempo, and play along with the track, trying out this idea at the top of a chorus.

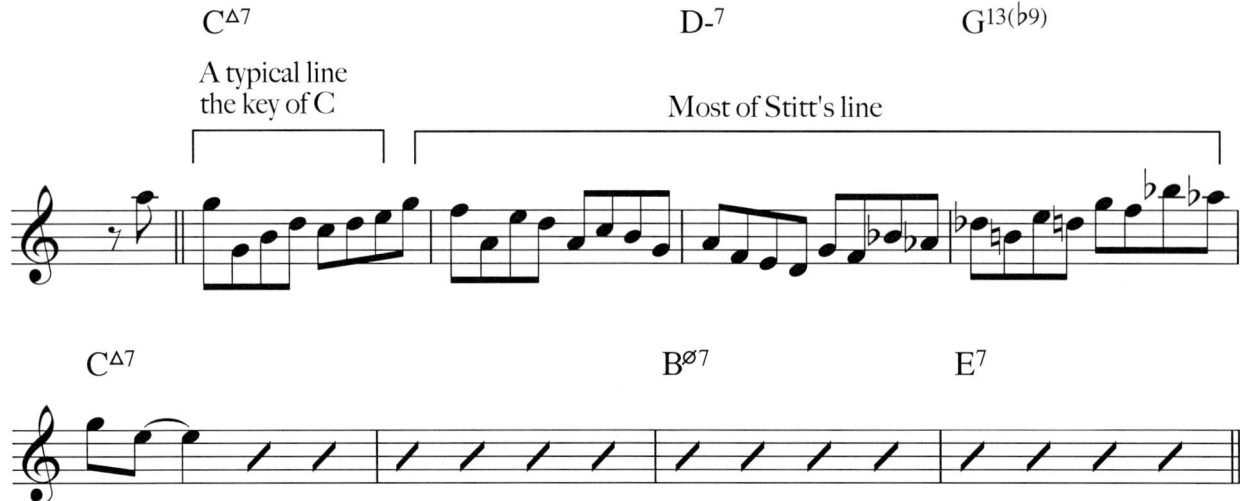

Speaking of Coltrane, he played one of the most famous and frequently copied diminished ideas of all time on "Moment's Notice," from *Blue Train*. Here's what he plays over the Bb pedal at the end of his second chorus:

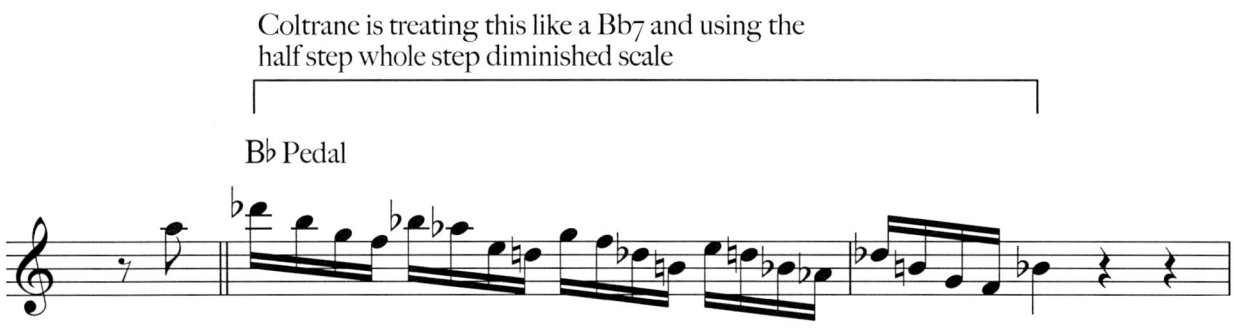

In the space of a few pages we've gone from Tom Harrell playing a laid back melody using the diminished scale, through Stitt triple-timing in thirds on a ballad, to Coltrane delivering a virtuosic pattern over a pedal—which brings us to a good subject for:

## A SHORT ASIDE: SHOULD I PLAY PATTERNS?

My answer: Go for it!

My follow up question: Are you going to play the pattern the same way every time?

There is absolutely no reason not to use patterns, and the diminished scale is a source for all kinds of interesting ones. The thing to watch out for, though, is whether it sounds like you're repeating something you rehearsed, which can pull you out of the moment and sound stiff. Just like in a conversation, you want the content to be related to the moment at hand.

If you have a regular gig once a week at a club with a house band, so the members of the group are the same every week, you wouldn't greet everyone with the exact same set of questions every time you saw them, would you? You'd become predictable and monotonous if you said the same things the same way every week.

Herbie Hancock is a prime example of someone who has mastered the materials of his craft to the point where he is able to improvise effortlessly with them in real time. As a result, something that could be merely a display of craft or technique in lesser hands, is transformed into art, right before your ears.

The following are two examples from Herbie's solo on, "Oliloqui Valley," the opening track of his recording, *Empyrean Isles*. At around 1:08 in the track, Herbie starts a pattern using the F melodic minor scale and transforms it seamlessly into the diminished scale along the way:

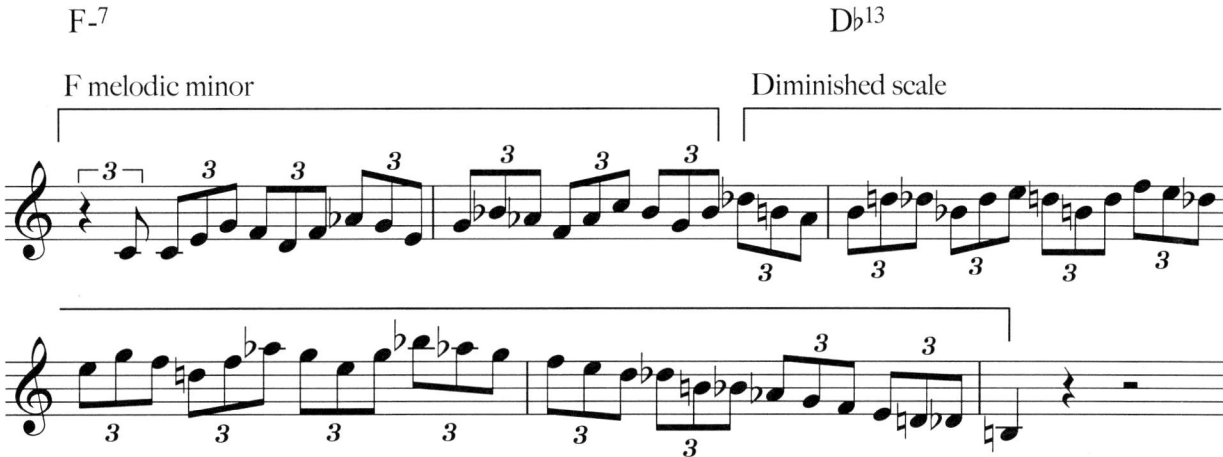

And here's Herbie using a pattern, but improvising with the rhythm, so that your ear can sense the pattern, but is constantly surprised along the way. He plays this at around 1:27, over the same harmony:

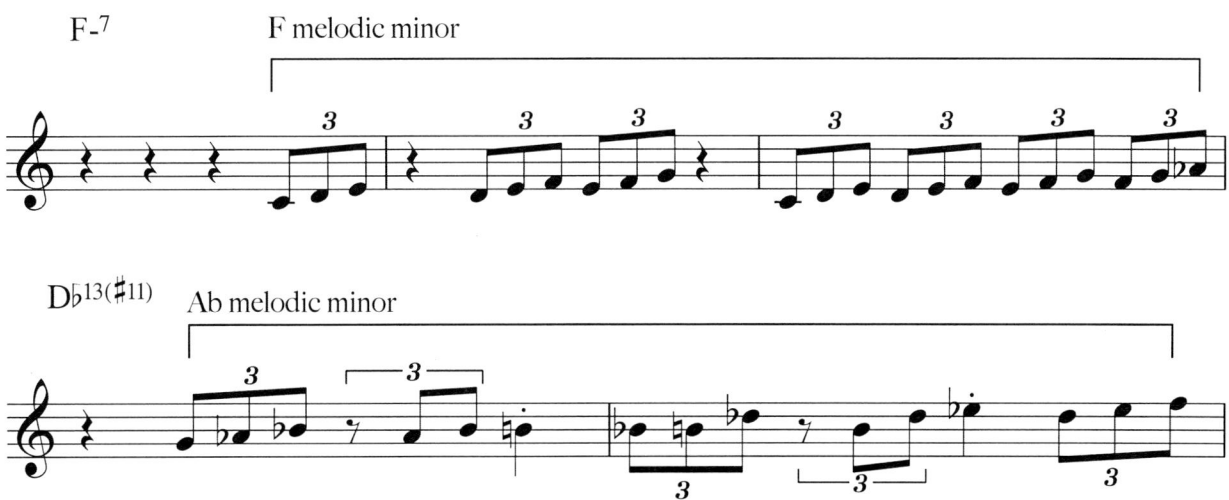

Notice how Herbie is not only tinkering with the rhythm of the pattern, but is also improvising with the quality of the Db13 chord from chorus to chorus. The first time through the form he uses the diminished scale, and in the second chorus he changes it up and goes with melodic minor. That's the mind of a master at work.

## WRAPPING UP THE DIMINISHED SCALE (FOR NOW)

That should give you a start on working the diminished scale into your vocabulary…!
There are some more avenues for exploration—here we've focused mainly on the uses of the diminished scale over functional harmony. In Chapter 19 we'll seek out some more ways to mine the diminished scale for ideas.

For now, here are:

## SOME THINGS TO PRACTICE

1. Get the three diminished scales under your fingers.

2. Sit at the piano and play the scales, using the whole step, half step pattern over diminished 7th chords.

3. Do the same over dominant 13(b9) chords, using the half step, whole step approach. Notice that the same scale works over all four dominants that are a minor 3rd apart. Prove this to your ears by playing the chords at the piano and blowing through them, and then try playing the diminished scale in some II-V-I situations in standards.

4. Pay attention to lining up the scale with the beat—whole steps on downbeats, half steps on upbeats.

5. Find some different ways to play the pattern Coltrane used on "Moment's Notice," for example:

6. Find more patterns of your own, and work on improvising with them so that you can play them differently each time.

7. See if you can play the diminished scale in a melodic way, like Tom Harrell showed us.

8. See if you can keep exploring the diminished scale for forty years.

# CHAPTER 17 · TRITONE SUBSTITUTIONS

When I first asked a musician what he meant by the term "tritone substitution" I got a quick and cursory explanation that didn't help much. That basically went,

"Oh, that means that you can replace a dominant 7th chord with the dominant 7th which is a tritone away."

I actually had enough knowledge to understand how it worked at the time, but the knowledge I had was like individual puzzle pieces that hadn't been put together to make a coherent picture yet. I had the pieces, but didn't know how they fit. My hope here is to save you the time it took me to figure something out that remained vague in my mind for some time. If you are coming straight to this chapter in the book rather than proceeding in order, it would be worth your while to read and play through the chapter on the melodic minor scale as preparation. If you are proceeding in order, it wouldn't hurt to have a quick re-read of the melodic minor chapter. Having the melodic minor clockwork diagram fresh in your mind will help to absorb the information here.

Let's take a different tack this chapter. Since the explanation takes a little while to get through, let's get the sound in our ears before diving into the grammar of the tritone substitution. Here are some examples of masters using the tritone substitution sound through some dominant 7th chords:

Remember the beautiful melodic minor line Hank Mobley played in the bridge of his second chorus of "The Best Things in Life Are Free?" Here's what he played right after that, at around 1:57 in the track:

And here he is in a different key, using the same scale sound on "Ceora," from Lee Morgan's recording, *Cornbread*. This is his second to last phrase, at about 3:56 in the track:

And now that you have "Ceora," cued up, listen to Herbie Hancock's exquisite solo. An entire book could be written about everything he does in that solo, but our purpose at the moment is to concentrate on what he plays in the last 8 bars. Listen to the sounds he uses over the dominant chords F7 and Eb7 in the III-VI-II-V-I progression starting in bar 27 of the form. Bar 27 starts at about 4:52 in the track.

Here are the changes:

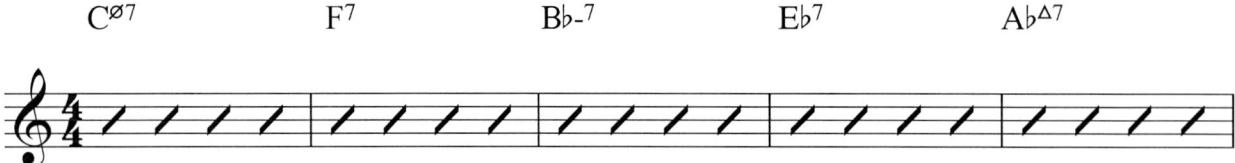

See if you can learn to play the lines he plays through that section.

If you've done that, and learned to play those two lines from Hank Mobley, you now have a couple of licks. As we've discussed before, the criticism of "lick players" is that they play a lick exactly the same way every time. You can do two things to head that criticism off at the pass:

- Challenge yourself to improvise with the licks you've just learned. Tinker with them. Move them around. Add and subtract notes and see how it makes a difference. Try playing them on different beats.
- Herbie Hancock describes himself as a tinkerer. People like Herbie who are curious and persistent wind up becoming inventors…

And

- Learn the underlying grammar of the lick—see if you can figure out which scale it comes from. If you've gotten familiar with the available scales and recognize which one your lick fits into, you can make up your own licks using that sound.

Take your time working on this chapter. There are a few important building blocks here, and it helps to get them in place one at a time, so your foundation is strong.

Let's break it down. First of all, what is a tritone?

A tritone is the interval you get when you divide an octave in half.

There are twelve half steps in an octave. If you count six half steps up from C, you'll land at the note F#.

And if you keep going, the sixth half step counting from F# will land you on the next C, one octave higher.

If you're not already sitting at the piano, let's get to it! We just learned how a tritone comes to be, but primarily our interest is in how one *sounds*. With the sustain pedal down, play the interval formed by C and F#. Find that on your horn.

If you remember Joe Henderson's composition, "Inner Urge," from Chapter 4, the first two notes of bar 5, F and B, are a tritone:

Two other songs people use to remember the sound of a tritone are "Maria," from *West Side Story*, and the melody from "The Simpsons."

Since there are 12 notes, and tritones come in pairs, there will be six pairs, right? I'll leave it to you to find the rest of them. While you're working on that, you might also take note of the fact that there are two more ways to find a tritone.

- One is to go up three whole steps. One whole step from C is D, from D is E, and from E is F#. There it is: three whole steps make a tritone.

- The other is to go up two minor thirds. The minor third of C is Eb, and the minor third of Eb is Gb (F#). Voila.

One more shortcut:

- A tritone is the same as a flatted fifth. The fifth of C is G. Flat the G and you get a Gb (enharmonically an F#).

## A SHORT ASIDE ON ENHARMONIC SPELLINGS IN JAZZ

This is a heads up to point out that jazz musicians tend to value clear, concise naming and shortcuts over precise adherence to the strict laws of harmonic spelling. The main reason being that they have to make lots of split-second decisions in real time, and anything that looks confusing on the page can cause a hiccup in the flow of the music. A few situations where you might see a difference to a classical approach:

- Oftentimes it makes more sense to write a jazz composition with no key signature, especially if the tune moves through multiple key centers. The goal is to make it easy to read by reducing potentially confusing accidentals. If, for example, you write a tune in the key of Eb, but have multiple bars with an F#-9 chord in them, the G#, which is the 9 of the F#-9 will appear in the key signature as an Ab. But an experienced improviser might see the note A in a bar with an F#-9 chord above it, and naturally interpret that note as the minor third of the chord, causing a disconnect in his mind. To avoid cases like this it often makes more sense to have no key signature, and let the A natural be an A natural, and write the 9 of the chord as a G#.

- When writing parts for pianists and bassists, if you have both chord symbols above the bar and notes within it, take care that the chord symbols and notes are in enharmonic agreement. I got scolded by a bassist for writing the note C# in a bar that had the chord symbol Db7 above it. He didn't take me to task saying, "This note is technically a Db, not a C# in this key." What he said was, "My eyes are telling me C# but the chord says Db7, so the disconnect caused me to stumble over that spot."

- If a piece is written in the key of Gb, the note B natural will be spelled as a Cb, which is correct, because the Gb major scale proceeds: Gb, Ab, Bb, Cb. But in jazz, the key of Gb is relatively uncommon to find as a key signature, and the spelling Cb is generally avoided. The aim is to reduce the hesitation that might be caused by the appearance of a relatively rare Cb. To that end, Cb is usually spelled B natural by jazz composers. B#'s, Fb's and E#'s likewise are generally avoided around jazz musicians.

- As in many other areas of jazz, someone will definitely object to the above and say that strict adherence to the key signature is absolutely the way to go. I'm not saying they're wrong, just reporting what appears to be the norm.

- There's a good argument for spelling the note A# in a bar where the chord is an F#7 chord, for example, even if the chord isn't indicated above the bar, as a clue to the player about what's going on around him. However, in a jazz context there could easily be an F7 in that same bar, and writing A# at the beginning of a bar, and Bb later in the bar is another thing to avoid, so you don't create that momentary confusion. It's a bit of a judgment call, with legibility and clarity being the primary goals.

- Why are legibility and clarity important? In a rehearsal context, if the music is spelled consistently and laid out clearly, you won't have to waste time correcting notes, or answering questions about the road map—you can use the time to refine how the music sounds. In a professional gig context, you might be asked to play something for the first time in front of an audience. Imagine the difference between experiencing that situation with a clear chart, versus having to sight-read something that is illegible or illogical.

---

Back to exploring the tritone:

Let's dig into why two dominant chords a tritone apart can be substituted for each other. Remember our simple piano exercise from Chapter 5? We learned that the root, 3rd and 7th were the essential notes needed to convey the type of chord we are playing. Let's play a simple root position voicing for a C7 chord.

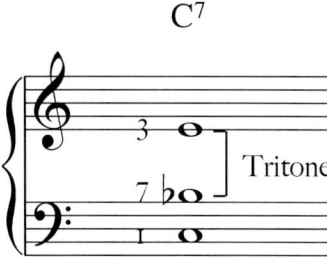

See how the interval between the 7th and the 3rd (Bb and E) forms a tritone within the structure of the chord? The tritone that appears between the 3rd and the 7th of a dominant 7th chord is what gives dominant chords their particular character and sound.

Now simply change the root to an F#.

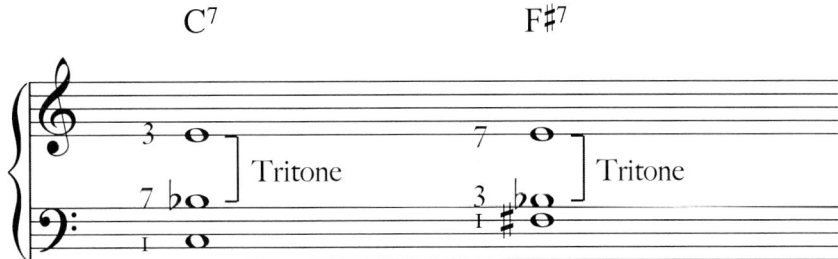

See how the 3rd of the C7 becomes the 7th of the F#7, and the 7th of the C7 becomes the 3rd of the F#7? The fact that the 3rds and 7ths interchange exactly, without altering the quality of the chord, is what makes the two chords work as substitutes for one another. You can change the root, but the new chord is still a dominant 7th.

(I've left the Bb spelled as a Bb to emphasize visually the fact that the note didn't change, though to be consistent theoretically, we should call the third of an F#7 an A#.)

Now that we know that C7's and F#7's are interchangeable because the 7ths and 3rds just flip over, let's see what happens in practice.

A regular II-V-I in F looks like this:

And if we substitute F#7 for C7, it looks like this:

See how the progression moves downward in half steps? It gives us a smooth linear harmonic motion with some heightened tension and release. Let's try playing both versions at the piano, starting with the normal II-V-I in F.

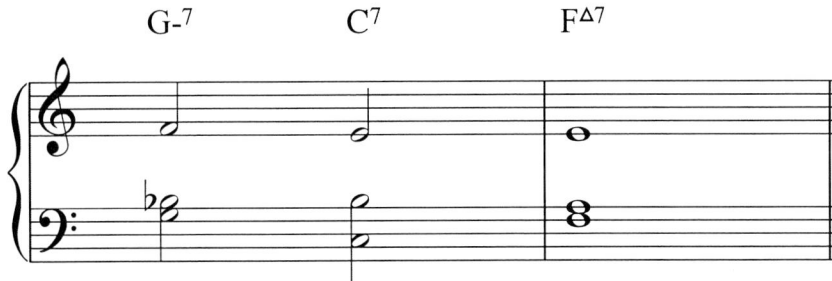

Becomes:

Staying with simple voicings, you could also play it like this:

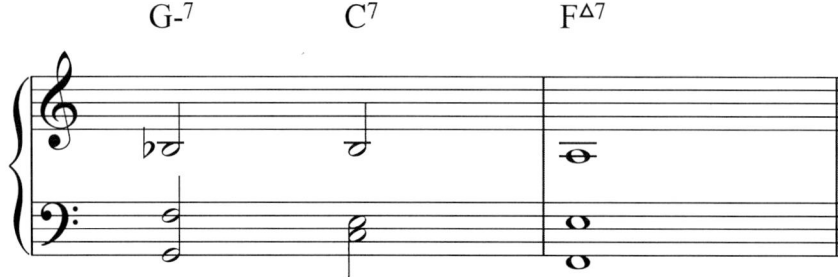

Becomes:

Now it's time to apply some of the knowledge of functional harmony we've already acquired. Much of the time, when we see dominant 7th chords, they are moving in V-I progressions. What about when a dominant is not moving in a V-I progression?

Think back to the melodic minor clockwork diagram. Remember that a dominant 7th chord appears in the 4th position of a melodic minor scale?

We discovered that, when a dominant is not moving in a V-I progression, we can think of it as a IV in melodic minor, which gives us a good sounding scale choice.

In the example above, we substituted an F#7 for a C7 chord. Now we have an F#7 that is not resolving as a V to a I, correct? To test yourself—in what major key would an F#7 function as a V resolving to I?

B major.

For an F#7 chord that is not moving in a V-I progression, ask yourself:

In which scale would I find an F#7 chord in the IV position?

Melodic minor is your answer, then you just need to figure out which one.

C# melodic minor has an F#7 chord in the IV position, so the C# melodic minor scale will sound good and travel smoothly through an F#7 that is *not* in a V-I progression.

If you're feeling confused, or didn't follow that process all the way through, go back and read it again, going slowly, and make sure you understand each step before you move on to the next.

Here it is boiled down into bullet points:

- C7 moving V-I
- For lots of tension, substitute F#7
- F#7 is not moving as V-I, so melodic minor as a IV, thus
- C# melodic minor

Try playing these chord progressions at the piano. The first is straight, with no added tensions, and the second is more complex. If you have a recording device handy, play them a few times, make a loop, and practice some lines over them.

Here are a few lines to test out how C# melodic minor sounds over an F#7(#11) chord moving toward Fmaj7.

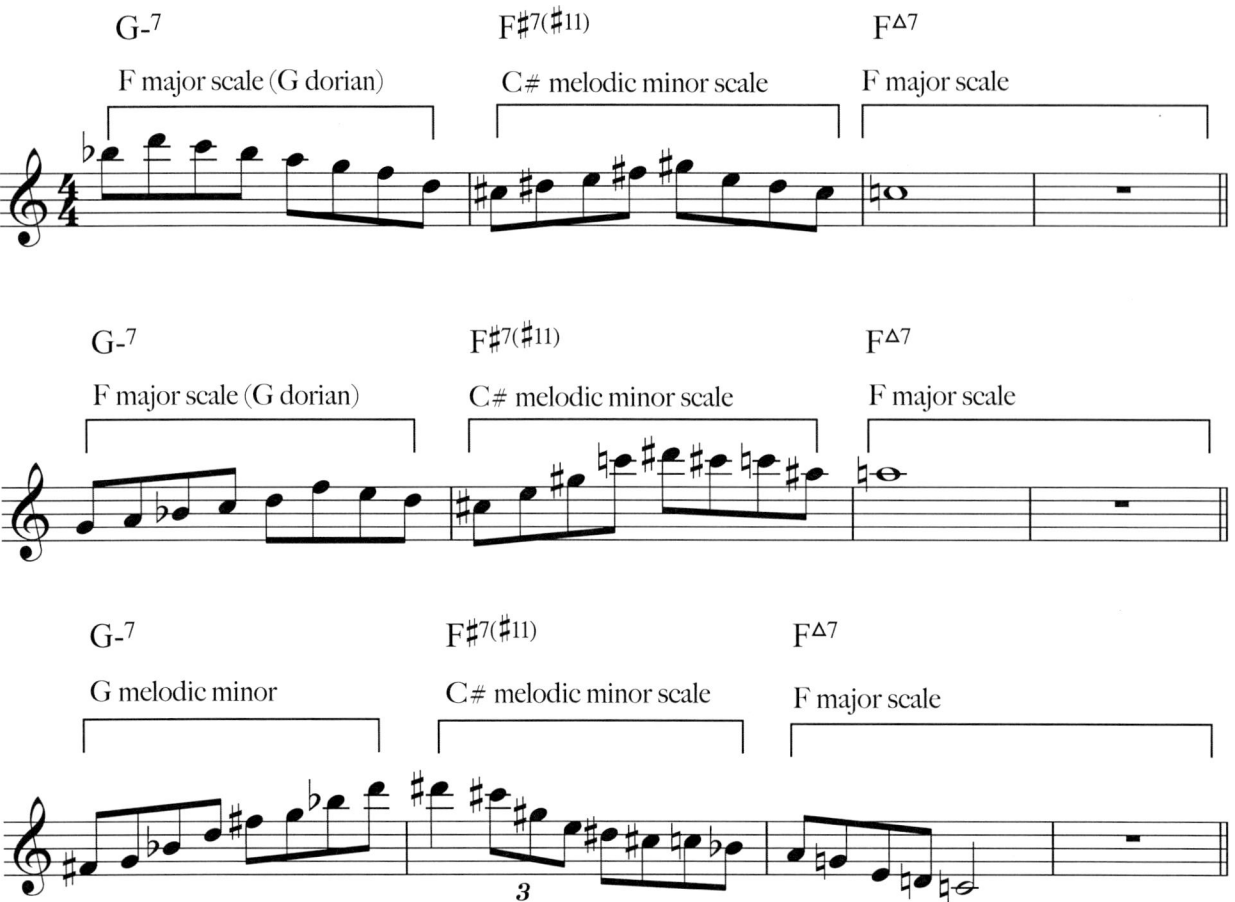

Try those lines out a few times over tunes with a II-V-I to F major, and then try transposing them to another key or two, so you get a feel for the way the harmony works more broadly. Personally, I prefer to take a more long-term approach to playing things in different keys. Some people like to take a new piece of information and immediately transpose it into all 12 keys. I find that that begins to feel like work, and I can lose the momentum of adding something to my improvising right away. My preference is to try something new in one or two other keys, keeping it fun, and trying immediately to tinker with it and get a feel for how it behaves. If you're the type who prefers to be thorough, and work things in all 12 keys, go for it. Just remember to improvise. Don't stop at simple repetition.

Now, the final step in this explanation.

If you decide to substitute an F#7 for a C7 as you blow through a II-V in the key of F, what happens if the rhythm section doesn't adjust and just plays a C7?

Since the C7 and F#7 are interchangeable, you won't have a clash, but you'll create lots of tension on that C7. A good piano player will hear that you're putting pressure on the C7 and can adjust the voicing to support the harmony you're playing in real time, but even if he doesn't, and you both keep moving and meet at the Fmaj7 chord, the feeling of tension and release will be satisfying if you execute well.

The thought process can feel a little convoluted.  Here are our bullet points again:

- C7 moving V-I
- For lots of tension, substitute F#7
- F#7 is not moving to I, so melodic minor as a IV, thus
- C# melodic minor

As a shortcut, you can simply think:

- C7—I want a smooth line with lots of tension
- Melodic minor a half step up from the root, thus
- C# melodic minor

The reason we're at pains to understand the underlying harmony is to build sensitivity to the different levels of tension that are created by the scale sounds we choose to play.  In this case, you wind up playing a C# melodic minor scale through a C7 chord, which is the most tension we've applied to a dominant 7th chord so far.

If the piano player recognizes the sound you are going for and wants to respond in real time, she will choose to voice a C7 which includes the #9.  Here are some piano voicings with some different spellings you may encounter, all of which will accommodate the melodic minor half step up sound:

If you have access to a piano, take a minute to play the C7 voicings with the sustain pedal on, and blow through the C# melodic minor scale to get a feel for how it interacts with the chord. You can alternate C7alt chords with F#7(#11) chords as well. Here's the same line analyzed against an F#7 and against a C7:

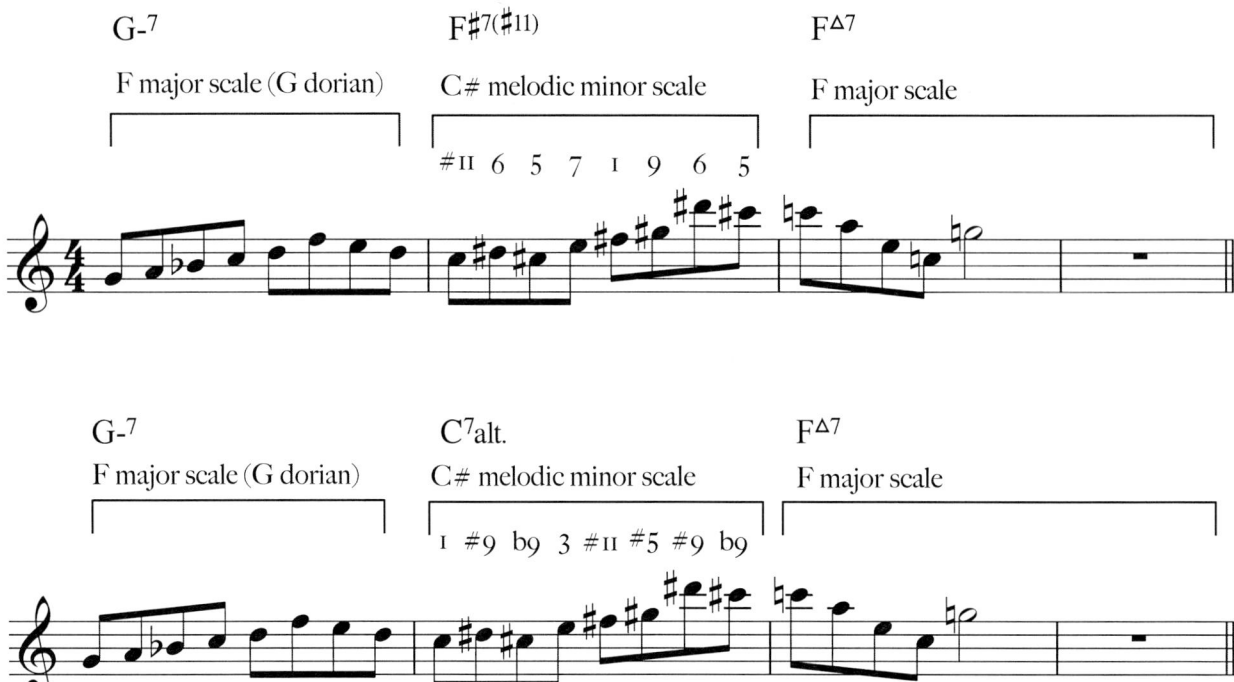

Look at the C# melodic minor line over the C7alt. The point we've been driving toward this whole chapter is the fact that that line contains 4 tensions on a dominant 7th chord. The b9, #9, #5 and #11 are all represented, and notice that the three remaining notes that are not altered are the 1, the 3 and the 7. Another way to say that is that the C# melodic minor scale gives us a smooth line traveling through a C7alt chord, using the three key notes—root, 3rd and 7th, and all four tension notes.

In practice, you may hear people talking about the "altered scale," the "super locrian" and the "diminished whole tone" scale. These are all names for what we are calling 'melodic minor half step up" here.

Let's get off the page and re-engage with the tradition for some illustrations of how people use this harmonic concept. We can revisit one of the most quoted melodies in jazz, the first phrase of "Cry Me a River," Arthur Hamilton's unusual take on a love song. (Check out the lyrics for a biting comeback from a broken heart.)

To get you thinking and hearing in a different key, let's look at the first phrase in E minor, Julie London's key from the first recording.

If you listen for it, you'll hear musicians quote this melody in a variety of ways, and over a variety of chords.

Our subject here is the melodic minor half step up, and jazz musicians love to quote "Cry Me a River" on altered dominants. If the original melody is in E minor, and assuming the melody will fit into an E melodic minor scale, which it does, where can we use it? Or, which dominant 7th chord is E melodic minor a half step above the root?

Eb7(#9) is the chord we're looking for. Try sustaining an Eb7(#9) chord at the piano and playing the first phrase of "Cry Me a River" over it.

And now you can use the scale to continue the line and resolve it into an Abmaj7 chord.

You can find examples of the use of "Cry Me a River" all over the jazz tradition. Here are a few other ways you might hear it:

Rather than transcribing examples here as we've done in other chapters, I'm going to send you on a treasure hunt. Some of Bob Berg's most inspired playing is preserved for eternity on Cedar Walton's deeply swinging recording, *Eastern Rebellion II*. You can find "Cry Me a River" quotes in Berg's solos on:

- "Fantasy in D"
- "The Maestro"
- "Sunday Suite"

See if you can find them. That should give your ears a good workout.

# A SHORT ASIDE ON RATCHETING UP TENSION, ONE STEP AT A TIME

This might be a good time to review the way in which you can increase the pressure on a dominant 7th chord by adding tension. Let's look at a C7 chord, adding one tension note at a time.

- A straight C7 chord with no tensions is fundamentally a V in the key of F major

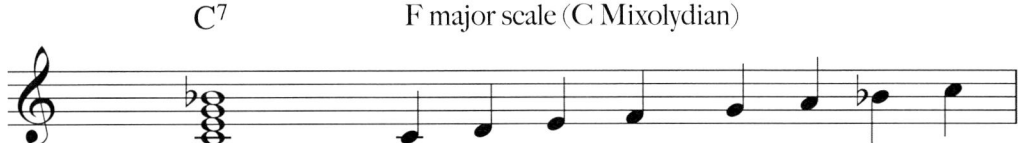

- C7(#11) has one note outside the key of F. The G melodic minor scale is a good choice on a dominant 7 that is not functioning as a V.

- The F harmonic minor scale works well through a C7 spelled with the #5 and the b9—two tensions

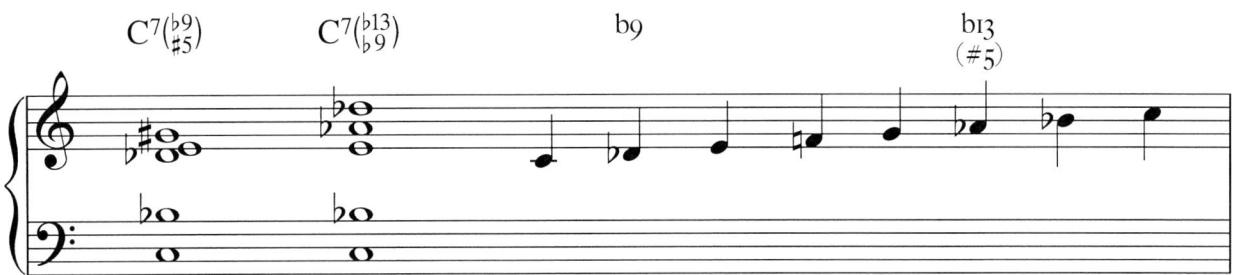

- A chord symbol indicating the natural 13 and the b9 calls for the diminished scale. In the case of a dominant 7th, the diminished pattern goes half step whole step

- If you see C7(#9), C7alt, or C7(#5#9), the melodic minor half step up shortcut will get you to C# melodic minor, which encompasses all four tension notes, and the critical root, 3rd and 7th.

Remember, if the piano player is playing a chord with no tension, you can choose to add as much as you want with your line, and it will work, as long as you resolve it skillfully across the barline into the next chord. On the other hand, the more tension the pianist or guitarist adds to the chord, the more it sounds better if you can hear it and choose the sound that goes with the type of tension they are adding to the chord.

That's why it's worth being familiar with each of these sounds, and spending time finding lines and melodies with the scales that match them. The voicings here are all in root position, which are useful for sounding the chords when you're practicing on your own. In a live situation, a pianist will more often leave out the root, since the bassist has the role of sounding the bottom of the chord. It's worth asking a piano player to show you how he might voice some of these different sounds in a playing situation. That question could lead to a discussion about how the pianist thinks, which could deepen your approach to playing, and your relationship with the piano player as well.

---

## TYING OFF A LOOSE END FROM CHAPTER 10

I promised in Chapter 10 that we would look here at one more usage of the melodic minor scale. Although this is not related to tritone substitutions, in keeping with trying to address harmony in a practical way, I chose to wait until now to add this so that we could take the time to build up a level of comfort with approaching chords from more than one direction. The situation we will address here is using the melodic minor scale through a half-diminished chord.

## THE HALF-DIMINISHED CHORD AS A VI IN MELODIC MINOR

So far we know that a half-diminished chord appears in the seventh position of a major scale, and in the second position of the harmonic minor scale. In my experience, using a major scale on a half-diminished chord is relatively rare, but worth having as an option.

We've encountered half-diminished chords most frequently in the context of a II-V-I resolving to a minor 7th chord, like the following example:

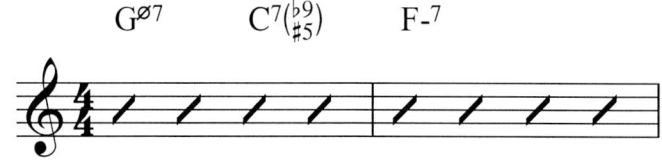

We know that the F harmonic minor scale contains both the Gmin7(b5) chord and the C7, so we have been playing the F harmonic minor through that progression, which gets us a smooth line like this to the F-7:

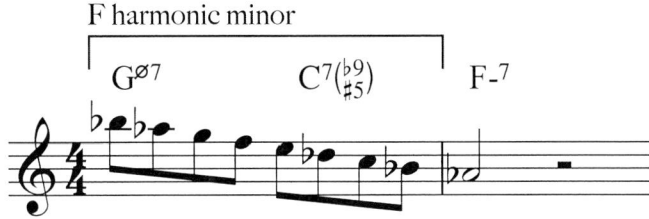

In a situation where you have a little more space to work with, like on "What Is This Thing Called Love," or "Woody 'N You," you can try the melodic minor on the half-diminished chord.

To refresh your memory, here's the melodic minor "Clockwork." It is transposed to the key of Bb, for the sake of visual clarity for the following examples.

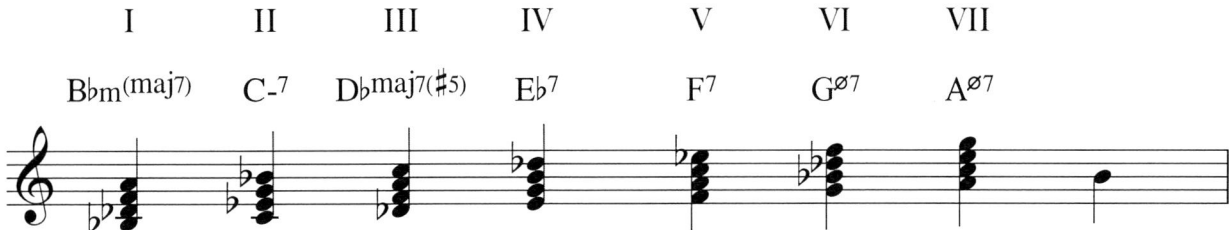

Notice the G half-diminished chord in the sixth position. That means we can play a Bb melodic minor scale through a G half-diminished chord, right?

Play the voicings at the piano, and try it out:

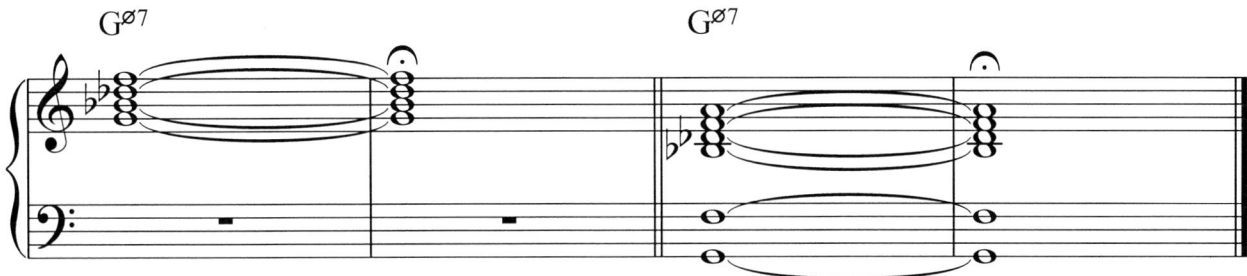

The thing to pay particular attention to is the note at the top of the second voicing, the A natural. That is the natural 9 on a half-diminished chord, which is a particularly attractive sounding note. Here are a couple of lines you can play to get a feel for this sound. Try working them out with a play-along of "What Is This Thing Called Love," or Woody 'N You."

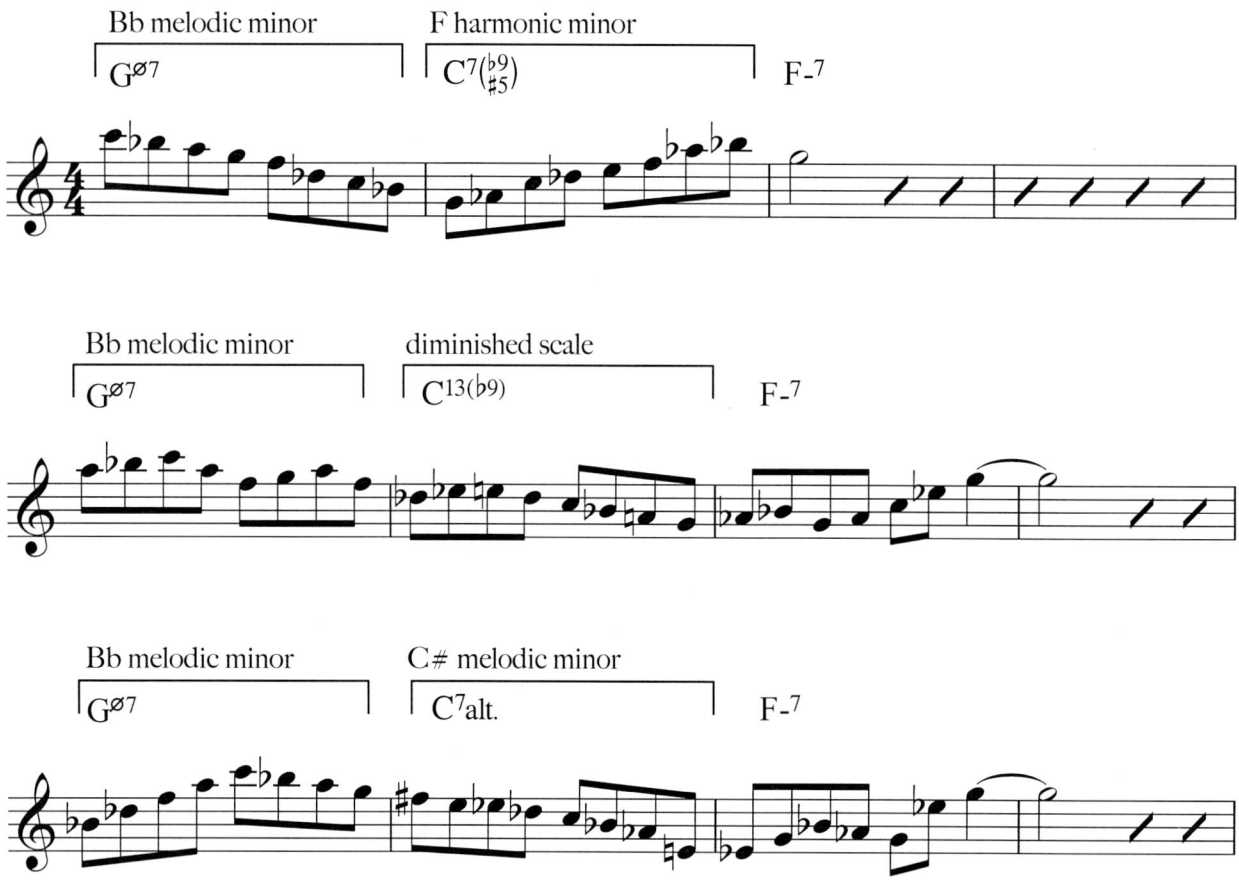

And just to bring it home for the chapter, here is a phrase using "Cry Me A River" to illustrate the use of two melodic minor scales working together:

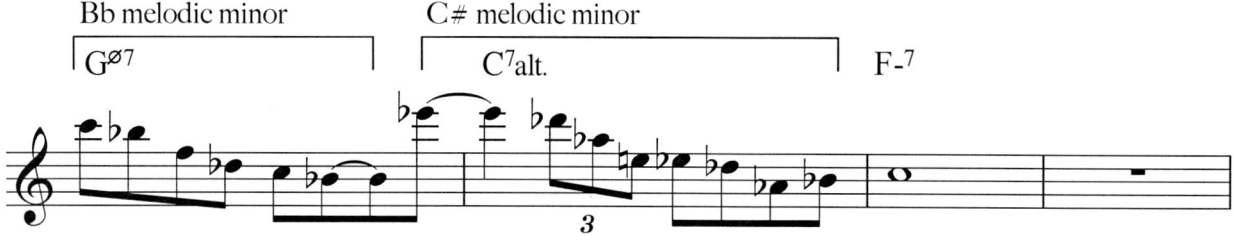

What we are calling "melodic minor as a VI" here, you may also see referred to as "Locrian #2." Note also that there are, typically, various spellings for a half-diminished chord. They include: Gmin7(b5), G-7(b5), G half-dim, and Gø7.

Go after it, and have fun. There are two recordings of "What Is This Thing Called Love" on the playlist for Chapter 17. See if you can find some examples of the use of Bb melodic minor on the first chord of the A sections (G half-diminished) in the solos there.

## SOME THINGS TO PRACTICE

1. Now that you're familiar with the derivation of the tritone substitution, go back to the Hank Mobley and Herbie Hancock examples at the beginning of the chapter and practice them again, knowing what you're playing.

2. We quoted "Cry Me a River," as a way to explore the melodic minor half step up situation. See if you can find some other melodies to use in the same way.

3. Take Hank Mobley's line from the fifth and sixth bars of the bridge of "The Best Things in Life Are Free," and transpose it for the seventh and eighth bars of the bridge, to make a question and answer pair of phrases:

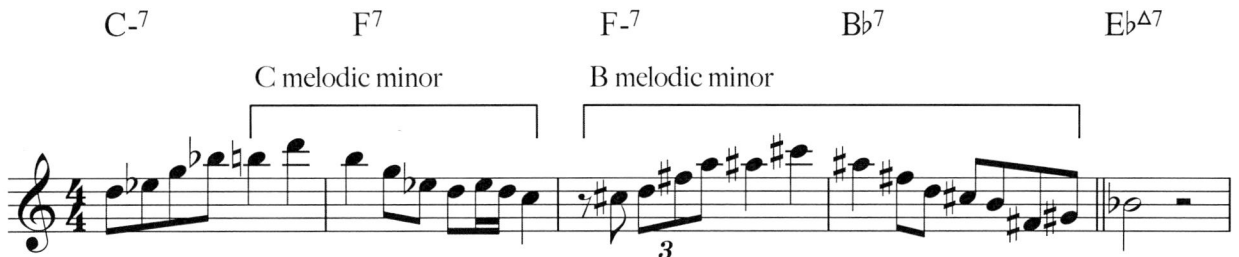

4. See if you can make up some Q and A pairs of your own.

5. Find some other tunes with this type of chord progression and transpose Mobley's phrase to fit the situation. Find some of your own. Some examples of tunes with this type of progression: "The More I See You," "Just You, Just Me," "It Could Happen To You," "There Will Never Be Another You," "There Is No Greater Love."

6. Count off a tune and blow for a while on your own. See if you can quote "Cry Me a River," but changing it slightly every time you do it, so it never comes out exactly the same way.

7. Here's one more shortcut to try. Our last bullet points went like this:

    - C7—I want a smooth line with lots of tension
    - Melodic minor a half step up from the root, thus
    - C# melodic minor

An even shorter version is:

    - On a C7—I want an angular shape, with lots of tension
    - Try thinking, "major pentatonic a tritone away."

This will get you the following five-note scale. F# Pentatonic:

If you play that against a C7 it will give you the 7th, and all four of the alterations.

All five of those notes are in the C# melodic minor scale, so the F# major pentatonic is not a new harmonic concept here, but a way to organize the notes of the C# melodic minor to create a different type of line. Give it a try and see how it feels.

We haven't addressed pentatonic scales in this book for two reasons. The first is that there is plenty of literature out there already on pentatonics. If the shape and the feeling of it appeals to you, by all means delve deeply into it. The second follows from what we just saw—that the pentatonic falls within a scale, rather than representing a new harmonic idea. If you understand the functional harmony in this book, you can use it to create context for pentatonic scales of all kinds. Happy tinkering.

# CHAPTER 18 · HARMONIC IMPROVISING—PASSING TONES

To illustrate the use of the different scales by the masters of modern jazz, I made a conscious effort to find examples that used the scale straightforwardly. That was in the interest of clarity of explanation. In practice, though, improvisers often use passing tones, or chromatic movement, within a scale. This is done for a variety of purposes:

- To smooth out a line
- To make a line lay better in the beat
- To help match chord tones with downbeats
- For variety, to find other ways to travel through a chord
- To aid in creating a smooth transition from chord to chord over the barline
- To lengthen a line, for example when playing double time

You can use passing tones within all of the scale types we've discussed. The trick is not to overuse chromaticism, which can result in loss of the clarity of the scale sound—making it harder for the piano player to pick up what sound you're going for and deliver voicings that complement what you're playing.

Here's a two bar line over a simple progression that uses just the scale:

Notice how the note F lands directly on beat three of the first bar. That's something I might not ordinarily do, since I'm generally aiming to line up chord tones with downbeats and non-chord tones with upbeats. In this case we're playing the scale straight down, and the note moves immediately to E, so it flows smoothly enough.

Now try this modification of the line:

Now the note F has been moved onto an upbeat, which makes is flow a little more smoothly. The other effect of the added passing tone is to make the line land on the note C across the barline, as we enter the G7 chord. This is another thing I wouldn't ordinarily aim for, since it throws off the rhythm of landing chord tones on downbeats, but I can make it work by continuing the motion until it resolves two beats later. The result is a feeling of delaying the arrival into the G7 chord until the second half of the bar—so it makes for an interesting variation.

That same passing tone, Ab, can be used going up, too:

And here's another iteration of that, using a few more passing tones.

Notice how the passing tones are all on upbeats. The sound of the C major scale is preserved by lining up the scale tones with the downbeats, and using passing tones between them. Releasing the passing tones onto scale tones on the downbeats also gives the line a feeling of forward motion.

Here's a line that incorporates a commonly played phrase that uses passing tones to create a bluesy sound:

And here's one more line that starts with a favorite triplet figure of the beboppers:

Speaking of beboppers, Charlie Parker and Bud Powell were the two artists most instrumental in developing the harmonic lines that characterized the sound of Bop in the 1940's. The timeless lines they created still sound fresh and are a great source for content that balances the clarity of scales with the smoothness of passing tones. Here are a few examples, with references to where you can hear them:

Bud Powell combined chromatic harmony, passing tones and anticipation to create a happening piece of melody in the 5th bar of his composition, "Celia:"

Bud's great solo break on the same tune is illustrated in Chapter 8.

Here are a few lines from Charlie Parker's classic solo on "Koko," that make use of passing tones.

From the 9th bar of his first solo chorus (0:32 in the track):

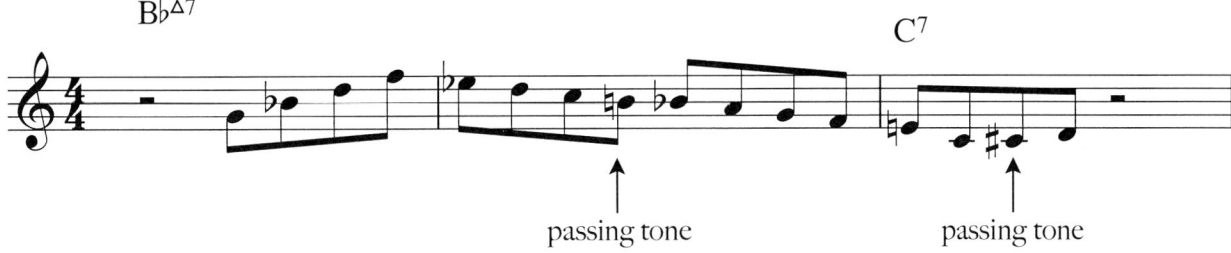

And leaving the bridge of his first chorus, at around 1:02 in the track, you'll hear a typical Parker phrase, where he uses multiple passing tones over the G-7 chord, followed by a clear use of the major scale over the C7, without any passing tones.

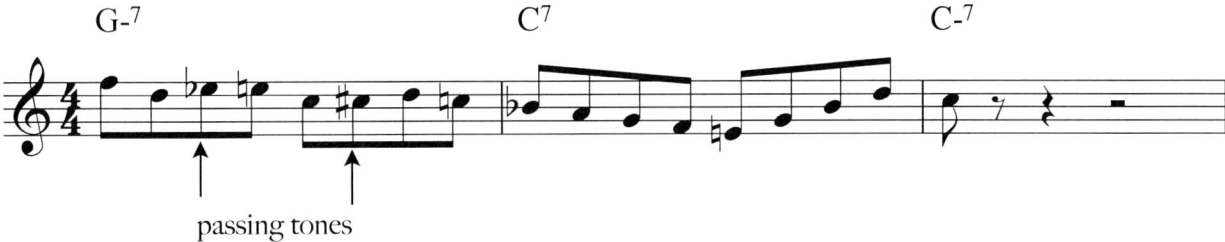

You can also use passing tones on the harmonic minor, melodic minor, diminished and whole tone scales. Here are a few examples to get you started.

Here's a common move on a D7 chord resolving to G-7, using harmonic minor with a passing tone:

Here's a similar line, with two passing tones:

And here's a longer line over two bars of D7:

You can try this last one out as a double-time line at a medium tempo over one bar of D7…

And here's a line Sonny Rollins played coming out of the bridge of his first chorus on "Almost Like Being in Love," from the album he made with the Modern Jazz Quartet:

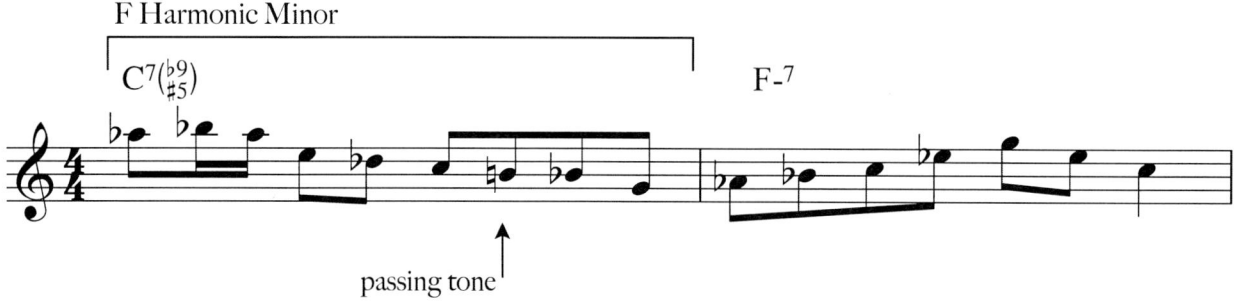

You get the picture—passing tones can help you smooth out a line so you're not just playing scales straight. See if you can find some lines of your own. The trick is to keep the flavor of the scale—finding the right balance of chromaticism and clarity takes some work.

For some more illustration, the transcription of my solo on "Soul Eyes" in Chapter 23 is filled with examples of lines using passing tones through various scales.

## SOME THINGS TO PRACTICE

1. Start practicing your major scales with passing tones, and get familiar with the spots in the scale where passing tones fit and help make a smooth line.

2. After you have a few lines to the point where they feel good, try them out against a timekeeper—a play-along track, a metronome, Drum Genius.

3. Grab a friend and play some duets. See if you can put your new lines to work in a real-time situation.

4. Use Bud Powell's "Celia" break as a starting point to develop some lines of your own. See if you can find some different places within the line to put passing tones.

5. See if Bud's line works over the first four bars of Rhythm Changes.

6. See if your iterations of Bud's line work over Rhythm Changes.

7. See if you can make some lines through a III-VI-II-V-I type of progression, where the second phrase echoes the first, using passing tones to make the echo subtly different. Here is an example of what I mean:

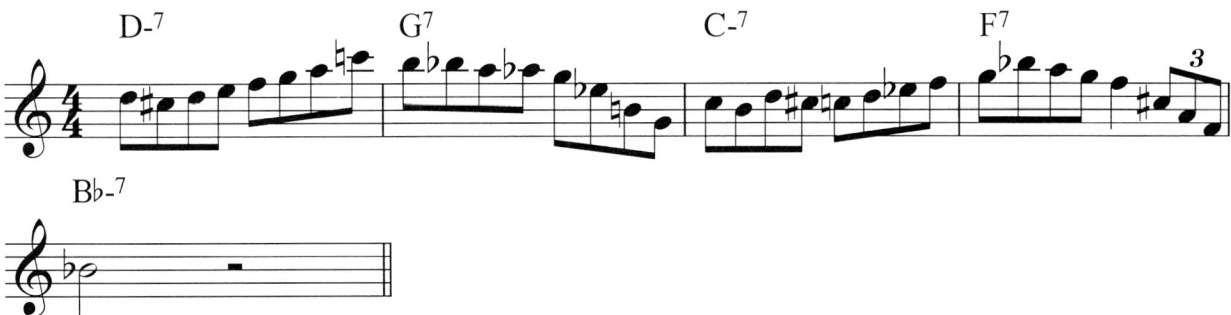

Here's another one, in a different key:

Here are a few other keys to try writing some of your own:

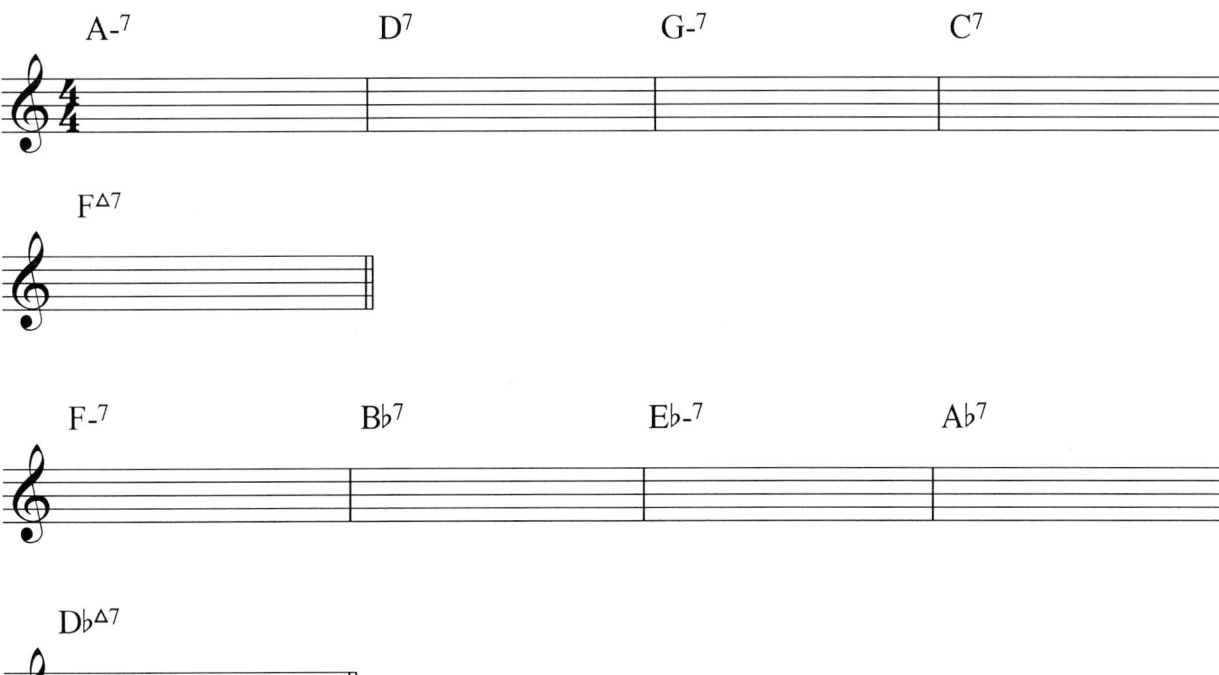

8. Practice using passing tones on melodic minor, harmonic minor, and diminished scales.

# CHAPTER 19 • PLAYING 'OUT'

Most of the time when students ask me about playing 'out' they are looking for harmonic information. They are ready to explore creating more tension and want to learn about playing "against the grain" of the chords. For many people the word 'out' does mean "outside the chords," but 'out' can also mean playing free. 'Free' can mean completely free—no rules whatsoever, just start playing and see what happens. It can also mean playing in time with no specific harmony, and it can refer to letting the harmony develop spontaneously in tandem with an improvised melody.

Learning to get freer in the time and in your use of harmony and harmonic logic is an exciting stage of development. This chapter is designed to show that exploring freedom and trying out breaking some rules is not meant simply to invoke chaos—there are some systems in place and ways of thinking that will help you navigate the edgier corners of the music. Let's see if we can clarify these ideas and explore them a little more comprehensively.

First, let's place playing 'out' in the context of the development of the music. By way of an extremely condensed recap of jazz history:

- Early New Orleans jazz musicians around the turn of the 20th century got the ball rolling by playing traditional songs and the blues through multiple choruses, and searching for new ways to improvise with the *melody* with each successive chorus.
- In the late 1920's and 30's jazz composers were writing more and more sophisticated song forms for the movies, Broadway and the Swing Era big bands. Jazz arrangers were mastering *harmony*, and soloists began adding harmonic knowledge to their improvisational technique.
- The beboppers took that knowledge and ran with it in the 40's and into the 50's, adding long, harmonically rich lines to the vocabulary of the music. They were highly virtuosic, and created songs with complex chord motion, taking pride in 'making the changes.'
- By the mid 1950's some musicians started looking for alternative ways to play jazz where they could be freer to explore, and less confined by the demands of bebop. In the process, they broke away from the common song forms and began improvising with *form* itself.

Charlie Parker's virtuosity and mastery were so inspiring, and he set the bar so high, that a majority of jazz musicians chose to follow his example. But the music had evolved to the point by the mid 1950's, that more and more musicians were developing distinctive voices within the tradition. Some artists, like Ornette Coleman and Lee Konitz, decided to go a different way, moving in an intuitive, or melodic direction in response to the beboppers. Others, like Miles Davis and John Coltrane, chose innovative harmonic pathways that led to new territory for exploration.

Both of these developments were considered 'out' at the time because they were breaks from the main stream of the music. They challenged listeners to follow them into uncharted waters. As players in the 21st century we can head out into those now well-charted waters in a boat—meaning we have access to the accumulated melodic and harmonic knowledge of the last 70 years. We could, legitimately, just swim on out into the open ocean and see what happens..........but we might get eaten by sharks. I'm all in for informed exploration. If you are thorough enough to become familiar with the known territory, maybe you can be the one to point toward the next frontier.

## ORNETTE COLEMAN EXPLODES THE FORM AND SHINES A LIGHT ON THE PATH TOWARD PLAYING FREE

In the YouTube playlist for Chapter 19 (search for Tim Armacost and The Jazz Saxophone Book, then Playlists) you'll find Charlie Parker at the top, playing on "Out of Nowhere," followed by three tracks from Ornette's first three recordings. Parker's solo on "Out of Nowhere" represents the state of the art at the time. Let's follow Ornette as he gradually pulls the elements of the music apart.

"Jayne," the second track on the playlist, is Ornette's contrafact, or new melody, on the chord changes to "Out of Nowhere." If you jump to the piano solo on "Jayne" without hearing Ornette's solo, you might assume that you are hearing a normal bebop group from the mid '50's. The approach to the music is straight ahead—Billy Higgins is swinging in 4/4, Don Payne is walking quarter notes, and Walter Norris's piano vocabulary is typical for the time.

Listening to Ornette's solo, though, you immediately hear that he is coming from a different place. If Charlie Parker's lines are beautiful strings of pearls, perfectly balanced with each note placed right where it belongs, Ornette's phrases are more like a necklace made up of abstract shapes.

His language includes raw vocalizations, and melodies where he chooses to follow where his ear tells him to go, rather than where the chords suggest he *should* go. Ornette took a lot of heat for playing sounds that followed his own internal logic rather than the conventions of functional harmony. But he didn't back down. Trusting his own instinct, he chose to search for a form that could accommodate what he was hearing, rather than forcing his playing to match the conventions of the era.

For his second recording, Ornette takes a few more steps away from traditional song forms. On his composition, "Tomorrow is the Question," which is also the name of the album, he abandons the piano and approaches Rhythm Changes in a highly personal way. His melody is in the key of G, which even today is unusual for Rhythm Changes. It has quirky turns of phrase, and has a bridge that is five bars long. Percy Heath still plays clear walking lines over the changes, but without the piano, Ornette's style of playing sounds more natural and less like it is clashing with the chords.

By the time he records "Lonely Woman," Ornette has completely upended the traditional way of playing. On his third recording, *The Shape of Jazz to Come*, Ornette had settled on his working band with Don Cherry, Charlie Haden and Billy Higgins—like-minded musicians who were willing to redefine the concept of improvising around Ornette's unique approach. On "Lonely Woman" Higgins is playing time, but he has become de-linked from a steady quarter note in the bass. Ornette and Don Cherry play the melody, which is a haunting, coherent set of melodic phrases, in a time feel that appears to apply only to the two of them. Each musician has a role he is playing, but they are not related by the bonds that held the beboppers together.

Ornette invented a way to set himself up in open space, where he could let his imagination run free, and allow the harmony to follow from his lines, in real time, rather than having to fit his lines into a predetermined harmonic path.

Ornette called his approach to improvising simultaneously with melody and harmony "Harmolodics." If you're attracted to this way of playing, there is a wealth of recorded material to absorb. Around the same time that Ornette was pulling apart the pieces of a jazz quartet, Cecil Taylor was following a similar path.

Although he may or may not have been the first one to try it, Lennie Tristano is generally credited with the first recording of a piece that is totally free—just starting out playing with no preconception about how or where it will go. Tristano's piece is called "Intuition," and is also available on the playlist for this chapter. Some other early notables on the trail blazed by Ornette Coleman are:

- Eric Dolphy
- Paul Bley
- Albert Ayler
- Sun Ra
- Roscoe Mitchell
- Musicians of the AACM and eventually the Art Ensemble of Chicago
- Pharoah Sanders
- And of course, John Coltrane

## JOHN COLTRANE GOES THE OPPOSITE DIRECTION, TAKING BEBOP TO THE LIMIT

Whereas Ornette's discoveries followed from his ability to pursue melody on his own terms, Coltrane's path toward free playing traveled a harmonic route. Along the way he was influenced by Ornette and Miles, and eventually arrived at the sounds that are now the basis of what most people mean when they talk about playing 'out.'

If you want to be like John Coltrane, ask yourself if you have:

- Curiosity
- A drive to do the work to master your craft
- Willingness to listen actively to music outside of your wheelhouse
- The openness of mind and strength of character to pursue an idea as far as it goes

If you know Charlie Parker's "Confirmation" well enough to play it, you're familiar with the demands of bebop—chord changes coming hard and fast, cycling through multiple keys, chorus after chorus. You have to have a solid, working knowledge of functional harmony to pull it off. While some musicians were starting to experience "Confirmation" as a kind of musical straightjacket, Coltrane embraced the challenge and decided to push himself even further in the direction of navigating difficult and fast-moving chord changes.

Trane embarked on a deep exploration of harmony, and began writing compositions with increasingly complex chord sequences. "Moment's Notice," is one of the first, from *Blue Train*, where Coltrane experimented with II-V-I based harmony, but with non-traditional left turns thrown in. Coltrane opened up his harmonic concept to include II-V's that did not resolve in any of the traditional ways—starting a journey that would eventually result in complete harmonic freedom.

In the process of mastering harmony Trane became fascinated by the circular relationship between major keys that are a major third apart. This is similar to the loop we found in the diminished scale.

Remember how, studying the dominant 7th chords appearing in the diminished scale (in Chapter 16), we found a continuous loop?  If we start from any key and move a minor third away, and then continue moving in minor thirds, after three minor thirds, the fourth one brings us back to where we started, like a snake eating its own tail.

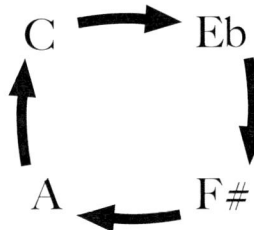

There is a similar loop created by moving in major thirds:

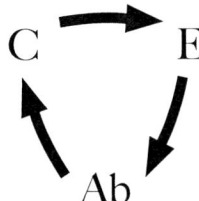

E is a major third above C; Ab (G#) is a major third above E; and C is a major third above Ab.

You may have encountered this relationship without realizing it while playing the bridge of "Have You Met Miss Jones:"

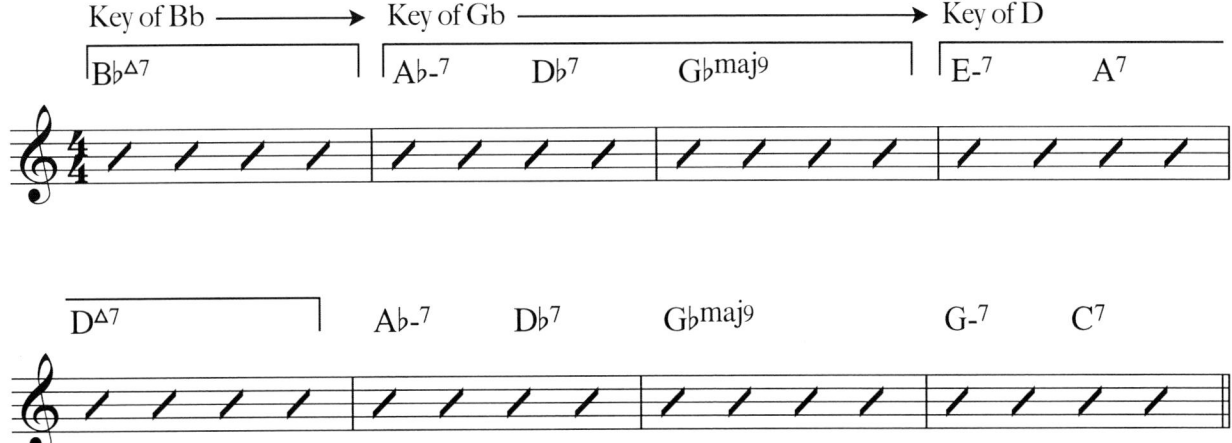

See how Bb leads down a major third to Gb, which leads down a major third to D?

If Richard Rodgers had wanted to keep the pattern going, he would have cycled back to Bb major in the 7th bar of the bridge, but there you have it—patterns are made to be broken…

This grouping of keys provided the inspiration for Coltrane's breakout composition, "Giant Steps." Let's take a look at the first 8 bars of "Giant Steps" to see how Coltrane cycles through the three keys of B major, Eb major, and G major, which form a continuous loop.

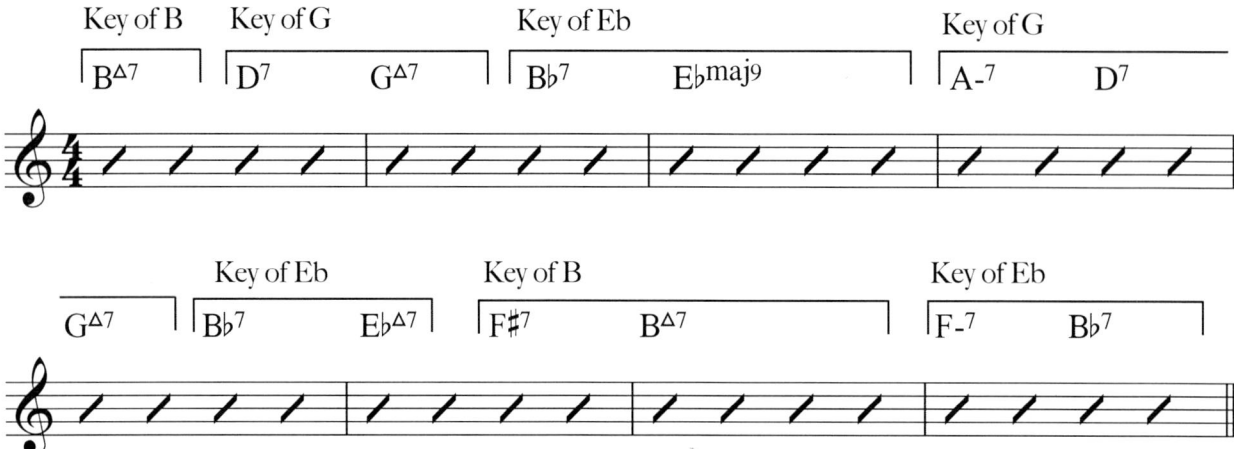

Notice how Coltrane uses dominant 7th chords to link the three keys. The result is an elegant, compact motion that is functional, but in a way that was unusual for the time.

Follow the root motion of the first five chords. It goes:

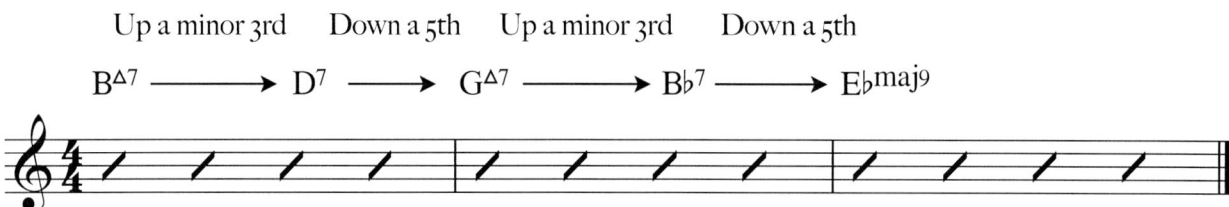

Two more important things to note regarding "Giant Steps:"

1. Coltrane is not using functional harmony to color a melody. He is pursuing a *harmonic idea* as the basis for the composition.
2. Coltrane's solo on "Giant Steps" has some passing tones, but is essentially a bebop solo in the sense that he is making the changes precisely. The chord motion is more difficult and faster than what has come before—so you could call it 'bebop on steroids,' but the way of improvising has not yet entered the territory of playing 'out.'

Having discovered a new kind of cadence—similar to a turnaround but cycling through three major keys in quick succession—Coltrane proceeded by applying this new idea to a batch of standards. The first, also on the album, *Giant Steps* is "Countdown," which is a re-harmonization of "Tune Up," the composition made famous by Miles Davis.

Here's your normal II-V-I in C major, which is the first four bars of "Tune Up:"

And here is Coltrane's reharmonization:

Once again, Coltrane's solo is pretty literal. He's playing a lot of arpeggios and clear lines defining the chords. He's not playing 'out.' He is making the changes, which is probably the most challenging set of changes anyone had ever played over to that point, and at a blistering tempo to boot.

This is a general rule you can follow as you start exploring playing 'out'—if the harmonic motion is dense like in "Giant Steps" or "Countdown," you don't actually need to play out. The changes are already doing the work for you. If you can successfully navigate "Giant Steps" with clarity, that will already sound good. (If you master "Giant Steps" and feel the desire to create some additional tension over the changes, go for it, but be aware of the possibility of creating 'too much of a good thing.')

The way toward playing 'out' became clear as the harmony got more spacious, which brings us to Miles Davis and modal jazz.

## MILES DAVIS SIMPLIFIES THE CHANGES

Wow, six pages of words before getting to the point. That's a new record. Bear with me—this is all leading toward ways to play 'out,' I assure you. Part of the object of describing Trane's approach to soloing on "Giant Steps" as bebop is to emphasize this guideline:

If you want to try energizing the music by playing 'out' it helps immensely to be able to play 'in' first. Playing 'out' gets its bite from the contrast to playing 'in.'

We're almost there, but first we have to know about the role that modal jazz played in creating the space for Coltrane to explore playing 'out.' Around the same time that Ornette was deconstructing bebop and Coltrane was taking it to it's logical conclusion, Miles Davis had his own response to the density of bebop harmony. Remarkably, *Something Else*, *Giant Steps* and Miles' *Kind of Blue*—the first modal jazz album—were all recorded within 14 months of each other in 1958 and '59.

If Ornette's approach was leading to the opening up of the song form, and Coltrane's was moving in the opposite direction toward highly complex new song structures, Miles' approach split the difference by playing over standard song forms, but with simplified, wide-open harmony. His composition, "So What," happens over a 32 bar AABA form, the most common form in the American Songbook, but the twist was the absence of functional chord movement. The A sections are eight bars of D minor (Dorian mode) and the B section is Eb minor (Dorian).

In 1959, playing over a long space of one chord was a new idea to American musicians, so if you listen closely, the soloists stay almost entirely in the Dorian mode throughout the track. They're not playing 'out' yet.

Coltrane played on Miles' *Kind of Blue*, of course, and it is significant that he was in the middle of the move toward modal playing at the same time that he was maxing out on complex harmony. Trane was primarily responsible for fusing these two strands together.

There's an indication of things to come on 1959's *Coltrane Jazz*.

On *Coltrane Jazz*, Trane wrote a contrafact over the changes to "What is This Thing Called Love," which he called "Fifth House." The tune is significant for a few reasons.

- Coltrane "modalized" the A section by removing the traditional II-V-I harmony, and using a bass ostinato in its place. Coltrane's melody happens over the following figure:

- He then set the following melody against the ostinato in the first four bars

- Since the piano is doubling the bass part and not playing chords, you might think Coltrane was experimenting with an alternate scale. The following scale appears in Yusef Lateef's *Repository of Scales and Melodic Patterns* as "Bharavi 2 or Bhairon" scale (pg 84) and as the "Persian Scale" (pg. 114).

(Shown here transposed up a fourth to match Coltrane's melody)

A closer look, though, reveals that the melody fits over a version of the "Countdown" style changes:

- And if you listen to Trane's solo, you'll find that he is blowing over those changes—in other words, he is *superimposing the changes on top of the modal line played by the bass.*

This is a key moment in the development of playing 'out,' which is way of saying "creating tension by playing polytonally." Coltrane has mastered harmony to the point where he can play a chord progression that creates intense friction with the underlying harmony, and trust himself to resolve that tension by releasing it back into the key he is playing "against."

You might also notice that the rhythm section, which was Miles Davis' working unit at the time, then plays over the traditional changes to "What Is This Thing Called Love" for Wynton Kelly's piano solo. "Fifth House" is halfway 'in' and halfway 'out.'

For another example of Coltrane's early experiments with 'out' sounds, listen to the version of "So What" on Trane's last tour with Miles Davis in 1960 (on the YouTube playlist for Chapter 19). You can hear flashes of his attempts to superimpose these new progressions onto the modal A sections of the tune. This music also sounds half 'in' and half 'out'—Coltrane is searching for something new, and trying to fit it over a rhythm section playing in the style of the day. Audiences famously booed Coltrane on that tour, unsettled by the high tension Trane was creating in the music with his as-yet-unfinished project.

It makes sense that Coltrane would leave Miles' band shortly afterward to look for a rhythm section that would invent a way to play that could support his polytonal improvising. Elvin Jones, not surprisingly, would respond with a level of *polyrhythmic* drumming that could complement the tension created by Trane's use of polyharmony.

Part of Coltrane's genius was his choice to embed his harmonic explorations in standard songs. This allowed him to test them for playability in the context of something familiar. The audience also had something recognizable to relate to while they were getting accustomed to the new sounds coming from Trane's great bands. On *Coltrane's Sound*, Trane explored these new ideas at length, and the rhythm section of McCoy Tyner, Steve Davis and Elvin Jones provided a new level of energy and interactive playing to match the electricity of Trane's ideas. The following are some examples of Trane's substitutions:

Here are the changes to the first four bars of the traditional bridge of "Body and Soul:"

And here they are with Trane's substitutions:

(You can find the entire Coltrane arrangement in the *New Real Book Vol. 3*)

"Satellite," a contrafact on "How High the Moon," gets a similar treatment:

Becomes:

This type of substitute harmony has come to be called "Coltrane Changes," for obvious reasons.

By the time Coltrane records "The Night Has a Thousand Eyes," things are really starting to get interesting. Coltrane reharmonizes the bridge of "The Night Has a Thousand Eyes" with some "Coltrane Changes," but what stands out on this track is what happens on the A sections. Trane makes the first eight bars of the form into a modal section in G, and experiments with superimposing the key of B on top of it during his solo.

See if you can make out what he plays in the fifth bar of his third chorus, at around 2:53 in the track.

It is apparent that Coltrane has accustomed himself to hearing two keys simultaneously—he can play a line in the key of B on top of the key of G. He's not just superimposing a chord progression anymore—he's playing freely in a related 'out' key, and finding his way back to the original key in real time.

Let's stop here to practice some things!

Try playing along with Coltrane's quartet on "The Night Has a Thousand Eyes." They're swinging like crazy, so work on things until they feel good, and it sounds like you're a member of the band. Here are some suggestions of things to try:

Superimpose some "Coltrane Changes" over top of the modal sections in G. At first, use what my teacher Bobby Bradford calls "doobaloopies." That was Bobby's humorous way of describing Coltrane's four note phrases (some people call them 'four note cells') on the changes of "Giant Steps." Trane often plays 1, 2, 3, 5 over a chord (the root, second, third and fifth). Outlining the chords like this sounds like "doopaloopy doobaloopy doobaloopy doobaloopy."

For example, over the first four bars:

Try superimposing:

See if you can play clearly enough to make those changes "sound" against what the rhythm section is playing.

Try starting that progression in some different places and see where you like it best. For example you could use a "Countdown" progression starting in bar 3:

Or, in that same spot, you could try playing the "Fifth House" melody over those same changes:

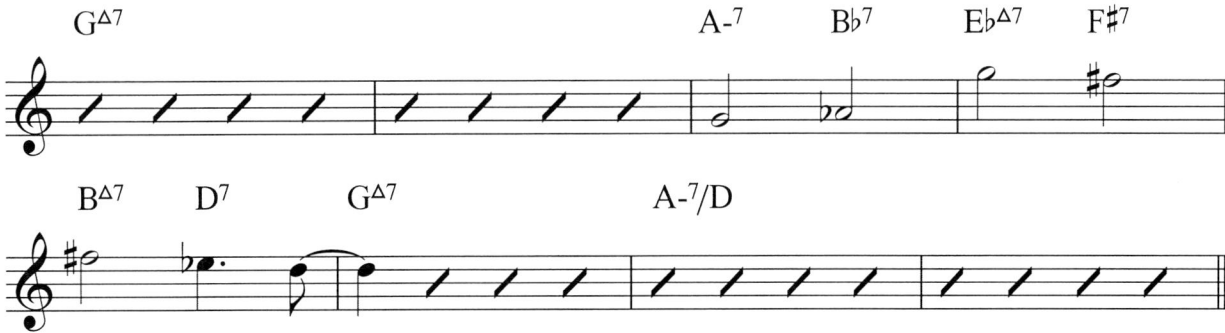

Which implies the Persian Scale:

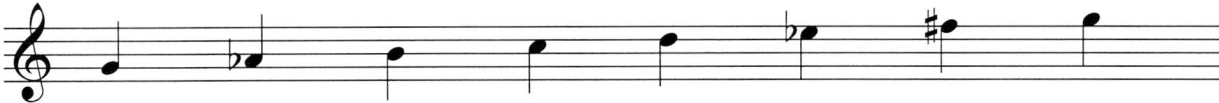

Try playing the Persian Scale anywhere in the eight bar section.  Here's a line I heard Bruce Barth play on a gig in Japan once, and have been using ever since. During the gig, I took note of where he played it in the tune, and asked him about it when the set was over:

On his landmark recording, *Blues and the Abstract Truth*, Oliver Nelson wrote the following melody in the bridge of his composition, "Hoe-Down:"

Try playing that line anywhere in the first 8 bars of "The Night Has a Thousand Eyes" and see how it feels…

Moving away from "The Night Has a Thousand Eyes" for a minute, that "Hoe-Down" line is also often played over minor chords.  Think about an E-9 chord.  If you start from the third of the chord, which is the note G, the next two notes in the series are B and D, which form a G major triad.

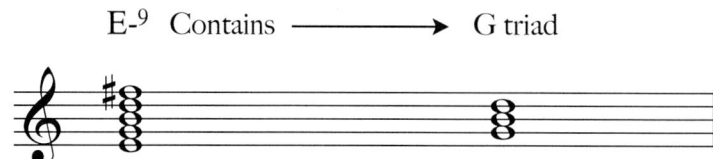

Try using the "Hoe-Down" line on an E-7 or E-9 chord and see how it feels:

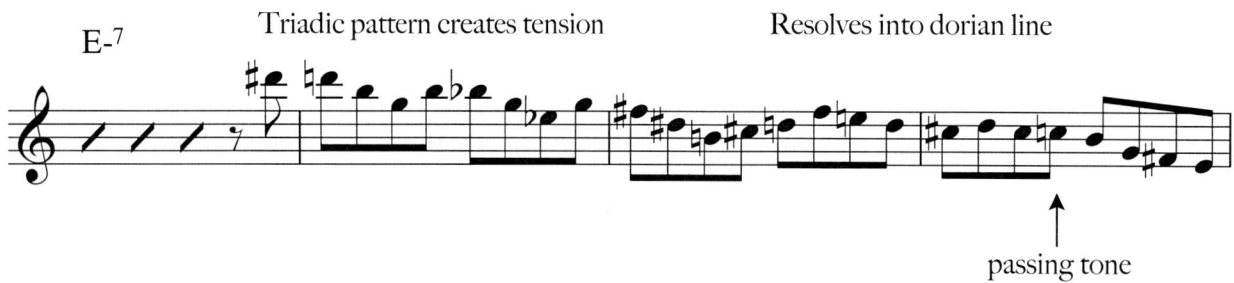

Another approach is to take those three triads and put them together to make a scale:

Try playing some lines with that scale and see how it behaves on the modal section of "The Night Has a Thousand Eyes" and on a modal section of E-7, Ab-7, or C-7. For example:

Or

One thing you may notice as you start experimenting with triads is that they have a strong character. A triad is recognizable to our ears even if it is played "out of place." This makes it a useful building block for lines and ideas that put pressure on the harmony. Improvising with triad pairs is a popular idea, and has been explained in detail by George Garzone. If you are inspired in this direction, Garzone's work, both as a player and as an educator, is highly recommended.

The idea of a triad being recognizable by the ear is also worth reiterating. It's not just *your* ears that can process the sound of a triad, but the ears of your band mates, and the ears in the audience are also involved. An important thing to keep in mind, especially when working on playing 'out,' is that the pressure you are putting on the music is felt by the audience, too. Working with the band to create a satisfying release of that pressure is important, but you can also offer the audience an invitation into your music by working with elements that are familiar on some level. Working with the melody is one obvious way to do that.

## MELODIC OUTNESS

In Chapter 11 we already explored the idea of moving a melody around in the beat, like Thelonious Monk does, and we can take a similar approach using harmony—shifting a familiar melody into a contrasting key, and then resolving the resulting tension. One of the simplest ways to create some tension and then release it is to play a melody, play it again up a half step, and then return to the original key. The melody of "52nd Street Theme" works great as a quote, and is easy to move around, since its shape is so clear. Here's the first four bars of a blues in F using the above-mentioned idea:

You could also start with the 'out' melody, and proceed from there, for example:

52nd St up 1/2 step    Same quote in Bb    Same quote down a half step. The Ear can follow the idea. Can you resolve it well into Bb7?

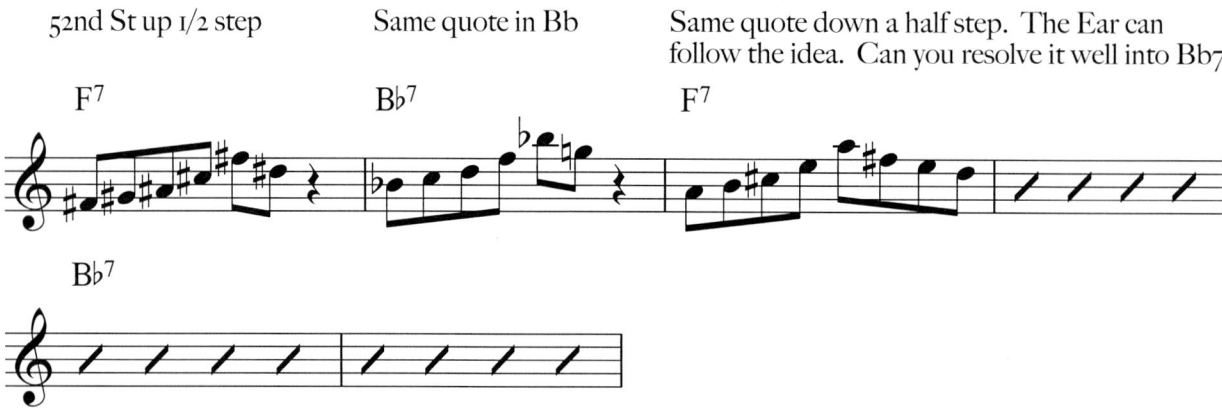

Another idea along these lines is to use the melody of the tune you are playing, but up a 5th. Here's the first four bar phrase of "On Green Dolphin Street" in Eb, with the melody of the first two bars transposed up a fifth:

See how that brings the #11 of EbMaj7 into play? It also lands you on the note Ab, the eleventh of the Eb-7 chord, which is a colorful way to enter that bar.

## THE WHOLE TONE SCALE

The whole tone scale is a bit of an odd bird that lives in its own space. It has a kind of symmetry that is similar to the diminished scale in the sense that it doesn't produce a wide variety of chords. It only generates augmented triads and dominant 7th chords. We can use the whole tone scale to create unusual sounding melodies and slightly off-kilter lines. We can also use its internal logic to move melodies around. There are only two whole tone scales.

Here's the scale starting from C:

Here it is starting from Db:

'Here is the C scale with the resulting triads if you arpeggiate it:

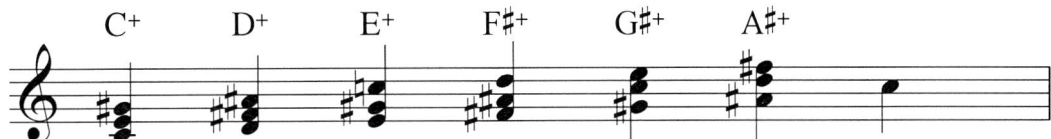

And, like the diminished scale, if you continue building chords using every other note of the scale, you don't get dominant 7th chords. The 7th of each chord is present in the scale, though, so you can build a dominant 7th for each degree of the scale:

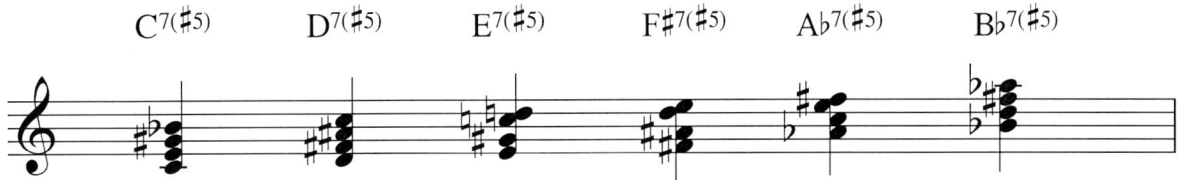

You'll often see these chords notated C+7, which can be confusing, since it can look like C with a raised 7th, so I've chosen to name them C7(#5) instead, for the sake of clarity.

We know that we can raise tension on dominant chords by altering the 5ths, 9ths, 11ths and 13ths. (See Chapter 17 for a refresher of how you can up the ante one alteration at a time.) In a functional harmony situation, like a V-I progression, you can use the whole tone scale in the same way you use the other scales, to carry you through the bar and land you in a good place across the bar line. The whole tone scale works well on dominants that are indicated with no tension, or with a #5 and a natural 9. Here's a line moving downward:

That line gets you two alterations, the raised fifth and the raised fourth, and the symmetry of all whole steps. That symmetry feels a little odd because it goes against the rhythmic grain—our bread and butter scales all give us half step resolutions down to the beat. Using the whole tone scale loses the smoothness that those resolutions provide, but the ear understands the logic intuitively, and can follow it. So in functional harmony situations the whole tone scale can be a great choice to spice things up a bit every now and then.

Here's another line, moving up:

And it sounds great to work with the augmented triad pairs when you have a little more space to make it happen, like over the two bar phrases in the bridge of a typical Rhythm Changes. Here's the first four bars of the bridge of a Rhythm Changes in Bb, for example, releasing the tension in the third bar:

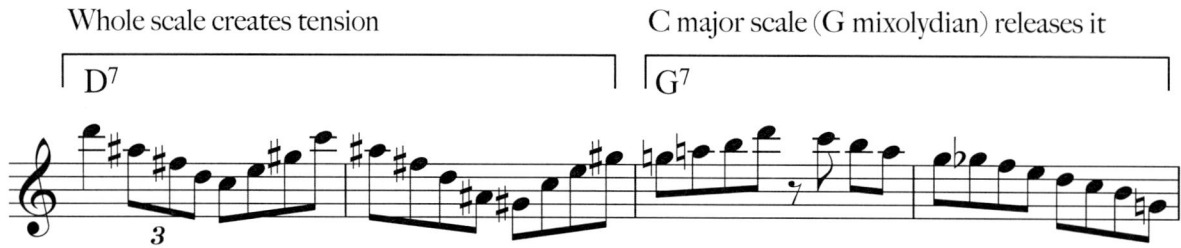

Or, you could adjust the pattern and keep it going on the G7:

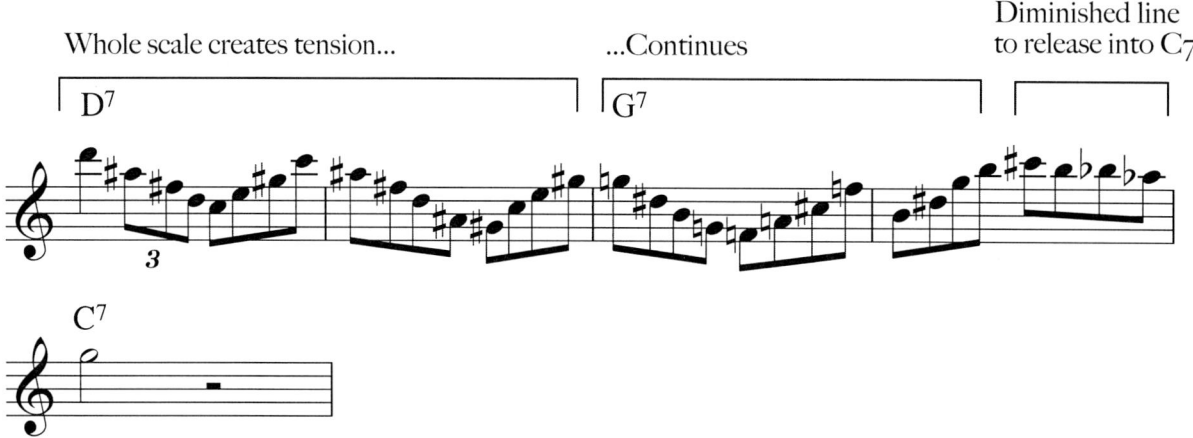

The fact that the ear can follow the symmetry of the whole tone scale makes it a great source for non-functional lines. Another idea I stole from Bruce Barth is starting a pattern in a major scale, then moving it into the whole tone to create a combination of harmonic and melodic tension. Here's what Bruce played on a longer space of an F major chord, like on "Bye Bye Blackbird:"

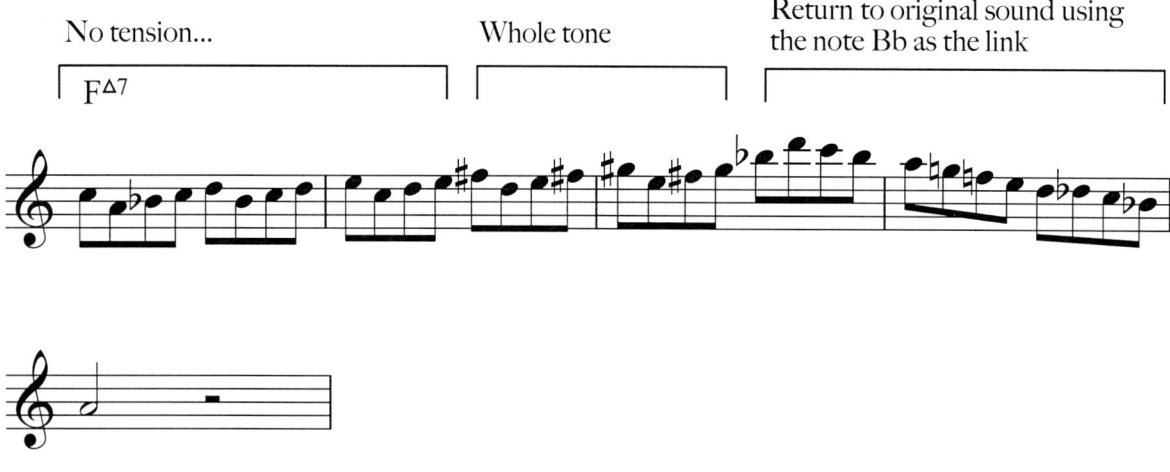

Although he could make the changes like a champion, James Moody also liked to open up the first four bars of Rhythm Changes and make it a space to play non-functional, but logical patterns. Here's one that I heard him use many times, always searching for a different way out of the pattern:

Bb△7

Pattern is: up a fourth, up a whole step, down a fourth, up a whole step

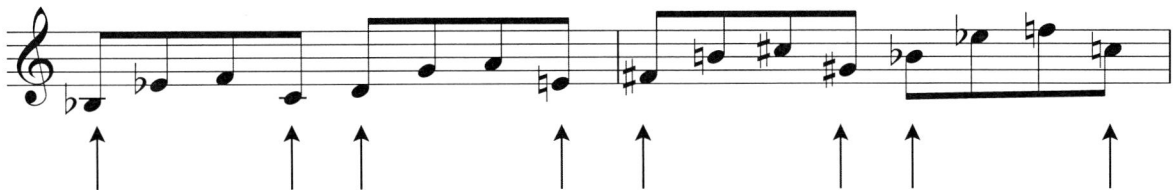

Bottom notes follow the whole tone scale

Another approach you can take is to play a melody, and then transpose it down in successive whole steps, and then see if you can resolve it. Try playing this one and see if you can find your way back to the changes in real time:

Bb7

Six note melodic pattern descending in whole steps

You can use the idea of transposing a melody in whole steps going up or down, and you can also start on an "in" note and proceed out, or start on an "out" note and let the pattern carry you back in. Herbie Hancock is extremely adept at "planing" melodies in this way.

Jackie McLean also liked to free up the harmony to break out of the predictable pathways on Rhythm Changes. Here's a line from his solo on "Red Cross" from the album he made with Gary Bartz titled *Ode to Super*:

Bb△7

Pattern is: down a fourth, up two fourths, up a whole step

That whole album is a goldmine for harmonic content that pushes the boundaries but is rooted in the tradition.

## PEDALS

One more subject and we'll bring this chapter to a close.

The first time I got to play with a seasoned professional rhythm section was also the first time I felt the music lift off when a bassist substituted a pedal into a II-V-I. Charlie Shoemake hired Bob Maize on bass and Carl Burnett on drums, who had just come off the road with Horace Silver, to accompany a handful of us students on a Sunday afternoon—to give us a taste of the real thing. We were playing "All the Things You Are," and Bob turned the rhythm section loose by playing pedals through the bridge of my second or third chorus. I didn't know what hit me, but I knew it felt incredible.

Pedals create a feeling of rhythmic and harmonic suspension in the music—tension that is looking for a release point. Rhythmically speaking, the bassist will usually leave the motion of the walking line and play a single repeated note or simple pattern. That repeated note will have the effect of simplifying and opening up the harmony as well.

The easiest way to explain the harmonic side is to play a major 7th chord and put the 5th of the chord in the bass. So if you have a GMaj7 chord, you can play a simple voicing, but put the note D (the fifth) at the bottom, like this:

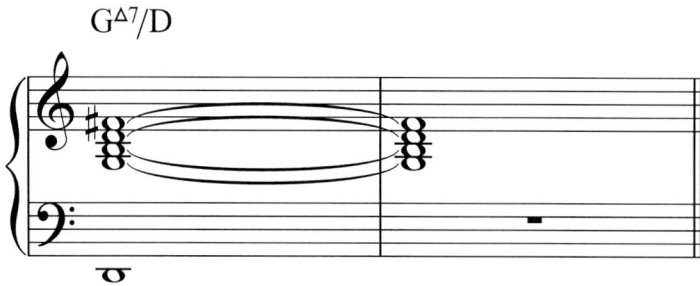

Try blowing over that chord to get the feeling for it. Play some other triads against it, and see what you can find. See if you can create some tension with 'out' triads, and then find an 'in' note for a place to resolve it.

Now that we have the basic idea, let's look at what Bob Maize did to the bridge of "All the Things You Are." He played the whole first four bars of the bridge with a D pedal. (Not just a D pedal over the GMaj7 chord.)

That looks like this:

Go to your piano and try playing each chord and then playing the note D an octave or two below it, to get a sense of how it sounds. Do it out of time at first so you can concentrate on the sounds and not worry about your piano technique. Here are some sample voicings to try:

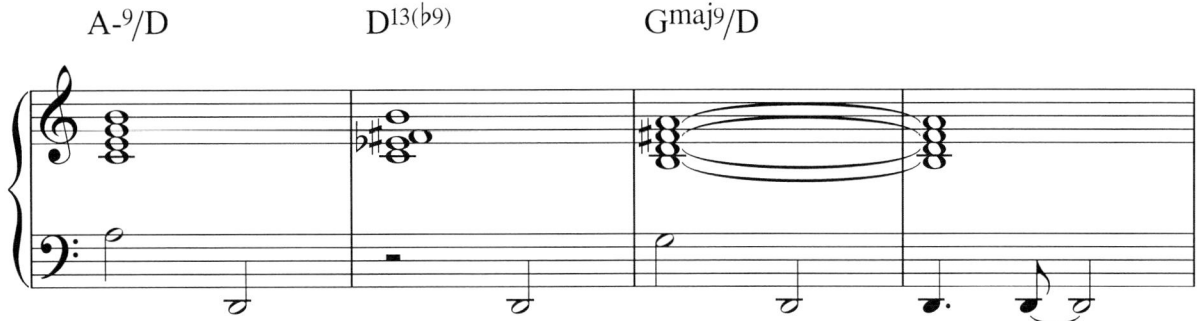

Bob then moved to a B pedal over the second four bars, in E major. See if you can find that at the piano.

After eight bars of suspension, he released the accumulated tension into walking lines in the C section.

Thelonious Monk's composition, "I Mean You," is one of the most familiar examples of a tune with pedals built into the arrangement. Check out the differences between the two examples on the playlist.

If you wanted to take it further out, you could have the bassist play a C pedal over the entire A section of "I Mean You," and have the piano player play *all* of the harmony on top of that, which could look like this:

See how the pedal frees up the harmony?

You could also try having the bassist play a C pedal for the whole A section, and tell the pianist to play whatever chords she hears on top of it. The pedal suspends the motion of the music, and the tension can build throughout the two A sections and release into the bridge.

You could use the 2 and 4 rhythmic pattern from the Monk arrangement, or you could write your own pattern for the bassist, or tell him, "play it rhythmically open."

Dexter Gordon's arrangement on "It's You or No One" uses the root and fifth together as a pedal for the statement of the A sections on the melody. They blow over the standard progression for the solos, but you could try using the pedal for the blowing as well…

We have just tasted the tip of the iceberg here, but it took us quite a few pages. Hopefully your curiosity is fired up at this point, and you can use some of the ideas here to jump off into the unknown. Here are a few suggestions to guide your explorations:

## SOME MORE THINGS TO PRACTICE

1. Learn a melody from one of Ornette Coleman's first three recordings.
    a. Try improvising with the melody itself, as we did with standards.
    b. See if you can find the structure of the phrases in Ornette's melody, and improvise by putting together a series of phrases that echo that structure.
    c. Play along with Ornette's recording and see if you can hear a tonal center from the bass. On "Lonely Woman," for example, the bass starts around the note D. See if you can improvise with D as your home. Play away from D and back again—see if you can tell a story that way.

2. Gather some musicians and try just starting out playing, without saying anything about where you're going. See what happens.

3. Try starting out free with a destination in mind. The destination can be a tune, so essentially you are freely creating an introduction to the tune together. Or the destination could be a bass line that you then use as the foundation for a composition that you invent right now.

4. With your free jazz compatriots, see if you can make up a melody on the spot, improvise on it, and then remember it (!) and return to it to complete the performance. (You can certainly do this on your own as well.)

5. Try playing "All the Things You Are" rubato from start to finish.
    a. You could play the first phrase followed by a improvisation on it, then the second phrase, and so on through the form.
    b. Or you could play through the whole melody chorus, then blow freely around the changes, and then the melody again.
    c. Or you could play halfway through the form and only improvise on the bridge…

6. Play "Impressions" and see how many different ways you can find to approach the D minor space.
    a. Try playing it with D as a pedal tone.
    b. Try playing it with A as a pedal. See what kinds of things that suggests.
    c. Try using some of the "Coltrane Changes" progressions to create tension.

7. Take a standard that stays pretty close to a home key, like "I Love You," and see if you can redefine it over a pedal.

8. Try playing the melody to "I Mean You" a tritone away from the original key, in the middle of your solo.

Remember, it's not just about the notes. Learn to become sensitive to the level of tension in the music. Is it rising? Falling? Does it need resolution? Where's the next good moment in the form for a release of tension?

Here are two short lists of some players to look out for who have mastered harmony to the point where they can use it creatively in the moment to inject energy into the music. From the straight ahead side, leaning out:

Sonny Rollins (mid '60's)
Jackie Mclean (especially late in his career)
McCoy Tyner
Herbie Hancock
Wayne Shorter
Woody Shaw
Joe Henderson
Gary Bartz
Dave Liebman
Steve Grossman
Michael Brecker
Richie Beirach
Kenny Kirkland
Branford Marsalis
Joe Lovano
Jerry Bergonzi
Kenny Garrett
Walt Weiskopf
Steve Wilson
Gary Smulyan
Chris Potter
Mark Turner

And a few whose music leans a little more toward the free side, but is deeply harmonic:

James Spaulding
Sam Rivers
Steve Coleman
George Garzone
Jorge Sylvester
John O'Gallagher

# PART FOUR
## DEEPER MASTERY

*What's Next?*

# CHAPTER 20 · HOW CAN I PRACTICE TO BECOME A CREATIVE IMPROVISER?

Let's start by pointing straight at the heart of the matter.

In my opinion, the essential core of improvisation is being able to deliver through your instrument exactly what you are singing in your mind's ear, immediately, without anything getting in the way.

That's worth repeating, here's another way to put it:

The essence of improvisation is imagining some music and singing it directly through your horn.

If that is my goal, what do I need in order to achieve it?

- Technical mastery of my instrument
- Musical language
- A well-developed imagination
- A disciplined practice routine

There's a saying you might have heard that goes, "A journey of a thousand miles begins with a single step."

That's true, but falls a little short for me. When I was starting out, my older brother Scott put it to me in a more inspiring way. He said,

"If you want to climb a mountain a mile away, and you can only take one step per day, if you take that one step every day, you *will* get to the top of that mountain."

That little push of encouragement helped me to embrace the idea of practicing with purpose, identifying goals I wanted to reach, and working steadily toward them.

One other quote that influenced how I organize my practicing is from Jackie McLean. When asked how much he practices, he replied,

"Three hundred and sixty-five hours a year."

Come to think of it, there's one more that a mentor said to me early on, which I often hear myself repeating:

"Ten minutes a day is better than 60 minutes on Saturday."

We could make a formula from those ideas.

Clear goal +
Long-term commitment +
Regular, steady discipline +
Familiarity =
Eventual mastery

## FROM THE INSIDE OUT AND FROM THE OUTSIDE IN

One more conceptual idea, and then we'll get to the actual work.

"From the Inside Out" refers to improving your ability to bring what's in your mind (the Inside) directly through your instrument (to the Outside world). Rather than having this ability just mysteriously appear after you've worked on your technique for some years, you can devise practice routines that *specifically address this skill every day*.

"From the Outside In" means teaching your inner singing voice new things to say—bringing vocabulary from the outside world into your inner world and expanding the range of your imagination. One of the other key lessons Charlie Shoemake taught me came in about the eighth month after I started studying with him. He said,

"Tim, you have pretty good ears, and you're doing well playing your solos by ear, but what you don't realize is that your ears will keep feeding you the same things over and over if you don't teach them to hear new sounds."

That's when I began to realize that learning the language of jazz is a life-long process. As we've seen a few times already, it's quite similar to learning your native speaking language. You can begin to communicate with a few basic words and sentences, but if you want to tell a good story, you need to have a rich vocabulary, and equally important, a deep well of life experience from which to generate ideas.

Anyone can do it, it's never too late to start, and no one ever learns it all.

## MY ONE-HOUR CORE PRACTICE ROUTINE

I have a routine I use for my first hour of practice time. I divide it into three segments of twenty minutes, and if I am not rushed, I'll make it a ninety-minute session, divided into three half-hours. You can see what works best for you. What I consider important is that each activity gets an equal amount of time. The three segments are:

1. Melodic exploration (Inside to Outside)
2. Vocabulary study (Outside to Inside)
3. Practicing to perform

I start with a few rules I follow for each section, and of course, I often choose to break them, especially if I'm having fun.

## FIRST 20-30 MINUTE ACTIVITY: MELODIC EXPLORATION (INSIDE TO OUTSIDE)

I start this activity by sitting at the piano with my horn at the ready. It's best if you have access to a real piano with vibrating strings. A digital piano will help, but one of the key elements of this work is to experience the way your instrument communicates with the vibrating strings of the piano. When I was first starting out and didn't have ready access to a piano, I'd rent a studio as often as I could afford it, so I could play in a beautiful space and use the piano.

I hold down the sustain pedal and play a fifth in the lower register of the piano, like C and G for example, and let it ring. Then I begin by *listening in my mind* for a note or a simple melody. The first rule for this time is:

- Hear it in your mind before you play it.
    - This is not a time for noodling, or playing something you already know
    - It is a time to play melodies you've *never played before*
    - This is a time to go slowly

If my goal is to be able to deliver directly through the horn exactly what is in my mind, this is a way I can work on that a little bit every day.

I listen for a note or a melody, play it, and then listen for what would make sense to play next. I am consciously working on matching my inner singing voice to the saxophone. I am not practicing melodies of songs that already exist. I am making up simple things, and seeing if I can accurately play on the saxophone what I hear in my mind's ear.

Sometimes students will ask, "What if I don't hear anything in my mind?"

My first response is, "Keep listening. Use your imagination."

And if you still don't hear anything, you can always get some inspiration from the outside. One thing I'll do sometimes is let my index finger drop randomly somewhere on the piano. Whatever note comes out of the piano, I'll see if I can sing it, either out loud or in my mind, and then imagine where that note is on the saxophone. Then I try to play that note on the horn—and next I try to listen for another note to play after it that would sound interesting.

You could also drop two fingers on the piano, and start out by making a melody with those two notes… or you could blow a note on your horn, find that note in your mind so you're syncing up with the horn, and proceed from there.

This is equally useful on the bandstand—sometimes I run out of ideas. What do I do? Listen! I can grab a melody from the pianist's comping. I could get a rhythmic idea from the drummer and put some notes to it, and I'm off and running again. Or I could listen to the direction of the bassist's line and either play something in the same direction, or go in the opposite direction.

If you're just getting started at this, remember, it takes time to build up some language. You won't get anywhere asking a two-year-old to reach into her mind and find and then express a creative thought. She has to learn some words, then some simple sentences, and then start to form thoughts and articulate feelings. A child masters her native language by learning a little bit every day.

Rule number two for this space is:

- Experience the beauty of playing in tune

That's why I like to be next to a piano. If I'm playing in tune, the piano will ring. The sounds I play will reverberate in the piano strings and will vibrate sympathetically. This gives me pleasure, and will give the audience pleasure if I can learn to fill the room with sound waves that are in sync with each other.

There is a video demonstration of this, called "Video 4: Make the Piano Sing," on the YouTube channel under "JazzSaxBook Ch. 2." (If you jumped into the book at this chapter, you can find the playlists associated with each chapter by searching "Tim Armacost and the Jazz Saxophone Book" on YouTube. Links are also available at www.timarmacost.com.)

Rule number three:

- This is a chance to get to know the weight of each note in relation to the key you're exploring.

I like the open fifth on the piano because it establishes a tonal center, but leaves me room to define it. If I'm sustaining C and G in the piano I can explore C major, C minor, or a C7 sound. I can play any note, and the idea is to begin to get a feel for whether the note is happy where it is, or wants to move. If it wants to resolve, in what direction? Up or down? If it wants to move downward, what happens if I go the other way?

If I play in the key area of C today, I'll pick another key tomorrow, and after twelve practice sessions I will have spent some time becoming more familiar with all twelve keys.

Last rule—these are really more like guidelines than rules…

- Explore melodic logic, and put together some short stories.

There is an abundance of literature about harmonic logic, and relatively little about melody. You'll find some resources in the Classical world, especially in the context of counterpoint, but there isn't a lot of guidance about how to create good jazz melodies. My suggestion for solving that problem is threefold:

1. Listen to a lot of jazz (!) and steep yourself in the music.
2. Continue to memorize new songs. There is no shortage of great melodic material.
3. Spend time making up melodies every day, to see if you can get better at it.

I usually start by making up short stories with an opening phrase, a development phrase, and a conclusion. I do that by:

- Listening for a melody in my mind
- Playing it
- Imagining a melody that follows from the first one, or develops it
- Playing it
- Finding a melody that leads me home to the root of the key I'm in, to tie off the story

• Video 28: Short Stories

Here are a few other shapes to try:

- Invent a simple melody
- Answer it starting from the last note of the first melody
- Do that again
- Bring it home

Or:

- Imagine a melody
- Play the same melody up a whole step
- See if you can find your way home from there

- Video 29: The Inevitable Note

Another approach:

- Start with the most tense note you can imagine and see if you can make a melody using it
- Answer that
- Bring it home

- Video 30: Off the Deep End and Back

Modeling the blues:

- Play a melody
- Play it again, adjusting for the changes in the fifth and sixth bars of the blues form
- Play a melody that brings it to a conclusion

If I still have some time left and am ready for the next level of challenge, I'll count off a tempo and try to do this in time. What I'm doing is practicing to *compose* in real time.

- Video 31: Composing in Real Time

After 20 or 30 minutes of melodic exploration, practicing to connect my mind's ear with what comes out of the saxophone, and getting familiar with a tonal center, I move on to adding a new word to my vocabulary.

## SECOND 20-30 MINUTE ACTIVITY: VOCABULARY STUDY (OUTSIDE TO INSIDE)

This is where we teach our inner ear to hear something new. We grab something from the outside, usually from the tradition, and add it to our inner world.

This can be a solo transcription I'm working on from start to finish, or a fragment of a solo that I like the sound of, or it could be a new song I want to learn by heart. The guiding idea is that I use this time to learn to play something that I consciously choose because I find it beautiful, attractive, hip—or simply that it sounds good.

In a nutshell here are the steps:

1. Find a phrase you want to learn, and listen to it a handful of times
2. Learn to sing it
3. Play it directly through the horn—Sing the phrase in your mind while playing it on the saxophone
4. Improvise with your new piece of vocabulary

For this stretch of time it is worth following those steps carefully. We're not focusing on *how much* of the solo or song you can learn. We're concentrating on the *quality* of the learning. After the core hour is complete, you can take a break, and then come back to learning more of the solo if you want.

Let's add some detail to those four steps.

1. The point of listening first is to internalize what you're about to learn. If I have the time, I like to listen to a song or a solo for a few days or a week before I ever try to play it on the saxophone. Remember, your memory lies in your mind, not your fingers. You'll hear people talk about 'muscle memory,' but that is not really useful to us here. Muscle memory describes the ability to do things unconsciously that you've done many times before. We're not dealing with repetition now. We are working on becoming deeply aware of what we're doing. Our goal is to improve at a specific skill—to imagine things on the spot and play them immediately. It's a way precisely to *avoid* going on autopilot.

2. Learn to sing it. You don't have to have a great singing voice, and in fact you don't even have to sing it out loud, although I think it's valuable if you can. As long as you can "sing" it in your inner ear, you'll be ready for step three.

3. If you can commit to doing this step regularly and with care, you'll improve quickly and you'll enjoy the feeling of rapid advancement. We've seen this before, but it bears repeating. Remember, here's the most important part:

You only get one chance to play something for the first time.

Let's take advantage of that.

- Sing the first chunk of the melody you're working on.
- Now, imagine where you think that should be on your instrument.
- Next, count off a tempo and tap your foot to it for a bar or two. It can be slower than the tempo of the tune or solo you are studying, if that helps.
- *Without trying to test it out at all* with your fingers, see if you can just play it, in time.
- If you miss, which you will, just keep the tempo going, and try again, in time.
- If you forget how the phrase goes, listen to the recording again, and confirm it, so you can play it with confidence.
- The point is to *do the searching for that melody on your horn in time.*
- After you feel like you have it, go back and play it along with the recording. Work on it until you can play it precisely and exactly—like the phrase that attracted you in the first place.

The end goal is to play what's in your mind straight through the horn, right? This is a way to get a little better at that each day.

- Video 32: Ask Your Fingers to Deliver the Melody in Your Mind

4. This next step is crucial. Remember when you first started studying your native language in school? Your vocabulary teacher, if he was any good, made you write sentences with the new words you were learning. It wasn't enough just to know how to spell a word, or to memorize its definition. You were taught to put it to use. Same with music. After you've learned to play your new piece of vocabulary, it's time to tinker with it—and put it into some sentences. Here are some suggestions:

- Count off a tempo and play your new phrase a few times, in time
- Now try changing a few notes—see if you can use your new phrase as a template for your own phrase.
- See if you can use your new phrase as a jumping off point for some more phrases of your own. Try playing something in front of it to set it up. Try playing it as a question and see if you can find some answers.
- It's a great idea to do this with someone else. Pass it back and forth. See if you can inspire each other to come up with more and more ideas.
- Grab a play-along or another musician, kick off a blues, and see if you can find a place in the blues progression where your new idea will work. Try it out.
- Pick a spot in the blues and play your new phrase in the same spot each chorus. So if you're going to play your new idea from the fourth bar into the fifth bar of the blues, see if you can improvise something in the first two bars, let a bar of rest go by, and then play your new phrase in bar four.
- Improvise your way through the rest of the chorus, and see if you can land your new phrase in the same place on the next chorus.

This is the activity that for me is the easiest one to get absorbed in, and forget about moving on to the third segment of the core practice hour. Charlie Shoemake made me set a timer for a while when it became clear that I was focusing on one activity at the expense of the others. Remember, you can pick up where you left off after the core hour is over, if there's something you want to spend some more time on.

The key point here is to spend equal time on a few activities that will all work together to make you a better improviser in the long run.

## THIRD 20-30 MINUTE ACTIVITY: PRACTICING TO PERFORM

I spend the third segment of my core practice hour *performing*. One thing I hear a lot from students is that they feel that they can't perform on the same level as what they can do in the practice room. There's a gap between what they know they *can* do, and what comes out on stage.
I think that's true for most people, and in my own experience, I've seen that gap widen and get smaller based on the balance between how much I'm practicing and how much I'm performing.

It is possible, though, to practice in a way that will address the closing of that gap.

How do we do that?

Start with a decision:

I am going to play a tune in time, and if I stumble or make a mistake I won't stop, but will keep going and work it out in the music.

It's simple—on stage if you make a mistake you don't get to turn around, stop the band and say, "Could we just go back a couple of bars so I can play that last line better?"

You have to figure it out in the moment, and try to make that little clunker you played fit into something so it eventually sounds like you meant it in the first place. It doesn't feel good in the moment, but if you can stay on your toes and work it out, that will often lead you into a place you couldn't have imagined, which is a big bonus.

It is quite challenging, though, to play alone in the practice room with the same intention you have on a stage, in front of an audience.

Which is why we practice it!

So kick off a tune and see if you can keep it going for twenty minutes. You may have to build up to that. Take your time.

Here are a few more things to think about:

- If you listen to a drummer in the practice room alone, you might hear him playing a single groove for a long time. He's playing it until it feels good, and then enjoying that feeling for a good long while. If drummers do it, we should, too. Play the tune until it starts to groove, then keep it going.

- If I can have the experience every day of playing a tune and working out the mistakes I make in real time, I will get good at making everything I play sound like that's what I *meant* to play.

- Generally speaking, if I play a tune for ten minutes, by the end of a few minutes I will have played everything I *know*. Now if I keep going, I really have to start *improvising*. Once I start following one idea with another and having fun, I'll get through twenty minutes in a flash.

- The goal Charlie Shoemake set for me in this exercise is: I should be able to play on the changes to "Confirmation" clearly enough that Charlie can recognize what tune I'm playing, without hearing me play the melody.

- Get yourself some feedback. Record yourself playing a solo performance. Listen back and see if you can snap your fingers or tap your foot to the beat you hear on the recording. Is it consistent? Does it feel good and sound good? What would you like to improve?

- You can also get visual feedback. Watch yourself play in the mirror. Or you can take a video. How do you look? Is your body relaxed? What about your face? Are you grimacing at your mistakes? If you are, you are telegraphing to the audience that you don't like what you are playing. If *you* don't like it, why would they? Think about the vibe you want to project to the audience with your body and face, and see if you can make that happen.

- Practicing by performing will help you strengthen your ability to solve problems in real time. Remember though, that actual performance, unless you're a solo act, involves other musicians. If you're improving at imagining melodies and delivering them in real time, that can also help you respond to what the other musicians are doing around you—if you make the effort to engage with them.

Naturally, you should try the ideas presented here and use what works for you. If something isn't lighting you up, move on and find a way that works better. I would, however, give it some time to sink in. Don't abandon something before you can really do it. These are things I've put together over many years of practicing, and they do a great job of putting me into a creative frame of mind. That's where I like to start my day.

# CHAPTER 21 • PHRASING

## NOW THAT I CAN NAVIGATE THE CHANGES, WHAT'S NEXT?

After I'd been studying with Charlie Shoemake for about a year, I was starting to get a handle on how to how to play melodies and create lines. It was exciting to be able to sound like I knew what I was doing a little bit, and around that time I got a chance to sit in with a high-level rhythm section for the first time. They were swinging the music hard, and I had that first experience feeling like the energy lifted me off the ground. It was an inspiring moment, and I practiced extra-long hours for the next few months, wanting to feel like I was ready for it the next time I got into a situation like that.

Charlie is one of those rare teachers who knows how to deliver a message just at the right moment, and with the right combination of reminding you that you're not there yet, but that you could be if you keep at it. He gave me a lesson that week that I've never forgotten and have passed on to many a student since.

After I played everything I'd been working on in the space of one solo, Charlie said something like this to me:

"Tim, when you go to play your solo it sounds pretty good and I can hear what you're working on and it sounds like you're starting to get a handle on things and you're putting some pretty good lines together but you never really give me a chance to hear what you just said because you're on to the next idea right away and I hear that you have some things you got from Hank Mobley and some things from Dexter Gordon and especially the influence of Sonny Rollins is strong but you're playing everything you know in every chorus and you're hardly ever stopping to take a breath or to hear what's happening in the harmony or maybe consider whether there are other ways to approach the solo besides lots of long harmonic lines and then you go ahead and play some more lines and..."

—pausing after running out of breath, taking a huge breath and then continuing—

"...then you're off and running and maybe working off the melody a little but mostly just saying everything you have to say all at once and then doing that again and then doing that again......."

—pause—

"You see what I mean?"

Charlie acknowledged my youthful enthusiasm positively, and then demonstrated in a way that was impossible to miss that I had some work to do if I wanted to play music that was tolerable to listen to...

A short while later, after moving to Europe to live for a while, I read an interview with Joe Henderson where he talked about thinking like a writer. He described how he would try to improvise in sentences and paragraphs, as if he were creating short stories.

Charlie's message was basically that I was using nothing but run-on sentences. With Joe Henderson's comments I started to understand better what phrasing means.

That prompted me to pick Joe's *State of the Tenor, Volume I* as my next purchase, on LP. Ah yes, the good old days. CDs were still a few years away. Anyway, I remember distinctly having the experience for the first time of hearing not just the notes he was playing, which had been my primary focus for a few years, but the *ideas* as well. It was possible to "watch" him move from one idea to the next, and that was a revelation. Not long after that Joe came to Amsterdam, and hearing him in person for the first time was another revelation.

Before I heard *State of the Tenor* the level of abstraction in Joe's playing was something I wasn't able to get comfortable with. The combination of reading the interview, hearing the recording where I could follow his train of thought and hearing him play in person with such a deep sense of swing, prompted me to figure out how to pay more attention to phrasing.

How can we start working on phrasing, then? Are there rules for phrasing?

If, like I did, you have a tendency to play too much, one option is to—

> Take the horn out of your mouth

—which was Miles Davis' reply when Coltrane said that he didn't know how to stop playing.

That's a bit of a blunt way to express it, but the idea is that a phrase has to have an ending point to be a phrase. Obviously it would be inefficient to take the horn out of your mouth after every phrase. We can think of it in more constructive terms by learning how to play ideas that are simple, clear and come to an end. Once we're able to make a complete musical statement, we can then work on linking one phrase to the next, and then we start to become musical storytellers.

As with most things, we can start by listening to the players who shone a light on the path before us in the tradition. Listening with intention is a great way to gather information. So in this case, listen to some solos specifically focusing on the length of the sentences, the way the players end their phrases, and how long the silences are between phrases.

Here's a list of players whose music you can seek out who are known for great phrasing. In no particular order:

- Miles Davis
- Sonny Rollins
- Charlie Parker
- Paul Desmond
- Lester Young
- Lee Konitz
- Tom Harrell
- Freddie Hubbard
- Hank Mobley
- Herbie Hancock
- Thelonious Monk
- Kenny Barron

The difference between improvising a great jazz solo with interesting phrasing and writing a novel or a short story, is that in jazz you don't have time to mull over what you want to say and try to find the perfect sentence that conveys your meaning exactly. If we get involved in thinking, it can take us a step away from being continuously present in the moment. What's the way in? To be a good phraser, you have to be able to listen..........to yourself. What I mean by that is that once you start paying attention to things beyond just getting the scales and chords right, your ear and your imagination become your guides.

As we discussed in Chapter 20, the main idea is that you play a phrase, pause, then imagine what an answer to the first phrase would sound like and play that. And then you can do that again. And you create your solo imagining from phrase to phrase.

As you get better at conjuring and delivering music, you'll also find some other ways to go about it. Phrasing doesn't have to be just questions and answers. You wouldn't write a short story or a novel composed entirely of questions and answers, right? Some other strategies might be:

- You could take a short phrase and see how many different ways you can play it—developing it over a whole A section or a whole chorus.
- You could pose a question, and see how many different answers you can find for it.
- You could pose a question, go on a tangent with a handful of seemingly unrelated phrases, and then come back and answer the original question...if you can remember it!
- You could start with a declaration, something really final sounding, and then take it apart piece by piece.
- Or you could throw phrasing out the window and just wail a long screaming emotional note for a few bars and see what kind of response that generates from the rhythm section.

The big idea here is that phrasing can help you organize your musical thoughts into a larger frame. You're not just thinking about notes and chords anymore—you're relating one thought or idea to the next one. Remember how, in Chapter 20, we played a note against the sustained fifth in the piano and listened to see if that note was happy where it was, or if it wanted to resolve? Now we're doing that with whole melodic phrases, not just individual notes.

If you learn to connect your thoughts so that they hang together over the course of a whole chorus, or a whole solo, you'll be saying to your band mates and the audience:

"Follow along while I make up this great story."

If you can tell a story that is interesting and surprising to yourself, chances are it will also grab the audience's attention. Then, once you're aware of phrasing as an element of improvisation, you can start challenging yourself to play phrases that are outside of your usual habits. The goal is to get comfortable throwing yourself into the deep water of music you've never played before and trusting yourself to swim.

All right, once again you're probably saying,

"Stop talking *about* phrasing and show me how to do it!"

Right. As I said, the gateway in is to become aware of good phrasing as something to strive for. Now that you're aware of it, there are some things you can do to work on it. Good melodies are built in phrases, and the blues is the bedrock of the music, so let's look at a few blues melodies and see what we can find out.

One of the simplest ones you can find is "C Jam Blues," so let's examine it, and see if we can build some phrases inspired by the shape of the original melody.

Here is what the first four bars look like. The whole chorus is this four bar phrase repeated three times.

One approach to using this little phrase for inspiration for practice can be to break it into three parts:

Then we can change the notes, and start using it as a frame to make our own phrases, like so:

That last example started on the flat 3rd. We could try one starting on the 5th, and with a few more notes:

To reiterate an idea from earlier in the book—we're not reinventing the language here. We're using something known, and improvising with it, which gives a simultaneous feeling of familiarity and not knowing where it's going. Taking a dive this deep into the details of how the melody of "C Jam Blues" works will also help us to play "C Jam Blues" when we're playing "C Jam Blues," rather than treating "C Jam Blues" as a blank slate to play everything we know all at once. Not to beat a dead horse here, but if you play a set of five tunes, and you treat them all the same, you'll wind up playing pretty much the same solo five times in a row, right? As an audience member, after the second solo, I'll start to lose interest. That's why it's worth your time to delve into everything a song has to offer and use it all to inspire your improvisation. That way you can keep it fascinating, for yourself and the audience, through the course of the set.

I think you get the idea, but let's look at one more tune to flesh it out a bit more.  Grab a lead sheet of "Secret Love" and see what you can say about the shape of the phrases of the melody.  Rather than the notes themselves, we're concerned here with the larger shape and direction of the phrases.  Here's my map:

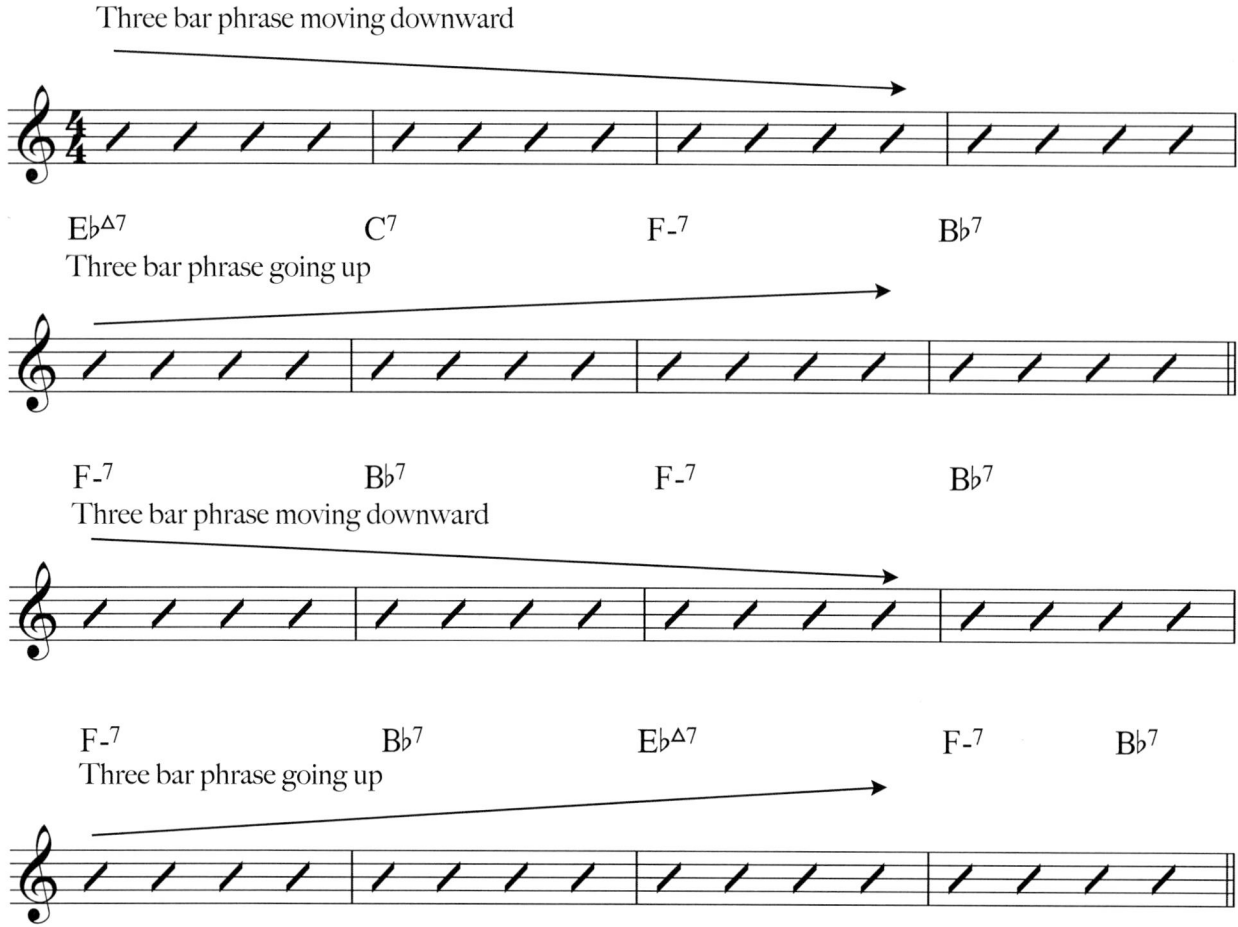

You now have a frame to work in, and you could start looking for phrases that fit the map of the first 16 bars of "Secret Love."  It could get annoying fast if you played an entire solo just with phrases that followed the map, although, come to think of it, I bet Sonny Rollins could pull that off…the idea is more intended as a way to guide you toward playing phrases—speaking in complete sentences, rather than random, run-on ones.

After you start to get an intuitive sense of what a musical phrase feels like, you can start challenging yourself to move from one phrase to the next in a way that is unpredictable to yourself.  Now you're taking that step into the unknown, letting the music guide you toward what to play.

If you get stuck and need a new approach, I love this quote attributed to Miles:

"Start on three and don't finish anything."

Remember, Hemingway is famous for short sentences and Joyce could write one that went on for pages—there are many different ways to express a thought.  With consistent practice and attention to detail, your personal style will gradually emerge.

## SOME THINGS TO PRACTICE

1. Listen to some of the artists mentioned in the chapter with the intention of becoming more aware of how they put their phrases together.

2. Listen to any blues solo from Charlie Parker for a master class in variety of phrasing and completeness of musical ideas.

3. Start listening to your own playing, while you're doing it, and see how it feels to let a phrase end and listen for where the next one should go.

4. Record yourself and listen "as a listener." Does the music make sense? Can you follow the ideas? Is there enough space? Are the spaces all the same length, or is there variety in the pauses as well?

5. Try making a phrase map for a few choruses of the blues. You can mix it up—draw some long lines and some short ones, big spaces and little ones, lines that move in one direction, and some that look like snakes. Then try to make music out of it.

6. If you haven't read it already, visit Chapter 20 for some ways to incorporate practicing phrasing into your daily routine.

# CHAPTER 22 · THE BLUES

The blues is a subject for an entire book, of course, and a few great ones have been written already. Amiri Baraka (aka LeRoi Jones) wrote *Blues People*, which is a deep look at the origins of the blues and the life experience of the Africans who were forcibly brought to the United States in the 17th century and beyond. Ted Gioia's *The History of Jazz*, now in it's third edition, is also an excellent resource.

In keeping with the overall aim of this book, we'll mostly focus on practical matters here, with some bits of philosophy and history added for context. When I was starting out I found so many variations of the blues that it took me a while to figure out what the standard forms were. The intention here is to collect a bunch of blues forms in one place, so that, in comparing them, you can zero in on what is essential and what is variation.

For starters, I'd like to pick a fight with the educators who give young musicians a blues scale and say, "Use that to improvise on the blues. It fits over all of the chords."

At its best, that approach is an honest attempt to get a person started improvising without filling her head with too much information. That's a worthy goal, but on the other hand, it is exactly what it is trying not to be—getting someone started by giving them *information*, rather than giving them *melody*.

To return to our language analogy, it's like saying to a two-year-old,

"The subject comes first, then the verb, then the object. Now, make me a sentence."

The answer might be pointing to a cat and saying,

"Kitty."

We talked about this earlier in the book, but it bears repeating—your parents and siblings, (or whoever taught you to speak your native tongue) supplied you with words, one at a time, long before you ever learned anything about the underlying grammar of language.

Your mother might have pointed to your eye and said, "Timmy's eye." Then she pointed to her own eye and said, "Mommy's eye." After some weeks of that, she might say, "Where is Timmy's eye?" And if you pointed to your eye in response, then you were starting to understand sentences, without ever being taught any grammar.

I think it makes more sense to start beginning improvisers with a simple melody. Without explaining it yet, show them how it fits across the chords of the blues by singing or playing it. Then introduce some variations to point them in the direction of improvising with melody. After learning a few easy melodies, students can learn how to combine them into simple sentences, and the process is off to a solid, organic start.

Here's a simple melody that suggests the essence of the blues:

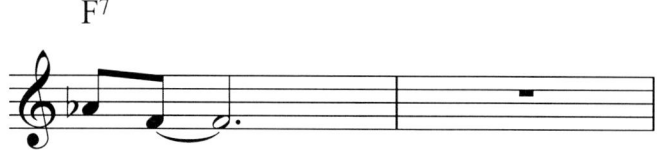

Listen to King Oliver's solo on "Dippermouth Blues" on the playlist for Chapter 22, (search for Tim Armacost and The Jazz Saxophone Book on YouTube) to hear a good example of this little melody being used as the basis of an improvised solo. The solo starts at 1:19 in the track.

You can "mine" that solo for variations or you can make up your own. Here are a couple of ways to add something to the front side of the melody:

And here are a few variations adding to the backside:

You get the idea...

There are a few things to point out about this essential little melody:

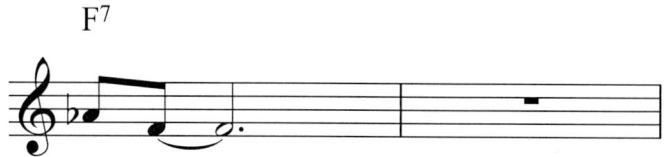

1. This is tension and release in a nutshell. The note Ab creates tension against the 3rd of the F7 chord, an A natural, and immediately releases it to the root.

2. If you listen to King Oliver's solo, he is *vocalizing* those Ab's. They are not just *notes*—they are personal vocal expressions. It is important to understand the distinction between scooping into a note and bending a note to express the spirit of the blues. Scooping is something inexperienced players do. It's usually unconscious, and it happens because the player is "guessing" at the pitch he wants to play. If you are hearing the note in your mind first, you can bend it in order consciously to express emotion. That is a different story altogether. With that in mind, listen to King Oliver's solo again.

3. On a more philosophical level, the presence of the both the major and minor thirds simultaneously is getting at the underlying meaning of the blues. It's deeper than what someone means when they say they've "got the blues." That usually means they're feeling down or unhappy. But if you think about the notes A and Ab rubbing against each other in that F7 chord—that's the major, or 'happy' sound, *coexisting* with the minor, or 'sad' sound. That is melancholy, or 'bittersweetness' boiled down to its essence.
But it doesn't end there. It's not just bittersweetness. You can also say that there is optimism expressed in the blues. The people who gave birth to the blues were living in brutal and oppressive conditions, yet the sound of the blues expresses hope for a better future at the same time that it describes the despair of the present moment. Further, this is not just blind hope that things will someday get better, either. It is hope *expressed*: "Despite all this pain, what I can do is play."

4. And on top of all that, there is a subversive element to the blues. In much of the American South, African slaves and their offspring, the first African Americans, weren't allowed to play their native African music at all. Their response to that was to use what they found around them—guitars, with Middle Eastern origins; harmony, with origins in Europe; and their African voices and musical genius, to imagine a new form of expression into existence.

Baraka explains this at length and much more eloquently than I ever could. I urge you to read *Blues People*, so you can approach the blues with some understanding of its origin.

Anyone can play the blues. The blues doesn't exclude. It is one of the most universal, arms-open-wide forms of art ever invented. For me, the people who developed such an art form while suffering harsh personal oppression deserve our unconditional awe and respect.

One last thing for clarity before we get to the nuts and bolts: The blues is the foundation of jazz, and has also developed into an electrified form of its own, as exemplified by artists like Muddy Waters and B.B. King. It has also informed Rock and Roll, R & B, and most of pop music in one way or another. These styles are all potential sources of information and inspiration for jazz musicians, but we'll be focusing on the jazz forms of the blues here.

Recording technology didn't exist when the first blues singers accompanied themselves on the guitar in the area around the Mississippi Delta, so we don't know exactly how the earliest blues sounded. We do have recorded examples of 20th century Delta Blues singers, who continued the oral tradition handed down to them. There are a few examples from Charlie Patton, Robert Johnson, Blind Lemon Jefferson and Honeyboy Edwards in the playlist to inspire your own search for more.

You'll notice from the early examples that the form is somewhat fluid. Because the singer is accompanying himself, he has room to let the form accommodate the length of his vocal phrasing. The fundamental elements present are sets of three phrases, and a harmonic pathway that generally goes:

Idom7 >
IVdom7 > Idom7 >
Vdom7 > Idom7

Or, for an F blues:

F7 for the first phrase
Bb7 to F7 for the second phrase
C7 to F7 for the third phrase

As we said, the lengths of the early phrases tended to be intuitive. W.C. Handy is generally credited with solidifying the blues into the basic twelve bar form. Of the many things that are remarkable about this compact form is how closely the harmony colors the unfolding story of the lyrics. Here's a description of a clear example, as sung by Billie Holiday:

- First phrase – sung over the root chord, generally a dominant 7th
    - "My man don't love me. He treats me oh so mean."
- Second phrase – usually a reiteration of the first phrase, with slight variations. Harmony moves to the IV chord, then returns to the root
    - "My man, he don't love me. He treats me awful mean."
- Third phrase – concluding phrase. Usually starts from the V chord, returns to the root
    - "He's the lowest man, that I've ever seen."

(Lyrics quoted from "Fine and Mellow.")

Through the nineteen-teens and nineteen-twenties, the blues was the basis of a majority of recorded jazz. The foundational form looks like this:

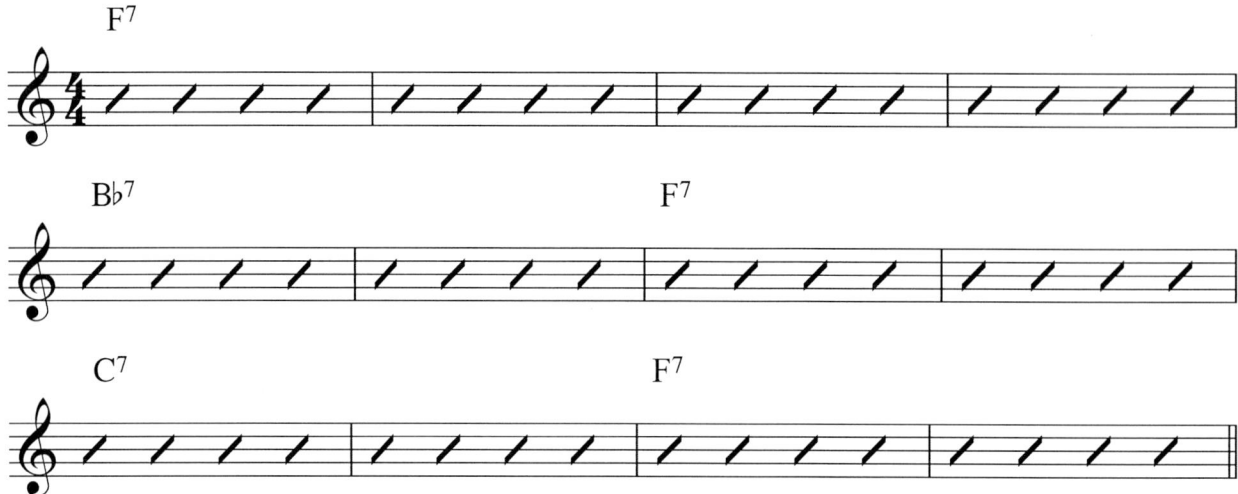

And a common variation added a Bb7 to the final cadence:

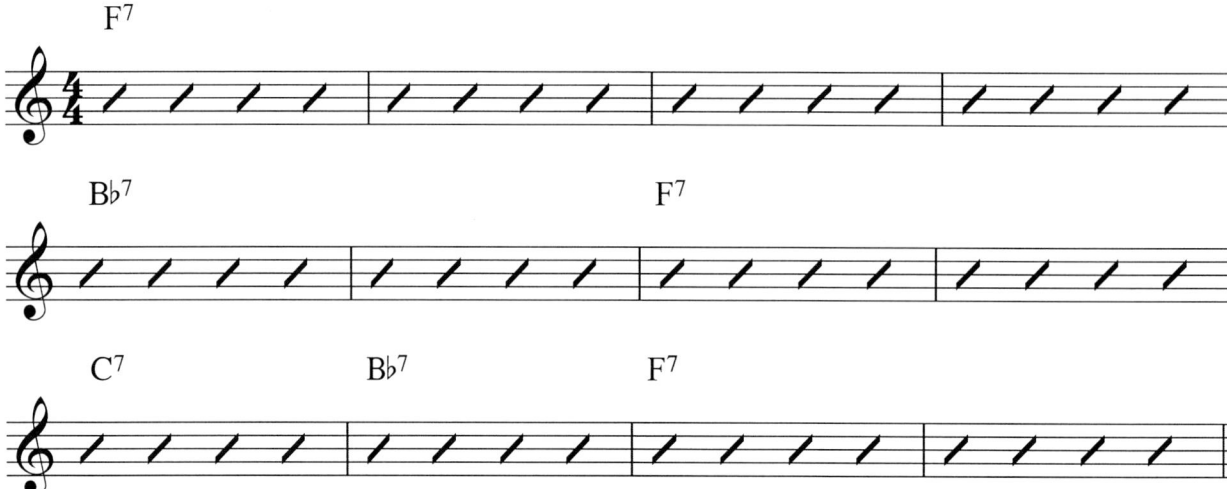

During the Swing Era, roughly the 1930's, jazz arrangers like Duke Ellington and Mary Lou Williams acquired a much deeper grasp of harmony, and started writing more sophisticated progressions. By the time the beboppers were playing the blues, there were new wrinkles in the common form, notably in the 2nd and 8th bars.

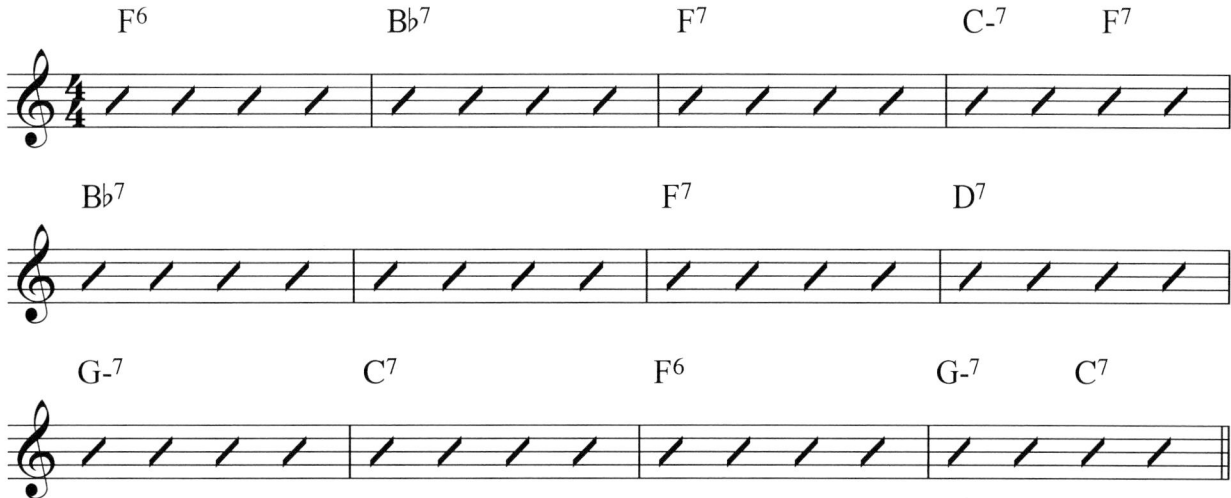

Notice how:

- A move to Bb7 happens in the second bar.
- The II chord (C-7) is added in front of the F7 in the 4th bar
- The II chord (G-7) is added in the 9th bar
- D7 has been added in the 8th bar to create a V-I cadence to the G-7 in the 9th bar

Charlie Parker led the charge to play over increasingly complex changes. Notice the addition of passing chords to the form of "Now's the Time:"

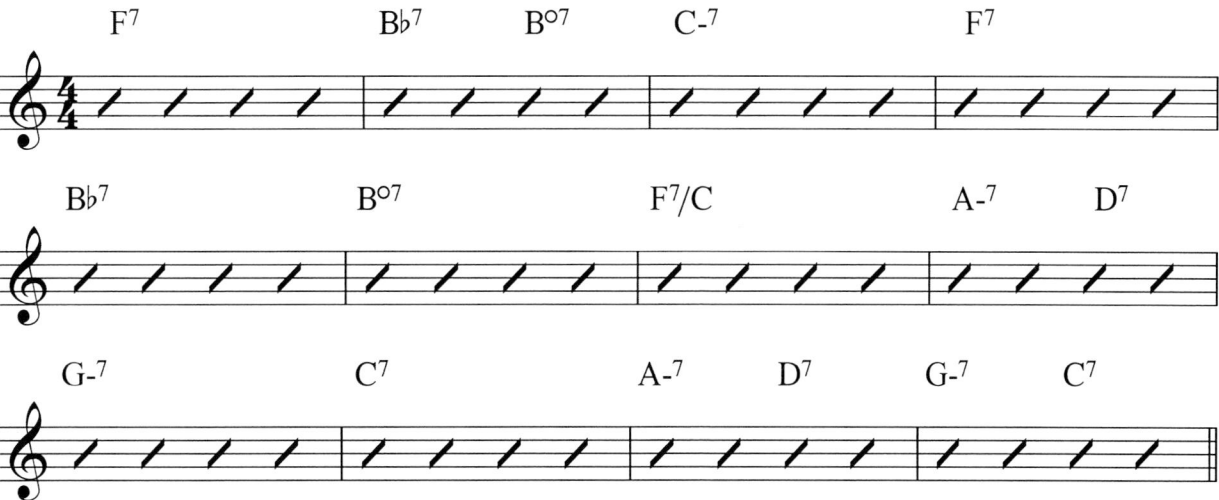

Now there's:

- A Bdim7 chord in the second bar, which makes an upward bass motion from Bb7 to Bdim7 to C-7, and the C-7 has been moved over to the third bar
- The same Bdim7 in Bar 6
- In the 8th bar an A-7 is added to make a II-V-I. Now it is A-7, D7 in the 8th bar, resolving to G-7 in the 9th bar
- Amin7 and D7 substituted in for F6 in the 11th and 12th bars to make a III-VI-II-V turnaround

Sonny Rollins, on "Mambo Bounce," adds more motion in the 7th and 8th bars, to make an interesting turnaround at that point. Notice that, even though the chord progression has gotten more and more complex, the bare bones of the original blues form are still right where they belong—the I chord is in the first bar, the IV chord starts the fifth bar, back to the I in the seventh bar, and home to the I again in bar 11.

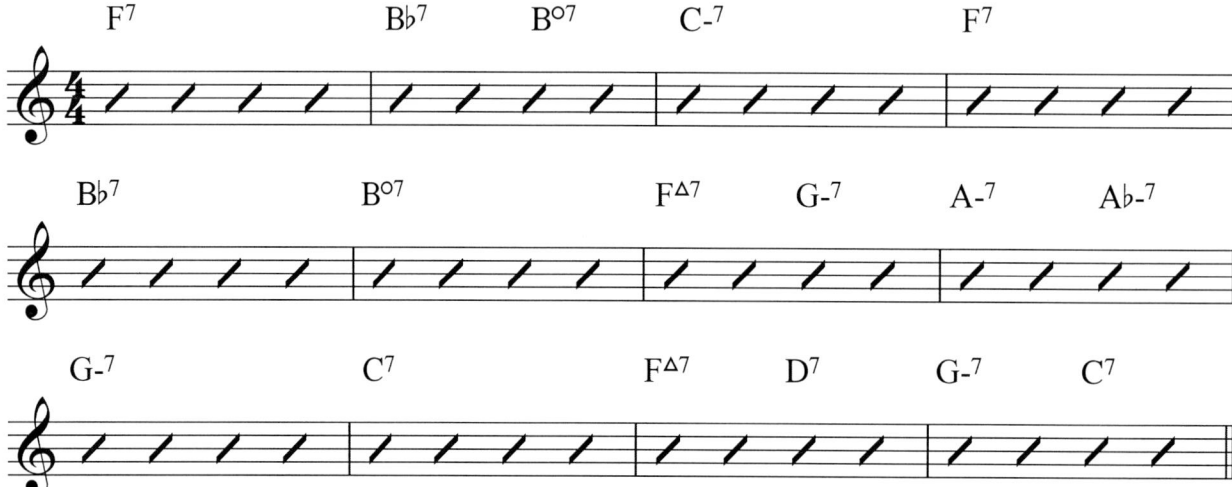

Bud Powell added a descending progression starting from bar 3, tritone substitutions in bars 4 and 10, and another pathway to get from bar 7 to bar 9. Have a look. (And you can listen to all of these on the playlist)

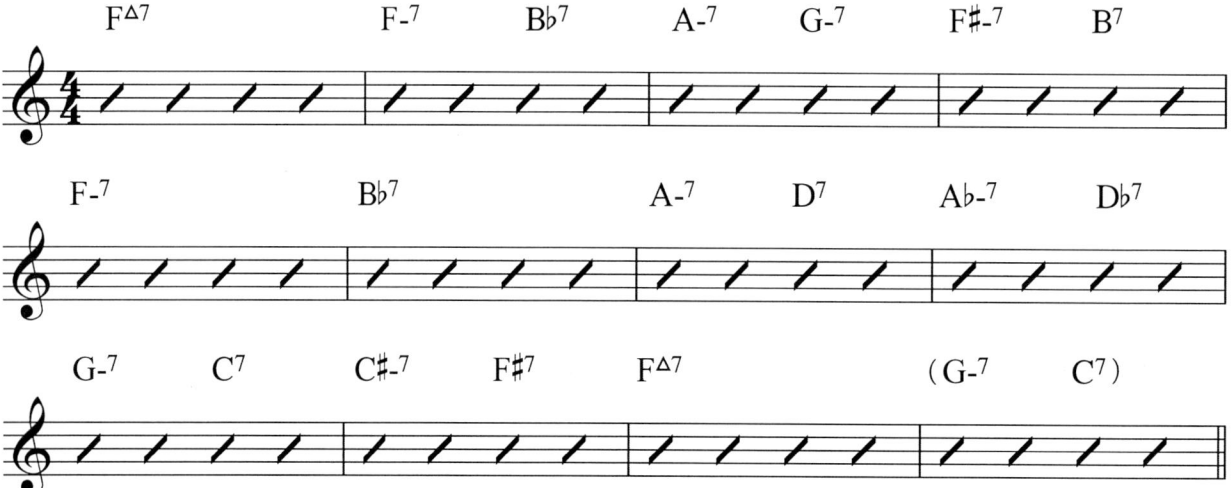

Parker maxed it out on "Blues for Alice," adding a cycle of fifths progression starting from bar two, and incorporating the "Dance of the Infidels" turnaround in bars 7 and 8.

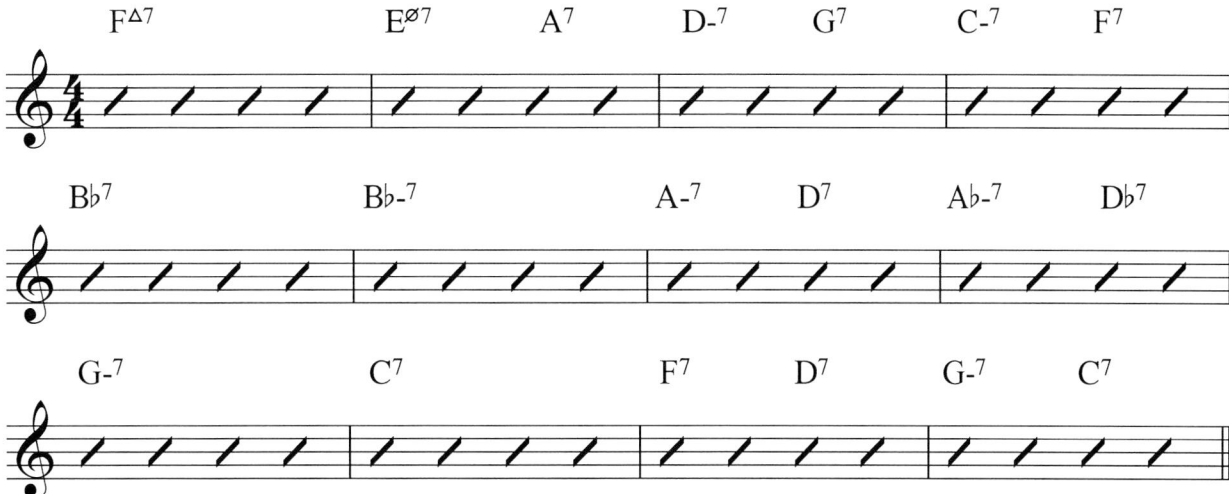

Now that you've seen a variety of progressions, and some different ways to navigate through the important spots in the blues, it is worth repeating a concept from earlier in the book. It makes sense to learn how to play through each of these progressions and play them "as is." More importantly, though, hopefully you're starting to get comfortable with the idea that the changes can be different every chorus. You can mix and match moments from each of these progressions, and challenge the rhythm section to hear where you're coming from. And, of course, if the pianist or bassist hears that you're going for some different progressions and decides to challenge you back by throwing in the "Blues for Alice" sequence, you want to be able to catch that and play it with them.

The following are a few more progressions with additional options:

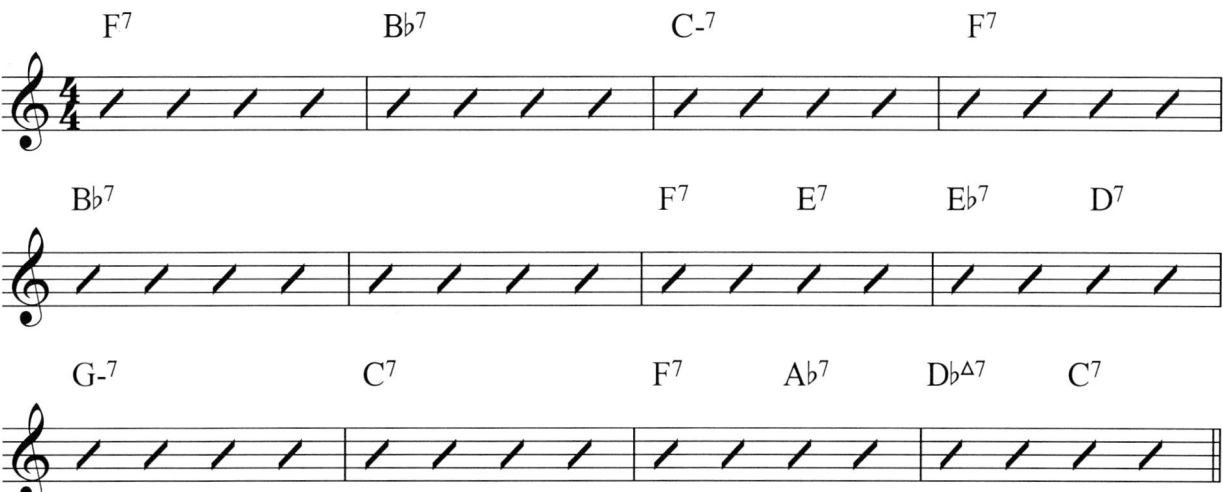

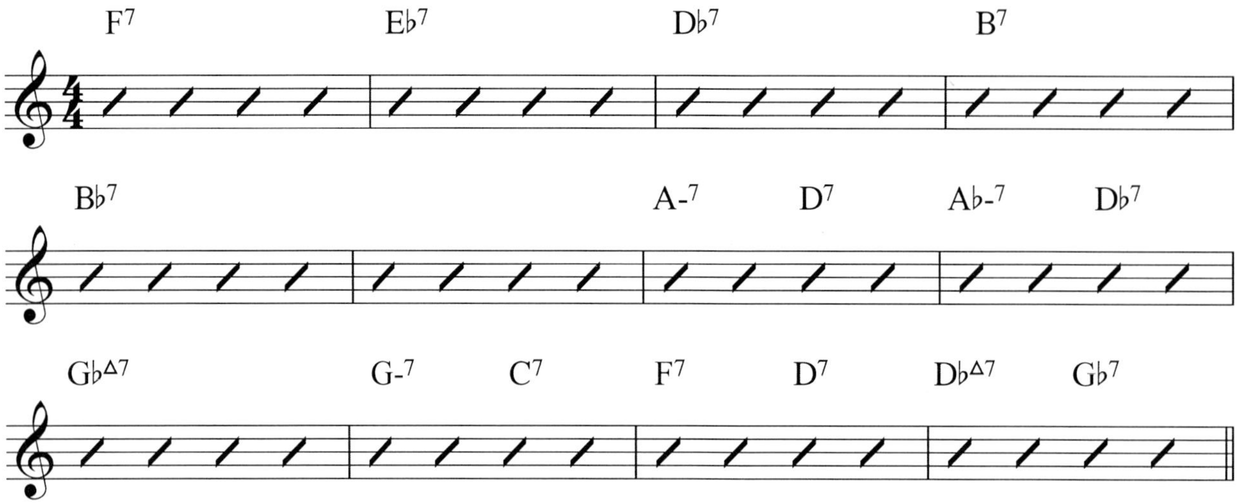

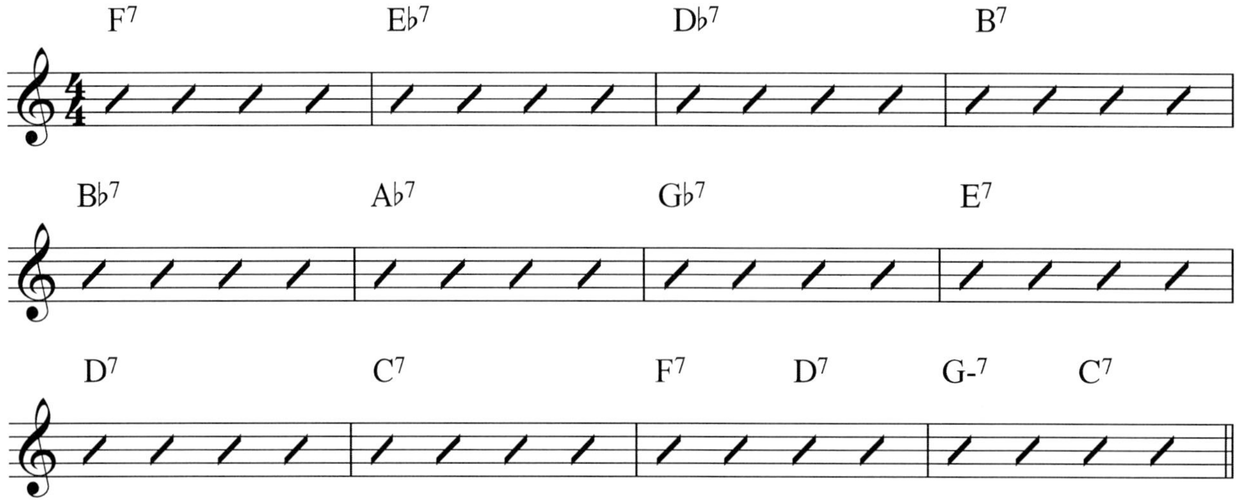

And here's a souped-up version of the "Blues for Alice" changes.

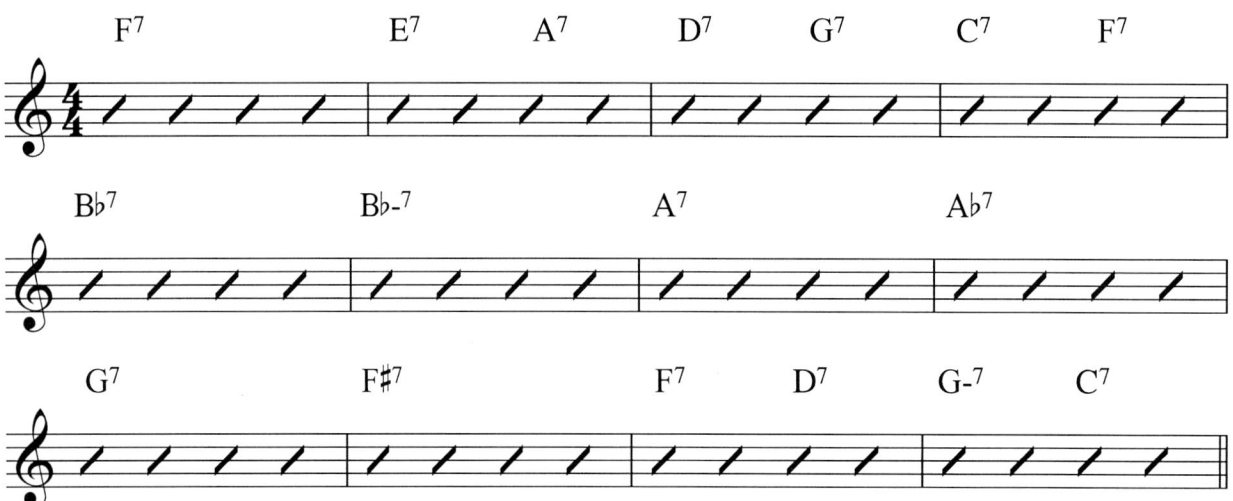

Remember how we said that a form that is dense with chords doesn't need you to play 'out?' That applies here. In order to make these chords sound, playing simply and clearly works best. The changes do a lot of the work for you.

Keep in mind as well that you can have fun substituting tritones throughout. The trick is to keep your antenna up for whether you are playing too much tension. Remember, tension eventually has to release to be tension. Tension on top of tension with no release becomes mush.

After a long journey into complexity it's always great to revisit the foundation. Another way to approach the blues is to take the basic form and use a different quality of chords.

Here's the basic form again:

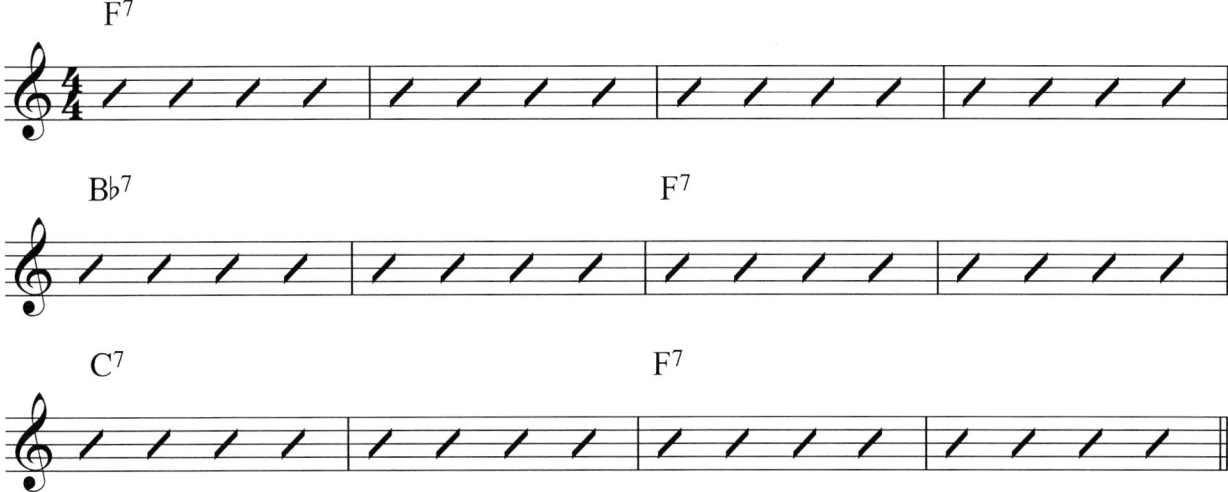

The most common approach to playing the blues form, but with a different harmonic color, is the minor blues. Duke Ellington's "Ko-Ko" (in Eb minor) is an early example. Coltrane's "Mr. PC" (C minor) and "Equinox" (Db minor) are frequently played songs that you should have in your repertoire.

To be consistent, we'll illustrate the minor blues form here in F minor. The half-step motion from bar nine to ten is the most commonly written form.

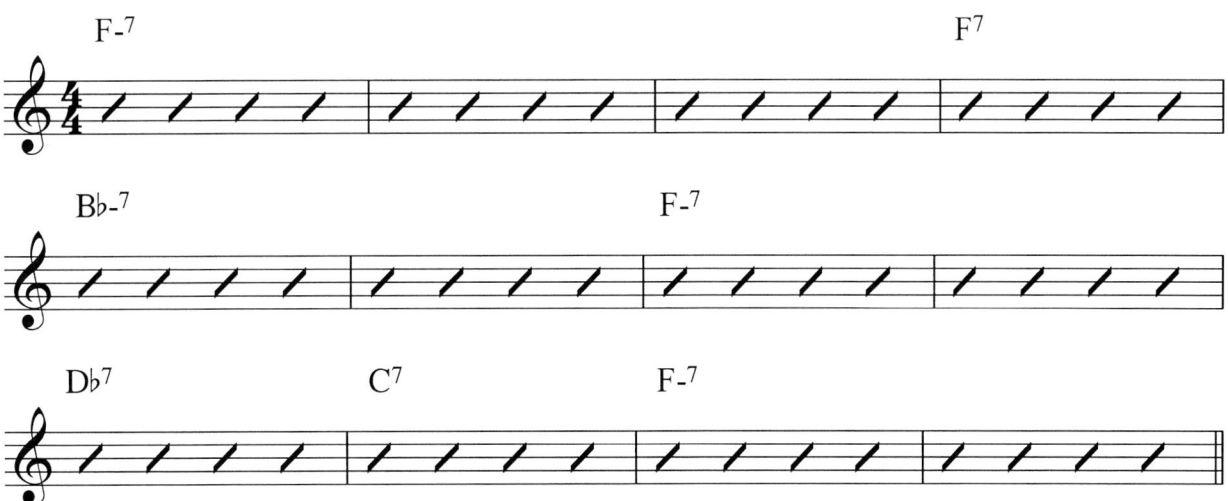

An alternate minor blues form, which is one of my personal favorites, goes to Db7 in the 5th bar instead of Bb-7. Dizzy Gillespie's "Birk's Works" and Woody Shaw's "Blues for Wood" are good examples of this form.

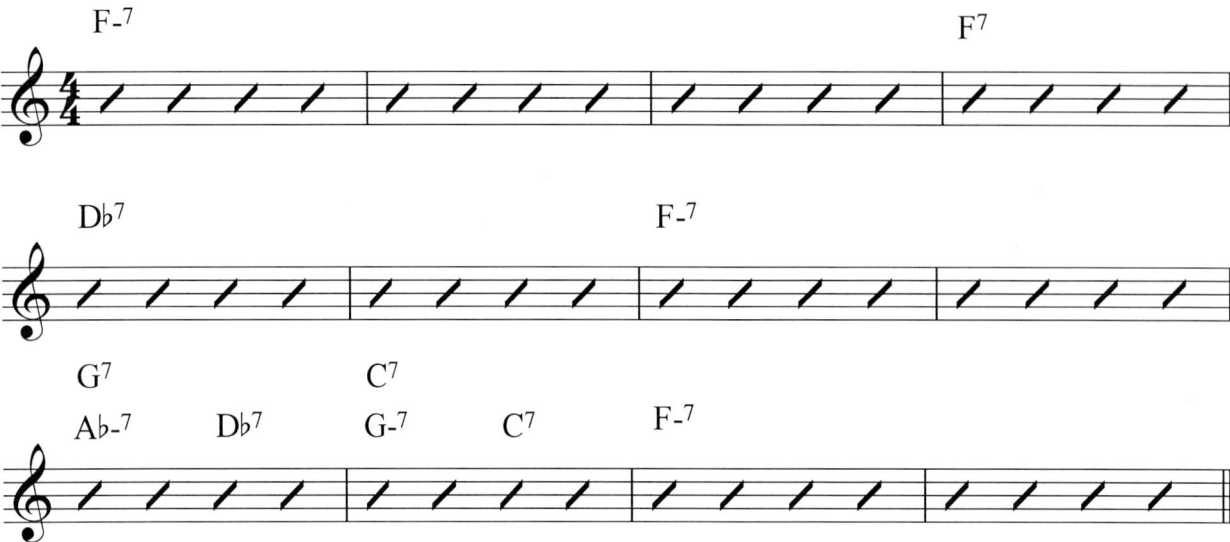

Another way to alter the sound and energy of the blues while keeping to the basic harmonic root motion is to use Sus chords. Here's what that looks like:

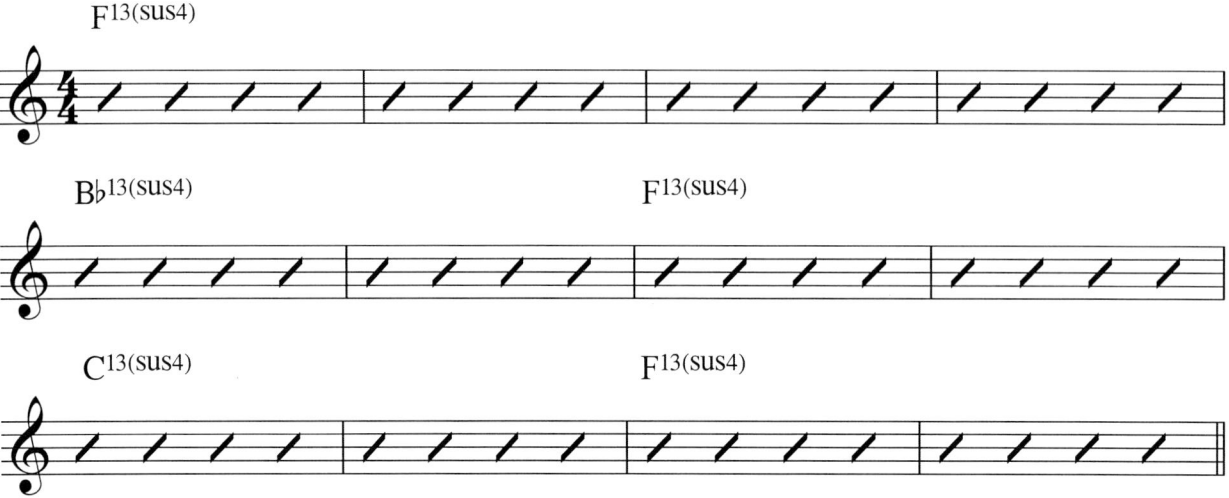

Coltrane's "Mr. Day" is a great example of this type of blues.

Again, you could play "Mr. Day" or write a melody over this form and play it 'as is,' or you could get together with a pianist and practice inserting this set of changes into the middle of your solo on a more traditional blues as a way of switching gears. Try it. If you have a creative drummer and bassist, you'll get a kick out of what happens when you get this sound going in the middle of your solo.

Now we have the opposite situation from the chords doing a lot of the work for you. Here you have wide-open spaces of Sus chords, which give you a lot of room to experiment with different 'out' sounds. The Sus chord can support lots of tension, and the blues form allows for regular releases of tension. It's a beautiful, compact little dynamo of a form.

Just for fun, here's the Sus blues sound with some more changes added:

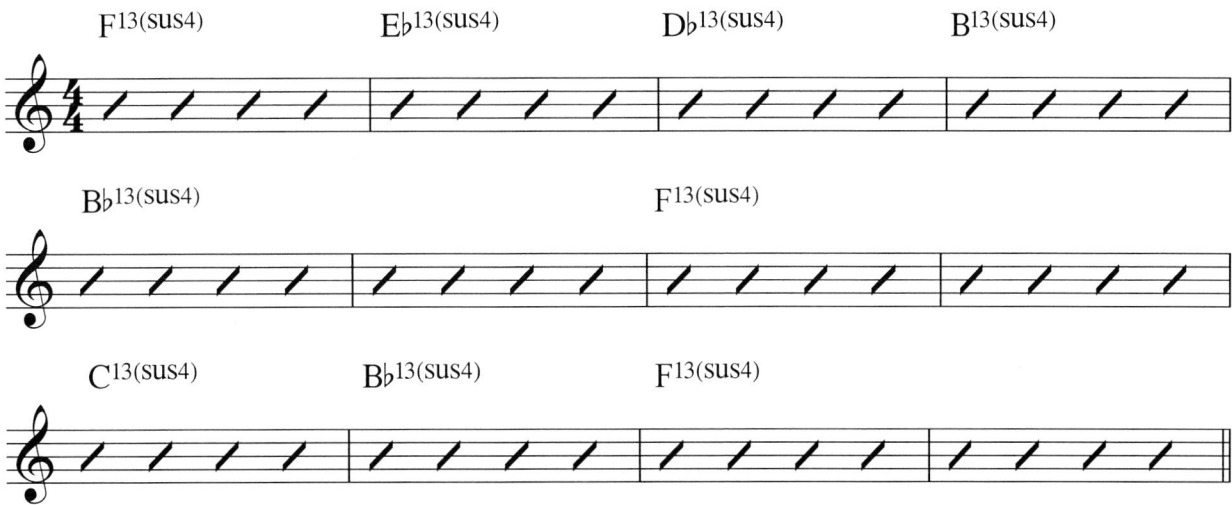

You can also find Coltrane's "Village Blues" on the playlist for the chapter. On "Village Blues" Trane takes a different tack—creating tension with an ostinato bass line. Listen to how he keeps the bass line the same all the way through the form. Your ear expects the bass line to modulate at the fifth bar, to match the harmony, but it doesn't. Trane keeps the ostinato exactly the same all the way through the form, which makes for a different kind of playing experience.

One more form, which is a great way to break things up when you feel like playing the blues, but need an added twist to keep it interesting, is blues with a bridge. It's usually played as an AABA form—12 bar blues, 12 bar blues, 8 bar bridge, 12 bar blues. The bridge is often a variant of a rhythm changes bridge, but it doesn't have to be. Four great examples are on the playlist:

- Sam Jones' "Bittersuite," in C, with a beautiful bridge featuring Sus chords (also spelled "Bittersweet")
- "Unit 7" also by Sam Jones, also in C
- Coltrane's "Locomotion," in Bb
- Joe Zawinul's "Scotch and Water," also in Bb, with a modal bridge

Below is the basic form in F:

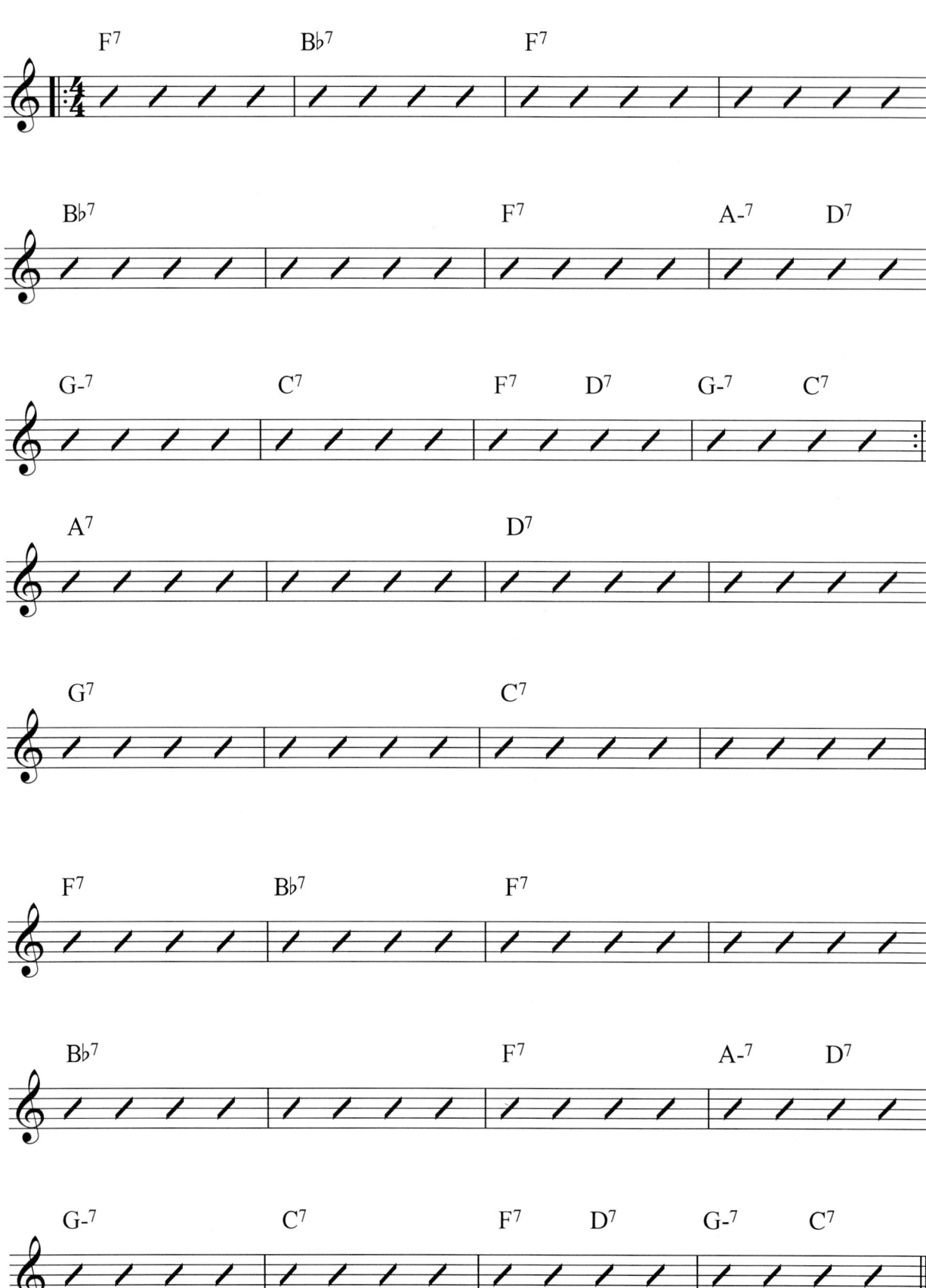

You might be wondering, should I learn the blues in all keys?

Yep.

How to go about that?

You've probably noticed by now that my main goals for the time I spend practicing are to have fun and feel inspired. There's work to do, and plenty of it, but I can do that work in a way that makes me happy. Remember, you are practicing to perform. What kind of performer do you want to be? Hardly anyone would answer,
"I want to sound like a robot that plays everything perfectly, and never has fun."

So when there's work to do, I try to find a way to be comprehensive without letting it get boring or mechanical.

There is certainly value in learning to play some Charlie Parker heads in all 12 keys, and if you enjoy that and love the challenge of it, do it! One benefit of doing that will be to give you some foundational language in all twelve keys. If that feels like work, and you're getting bogged down in it, I'd recommend taking a longer view—learn "Au Privave" in a couple of keys, and practice getting fluent interpreting that melody in those keys, and then move on.

As a way to set your foundation I would suggest that, instead of learning the same head in all twelve keys, you start by learning at least one blues head in each key. That way, if you feel like playing a blues in Eb, you can call "Sandu," rather than saying, "Lets play "Au Privave," but in Eb instead of F."

You could call "Au Privave" in Eb, but the disadvantage of that is that no one else is likely to have that head under his fingers at a moment's notice. If you call "Sandu" (and everyone knows it to play it) you'll get a stronger performance right off the bat.

Here again is a partial list—not meant to be comprehensive, but intended to get you started with a blues or two in every key. The idea is to point you toward some blues heads that most jazz musicians play, and also to expose you to a variety of sounds and artists.

## Key of C

| | |
|---|---|
| "C Jam Blues" | Duke Ellington |
| "Relaxin' at Camarillo" | Charlie Parker |
| "Cheryl" | Parker |
| "KC Blues" | Parker |
| "The Turnaround" | Ornette Coleman |
| "Village Blues" | John Coltrane |

## F

| | |
|---|---|
| "Walkin'" | Miles Davis |
| "Billie's Bounce" | Parker |
| "Au Privave" | Parker |
| "When Will The Blues Leave" | Ornette |
| "Dance of the Infidels" | Bud Powell |
| "Blues for Alice" | Parker |
| "Straight No Chaser" | Thelonious Monk |

## Bb

| | |
|---|---|
| "Blues Connotation" | Ornette |
| "Blue Seven" | Sonny Rollins |
| "Bloomdido" | Parker |
| "Bigfoot" | Parker |
| "Tenor Madness" | Rollins |
| "Blue Monk" | Monk |

## Eb

| | |
|---|---|
| "Sandu" | Clifford Brown |
| "Cool Blues" (Sonny Stitt version) | Parker (original key is C) |
| "Bessie's Blues" | Coltrane |

## Ab

| | |
|---|---|
| "Chichi" (Blues for Alice Changes) | Parker |
| "Freight Trane" (Blues for Alice changes) | Tommy Flanagan |

## Db

| | |
|---|---|
| "Equinox" (minor blues) | Coltrane |

## F#

I can't name a standard blues head in the key of F#. You, dear reader, will have to write a great one, have it become a standard, and then let me know, and we'll put it into the book!

## B

| | |
|---|---|
| "Mr. Knight" | Coltrane |

## E

| | |
|---|---|
| "Mr. Day" | Coltrane |
| "Only Half a Cup" | Jim Ridl |

## A

| | |
|---|---|
| "Bailey's Blues" | Armacost (I only include my own because I can't find another one!) |

## D

| | |
|---|---|
| "The Disguise" | Ornette |

## G

| | |
|---|---|
| "Jumpin the Blues" | Stanley Turrentine |
| "Stormy Monday" | T-Bone Walker |

Thelonious Monk wrote all kinds of blues melodies, and many of them have quirks in the harmony that are unique to Monk's composition. He's a great source to take it to the next level.

## THREE SIGNPOSTS IN THE FORM

Here's one more thing to practice. This is a way to address the harmony of the blues that can help you be grounded in the form, while aiming for notes that anchor the passage of the three phrases. You can think of the three notes as signposts or landmarks as you make your way through a chorus. Here's the basic bebop form with the landmarks added:

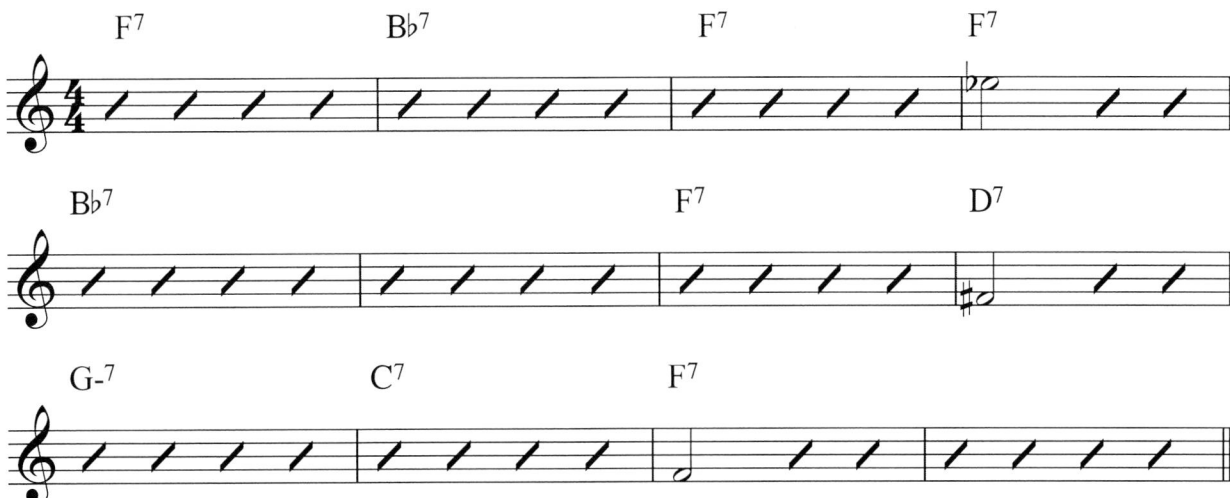

In the first four bars, ending the first melodic phrase with the 7th of the F7 chord—the note Eb in this case—is very common. I don't have a theoretical explanation for this, it's more something I've observed in practice. It's a way of ending the first statement that leaves a feeling of an open question waiting for an answer.

Sonny Rollins ended the opening phrase of his solo this way on "Mambo Bounce:"

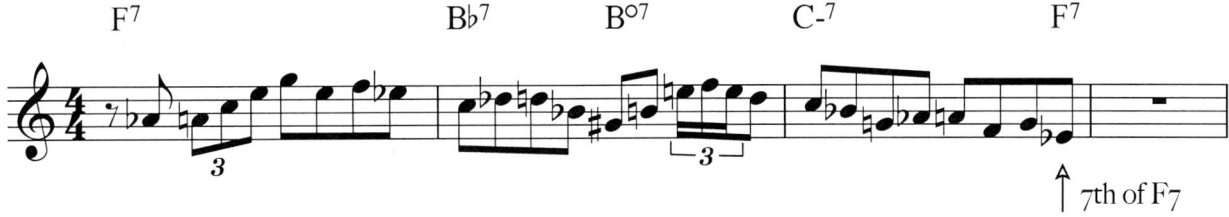

The melody in the first four bars of Charlie Parker's "KC Blues" is a classic example in the key of C:

On his debut recording, Libra, Gary Bartz plays a great solo on Parker's "Bloomdido." Here's what he plays in the first four bars of his second chorus, starting at 0:53 in the track. We're in the key of Bb:

The signpost to aim for in bar 8 is the 3rd of the D7—the note F#. This note is completely outside of the home key, so it creates a lot of contrast, is a strong sound on the D7 chord, and wants to move hard toward the G-7. It gives the second phrase a feeling of having developed the idea of the first four bars, but with a need for resolution.

Here's a strong concluding phrase, starting from the seventh bar of the form and taking it all the way home. Charles McPherson, grooving hard on Don Patterson's recording, *Boppin' and Burnin'*, plays this at 4:34 on "Now's the Time:"

Here's Coltrane on "Some Other Blues," also using both the 3rd of the dominant chord in the 8th bar and the root in the 11th bar. This happens at around 1:08 in the track:

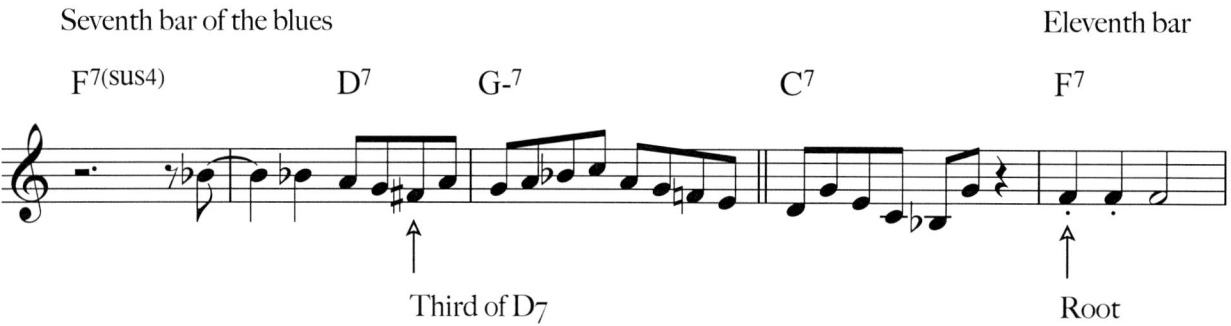

The recordings Woody Shaw and Freddie Hubbard made together in the mid 1980's with Kenny Garrett contain a deep well of modern post-bop language. Here's a phrase from Woody Shaw's first chorus on "Sandu," in the key of Eb. You can hear it at 0:57 in the track:

The note F in the eleventh bar brings the story to a close by resolving to the root. Here's a concluding phrase you'll hear used by musicians on all instruments. The example starts from G-7 in the 9th bar:

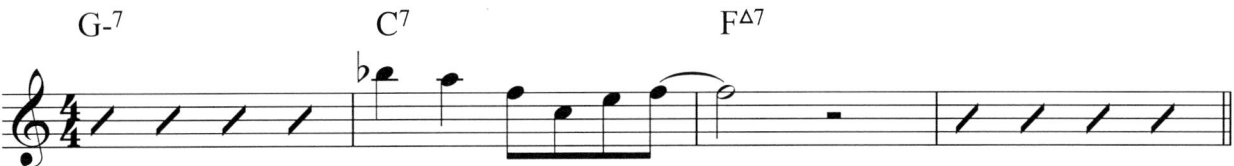

And a variation:

Harold Land is never far from the blues. Here's a great concluding phrase he played on the original version of "Sandu," with Clifford Brown. You can find this at the end of his first chorus, at around 1:38 in the track:

Check out the video for a demonstration of how it sounds to organize some choruses using these landmarks in the form.

- Video 33: Three Signposts in the Blues

Finally, the organ tradition is a great source for modern playing that is steeped in the language of the blues, but is also informed by contemporary jazz harmony. You'll find a few suggestions toward the end of the playlist for Chapter 22:

Stanley Turrentine with Jimmy Smith
Red Holloway with Jack McDuff
Sonny Stitt with Don Patterson
Gene Ammons with Jack McDuff
Joe Henderson with Larry Young

# CHAPTER 23 · ARMACOST SOLO TRANSCRIPTION ON NYSQ'S "SOUL EYES"

Including a solo of my own in this book seemed a bit presumptuous to me at first, considering the examples from the masters I've been using throughout the text. However, Chuck Sher convinced me that it would be valuable for the following reason: I can analyze and learn from someone else's solo by reading the notes and making educated guesses about what sort of ideas the soloist was exploring, but with my own solo I can explain pretty much exactly what I was aiming for. In the first conversation we had about creating this book, Chuck and I talked about the New York Standards Quartet arrangement of "Soul Eyes," on the recording, *Sleight of Hand*, so that seemed like an appropriate solo to use to talk about the way I experience improvisation.

I've taken the approach of outlining what harmonic choices I was making throughout the solo, with occasional comments about what happened along the way. I was surprised by two things in the solo:

- That I played a lot of passing tones(!)
- That I occasionally made choices based on the logic of the melody I was working out, rather than trying to be 'correct' over the changes

Going into an analysis of my own solo for the first time, I expected the scales to be clearer. I hadn't really thought about this before, but using a lot of passing tones creates a smooth feeling, like sanding the sharpness off of a wooden edge. That smoothness is something that I've always held as a goal, and it was interesting to see one of the ways I've created it, without having articulated it clearly to myself. Another way to think about it is the difference between a line drawing:

and an image created with shading:

One of them is not necessarily better than the other—it's just two ways to go about it. One is clear and direct, and the other is more mellow and roundabout.

As for melodic choices, I was happy to see some things in this solo that were "incorrect" in the sense that I played a combination of notes that doesn't fit in any commonly used scale. These melodies happened in the heat of the moment, and I was working them out in real time, trying to use my imagination to solve puzzles as they came up. Some of the solutions make me happy, and others make me cringe, but I can live with the overall result.

In the interest of keeping things simple, I have indicated mostly major scale choices rather than saying Dorian for a minor 7th chord, or Mixolydian for a dominant 7th, mainly because that's also the way I think. I put a few modes in parentheses at the beginning, but left them out after the first mention. In the case of melodic minor and harmonic minor choices, I've just indicated the scale, and the explanation can be found in the chapters on those scales earlier in the book.

Lastly, before we get to the solo itself, a word about thinking. When we started out in Chapter 1 we were just singing some simple melodies, trying to play them through the horn while we sang them in our minds. That is the essence of improvisation. When you decide to dive more deeply into the language of modern jazz and study harmony, there follows a years-long process where learning to think quickly and accurately can feel like it's too much thinking and not enough music. Transforming the things that you've *studied* into things that you *hear* is the trick. Maintain the connection to your internal singing voice as you work—and always try to practice something until it feels good when you play it.

After you've trained your ears and gotten familiar with the different sounds available to you, you'll be able to hear things on the fly, and execute them in real time, and at that point you start to become a mature improviser. You're still just trying to imagine things, and play them straight through your horn, but now your inner ear is informed by a wealth of information and musical intelligence.

When I was living in Amsterdam many years ago, I had a chance to ask Kenny Wheeler a question after a gig I heard him play one night. Because he sounds so free over the changes I asked:
"What are you thinking about as you're making your way through the changes?"

He answered,
"I try to know the changes so well that I don't have to think about them at all."

With that in mind, here is a snapshot of the way I speak the language of jazz. I'm still working on it...

# Soul Eyes

**Concert Key**

Tim Armacost's Tenor Saxophone Solo
From the Album *Sleight of Hand* by NYSQ (New York Standards Quartet)

Mal Waldron
Arr. Tim Armacost
Transcription by Lorenzo Bisogno

**A**

Starting out rhythmically interpreting the melody

Whoa, was aiming for F, landed on Gb, better work it out melodically

Ok, safe landing — First line - Eb major scale with multiple passing tones

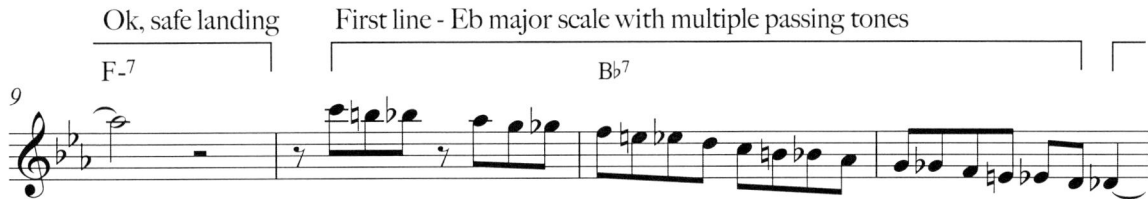

Bb melodic minor with passing tones — Db melodic minor — Working

on a little fragment here based on the melody — Went with A-7 here

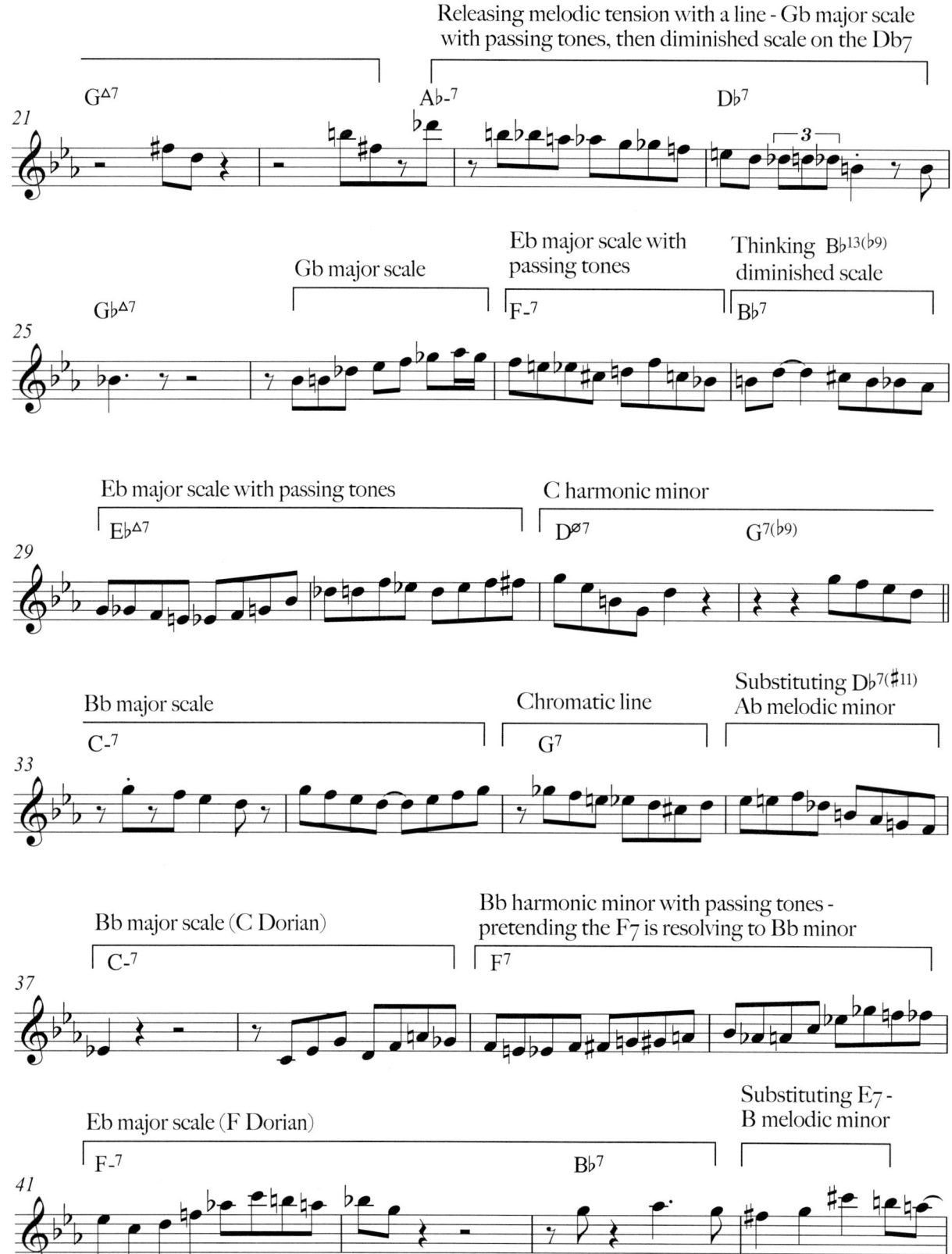

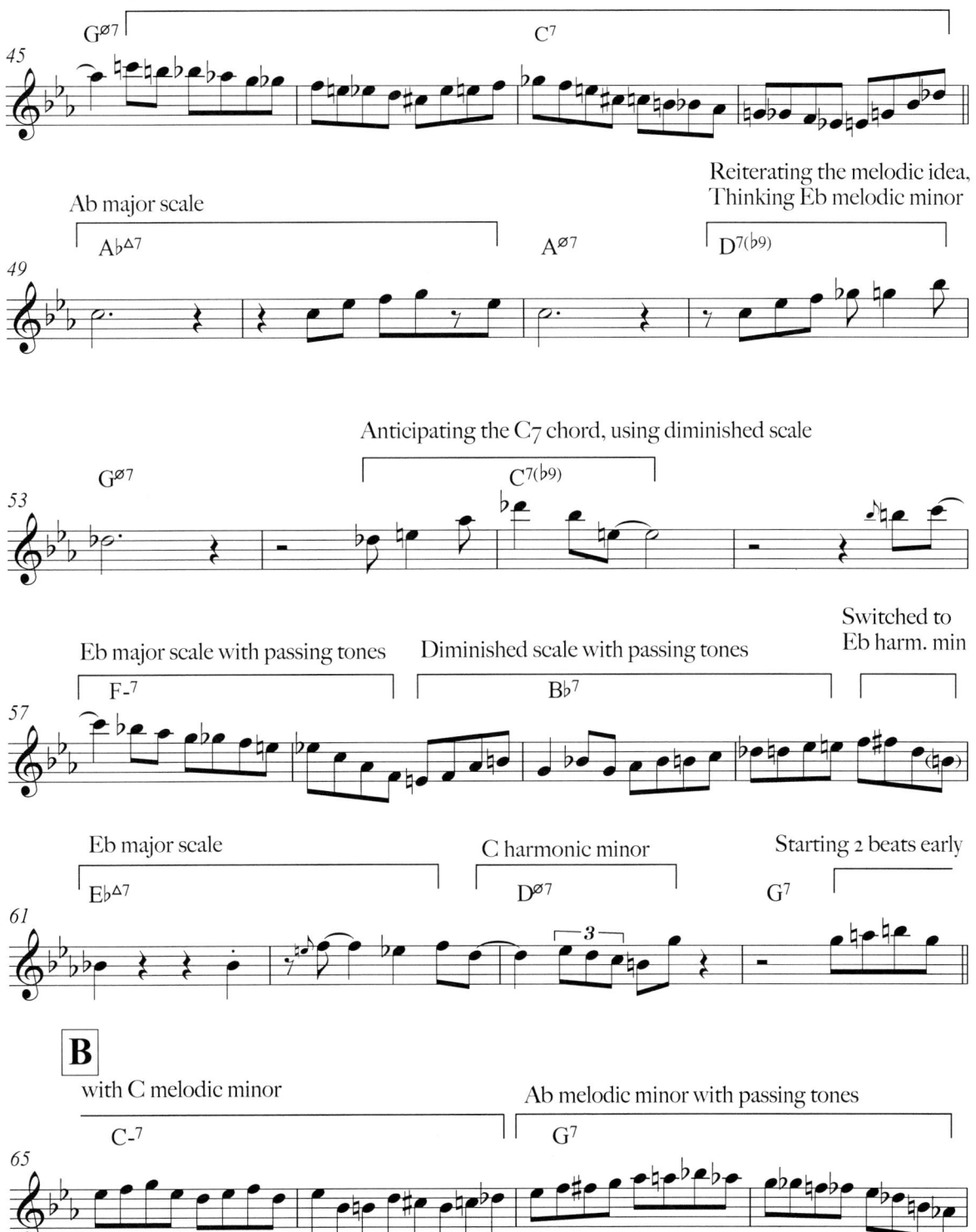

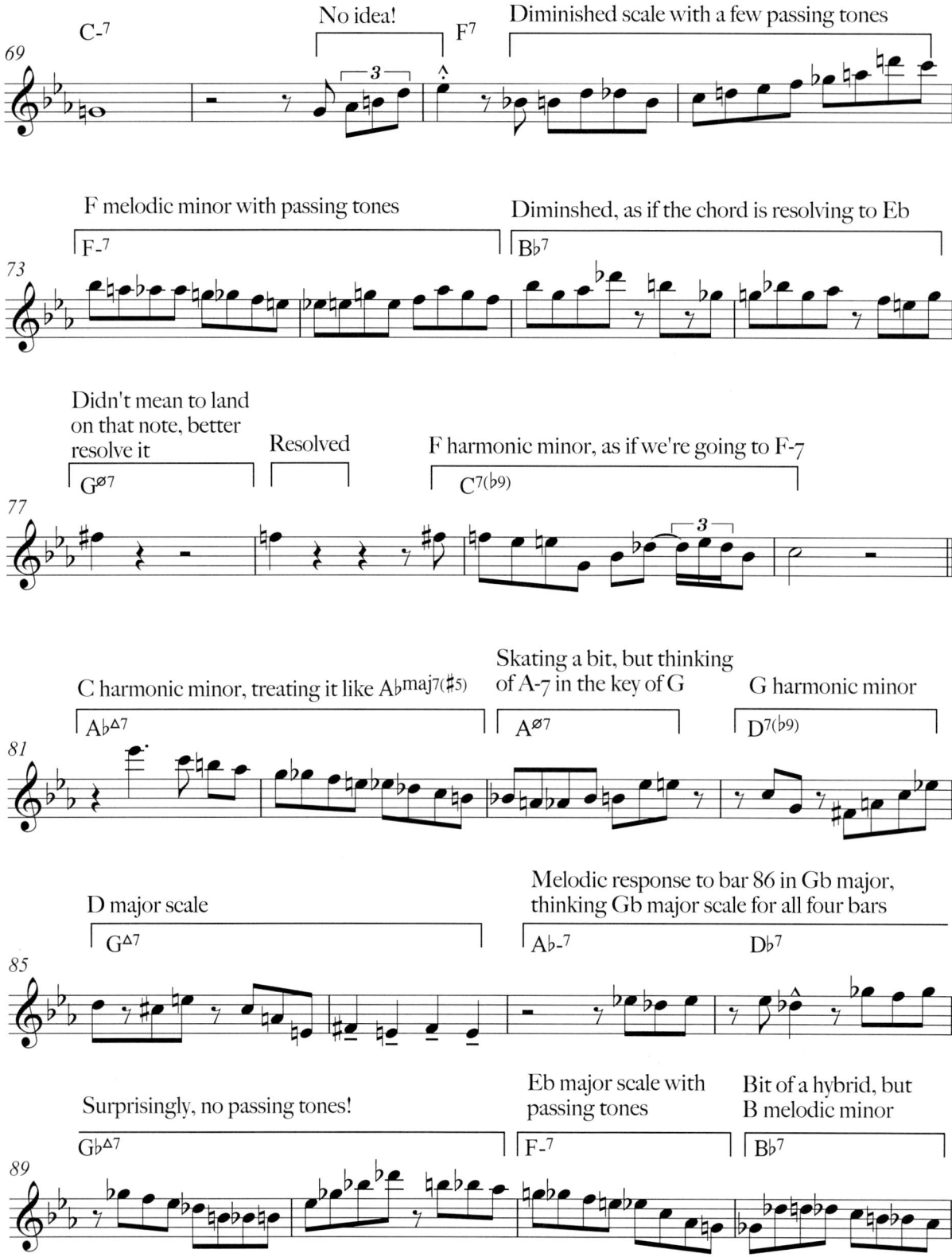

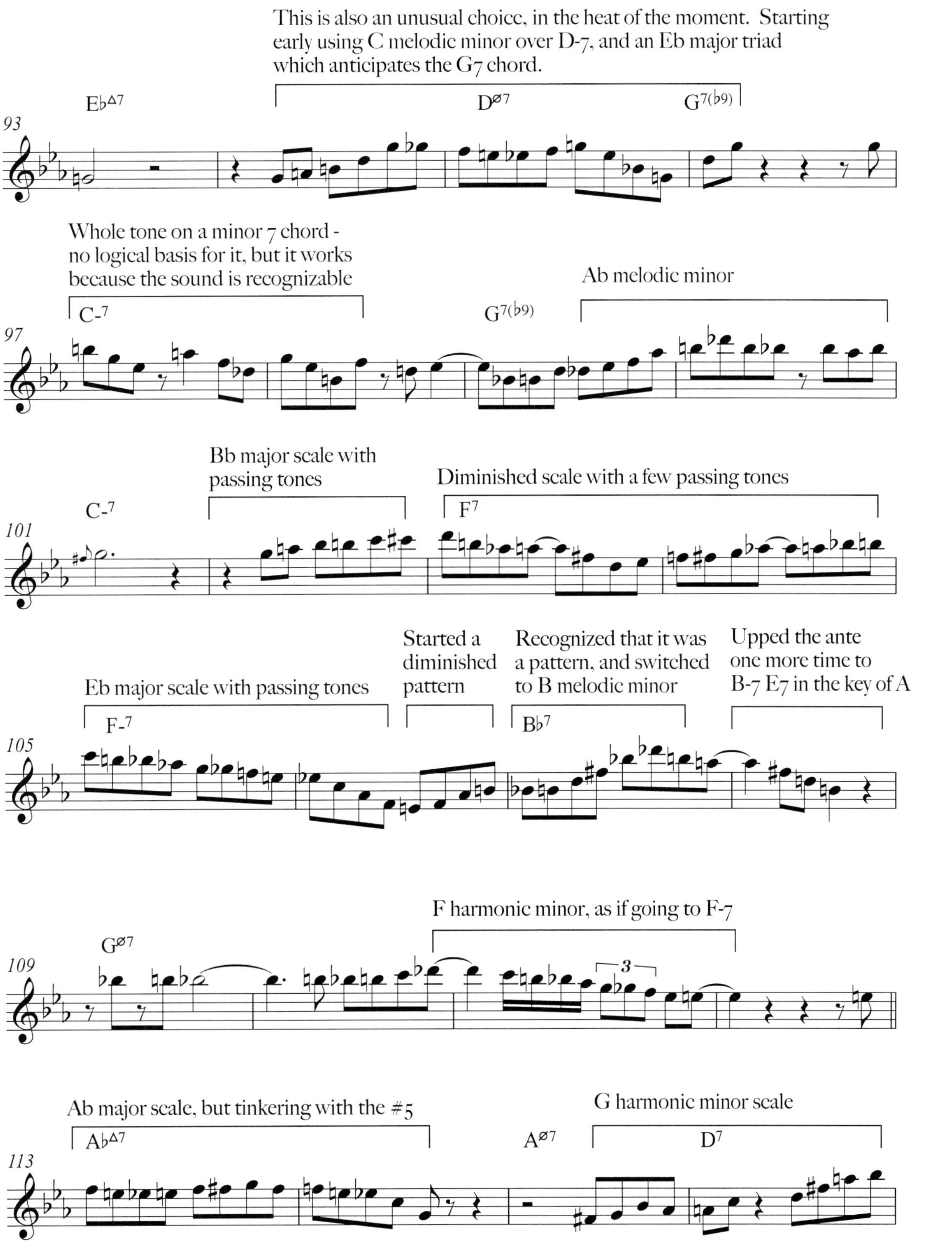
This is also an unusual choice, in the heat of the moment. Starting early using C melodic minor over D-7, and an Eb major triad which anticipates the G7 chord.
93
Eb△7
DØ7
G7(b9)
Whole tone on a minor 7 chord - no logical basis for it, but it works because the sound is recognizable
Ab melodic minor
97
C-7
G7(b9)
Bb major scale with passing tones
Diminished scale with a few passing tones
101
C-7
F7
Started a diminished pattern
Recognized that it was a pattern, and switched to B melodic minor
Upped the ante one more time to B-7 E7 in the key of A
Eb major scale with passing tones
105
F-7
Bb7
F harmonic minor, as if going to F-7
109
GØ7
3
Ab major scale, but tinkering with the #5
G harmonic minor scale
113
Ab△7
AØ7
D7

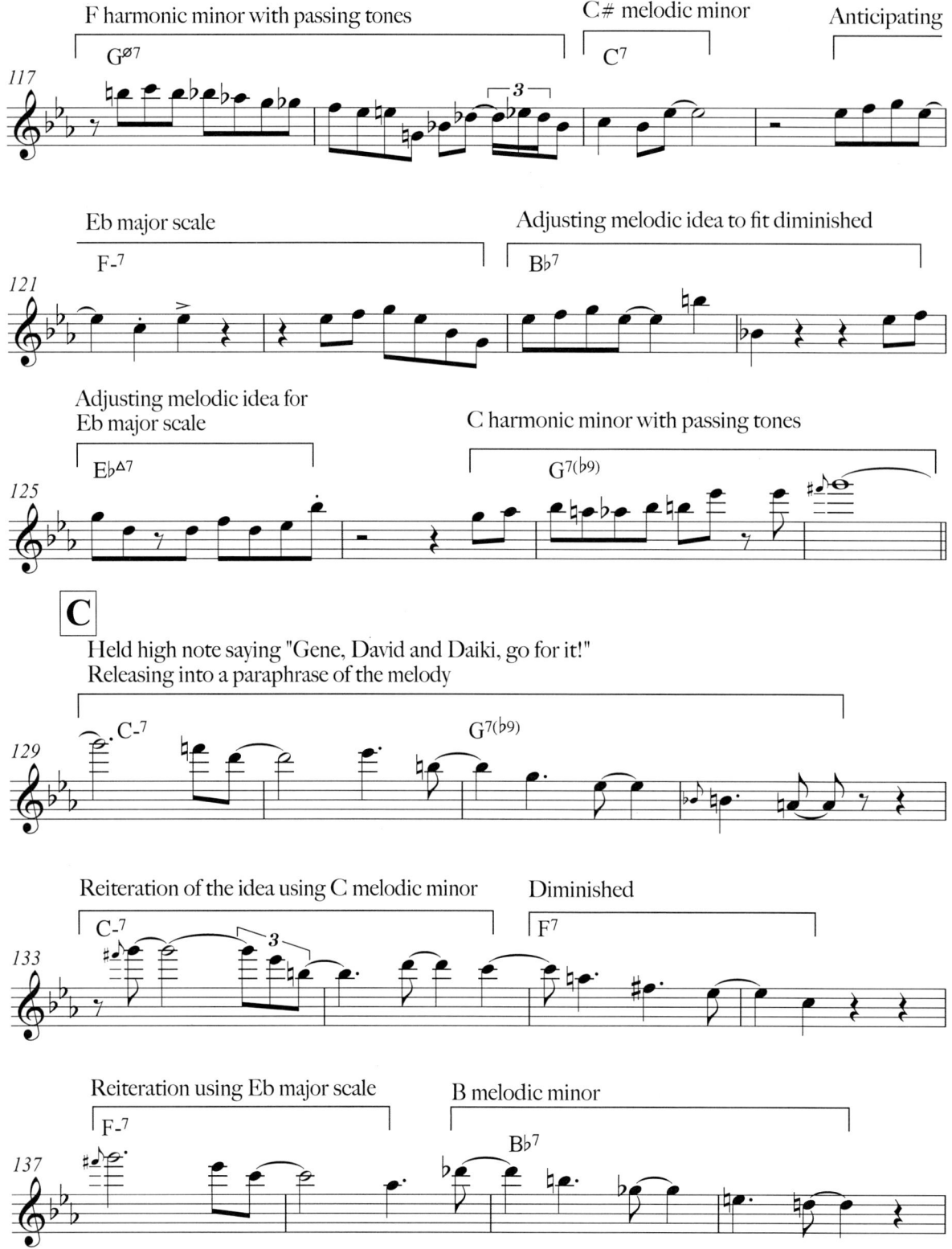

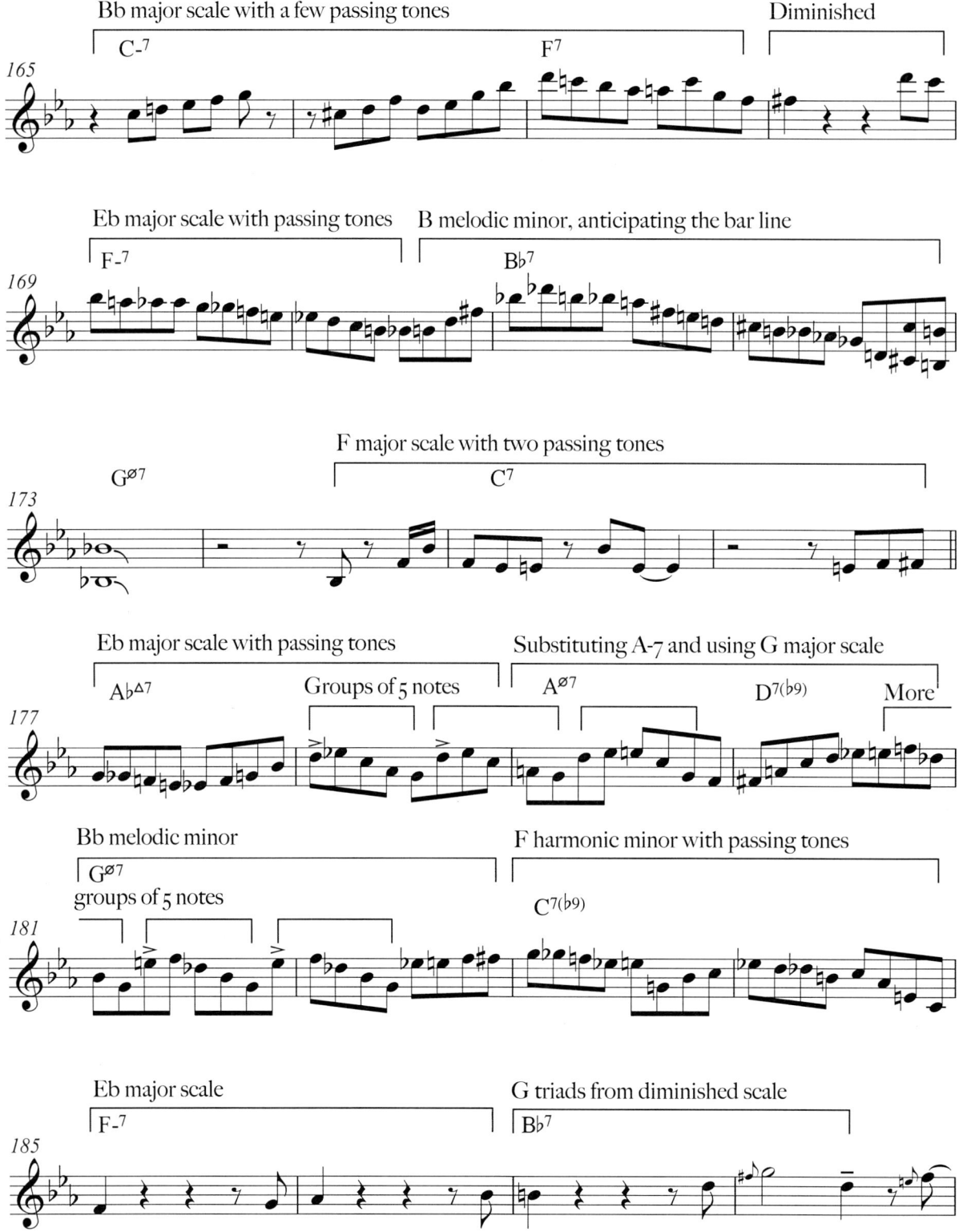

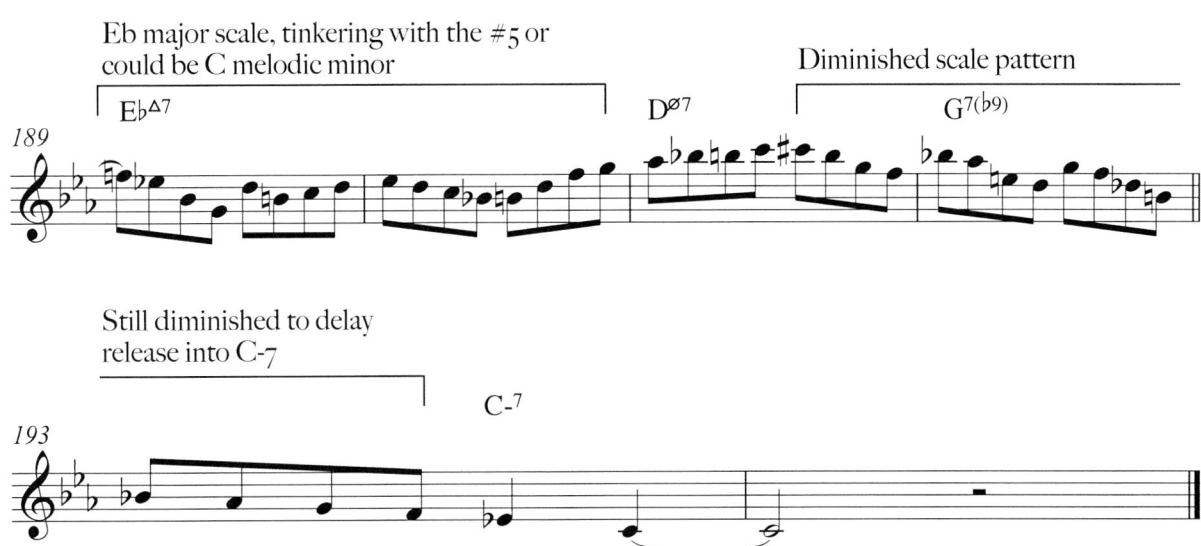

# SPECIAL THANKS:

I am blessed to have been born into a loving family, the members of which are all teachers, either in practice or by example. Maybe growing up around them trained me to look for good teachers out in the larger world. This book is dedicated to the people who pointed me in a good direction. Thank you, one and all.

Mom, Dad, Scott, Chris and the extended Armacost Family
Niki, Zak and Colson, and the extended Cunningham Family
Olivia Gutoff
Ron Doberstein
Doc Ross
Earnest Bradley
Margaret Dornish
Keido Fukushima Kancho
Jeff Shore
David Blum
Charlie Shoemake
Bobby Bradford
Jorrit Dijkstra
Peter Guidi
Craig Bailey
Marion Skelly
George Kormendi
Miriam Cooper
Nanette Walsh
Clare Stelling
Barbara Blum
Valery Ponomarev
Billy Hart
Ray Drummond
Bruce Barth
David Berkman
Gene Jackson
Michael Carvin
Michael Mossman
Howard Brofsky
Antonio Hart
Dennis Mackrel
Jamey Aebersold
Linda Boyd
Donna Doyle
David Schober
Bennett Paster

# BIBLIOGRAPHY/RECOMMENDED SOURCES

The following are resources that have either been mentioned in the book, or that have provided me with some inspiration.

| | |
|---|---|
| David Berkman | The Jazz Harmony Book |
| | The Jazz Musician's Guide to Creative Practicing |
| Mark Levine | The Jazz Theory Book |
| | The Jazz Piano Book |
| Ted Nash | Ted Nash's Studies in High Harmonics |
| Sigurd Rasher | Top-Tones for the Saxophone |
| Sher Publishing | The New Real Book Vol. 1 |
| | The New Real Book Vol. 2 |
| | The New Real Book Vol. 3 |
| Jeb Patton | An Approach to Comping: The Essentials |
| Nicolas Slonimsky | Thesaurus of Scales and Melodic Patterns |
| Gary Campbell | Expansions: A Method for Developing New Material for Improvisation |
| Walt Weiskopf | Giant Steps: A Player's Guide to Coltrane's Harmony |
| John O'Gallagher | Twelve-Tone Improvisation: A Method for Using Tone Rows in Jazz |
| Charlie Parker | The Charlie Parker Omnibook (Transcriptions by Jamey Aebersold and Ken Slone) |
| Thelonious Monk | Thelonious Monk Fake Book (Transcriptions by Steve Cardenas) |
| Ted Gioia | The History of Jazz |
| | The Jazz Standards |

Websites:
Tim Armacost and the Jazz Saxophone Book on YouTube:
https://www.youtube.com/user/timarm8

www.timarmacost.com
www.jazzstandards.com
www.musicnotes.com
www.sheetmusicplus.com
www.shermusic.com
www.jazzbooks.com

# The Sher Music Co. Catalog
VISIT SHERMUSIC.COM FOR MORE INFORMATION AND TO ORDER ONLINE

## BEST-SELLING BOOKS BY MARK LEVINE
The Jazz Theory Book
The Jazz Piano Book
Jazz Piano Masterclass: The Drop 2 Book
How To Voice Standards at the Piano

## THE WORLD'S BEST FAKE BOOKS
The New Real Book - Vol. 1 - C, Bb and Eb
The New Real Book - Vol. 2 - C, Bb and Eb
The New Real Book - Vol. 3 - C, Bb, Eb & Bass Clef

The Real Easy Book - Vol. 1 - C, Bb, Eb & Bass Clef
The Real Easy Book - Vol. 2 - C, Bb, Eb & Bass Clef
The Real Easy Book - Vol. 3 - C, Bb, Eb & Bass Clef
The Latin Real Easy Book - C, Bb, Eb & Bass Clef
Drum Supplement for Real Easy Book - Vol. 1

The Standards Real Book - C, Bb and Eb
The Latin Real Book - C only
The Real Cool Book - Octet charts from the 1950s
The All-Jazz Real Book - with selected audio
The European Real Book - with selected audio
The Best of Sher Music Real Books - C, Bb & Eb
The World's Greatest Fake Book - C only
Jazz Arrangements of Public Domain Songs
The Yellowjackets Songbook - separate parts

## LATIN MUSIC BOOKS
Contemporary Latin Jazz Guitar - Vol. 1&2, by Neff Irizarry
Decoding Afro-Cuban Jazz - by Mauleon & Valdes
The Salsa Guidebook - by Rebeca Mauleõn
101 Montunos - by Rebeca Mauleõn
The Latin Bass Book - by Oscar Stagnaro & Chuck Sher
The Latin Real Book - C only
The True Cuban Bass - by Carlos del Puerto
The Brazilian Guitar Book - by Nelson Faria
Inside the Brazilian Rhythm Section - Faria/Korman
Conga Drummer's Guidebook - by Michael Spiro
Language of the Masters - by Michael Spiro
Introduction to the Conga Drum DVD - by M. Spiro
Afro-Caribbean Grooves for Drumset - JPhi Fanfant
Afro-Peruvian Percussion Ensemble - H. Morales
Flamenco Improvisation - Vol.1-3 by Enrique Vargas
Muy Caliente! - Afro-Cuban Book & Play-Aong audio
Music of the Arará Savalú Cabildo - Galvin & Spiro

## DIGITAL FAKE BOOKS
The New Real Book - Vol.1 - C, Bb & Eb
The Digital Standards Songbook - individual songs with lyrics, plus C, Bb, Eb, High Voice & Low Voice
The Digital Real Book (650 songs from all our books)

## THE DIGITAL SONGBOOK SERIES
The Kenny Barron Songbook
The Carla Bley Songbook
The Tom Harrell Songbook
The Oscar Hernandez Songbook
The Alan Pasqua Songbook
The Horace Silver Songbook
The Steve Swallow Songbook
The Ralph Towner Songbook
The Wayne Wallace Songbook
The Kenny Werner Songbook
The Randy Brecker Songbook
The Larry Dunlap Songbook
The Barry Finnerty Songbook
The Benny Golson Songbook
The Steve Khan Songbook
The Doug Morton Songbook
The Andy Narell Songbook
The Enrico Pieranunzi Songbook
The Dave Tull Songbook
The Denny Zeitlin Songbook

## FOR STUDENT MUSICIANS
The Real Easy Book - Vol. 1 - C, Bb, Eb & Bass Clef
The Real Easy Book - Vol. 2 - C, Bb, Eb & Bass Clef
The Real Easy Book - Vol. 3 - C, Bb, Eb & Bass Clef
The Latin Real Easy Book - C, Bb, Eb & Bass Clef
Drum Supplement for Real Easy Book - Vol. 1
The Blues Scales - C, Bb, Eb, Bass Clef & Guitar
Rhythm First! - C, Bb, Eb & Bass Clef - by Tom Kamp
Guitarist's Introduction to Jazz - by Randy Vincent
Walking Bassics - by Ed Fuqua
Foundation Exercises for Bass - by Chuck Sher

## CDs
Poetry+Jazz: A Magical Marriage - by Chuck Sher
Play-Along CDs for The New Real Book - Vol.1
The Latin Real Book Sampler CD

# SHER MUSIC CO. JAZZ METHOD BOOKS
*available in both print & digital forms*

## GUITAR
**Jazz Guitar Voicings: The Drop 2 Book**
 - Randy Vincent
**Three-Note Voicings and Beyond** - Randy Vincent
**Line Games** - Randy Vincent
**Jazz Guitar Soloing: The Cellular Approach**
 - Randy Vincent
**The Guitarist's Introduction to Jazz** - Randy Vincent
**Contemporary Latin Jazz Guitar, Vol. 1&2** - Neff Irizarry
**The Jimmy Raney Book** - Jimmy and Jon Raney

## PIANO
**The Jazz Piano Book** - Mark Levine
**Jazz Piano Masterclass: The Drop 2 Book** - M. Levine
**How To Voice Standards at the Piano** - Mark Levine
**An Approach to Comping - Vol. 1** - Jeb Patton
**An Approach to Comping - Vol. 2** - Jeb Patton
**Introduction to Jazz Piano: A Deep Dive** - Jeb Patton
**Playing for Singers** - Mike Greensill
**Wisdom of the Hand** - Marius Nordal
**The Jazz Solos of Chick Corea** - Peter Sprague

## SAXOPHONE
**The Practice Notebooks of Michael Brecker**
**The Jazz Saxophone Book** - Tim Armacost
**Logic and Critical Thinking in Jazz Improvisation**
 - Vincent Herring

## VOICE
**The Digital Standards Songbook** - individual songs
 with lyrics, plus C, Bb, Eb, High Voice & Low Voice
**The Jazz Singer's Guidebook** - David Berkman

## DRUMS
**Syncopation Companion** - Bryan Bowman
**Inner Drumming** - George Marsh
**Drum Supplement for Real Easy Book Vol.1** - Alan Hall
**Afro-Caribbean Grooves for Drumset** - JPhi Fanfant

## BASS
**The Improvisor's Bass Method** - Chuck Sher
**Concepts for Bass Soloing** - Marc Johnson & C. Sher
**Walking Bassics** - Ed Fuqua
**Foundation Exercises for Bass** - Chuck Sher
**Walking Bass Line Construction** - Bob Sinicrope
 F Blues, Bb Blues and C minor Blues
**Bass Foundations** - Chuck Israels

*Sign up for our monthly discount newsletter
by writing shermuse@sonic.net*

## JAZZ THEORY AND HARMONY
**The Jazz Theory Book** - Mark Levine
**The Jazz Harmony Book** - David Berkman
**Forward Motion** - Hal Galper
**Metaphors for the Musician** - Randy Halberstadt
**Minor is Major!** - Dan Greenblatt
**Rhythm Changes Guide** - Lukas Gabric
**Jazz Scores and Analysis - Vol.1** - Richard Lawn
**Jazz Scores and Analysis - Vol. 2** - Richard Lawn
**The Blues Scales** - C, Bb, Eb, Bass Clef & Guitar
 - Dan Greenblatt
**Logic and Critical Thinking in Jazz Improvisation**
 - Vincent Herring
**Major is Harmonic** - Randy Vincent

## PRACTICE GUIDES
**The Practice Notebooks of Michael Brecker**
**Jazz Musician's Guide to Creative Practicing**
 - David Berkman
**The Serious Jazz Practice Book** - Barry Finnerty
**The Serious Jazz Book II** - Barry Finnerty
**Building Solo Lines from Cells** - Randy Vincent
**365 Days of Practice** - Rick Margitza
**Bob Mover Jazz Lexicon** - 2nd edtion - Bob Mover
 - Bass & Treble Clef versions

## EAR TRAINING
**The Real Easy Ear Training Book** - Roberta Radley
**Reading, Writing and Rhythmetic** - Roberta Radley

## TRUMPET
**New Orleans Trumpet** - Jim Thornton
**Modern Etudes for Solo Trumpet** - Cameron Pearce

## RHYTHM SECTION GUIDES
**Essential Grooves** - Moretti, Stagnaro & Nicholl
**Inside the Brazilian Rhythm Section** - Nelson Faria
 & Cliff Korman
**The Salsa Guidebook** - Rebeca Mauleõn
**Decoding Afro-Cuban Jazz** - Mauleõn & Valdes

## BILINGUAL OR LIBROS EN ESPANOL
**101 Montunos** - Rebeca Mauleõn
**Muy Caliente!** - Afro-Cuban Book & Play-Along
**El Libro del Jazz Piano** - Mark Levine
**The Latin Real Book** - C only

## MISCELLANEOUS
**Method for Chromatic Harmonica** - Max de Aloe
**Jazz Songs for the Student Violinist**
 - Kevin Mitchell & Joanne Keefe